To Ella

Hope it's worth the wait!

Liz
x

THE SECOND SON

LIZ WARHAM

authorHOUSE®

AuthorHouse™
1663 Liberty Drive, Suite 200
Bloomington, IN 47403
www.authorhouse.com
Phone: 1-800-839-8640

AuthorHouse™ UK Ltd.
500 Avebury Boulevard
Central Milton Keynes, MK9 2BE
www.authorhouse.co.uk
Phone: 08001974150

First published by AuthorHouse 10/10/2007

ISBN: 978-1-4343-1112-2 (sc)

Printed in the United States of America
Bloomington, Indiana

This book is printed on acid-free paper.

GLENSHELLICH

It was the devil's weather. Icy gusts funnelled from the high corries, hurling piercing swathes of sleet down the glen. The taller rider wrestled his mare from the swamp's clutches with a curse.

"Hell take the Old Fox," he muttered, "if this is his conjuring."

His companion squinted up at the Mountain of the Eagle, its twin peaks menacing beneath their shroud of swirling cloud. The wind carried a scent of the snow it was sweeping from the summits. Lowlander though he was, Archie Fraser knew that April was no month for journeys: but he knew better that when his master's mind was set it would take more than a blizzard, even one summoned from Hell itself, to change it. North of the Great Glen he was MacSomhairle, a title proudly held by the Stewart chieftains of Glenshellich since the first Samuel crossed the sea from Ireland. Fraser shook the water from his bonnet for the umpteenth time and slapped it across his saddlebags.

"Now he's sprouted horns and cliffit hooves at last," he quipped as they drew rein, equally reluctant to steer the horses into the writhing clump of stunted willows that sheltered Kilclath's fertile plain. Ahead stretched the field of stones that gave the valley its name, leaning like jagged teeth at the mouth of its dark mountain corridor.

Fraser was doubly uneasy. The weather had been against them from the moment they had left the Glen of Black Cattle, venting its disapproval of the mission every bit as forcefully as he had done himself. Bartering with beasts was one thing, but dealing in children's futures quite another. He shivered and wrapped his plaid tighter, with the nagging sense of shielding himself from something more sinister than the wind or the rain.

The gusts grew fiercer as they entered the pass. Generations of MacSomhairle's clan had plundered here, lifted cattle and seized women, cut countless Campbell throats in days when the power of the chiefs reigned supreme. But these days were different. Laws were at last upheld in the glens, and even chieftains were bound to obey them. Another squall snatched at Fraser's plaid and an unpleasant trickle ran down his neck. Rain, or the whisper of restless ghosts? He pulled himself together and pressed his heels firmly into his garron's side, urging the sturdy little horse around the gleaming boulders, further and deeper into Kilclath.

Kilclath, the Valley of Stones, gouged by ice between two towering volcanic crags was a desolate place even on the brightest of days. Part of the spreading Campbell empire, it was presided over by the Master, Alexander, better known throughout Scotland for his cunning as "The Fox". Holed safe in his den he could ignore the ancient enemies surrounding his lands on every border, for what had he to fear from clans whose own misguided allegiances had stripped them so thoroughly of influence and power? Clans like the Stewarts of Glenshellich, his closest neighbours, had sealed their destiny fifteen years earlier when The Old Pretender had taken ship for France. The price of loyalty to the old regime was increasing irrelevance to the new.

The two riders passed slowly under the looming shadows of the big and little mountains, their concentration so fixed on the treacherous valley floor that they were completely unaware of three figures on horseback, still as statues, perched on a slight rise where the valley briefly widened.

"It is the oak on their bonnets," muttered one, narrowing his eyes against the stinging rain. The figure in the centre stiffened, almost as if the information gave offence. A flicker of uncertainty crossed his handsome features before he drew his black eyebrows into a frown.

"They take a risk, then, do they not ….?" His voice was mellow, cultured beyond its seventeen years, a voice befitting the son of a chieftain. His companions exchanged sharp glances of anticipation. At George Campbell's right shoulder was Hughie McIvor, most trusted ghillie of the Master of the Stones and sworn protector of his heir. At his left was Hughie's cousin, Rob the Half Blind, who had lost an eye to a drunken cattle dealer in Crieff but could smell trouble sooner than a hungry man could smell a steaming pot. He sniffed now as Hughie's hand slipped beneath his plaid.

"I am aware of no request for passage from gentlemen by the name of Stewart," the young master continued. "What say we spur them on their way?"

A wolfish grin crept over Hughie's lean features. It was not every day he found himself in so powerful a position, a loaded pistol in his hand and trespassers in the glen. He waited until the riders had plodded unconsciously within range and then, slowly and deliberately, raised his arm and fired a single shot.

In the pass below John Stewart's mare reared in panic, cantering out of control. But Fraser's garron was less highly strung and the groom soon recovered the balance he needed to pull his own pistol from his belt. Quite calmly he fixed his eyes on the hillside and steadied his hand until a swirl of mist revealed the vague shapes of their ambushers. Then he took aim and fired.

Through the smoke and drizzle he made out a figure toppling slowly, almost gracefully, into the heather.

In an instant the heir to the Master of the Stones had leapt from his horse and was on his knees beside his servant's body. Fraser's bullet had passed clean between Rob's eyes and blown away most of the back of his skull. The young master turned his disbelieving eyes onto Hughie who remained frozen in the saddle, his gaze fixed impassively ahead.

3

Hughie waited discreetly as he heard the sob that tore itself from his master's throat. It would be less fitting still to witness any sign of weakness in the son of his chief.

Below them John Stewart continued to struggle with his terrified mare, striving in vain to bring all four of her hooves to the ground. Cursing his trembling hand, Fraser fumbled to reload his pistol. While the seconds stretched around them the Master's heir finally raised himself from his servant's lifeless body. With the briefest of glances in Hughie's direction he drew his pistol, tightened his fingers around its sparkling hilt, and took cold and careful aim.

* * *

Remnants of the same storm clouds darkened the Glen of the Little Oak Trees a dozen miles distant, and the dampness seemed to seep into the spirit of the small boy who gazed steadily eastwards along the invisible track. On a different day he would have looked across a view of unrivalled beauty, for it was said that no stranger passed the Watcher's Stone, granite sentry to Glenshellich, without finding themselves captivated by the tumbling landscape of mountain and loch, somehow less wild, less barren, than the regions to the east, north and south. Further west it was scarcely possible to go, unless on a passage to America.

"My mother says you must come inside now, Domhnull."

Another boy, taller and sturdier, had appeared at Donald's shoulder, his face full of concern. "It is a death this cold will be giving you. You are drenched and must be frozen. And you know full well your standing out here will bring him home no sooner."

Donald made no reply, for he did indeed know that Euan was right. His foster brother gave sound advice on most matters but Donald was not obliged to heed it. He and not Euan MacMichael was the son of the chieftain, and would be MacSomhairle one day. It was Euan's duty to protect and counsel him, not to give him orders. Donald had watched for his father's return all of the day before and now for most of this. He let out a deep and heartfelt sigh.

4

"Yesterday I was excited, Eochain," he said at last. "Yet today I am afraid. Why would that be?"

"It is only your mind playing tricks on you. Please come now, Domhnull. My mother will half-slay me if I go back without you."

Donald leaned defiantly into the shelter of the dyke.

"Do not go back, then," he replied. "Stay and wait with me."

Euan gazed helplessly at his friend, his brother as Donald was, for they had shared the same breast milk. He wrapped his plaid tighter around his body. Surely it could not be so much longer now? Preferring the prospect of his mother's wrath to Donald's displeasure, he hunched closer to the wall behind the Watcher's Stone and waited, as he had been bidden.

* * *

Fraser pressed gently on the bullet wound already spreading its black stain on his master's plaid. Why had he been the one his chieftain had taken with him to the Glen of the Black Cattle? Why had MacSomhairle not chosen his usual companion, his foster brother, Euan, the healer? Euan would have known how to staunch the wound, known how best to lay his chieftain across the saddle, known the soothing words of comfort in the language that could never spring naturally from a tongue schooled in the back streets of Leith. Hardest of all for Fraser to bear was his growing certainty that if Euan had been with his chieftain there would have been no need for his skills. The first shot had been a warning, no more than a gesture, and Fraser had little doubt that the second had been provoked by his own rash response. As gently as he was able he hoisted the dead weight of his chieftain's body onto his horse, and turned his face westwards.

The clouds outpaced them as they followed the glinting path between the mountains. From high above Fraser caught the fractious cry of a lone bird: not an eagle but a herring gull swept too far from the sea. In the distance rose their own Beinn Feodag, the giant's mountain, and as they emerged from Kilclath's shadows its sharp peak pointed white above the clouds. Before long their horses were wading into the churning waters that carved the boundary between the Valley of Stones and Glenshellich, the Bloody Burn, christened in memory of Samuel's most infamous son, An Ciobar, blackmailer, thief and murderer. On a day much like this one, with the wind in the north, An Ciobar had slaughtered twenty Campbells who dared breach his glen and drive off his cattle. As many of his own men had died in the bloodbath and their bodies had turned the water red for days.

But the rain clouds ahead were dispersing, drifting southwards. Their horses clambered onto the opposite bank and Fraser felt the slightest stirring of hope. For had he not saved MacSomhairle before? Saved him when the redcoats purged the city and there seemed no escape? Surely the mountains of Glenshellich would prove safer refuge than the ramshackle wynds of Leith? Why should his master die from a bolt that pierced the rain .....?

The words rushed unbidden to his head, their force almost jerking the reins from his fingers. Was he becoming as fey as the old men at the fires with their portents and prophecies? Yet other words followed, words that in ten years had become as familiar to him as a catechism, and with them came a strange reassurance.

"And when the boy is a man will the time fall, when the last son of Samuel leads his clan to the death of their hearts."

* * *

The old chieftain sat behind his desk in the House of the Eagle. His white hair was unpowdered and his expression benign. Only the select few he could count his intimates would recognise that the innocuous manner of The Master of the Stones was just another of his craftily baited traps. He leaned back and allowed a soft sigh to relax his fine features. An English client for his Edinburgh law firm was always reason for satisfaction, a further sign of his ever-growing influence.

His complacency was banished by the dramatic appearance of his son and heir. "There has been an incident," the boy began, but his eyes immediately shrank from the old man's scrutiny.

"Indeed," Kilclath answered, in a dangerously benevolent tone. His glance flickered from his son's trembling hands to the pulse that came and went on the side of his temple. He raised one eyebrow and his voice almost imperceptibly changed. "And a serious one it would appear."

"A man from Glenshellich has shot Rob dead."

This time the transformation was total. "Explain!" Steel had replaced the silk. There could be no mistaking the impact of this news. The young master slumped to a chair. He clutched his head and his delicate fingers flexed white against stray strands of black hair. When he dared look up his expression held the same blank despair as when he had knelt beside Rob's body. Yet his father's instruction must be obeyed. He drew a tentative breath and began his account.

The old man listened keenly. When his son had finished he murmured, "And how accurate was your aim?"

"I did not wait to see."

Another silence fell.

"You did not wait to see," echoed the old man at last. "That was indeed unfortunate." He let his words die slowly before he went on. "So we have a new scratch to the old wound. A deadly scratch, I fear, for it was MacSomhairle himself who was crossing Kilclath today." He paused. "With permission." He paused again. "From no lesser authority than myself."

His son stared back in horror as the information crossed the cold space between them. At last The Master rose to stand at the window, looking out in the direction of his mountains, which he seemed to be addressing rather than his son as he continued. "Our lands prosper. Our name is respected throughout the realm. Yet with this folly you have made yourself as culpable as our enemies."

A bitter flush had spread itself on his son's face, but for the first time something like defiance shone from his eyes. "Have you not raised me to follow the instincts of my namesake, the eagle?"

The old man turned and studied him for some moments in silence. When he next spoke his mood seemed to have mellowed. "Then it is time to choose your prey with more care. And to learn to keep a clear head"

Again he was unprepared for his son's reply.

"As you have always done?"

The Master of the Stones let his glance waver for less than a second, but when he replied all trace of menace had left his voice. Positions had shifted and he spoke more in the manner of one conspirator to another.

"My son, my son! All your life I have sought to impress upon you that the old clan feuds are over. Our kin are ascending and will remain the victors if we understand the future. It is not our wrong, nor the wrongs done to us that need concern us now." He drew a long sigh, hobbled back to the desk and closed the ledger that still lay open, its contents now almost a mockery. "So come," he said at last. "We must attend the McIvors immediately to pay our respect before we ride to Glenshellich."

* * *

Fraser finally dared to steal a glance at his master's face, grey as ash against his horse's flank. The rain had dwindled to a steady drizzle as the afternoon darkened, yet Fraser knew he could risk travelling no faster. He feared each jolt was nudging the bullet fraction by fraction closer to MacSomhairle's heart.

"What kind of a story will this make?" he muttered to himself, for Fraser was a man who lived as much on stories as he did on meat and drink. Stories were life and life was a story, be it short or long, thrilling or dull, joyful or tragic. His own was a mixture of all those things, as was his master's, and through their fifteen years together they had

8

retold and relived them time after time.   Stories had never yet lost their power to lift MacSomhairle's spirits and even though he might be beyond hearing them, they were still the only comfort his servant had to give. Fixing his gaze westwards Fraser drew a determined breath.

"So now we're out of that God-forsaken glen, presided ower by the progeny of whores and traitors, I'll remind you of a better one," the lowlander continued grimly. "The one we're bound for, the story we're still in thegether. We're far from finished yet, MacSomhairle, you and me ..."

He paused for a moment and raised his hand to brush the water from his face, warm water that owed nothing now to the rain.

"So Dear Lord in heaven," he whispered, "Gie' him breath enough to see the shining side o' the Watcher's Stone."

* * *

Catriona MacMichael paused at the door of the House of Glen-shellich and glanced towards the silent stables. It was strange, she thought, how you missed the sound of Fraser's singing, so tuneless yet so full of heart. Surely they could not be far from home now? Catriona had no need to wonder why her spirits were heavy. Donald and Euan still crouched beneath the Watcher's Stone, their small figures pressed into the wall for shelter. When the veils of mist swirled and lifted she could see that dusk had begun to creep over the lochan to merge with the vast shadow of the Giant's Mountain. Catriona could not ignore her hollow sense that all was not well. She pulled her shawl tighter, feeling the familiar trickle of pain pass from the two fingers, which were all that remained of her left hand, along the scarred wrist and up to her elbow. It was a pang she felt without fail each time her sons were troubled.

She drew her fine eyebrows into a frown. Much as Catriona loved, revered, her chieftain, she had been unable to give her blessing to the venture that had taken him to the Glen of the Black Cattle. Forcing the disquiet from her mind she directed her feet away from the house and through the gate, along the track to the Watcher's Stone, quickly at first, then, when she could identify the distant shapes approaching, desperately, spurred by the certainty that she must reach Donald and Euan first.

Fraser rounded the bend in the track and cursed as he saw the boys step from the mist. He reined his garron sharply and called out to them

"Run the two of you! Run for your father, Euan. Run for the healer!"

His tone should have made them obey immediately, but they had seen MacSomhairle's horse and its swinging burden. They stood rooted to the spot as the riders drew closer, and despite the darkness Fraser was aware that all trace of colour had drained from Donald's face.

"You must go for the healer, laddie," he repeated, but this time more gently, and finally Euan understood. He tugged at Donald's arm and dragged him with increasing speed down the track in the direction of the clachan. He knew his father would be securing the herd. He knew exactly where he would find him.

As their footsteps faded Fraser dared at last to look into the face of his chieftain. Was it his imagination, or was there a tiny movement at the corner of John Stewart's mouth? Fraser leaned down and gently touched the tangled hair. Had his master heard and heeded his ramblings? Was it not his death after all that was to come in smoke from the Valley of Stones? He led the mare forward until Catriona MacMichael's stricken grey eyes were level with his own.

"You take the reins now, Catriona," he said softly. " We'll take him the rest of the way together."

* * *

Euan MacMichael's deft knife glinted in the lamplight. Concentration had carved deep lines on his brow and at the sides of his mouth. Beside him Catriona clasped the bowl of water and wiped the wound as her husband instructed, while Fraser's goblin-like shadow performed a distorted dance above the bed. The smallest of the three boys crouching in the corner crept to Catriona's side.

"What is he doing now?" he whispered. The question seemed to drift for a long time through the silence.

"I am …," the healer paused and gave a small gasp as he achieved his task, "…..I am removing Kilclath's bolt – " He stopped himself suddenly as Fraser and Catriona drew what seemed a single sharp breath. "That is to say.. . . .. his bullet." But the correction had come too late. Euan pretended not to notice the reaction as he smiled at the boy. "It will do your father no more harm." He twisted the tool in his wrist and held the bullet against the light. "Now, Andrew," he went on. "Since you imagine you will be my successor one day, go down for the sphagnum moss and we will lay it on the wound together." He stood back, well satisfied with his work. "Come you closer, Domhnull, and see how your father's face is grey no more. Look how calmly he sleeps. It is sleep that will bring the healing now."

Donald crept to the edge of the bed. What Euan said was true. His father seemed at peace, free from the pain he had cried out with, even though unconscious, when Euan had probed his flesh. Euan himself was passing weary. The healing was an exhausting business and this one doubly so, drawing from the very depth of Euan's spirit. Understanding how it was for him, Catriona gently smoothed back his hair. Her hand, maimed though it was, brought an almost instant calm.

Andrew returned from his mission and began to help Euan dress the wound. Fraser was so engrossed in watching them that he scarcely heard the horses' hooves, faint at first, then growing more insistent as they clattered over the smoothed path leading to the outbuildings around the house. But Euan had heard them. With a nod towards Catriona he stood up and moved to the window. He pulled aside the drapes and peered out, waiting until the light from the burning outpost fire showed him who the visitors might be. Three men came into view, though Euan MacMichael recognised only one. He let the drape fall back, and when he turned to face him Donald had never seen his expression so dark

"So they've come," Fraser muttered.

Euan remained at the window. "Kilclath himself," he pronounced at last.

Fraser moved a hand instinctively to his pistol. "Let me at the devil."

"No!" Euan's order was less than a whisper. "It is a duty for myself." But he stepped back and seemed to hesitate before he added, " I will take the boy."

Keeping close to the walls Catriona slid towards Donald and put her hands on his shoulders. "You cannot take Domhnull," she breathed.

Donald's eyes darted from one to the other. Euan's face seemed to have lost all expression. "Fraser will remain with you beside MacSomhairle's bed," he instructed. "None of you will move, even so far as the doorway. I will speak with Kilclath in the study."

Donald could be in no doubt that his father had received a wound from his enemy, a wound which but for the grace of God and his foster father's skill should have killed him. Although he was only eight years old he understood perfectly that he might have been called upon to accompany Euan downstairs in an altogether more alarming role. He moved to the healer's side.

The rasp on the front door rang like a summons. It was not a sound that implied remorse. Once again the three adults exchanged lowered glances.

"May I have strength left in me….." Euan whispered, but only Donald was close enough to hear his words. Then the healer closed his eyes, drew a faltering breath and held out his hand. "Come, Domhnull. Let us go greet the men from the Valley of Stones."

As the door closed behind them Euan's son crept across to the window and tweaked back the heavy velvet. Below him were the shortened forms of two men standing in front of the door: one old, one young. Further back, holding their horses, was a lean and wiry clansman wrapped against the night in a shabby plaid. So unremarkable was his appearance that the young Euan MacMichael could almost have mistaken him for someone from his own clachan. Yet he quickly dismissed such an unworthy notion. The man was his enemy. He was a Campbell from Kilclath.

Eilidh of the scarlet face, servant to the house of Glenshellich, stood at the door gazing up the wooden stairway, awaiting her instruction. It was Eilidh's duty to admit Glenshellich's guests, and she had gleaned enough in the few hours that had passed since the return of her chieftain to have little doubt as to the identity of these.

At last Euan MacMichael and the son of MacSomhairle appeared at the head of the staircase. Euan gave a brief nod and Eilidh obediently lifted the iron bar.

The men from Kilclath stepped inside and the front door groaned as it closed behind them, as if the very fabric of the house grew uneasy with their presence. Glancing quickly at Euan, Donald felt a sudden, inexplicable fear. He had never doubted his father's right hand man before. Euan was the strongest, most skilled, most fearless in all the clachan, and competent for any task. But he saw Euan hesitate again as Eilidh nervously ushered the visitors across the stone flagstones of the hallway and into the study.

"I had hoped to be speaking with MacSomhairle himself," began the Master of the Stones.

"He is indisposed," Euan replied levelly. "By a bullet from Kilclath."

Donald slipped quietly through the door and took his place in the shadows by Euan's side.

"Ahhh," breathed The Master at last, his shrewd gaze resting for some seconds on Euan's face. The healer's eyes were dull from the effort of his work, his features set in a tight mask, yet Donald understood how overwhelming was his urge to look away. Kilclath seemed to be prolonging the silence, emphasising his power even in the house of his enemy.

"Not fatally indisposed?" he murmured at last.

"We pray not."

Donald watched as the younger man's glance strayed uncomfortably around the room. For a moment he saw it himself as a stranger might: the walls lined with rows of books tumbling indiscriminately on makeshift shelves, the solid oak desk and chairs, the huge fire blasting the room with warmth and flickering orange light. It seemed to Donald that the Master's heir was no more at ease with himself than was Euan MacMichael, but any sympathy he might have had for him was to be short lived as The Master's soft voice insinuated again.

"My son will make his own apology." In the silence that followed he added, "George?"

George Campbell cleared his throat. His voice might have faltered, but arrogance still shone from his eyes. "No injury was intended. My ghillie's shot was fired only to warn." He paused, again uncomfortably aware that he lacked his father's skill in making words his weapons. "If your own man had not responded as he did the matter would have ended there. We had no reason to believe that those of your persuasion would carry arms...." His voice faded. His apology lacked grace. His father had advised humility. The old man's eyes glinted in reproach. Although the Stewarts were not licensed to bear weapons no highlander could reasonably be expected to travel abroad without proper protection. It was a law not even the Old Fox would seek to enforce. George Campbell swallowed and continued. "As you must be aware, we have never had occasion to welcome men from Glenshellich into our lands."

Another silence fell before Euan replied softly, "I am aware of it," and then, to Donald's horror, he turned away.

Outraged, Donald stepped forward, unable to believe that Euan could so sacrifice his clan's honour. No Stewart of Glenshellich, least of all his chieftain's foster brother, would turn his back on their enemy, especially a enemy of such long standing. But straightaway he felt Euan's hand like a vice on his shoulder. The healer pulled Donald backwards and when the boy glimpsed his face he saw that the expression on it was truly terrible. Trembling at it himself, he retreated to stand once more behind Euan, who tendered his hand with an almost heroic effort.

Neither of the men from Kilclath made any move to take it.

"I will accept from MacSomhairle your apology," Euan said finally, looking from one to the other, before letting his hand drop back to his side.

Kilclath eyed him with cold disdain. "As my son has observed, we have never been friends, which gives me cause to deplore this deed all the more. Violence can so often breed upon itself. I hope the incident will not lead to further hostilities."

"MacSomhairle desires peace above all else," said Euan. "He has no interest in settling scores." He extended his hand a second time. "Old ones or new."

Hesitantly, and without once looking in his father's direction, George Campbell reached out and took it.

"Then please convey my genuine regret to your chieftain." His voice was scarcely a whisper

"I will do so," said Euan simply, still with the young man's hand in his.

Donald glowered by Euan's side. "I would not offer my hand to a man from Kilclath," he muttered darkly.

At once the attention of all three drilled him, but Donald did not flinch. He returned their stares defiantly. The Old Fox gave a thin smile, bent down and placed a pale cheek next to his.

"This young son of Samuel would do well to study the lessons of history." His delicate features advanced closer. "It would be unwise indeed to plant a new seed of enmity between our families." The breath that issued from the Master of the Stones was strangely sweet, yet to Donald it seemed to carry the essence of pure poison. The smile that briefly crossed his lips was betrayed by the expression in his eyes.

"As you say, Donald is young," Euan replied. "His father will teach him well."

"His father is an honourable man, if a misguided one," Kilclath countered. "But I trust we can take our leave assured of his pardon."

Euan's hand once again gripped Donald's shoulder in fierce warning. He said nothing but only inclined his head as he followed the visitors into the hall. They watched the two men pass through the doorway and out to where Hughie McIvor waited with their horses. They stood together as the drumming of hoof beats faded and merged with their own measured breathing, then both instinctively turned their heads towards the staircase.

Not a single sound could be heard from the room above.

* * *

Thin May sunshine filtered through the east wing window of Glenshellich House and spread to all but the furthest corners of the chieftain's bedroom.

"Story-time," demanded Donald mischievously, and stretched himself like a cat across the foot of his father's bed, at the same time throwing a wink in his brother's direction. Andrew grinned back. Outside a mist was creeping down the Giant's Mountain revealing the last of the winter snows sparkling on its summit.

"And which story might you have in mind?" asked Fraser, delicately laying a bowl of oatmeal and milk on his chieftain's bedspread.

John Stewart smiled. "And who to tell it?" he added, his eyes twinkling in the direction of his younger son who sprawled in the seat of the same window young Euan MacMichael had looked down from three weeks earlier. This time not the ghillie from Kilclath but Euan himself was the prospect, scampering past the stables, scattering squawking hens in his wake.

"My days were a' spun out in that wee dark chandlery, reeking o'wax and tobacco, more French and Spanish tongues to be heard than honest to goodness Scots ......" Donald recited.

".... crying out for claret when I stocked nothing but rum, gabbing for a decent ship's biscuit......" Andrew continued with an even better talent for mimicry.

John Stewart laughed out loud. "You see, Fraser, though they never tire of hearing it they have it by heart. Your story, my friend."

"Our story," Fraser corrected him. "All our stories," he added, as Euan appeared breathless in the doorway.

"And is now not as good a time as any to relive them?" smiled John Stewart, taking a mouthful of his breakfast and chewing conscientiously. "Now that my future seems to have been returned to me?" Though he could not deny that in the last weeks it was his past that had come to loom larger. What had there been in that bullet from Kilclath, he wondered, to work such sorcery? Still, he knew he owed it to them all to regain his strength. He fully intended to do so.

"And I mind to this day the exact first words your father said to me," Fraser went on, rising as ever to the bait, unable to resist the opportunity to relive the most momentous day of his life. Fifteen years earlier he had been a ship's chandler with a wily eye fixed on business and a shrewd mind bent on profit. There had been little to inspire a man in Leith's squalid dockland, only taverns teeming with drunkards and whores, stinking alleys turning blind eyes to blades in the dark. Fraser had not become the man he was destined to be until he had found himself face to face with the ragged men from the north. He had been in absolutely no doubt of their identities: fugitives from the Old Pretender's ill-fated war, men whose strange lilting voices sounded more foreign to his ears than the accents of the French or the Spanish sailors he bartered with daily.

""In God's name this stink is worse than MacCombie's tanners," Donald declared.

Fraser grinned, then his expression changed. His stories kept their memories alive, but the past could find other ways of shaping the future. Cairnill had leaned over his counter next, Cairnill who was now master of the sweeping Glen of Black Cattle, father to four sons and one daughter, Cairnill who had long since learned the wisdom of paying lip service to an alien government. But a different prospect had stretched before him then, and Fraser could still smile at the memory, though Cairnill had, as ever, been the first to recognise an opportunity when he saw it. Behind the smell of greased ropes and hemp he had caught the more enticing possibility of a berth across the channel.

"A passage," says you," went on Andrew.

"A passage," says I," Donald chorused.

But Fraser was accustomed to their interruptions. He nodded shrewdly and narrowed his eyes. "So I kent then who the two of them might be and what failed business had brought them to my door, though I bided my time till I learned more, names maybe, all the while reckoning up the likely gains from handing over such traitors to the lawful authorities. For that old Archie Fraser kent only too well what a handshake with a redcoat might lead to......."

His voice faded. Those old dreams might have belonged to a different person, but he had smelt in the hot rebel breath a world of romance and glory, loyalty and legend, a world he had only ever encountered in songs and stories. Archie Fraser had spent his life trading with foreign cutthroats, wrangling and dealing, cheating and being cheated. All these years later it was still hard to explain how a handful of desperate strangers could so easily turn a canny merchant into a man prepared to gamble his own future as recklessly as they had gambled theirs.

But it was Euan's turn to interrupt, with the line he somehow always liked best.

"So are you for the one true king?" you demanded."

"Indeed I am, said I," went on Donald, taking his cue, "kenning myself a loyal subject of King George, and the last man on God's earth to give support to his enemies....."

But it was always better to hear the story from its source. They leaned back expectantly and waited for Fraser to take up the thread. With a sigh and a half-hearted show of reluctance he obliged.

"Not that politics was muckle concern of mine, any more than the treacherous dealings of men from the north - where I'd heard they ate babies and wrestled bears." He winked at his master, knowing how well he too could remember the hollow dread of capture, the prospect of the noose and the worse things that followed it.

""Damn you, man," you cursed. And you held out your hand and opened it up, and there lay five gleaming gold coins. Five gold coins for five berths. But there were only the two of you standing behind my counter. That was when the quiet gentleman with the sad face stepped inside the doorway. And the two others after him...."

He reached out and patted young Euan MacMichael's head. "That was when I kent there would be no going back." He turned again to John Stewart who was scraping his bowl. "Could you manage a drop more?" The chieftain shook his head and motioned his old friend to go on. Fraser looked around and saw his audience was waiting.

""Let me introduce you to my foster brother," this red bearded ruffian said. And I kenned fine what that was polite speak for. "This is my man and you'll have him to deal with if you put a foot out of line. I'd no' gie muckle for your chances, would you?"

Young Euan MacMichael grinned. He had been told many times how his father had fought like three men at Sherrifmuir. He still had the scars and a bullet from the battle in his chest.

"And then you telt me the rest o' your names, music to the ears of a' the informers south of the River Tay. John Stewart, second son of Glenshellich in Appin, The Master of Cairnill, the Glen of the Black Cattle, and for good measure the most valuable prize of all, James Hamilton, Laird of Allomore, with rents that stretched from Perthshire to the Moray Firth, the best kenned fool in Scotland for the Pretender. There couldna be a man in the land hadna heard tell how Allomore flung his riches at the Pretender like muck at a midden, and ended up wi' nothing in return but a price on his head high enough to furnish me twenty shops." Fraser's eyes sparkled from his leathery face as he turned again to the son of the healer.

"But I was still counting and it was still only four," obliged Euan.

"And that was when," said Fraser. "I saw your mother."

He would never forget that first vision of Catriona MacMichael, framed in his doorway, her head almost touching the splintered oak beam. Gazing into those unfathomable grey eyes he had known beyond any doubt that he would do whatever the red-bearded Highlander asked of him, do it if it meant the sacrifice of his shop and everything he had ever worked for. Catriona clung to her husband's arm as if for her very life, clung with a hand that was only a thumb and two fingers and a scar running red and angry to hide itself under the folds of her cloak. Aware of Fraser's stare, with the gentlest of gestures, Euan had covered it with his own huge fist.

As it turned out it had been an easy enough task for the chandler to find his old sparring partner, Captain Merclere of The Petit Dauphin, in the Half Moon Tavern and persuade him to take the gold. The buccaneer was renowned for an adventurous nature and more than a glancing sympathy for the Jacobite cause. He was also a man with little time to spend ashore and less to waste on bargaining. The rum in his stomach had fired his spirits and he had waited all morning for the girl who wriggled on his knee. No one in The Half Moon suspected informants might be skulking in cobwebbed corners and the hapless chandler had returned proudly with news of a successful deal.

"But I aye had the feeling Cairnill wasna easy in his mind..." Fraser went on, glancing shrewdly at Donald. "Even though he was a man comfortable enough with duplicity." His tone was meaningful and this time his words were directed at MacSomhairle. "And you and I saw another change of heart last month," he added grimly. "He'll no rise for your cause again, mark my words ......"

The chieftain made an irritable gesture that commanded silence. But for the first time it occurred to Fraser that his master might have had a more devious motive for their journey to the Glen of the Black Cattle. Did MacSomhairle himself understand that their old dreams might be gone forever? Was he mapping out a safer path for his son, a different destiny for his clan? The old groom sighed. Only time would tell.

"We are not out of this peril yet, John," Cairnill had warned as the shadows lengthened, and once again he was proved correct. At six after midday the fugitives had taken their leave and made their separate ways to the dockside. They wove among the evening crowds jostling through the narrow streets: Euan MacMichael, stooping like a big bear, sheltering his woman in the vast folds of his plaid, Glenshellich and Cairnill, furtively threading their separate ways to the harbour, and finally Allomore, quietly slipping through hidden alleyways that would lead no further than the end of his dreams.

And quietly shadowing them, with an uncanny desire to see them safely boarded, was Archie Fraser, whose time as a chandler of Leith was about to be counted in minutes. In the afternoon they had spent together he had learned something of what had led the rebels to the unlikely shelter of his roof. He had heard how John Stewart's brother, the chieftain of Glenshellich, lay under sentence of death, how the three chieftains and Euan MacMichael had followed the cause of their King James until all hope was gone. Then they had made their way to the Glen of the Little Oak Trees where John Stewart held his own portion of land. But his land had no longer been safe. Glenshellich's neighbour, the Campbell chieftain of Kilclath, had heard of their return and his sense of justice demanded they should stand trial. They had fled quickly in the night and made their way south, passing with heavy hearts through the wasted lands of Allomore, until fate had finally led them to Archie Fraser's dockside chandlery.

When dusk had settled and the lights of The Petit Dauphin flickered on the water Fraser had watched from the shadows behind the wharfside. The tide had turned. He heard the ship draw anchor. The ropes were cast loose, and with a creaking and grinding the vessel began to circle slowly in the water and make her way towards the open sea. The wind flapped in her sails as the distance separating the men of the north from their homeland grew heart-breakingly safer.

Then had come the sound of running feet, the bark of harsh orders, the blur of red coats, and finally the curses of men who realised they were too late. Fraser let a half smile pass his lips as he watched the waves gently caress the stern of the Petit Dauphin. But before he could turn for home he felt the grip of a hand on his shoulder.

"The wee rat Moncart," exclaimed Andrew. They had reached his favourite part of the story. He loved to picture Fraser spitting into the informer's treacherous, pockmarked face. "Aye with an eye to the main chance, as twisted as his own greased ropes. For you had escaped, and I was the prisoner...."

"Then I heard your voice borne over the water ....." joined in Euan, for he too had relived that scene times without number in his dreams.

21

The names shone like beacons in his mind. Cairnill, Allomore, Glen-shellich, heroes every one. And his own father and mother had been with them, standing on the same deck, part of the whole magnificent adventure.

"The ship, man. You can make the ship, Archie Fraser, chandler of Leith. Swim out to us, man! Swim to the ship!" John Stewart had yelled.

"Would I have done it if I'd kent just how strong the evening tide was?" Fraser took up his own story. Or if he had known how melancholy those next years would be, hearing of indemnities granted, tales of leading Jacobites pardoned and restored to their estates. They were tales that at once heartened and depressed them, for it needed but a signature, a token of lip service to a despised government, and they could return. What did it matter, Fraser tried to tell them. What did a scrap of paper signed with their hands signify against the undying loyalty imprinted on their hearts?

One by one they had come to their senses. First Cairnill, who had left two infant sons in the Glen of the Black Cattle and a wife grown weary with the burdens of their estates, had sought and been granted pardon. And then had come the news that John Stewart's son, a baby when his father had taken up the standard, had fallen ill and died of the flux. His wife arrived weeping at their lodgings in Paris and in her misery had cursed them all. She had suffered too much since he had had plucked her from the city and abandoned her to the lonely silence of Glenshellich, she who had been used to crowds and company, society and entertainment. She was tired of living alone in a bitter land bled dry by his brother, a fugitive who milked his tenants only to gamble and drink and squander with the banished plotters. She brought with her the offer of his pardon and told her husband he must decide where his true loyalties lay. The clan or the king was the choice she presented, but if he chose the king she would return to her father in Edinburgh. They had spent most of their marriage apart, and he had never once set eyes on the son she now so desperately mourned. But it was not a choice he could easily make. His brother was the chieftain. The responsibility for the clan was his.

It had fallen to Catriona MacMichael to persuade him. Over the years of their exile the fear had left her eyes, but when she spoke, just for a moment, Fraser had seen its shadow cross them again.

"We should go back," she had told John Stewart. "Janet has suffered more than you know and has borne her grief alone. It is time."

So they had made their arrangements to return. Only Allomore remained in France, preparing to make his lonely way to King James' exiled court in Rome. Fraser's last memory of Paris was of his slight figure, standing alone outside his grimy lodging house, watching with empty eyes as their carriage drove away. Ahead for Allomore lay a life of exile and a nickname for posterity. He would pass into Jacobite annals as "The Plotter". For him there would be no amnesty and no homecoming.

In Glenshellich it seemed to Fraser that he had arrived in a land more foreign than France, a land with no welcome for strangers such as the Leith chandler and the wife of Euan MacMichael. For a long time the folk of the clachan turned from them with suspicion and hostility, muttering and mumbling, and calling them by unintelligible names in their outlandish tongue. Then had come another futile uprising for King James. In 1719 the banished chieftain of Glenshellich returned with a Spanish force only to be blown up in a burst of mortar fire in the skirmish in Glensheil.It was the end of an old forlorn story: or so Fraser hoped.

He looked across at his chieftain. His eyes were closing. There had been enough memories for one day.

"Be off now, the three of you," he instructed. "And let MacSomhairle sleep. He's a way to go yet before he'll be fit to clear the giant's snows."

John Stewart waited until he heard the door close behind them.

"Too long a way now, I fear, Fraser," he replied softly.

Fraser drew breath to argue, but something stopped him and he watched the chieftain drift back to sleep. He pushed a stray strand of hair from his forehead and wondered if this would prove an end to his misfortunes. It was an odd old world to be sure, he reflected, as he continued to study his chieftain's calm face, and a cruel one at times. Though not this time it seemed, and for that the old servant could only send up a sincere prayer of thanks.

* * *

They said in Glenshellich that in a time beyond the reach of men's memory the mighty giant Feodag had stood on the highest peak of his mountain and hurled boulders down upon the brothers who had dared to challenge his power. Some had landed in the lochan, making tiny islands that rose and fell on its surface at the whim of the tide. Others had splintered and scattered down the hillside where they marked a haphazard path to the clachan. Feodag's final and heaviest weapon had embedded itself on the border of the glen where it had stood steady guard ever since, known to untold generations as the Watcher's Stone.

As the sun's light forced its way through the clouds Donald stood on one of Feodag's smaller missiles and watched his father making a slow and painful way towards him. MacSomhairle stopped every few yards to gather his breath before dragging himself higher, glancing ever upwards, into days when he could run as nimbly up the slopes as his son. When he was forced to admit defeat he motioned Donald to his side. After the moment or two it took him to recover his breath he bent down and reached inside his stocking. Even that effort seemed to tire him further, but Donald waited patiently until his father was ready to speak.

"One day, Donald," he began at last, and took another shaky breath as he looked towards the mountain's peak. "One day you will be master of this glen. Not too soon," he added quickly, seeing the growing dismay on the boy's face, "I think I can now safely promise."

Then he opened up his hand and Donald saw that a tiny knife rested in his palm, a skean dhu, its hilt studded with rubies red like drops of bright blood, its blade gleaming in the sunlight. "Your uncle carried this knife into battle," John Stewart went on, "and, because he died with no son, it was given to me. It is a talisman, a symbol of each chieftain's link with the past and the future. It should be passed on in life from one chieftain to the next, and it is said that each of us will know when the time for that comes. It was not so with your uncle, could not be so, but I believe the time for my duty is now." He placed the hilt in Donald's hand and tightened his fingers around it. "Keep it safe, Domhnull," and then he added, in scarcely a whisper, "for your own son."

A cloud passed briefly overhead as Donald stared down at the knife. At last he slipped it inside his own stocking as they turned to retrace their steps. He no longer raced ahead but matched his pace sedately to his father's, and with each step he felt the thrill of the blade's cold steel against his warm flesh.

MacSomhairle's younger son watched from his bedroom window as they returned along the track. Andrew had never grudged Donald his special place in their father's heart. He had his own plans for a future free from a chieftain's burdens. Quietly and determinedly he was already making it his business to study the skills of Euan Mac-Michael, for as long as he could remember it had been his dream to follow in the footsteps of the healer.

Donald wasted no time in showing him the skean dhu and Andrew gazed at it, drawn by the power of its beauty and its history. He touched the tip of the blade and suddenly felt his heart quicken and heard the blood course through his veins. His head spun and his vision faded. He was no longer in his room with his brother but on a battlefield where clansmen ran and stumbled through smoke across the stubble of a cornfield. Then came one clansman in particular, charging madly, screaming and brandishing a broadsword. Above the clansman's stocking gleamed the very jewelled knife hilt he was holding in his hand. Andrew squeezed his eyelids tight and turned away. He remembered the last time his head had spun like this. It had been the morning his best friend in all the clachan, Meg, the witch's grand-daughter, had fallen on the shore and cut her knee open on the sharp mussel shells.

Andrew remembered how Kenneth MacCombie, MacSomhairle's piper, had rushed from his boat and bathed away the blood until her crying stopped. He remembered how Kenneth had lifted her into his arms and high into the air. And as Andrew's head had spun with her she had been a child no longer, but a woman with blazing eyes and raven hair. But Kenneth was still holding her high against the skyline and she was still laughing down at him. He had told Meg what he had seen, and she had not thought him crazy or mocked him. She had only looked at him in the strange way she sometimes had, and nodded, as if she might even be part of the same secret.

Donald was also looking at him strangely. Then, as the haze cleared before his eyes he realised it was not Donald, but the same man, tall and tanned and troubled. He was standing in a cluttered room, his back to a window through which came many different sounds, shouts, orders, the pounding of horses' hooves. Then Andrew saw the man stretch out his hand and give the skean dhu to a woman. He could not see her clearly for the light was against her, but he could make out that her hair was a deep golden colour and her eyes were blue, so blue that the sun seemed to shine from the very depth of them. He knew too that she did not want to take the knife, and that her heart was already weighed down with too many burdens.

"Andrew!" Donald's voice finally broke into his fantasy. "Andrew what is it?"

Andrew pulled himself back.

"I saw a man," he said at last, "a man who made me think of you. I saw him give the knife to a woman."

"Ach, Andrew, what is it you say?" scoffed Donald. "Do not be so daft. It is my own son I will give it to."

Yet Andrew could not deny the vision to himself as he handed back the knife, anxious now to be quickly rid of it. Donald ran his finger almost reverently down the blade, but suddenly drew back, eyes bewildered as the blood streamed over his hand. Without a second's hesitation Andrew pulled a strip from his shirt and bound the wound tight, while Donald could do nothing but stare in stunned silence.

"It cut so deeply!" he whispered at last. "Yet I felt nothing at all." He forced a weak smile. "But you have sorted it, Andrew. It is a healer you are, as good as Euan MacMichael himself." Then he paused and looked puzzled. He glanced at Andrew as if trying to make up his mind. At last he said, "I was thinking something."

"What?"

"Perhaps it was a wrong thought."

Andrew looked into his eyes and knew exactly what the thought had been.

"You were swearing vengeance on the man who shot our father."

Donald touched the blood-soaked bandage, and his voice came softly.

"MacSomhairle will not climb Beinn Feodag again, Andrew. He will never run with us by the lochan or swim from shore to shore."

"His injury was not intended. MacSomhairle does not seek revenge."

Donald's hand began to throb. He shrugged and tried to smile.

"Perhaps the knife is enchanted," he said finally.

But Andrew did not smile back. His brother knew as well as he did there was no enchantment in knives. But he knew nothing of the other enchantment, the one the clachan only whispered and even then on pain of death. He knew nothing of the curse that had stalked him since the day he was born. Donald was the second son of the second son of MacSomhairle. His coming had long been expected and dreaded, for to his clan he was the last son of Samuel and on his shoulders rested all their destinies.

DONALD

"We are ever prepared and ever ready!"

The scribe of Ardallan's shrill voice piped with all the passion of his conviction. "Our liberties are constantly eroded by a corrupt government that cannot comprehend our unique and ancient society.........."

Donald stifled a yawn. Even Andrew, usually attentive, seemed to be struggling to keep his eyes open. Outside the window the distant clamour of the herring gulls told him that the boats were returning to the jetty. He longed to be among the fishermen, pulling in the creels and the nets, wading through the clear water, turning his face to the warmth of the sun.

Despite what their tutor preached, the third decade of the eighteenth century had been a quiet time in the Highlands. Many chiefs from the ancient lines, the old orders that had renewed themselves generation upon generation, had found practical reasons to reconsider their loyalties. Others paid lip service to The King over the Water while profiting from their dealings with his German cousin. In ascendancy overall were the judicious entrepreneurs, men like the new young Master of the Stones, dedicated to establishing their own satellites in the forfeited lands, while the exiles, sad men like Allomore, lived out lonely existences obstinately waiting for the day when the true king would be restored. It was a day that seemed to grow more distant with each year that passed. Most dangerous of all to zealots like the scribe of Ardallan was the embryonic notion called progress, insinuating its message through the glens, seeping inevitably into the roots of tradition. And always there was the controlling presence of the soldiers to remind them, foreign accents in the air around Fort William, Fort Augustus and Inverness, speaking of another world to tempt the clansmen away from their huts and their dependence.

"Yes, Parliament is uneasy and has cause to be. We in the glens will not forsake our old allegiances. The day will come when we will rise again and regain for them what has been lost...."

Donald did not disagree with his tutor's sentiments, but he was sick to death with his tedious rantings. There were plenty enough books in his father's study to teach him more than he would ever need to know in order to take his place as chieftain. From the scribe they had learned little more than how to recite their own genealogy, which he could accomplish backwards or forwards, together with the lineage of the royal house of Stuart. He looked again at his brother, still gazing out at the skimming clouds. Andrew craved to know why the world turned, to study science and medicine, to learn the ways of the future instead of burying himself in a disappearing past. If Donald could have given his brother that opportunity he would have done so gladly. Instead such benefits were about to fall to him, who would appreciate them not at all. But it was required of a chieftain in waiting to avail himself of the best education, and soon Donald would be southbound, to his country's capital, where he would acquaint himself with the intricacies of philosophy along with the histories of classical Greece and Rome. Andrew would remain in Glenshellich and wait for an opportunity to come his way, perhaps, like so many of their friends and neighbours, in the shape of a commission in the army of France. One thing was certain, whatever his future, he would learn more waiting for it from Euan MacMichael than ever he would from their opinionated "scribe" of a cousin.

"Again you are guilty of inattention, Andrew," the tutor complained and as Andrew turned his soft brown eyes apologetically back to him anger surged through Donald's heart. Why should Andrew always be blamed for the faults that lay in him? He knew that in the scribe's small mind the son of the chieftain was above censure, but that did not mean the same son should have to tolerate it. He sprang to his feet, loudly scraping back his chair.

"I am in no mood for history," he announced and stormed from the room, slamming the door behind him.

John Stewart watched him stride across the yard and onto the track that led to the clachan. There was no mistaking the darkness of Donald's mood and the old chieftain shook his head in concern. Leaning heavily on his stick, as he had to do so often these days, he began to make his slow way towards the stables. From inside he could hear the tuneless notes of an old melody and he smiled as he paused to listen. But as he limped inside his expression became serious again.

"Donald grows more headstrong by the day," he observed. " I fear I have spoiled him."

Fraser did not like his chieftain's colour or the sharp shallow sound of his breathing. "Ach!" he snorted. But he did not disagree.

"And kept him here longer than perhaps has been wise," MacSomhairle added. He pushed the piece of paper he was carrying towards his old servant, and Fraser saw that it was a letter. He eyed his master shrewdly.

"Newly dispatched from the Glen of Black Cattle," MacSomhairle announced. "An invitation to myself, and to Donald."

Fraser tried to respond with enthusiasm.

"Good news then."

"Indeed."

But Fraser wondered if he heard a note of misgiving. He decided to act on it.

"You canna' legislate for the laddie's heart."

"What more could a man ask for than a wealthy and beautiful wife?"

Fraser turned away without an answer and the chieftain made a gesture of impatience. "My own marriage to his mother was arranged under similar contract."

Fraser's eyes narrowed. "But you hadna' placed your heart elsewhere."

This time he had gone too far. MacSomhairle's reply was sharp. "The witch's grand-daughter could never be Lady of Glenshellich."

"Perhaps no'," Fraser agreed, remaining calm. "But while she fills his mind there'll be no room for another, and he'll no' help your cause in the Glen of the Black Cattle." He paused again. "Maybe his brother would serve your schemes better."

John Stewart seemed to give the suggestion serious thought. Fraser could well be right. It would be unfortunate if Donald's hot headedness spoilt plans so carefully constructed over so many years. Recognising his master's indecision Fraser ventured further.

"There's some still think the match ill-omened." He was referring to the journey home on the occasion it had first been proposed, the journey that had taken them through the Valley of Stones. But John Stewart was quick to dismiss him.

"Some in this land attribute too much to omens – even you, my friend, despite coming from a place where folk are held to possess some common sense. More moonshine has rubbed off on you here than is good for you, it seems."

"Meaning I've turned into a more fanciful body than yoursel'?"

John Stewart laughed. "There are few less fanciful then I, as you well know," he replied, but it occurred to him that Fraser might have provided him with a convenient solution to the problem of Donald's visit to the MacLeans of Cairnill. Why not take Andrew instead? Certainly there would be no fear of his younger son compromising the arrangement by rash words or rasher actions. The more he considered it the more practical Fraser's suggestion began to appear. He gave him a genial slap across the shoulders before hobbling back in the direction of the house

Donald had taken a different direction. Lying beside him on the slopes below the shielings Meg MacLeay made no attempt to cover her nakedness. She relished the roughness of the heather against her skin, the warmth of the sun on every part of her. Donald rolled himself onto his back, his body singing and spent, and laughed into the drifting clouds. He had laughed when they were children together racing along the loch-side and swimming through the summer waters with Euan and Andrew and the other children from the clachan. He still laughed, and Meg laughed with him, thankful for the fire and the passion and wildness of their snatched moments. Her eyes were directed upwards, to the place where the blue line of sky met with the mottled granite of the giant's mountain and, focusing them, she could just make out the fissure beyond the corrie that marked the entrance to Feodag's cave. Following the direction of her gaze Donald stroked her cheek and kissed her neck.

"What are you thinking?" he asked, his breath warm on her face.

"I am thinking of the day you saved Euan MacMichael's life."

"And why would you be remembering that day?"

"Because it was so like this one. I remember the smell of the lilac in the warm wind. All the time I was watching you my heart was in my mouth and the lilac was in my nostrils. And now each time I catch that scent I think of it."

Donald sat up and gazed out across the lochan. The last fishing boats were returning and he watched the men hauling their nets onto the shore. They were too far off for him to catch the sea smell of the mussels and shrimps, but still he could not imagine the scent of lilac, unless it was in the musky perfume that came from the black strands of Meg's hair. He raised his eyes all the way from the water to the summit of Beinn Feodag. It must have been more than a year since he had climbed to the cave. There was no challenge in reaching it now, though Meg was right to remember that once the climb had almost cost his foster brother his life.

"You never knew I watched you," she went on, " though Andrew did. I watched the three of you, each day climb higher and higher, each

33

time determined to reach a little bit further. Andrew discovered me on the morning he knew he had climbed high enough." She smiled and the beauty of her expression caught Donald's breath and twisted at his heart.

Meg fell silent as she remembered how Andrew had stumbled over the heather, tears blinding him to the witch's grand-daughter sitting small and still, hidden in the bracken that clothed the lower slopes. When he did notice her it was too late. She had seen his tears. She was witness to his shame as he ran, crying like a girl, while his brother and Euan MacMichael still had the courage to pursue their goal. But she had smiled and told him she was only glad he was safe.

"Why would you be climbing to the top of mountains?" she had asked him, sensing then, as now she was certain, that Andrew would have different heights to scale. The two of them shared a special secret, the rare vision that whispered and hinted to them of things yet to come. Some called it The Sight, a bitter gift, better described as a burden, and Meg knew that she possessed only a fraction of Andrew's share. From the beginnings of time each clan had their seers, wise beyond the world's ways. Their ancient powers might have dwindled, but they had not died, and the intangible bond between the lingering few who shared them was strong. But while Donald could not fail to sense the spirit of the girl who had come to him so naturally, it was her body he craved, with all the hunger of his seventeen years. For the moment his craving was satisfied and he was in the mood for conversation. He too thought back to the day she had mentioned.

"Eochain MacMichael and Domhnull MacSomhairle were too proud to be seen in the company of the grand-daughter of Beathag the witch. And too foolish not to know when they had climbed high enough." He grinned. "We never told Catriona – even to this day she does not know what we did."

Fortunately so, thought Meg, for she had witnessed too vividly how close Catriona's son had come to plunging to his death, drawn by the dangerous legend of a hidden cave. It was said that once it had been reached other, safer, routes could easily be spotted. The way that

Donald and Euan had conquered was the most perilous, a way a person would choose to venture only once.

Donald squinted into the sunshine. He and Euan were bound in ancient ways, but that day had made their bond stronger. He would never forget his foster brother's face, stricken with fear as his ten-year-old legs kicked wildly, desperately seeking a hold on the rock-face beneath the scree, his fingers slithering inside and around Donald's grasp. He would never forget the sound of his own frantic gasps and the knowledge that at any moment he might tumble with the weight of the more muscular boy, over the edge of the ridge and down the sheer slope to a certain death. Both their hands had grown treacherous with sweat. His arm had cracked and torn in its socket, his muscles had stretched and twisted and cried out, but somehow each of them had found the strength for Donald to heave Euan back onto the ridge. From there they had crawled onto the ledge that widened towards the mouth of Feodag's cave. Since that day they had stood on the ledge many times, looking down on the clachan, dwarfed and distant, and over the scattering of isolated cottages and crofts that clung to the lower slopes. At the mouth of the giant's cave they shared an eagle's view, a view not granted lightly.

Had Donald been there now he would have seen his father's piper, Kenneth MacCombie, pulling his grandfather's nets, heavy and rustling with their haul of shellfish from the lochan. Had he been on the shore he would have seen Kenneth's steady eyes scan the heather clad slopes and grow strangely sad.

Old Angus Ban secured his boat then followed the direction of his grandson's gaze.

"Eilidh of the scarlet face would still be your woman, Kenneth Mhor," the old man murmured. "If your eyes were not imprisoned by the grand-daughter of the witch."

"I cannot choose the direction these eyes take," Kenneth replied. "And you know they have watched her from childhood."

"And did I not warn you then, my grandson, that she would come to you second? And she would not come alone."

Kenneth made a gesture of irritation. He turned his attention away from the hillside and back to the nets.

"I am minded with my chief," he retorted. "I will not heed the old and dangerous words of the seers."

"Then your chief and you perceive ill, for be sure the time is closer than you know. You of all people need no reminding how the boy has become a man." The tone of Angus' voice grew softer, but it did not waver. "It might be wise to be making in your music some strains of lament."

Kenneth's eyes narrowed as he stared out across the darkening loch. The blue sky would soon disappear under the cloud that approached from the west. His weathered face took on a distant expression. He had waited a long time, but he was prepared to wait longer. For the granddaughter of Beathag the witch he knew he would be prepared to wait forever.

* * *

The cottage of Euan MacMichael was the largest in the clachan and stood at its eastern end. At daybreak on summer mornings the shadow of the Watcher's Stone could stretch almost as far as the divots on its outhouse roof.

Euan held the largest tract of the clachan's arable land. This was the fifty yard wide, seaweed enriched strip that extended from the eastern shore of the lochan for over a mile to the last outlying croft. On this uniquely favoured soil grew the corn and oats to feed the clachan, small plots individually husbanded, their produce communally stored in the ramshackle huts and barns that tumbled beside the larger cottages.

Euan had his own barn and his own smokehouse. His cattle grazed freely over the acres of his leased land, from the foothills of the giant's mountain to the eastern shore of the lochan. Recently he had been at pains not only to increase the number of his herd but also to improve its quality, keeping his best beasts behind for breeding and buying stock as well as selling it at the Crieff trysts. The special care that he and his son took with the new calves was the subject of much talk in the clachan.

"Would you be trading the healing for the husbandry?" old Angus Ban had taunted him one evening as they sat at the fire telling old tales.

"I would be looking for some reward from my labours," Euan had retorted. "For the healing might be much in demand but it affords a poor return. I have a notion to ease my old age with some silver. They say that in the south the farming is a very profitable business."

Angus was not sure if he should take the healer seriously. He had nothing but scorn for the south and its new fangled notions of trade. What good was silver in Glenshellich where a man could meet all his needs without a groat to his name and live a long and healthy life into the bargain? He was disappointed in Euan MacMichael, who had no doubt been fed the farming nonsense from the woman he had brought back with him from The Rising. Better to have left her where she was and found a wife from among his own clan, a wife with less interfering ways. It would end badly, of that Angus was certain.

John Stewart was also reflecting on his foster brother's uncharacteristic materialism as he watched Euan's dogs dart and crawl around the shaggy black beasts. But his thoughts were interrupted by the appearance of Catriona's tall figure in the doorway of the cottage. Seconds later a dozen or so ragged children spilled from behind her into the sunlight and their shouts rang through the still air as they sprinted along the shoreline. Their chieftain reined his horse and watched them with an expression of deep satisfaction.

"I will soon preside over the best educated glen in the north," he said as Catriona came to stand beside him.

Her eyes followed her young charges as they dispersed through the clachan. "They are hungry for knowledge," she answered. "One day there will be real schools in the glens, and proper teachers to instruct them."

"But not in my day. Or even in my son's, I fear."

"Why not, if we all strive for it?"

"I doubt there will ever be a teacher in Glenshellich as gifted as the one we already have," the chieftain replied with a smile. But she did not appear to be listening. Her eyes were on the shore where her husband and son moved around the cattle, slow figures in a purposeful dance. Her next words told him that her thoughts moved with them.

"And no healer as gifted as Euan?"

He suppressed a sigh and looked away, understanding her inference only too well. "There is sufficient capital only for Donald," he said briefly.

"Donald will not thank you for a city education. Everyone in the clachan can see that his choice would be to remain in Glenshellich."

"It is the way, Catriona."

But he sighed again and wondered how long he would be able to fall back on such excuses. Tradition was fast becoming their enemy, and he had never yet produced an argument convincing enough to counter Catriona's opinions on the education of his sons.

"Have you asked Donald what his wishes might be?" she persisted.

"It is not a subject for discussion - with him or with yourself."

Catriona turned her head away in frustration and her eyes drew distant as she watched her husband and son call in the dogs. The herd were gathered close and safe and would be well guarded.

"The shadow is creeping over Euan's heart," she murmured at last. "Sometimes I watch him when he sleeps and I see it. I fear we have placed too many burdens on him, MacSomhairle."

"We all have burdens to bear," he answered sadly. "There are shadows on all our hearts. We can only be thankful that our sons will be heirs to better times."

Catriona expression grew earnest again.

"You know that all Euan's hopes lie with Andrew. The hands of a healer are not passed through blood. They come through the pathways of the spirit. Only one who has the gifts can distinguish it in another. Andrew has the healing in him and he has the sight. Do not send him for a soldier, MacSomhairle."

John Stewart sighed. All those closest to him were of similar mind: Fraser, Catriona, Euan, even Donald himself, who seemed always to find a reason to delay the day he would leave the glen for the education which was essential for him to take his proper place in the world. It was Andrew they all believed should go to Edinburgh, to study medicine, for it was his dream and perhaps his destiny, while Donald could not concentrate for five minutes on any knowledge that was to be found in books. But his father could not condemn him for it. Progressive as some of his views might be, John Stewart had come to his chieftaincy down ancient routes. A chieftain was a leader, learned above the others of the clan, equipped to inspire them in peacetime and in war. There had never been a time, in his memory or in the annals of his clan, when the chief had not been compelled to lead his men into battle. There would always be occasions when honour must be fought for. As he had already stated, that was the way.

"What advantage have your wars ever brought?" Catriona went on. "They only delay the way forward. Peace and prosperity is surely what you all want, whatever your title, whatever your allegiance."

"We must be ready to defend our beliefs."

"Yet beliefs can change." Her voice took on a sharper edge. "As your old friend's seem to have done."

John Stewart turned away. He was becoming old, too tired for argument, too stubborn to abandon his convictions. But he was honest enough to recognise some truth in what she said.

"If you refer to Cairnill, then indeed, his attitude saddens me." His expression grew thoughtful, but then he smiled. "Yet he still intends to honour our agreement."

Catriona turned away and her eyes fell once more on her husband and son who were now making their way towards them. She was struck by how alike they had become.

"For whose benefit was that agreement made?" she murmured softly. "Donald's or your own?"

Not for the first time she spoke as his conscience, voicing judgments that he knew none else, save perhaps her old ally Fraser, would dare to utter.

"I have decided what is best," he said abruptly. "For Donald and for Glenshellich."

Still she was not prepared to let the matter rest. "For now perhaps. But our sons will have their own way to find in their own world. Should they not be allowed to listen to their own hearts?"

He turned away. It grieved Catriona that John Stewart, usually so wise, could be so obstinate when it came to the subject of Donald. But with Donald lay the future of his clan and the succession of his bloodline. Catriona understood perfectly why it was a subject best left unmentioned.

* * *

In the summer months the heart of the clachan moved to the shielings, the sheltered pastures among the hills where the cattle grew fat for the autumn sales grazing on the sweet green grasses and the women and girls churned their milk into butter and cheese. For weeks they lived simply in huts of turf and branches, and made merry through the long summer days. Few unions in Glenshellich had not begun in the warm shieling nights when the sun had so short a time to set. Donald loved to join his clan there, listening to the old stories under silver skies, tending cattle with Euan and the dogs, and taking every possible opportunity to slip with the witch's granddaughter into the more private places still higher on the mountainside.

On a mid-June afternoon the barks of welcome from the house below told him that his father and brother had returned from their visit to the Glen of the Black Cattle. They would be expecting no less a welcome from him. Meg brushed the light hairs on his chest with her lips and let her breasts press down on the muscles of his stomach. He found it impossible to tear himself away. He could spend every minute of every day like this. He closed his eyes and sighed with pleasure and anticipation. As she often did Meg was taking control, placing him inside her, moving above him as much for her own pleasure as for his. His gasps grow louder and she placed a finger on his lips. Then she watched him, smiling and groaning gently, provoking and teasing him, until finally he cried out his release. Lazing among the cattle Euan and the other boys chuckled and winked to each other, and wished, not for the first time, that they could trade places with the son of their chieftain.

But minutes later Donald's loping strides were leaving the hillside behind, brushing the bracken between Feodag's stones. Walking between worlds he could still hear the laughter behind him. Soon he would arrive at the house and take up the weight of his responsibilities again.

He paused, as he did each time he rounded the boulder. Between worlds also was Meg's cottage, if it deserved that name, for it was little better than the huts at the shielings, tiny, smoke filled, with hardly a stick of furniture. Almost as if she had been expecting him, Meg's grandmother, Beathag, slunk to the doorway and Luath, her mangy hound, padded from the gloom behind to keep yellow-eyed vigil at her side. Donald's stomach tightened and heaved with the smell that wrinkled out with them.

The old woman neither moved nor spoke, but as he drew closer she gave a strange little smile that told him she knew everything, all he had done with her grand-daughter in the shadow of the giant's mountain. He tried to shrug off the cold chill that ran through him. He was the son of the chieftain. He had no reason to be afraid of half-deranged crones like Beathag. He forced himself to meet her glinting eyes. She smiled again, with a kind of satisfaction, and turned to fade backwards into the darkness of her den. With a low swish of his tail Luath followed her.

The clouds were gathering over the lochan and the air grew suddenly cooler. The wind was bringing Glenshellich the storm that was already breaking over the distant Mountains of the Eagles. Out on the water it seemed that MacSomhairle's piper had seen it too, for Kenneth had wheeled his boat around and was rowing quickly back towards the shore.

Donald strode on, his pace only slowing as he drew closer to the house. He had little doubt that the long planned union between Glenshellich and

Cairnill would have moved a step closer. He could hear Fraser singing softly inside the stables as he brushed down the horses after their journey, but he did not stop as he usually did to greet his old friend. Instead he drew a determined breath and strode into the house.

Andrew took some moments to answer his brother's knock on the door of his room, and when he appeared his face was flushed, his eyes strangely bright.

"I fell asleep," he mumbled.

Donald eyed him with suspicion but threw himself carelessly onto the bed.

"So tell me everything," he demanded. "That is, everything as you saw it."

Andrew turned away. He wondered what Donald would say if he knew how impossible that was. Everything as he saw it. So he must he tell him that the girl waiting for him in the Glen of the Black Cattle was now a woman, and the most beautiful woman a man could lay eyes on. He must seek the words to describe her gentle eyes, her delicate features, the smile that brought such a trembling to his heart. He should mention Helen's slim and perfectly proportioned body, the auburn sheen on her dark hair. Andrew could have found superlatives to describe his brother's future bride until the sun set over the giant's mountain, until even Donald could not fail to realise that he had completely betrayed his role as emissary by falling head over heels in love with her himself. Or perhaps he should tell Donald that even her father, for he had overheard him, believed that a match with a different son might represent a truer meeting of hearts, might even afford his daughter a greater chance of happiness.

"Do you imply that Donald will not make Helen happy?" an outraged John Stewart had charged his old friend.

Cairnill only shook his head. The two chieftains had known each other too long for any pretence. Yet although they had suffered exile together they had drawn different lessons from it. Andrew could not deny a sneaking respect for the wily cattle baron who reaped such rich rewards from his rearranged loyalties. It was also clear that while Cairnill might be as dedicated to his own dynasty as MacSomhairle was to his, his daughter's happiness would be his priority, always and at whatever cost.

"I confess to wondering if he will," Cairnill had replied calmly. "For instance, why is he not here with you? What matter could be more important to a young man than time spent with his future bride? Certainly I see true merit in his brother, but my own sons have taught me that brothers can be as different as moss from marble. A kind heart is worth more than a chest full of guineas, old friend, and something most fathers would go a long way to seek." He hesitated, and Andrew wondered if he should take the opportunity to make his own presence felt. Skulking at doors had a distinctly dishonourable feel. But the resentful tone of his father's reply stalled him.

"And your four sons will doubtless follow your lead."

Cairnill's voice was sharp. "Four sons, two sons. It is not a question of numbers."

Through the gap in the door's oak panels the words lost none of their impact. Listening, Andrew realised sadly how time could take its toll on old friendships, especially ones that ran counter to progress. Cairnill's clan had grown rich under a government he had once taken arms against. Andrew could understand the chieftain's dilemma. His father could not.

"I will say one word to you, Hector," John Stewart retorted. "Allomore."

It was less a name than an accusation, but still Cairnill did not concede. To survive they had all been required to adapt. Black cattle would roam over the lush pastures from Loch Ericht to Loch Laggan and the MacLeans of Cairnill would prosper with or without the blessing of a ruined man peddling dead dreams in a distant land. His retort reached Andrew's ears clearly.

"And I will say two to you, John. Dispossessed. Destitute."

There could be no doubting the silence that followed owed more to hostility than accord. Needing now to break it, Andrew had raised his hand to the door. But just at that moment Helen appeared at his

43

elbow, her finger pressed to her lips. How long she had been beside him he did not know. He felt his face redden with the shame of being discovered in the role of eavesdropper, but she drew him aside and looked earnestly into his face.

"I do still wish my future to be in Glenshellich," she breathed.

It was too easy for Andrew to imagine her there, bringing light and tranquillity to a house made harsh over his lifetime by the lack of a woman's warmth. Her presence was just one more gift destined for Donald, unsought, unwanted, undeserved.

Looking into his brother's eager eyes he felt his heart twist again.

"The contract is unchanged," he said simply.

Donald grinned. "But not to be acted upon in the foreseeable future."

"You might consider yourself fortunate to have the prospect of such a wife."

Donald looked briefly puzzled, then threw back his head and laughed out loud.

"In God's name, Andrew, you have become an old man in Cairnill's house. I know what I must do and I will do it." His expression changed. "But it is not fair that our lives must be so prescribed, when I am forced to leave for Edinburgh, a place that fills me with abhorrence, to study subjects that interest me not at all, while you, who would seize that chance with both hands, will be confined in this glen, the place I would never willingly leave in my whole life."

"Yet for all that," replied Andrew, finding it impossible to keep the bitterness from his voice. "For all that, you would not have chosen to be born second."

* * *

Later, as the soft evening light crept across the sky, Donald lay alone in the heather, out of sight and earshot of the huts on the hill pastures. Sometimes he craved such solitude, though not usually to dwell on gloomy thoughts. He had been away from Glenshellich on many occasions, on visits to old friends, to Inverness and Crieff with the cattle, to his aunt's in Edinburgh; but never for more than a few weeks, and never alone. His travels had broadened his outlook only so far as to convince him that everything he required for his contentment could be found in his own glen. He knew he would be happy to live forever under the giant's mountain, managing the beasts, stalking the deer, fishing the loch, hearing the old stories and being with his people. They were a part of him and he of them. He wished for nothing more than one day to be as honourable and wise a leader as his father.

He rolled over and listened for a while to the soft sounds around him, the distant lowing of cattle, the steady humming of bees. He thought of the noise of the city, the crowds, the noxious smells from every close and wynd. There was much for him still to learn, he knew, and he supposed he must learn it where they thought best. But his thoughts drifted as ever back to Meg, the delights of her body, the fascination of her wild, strange heart. He could do nothing now but abandon her to the dwindling sanity of Beathag and her darting, damning eye, the eye that always seemed to rest longest and most spitefully on him. In his darkest moments it seemed to Donald that he had indeed been cursed, born only to bring pain to those he loved best, the mother he had so briefly known and forgotten, the brother whose dreams he must steal, even Catriona, his protector and comforter whose face could hold such strange and inexplicable sadness, and most of all when her gaze came to rest on him.

Even as Donald thought of her, Catriona was gazing at her husband through the gloom of her cottage, trying to hide a sadness that was not at all difficult to understand. She imagined their son, up in the hill pastures, laughing with the girls from the clachan. Soon he would find a special girl for himself. Soon, Catriona was convinced, she would be alone.

As if the healer read her thoughts he whispered, "I have lived to see our son become a man. And still I feel the life strong in me."

"He may be a man, but he needs you still." Her voice faded to little more than a whisper. "As I do. As I will always."

He did not answer and she moved to stand behind him, gently stroking his shoulders until she felt the tension in them relax.

"Do you feel the soldier's bullet?"

"A little today," he replied quietly. "It turns near my heart and we must never forget, my dearest love, that one day it will turn too far. I do not have the powers to heal myself."

Catriona's eyes grew distant. "Each day is precious to me. Each day since I saw you. We have been given many days, Euan. Many more than ever I dared hope."

He took her hand and held it to his lips. "Yet you will have many more without me."

She gave him a tender sad smile.

"If we are to believe the old stories."

"There is but one man in this glen who can ignore them."

Catriona pulled herself away and took two steps towards the window. Out on the lochan the sun was setting. They had seen sunsets like this before, blazing red and orange, fingers of silver, pink and gold beckoning from the Giant's Mountain, pointing westwards. Only once had the dying sun set the lochan on fire. They did not expect to see such a sunset again.

"Then perhaps he is the wisest," she said softly.

"Perhaps," he agreed, knowing that neither of them believed it.

* * *

Old Angus Ban picked his way over the mussel shells that littered the shoreline of the loch. The clachan was quiet, almost deserted. Its soul had climbed with the cattle and the women who spun new threads to weave around old stories. They sang in the shielings, Angus remembered, and danced, and laughed for the joy of the life in their veins. What did it mater that the joy was short lived, as long as it returned each season to lift their hearts?

As the sky deepened from orange to red, Angus realised that he was not alone. A slight, hunched figure was approaching, stumbling awkwardly as the shingle clutched her feet, turning her head scornfully from time to time towards the drifting strains of laughter.

No one in the clachan could count as many summers as Angus Ban. He had sat times without number around the peat fires, alongside elders now long buried and themselves immortalised in tale. Few stories were unknown to Angus and no gossip forgotten. Age had not diminished his powers of memory and he did not need his dimming sight to recall another evening when the very same figure had taken an almost identical path.

He shook his head sorrowfully, remembering how Beathag had cursed her only child from the glen, close on twenty summers before, cursed her for the disgrace she had brought to the honour of the clan. It was said, though Angus himself did not entirely believe it, that Beathag's daughter had found a lover in Kilclath, a lover she met secretly on misty evenings under the mountains of the Eagles. It was said that the lover was the father of the girl who now turned all the men's heads in their own clachan, his own grandson's most of all. But the lover in Kilclath had tired of Beathag's daughter. She had been forced to flee with the child to her mother, only to be banished more cruelly still. Angus had heard tell she was a whore now in Inverness. He had heard that MacSomhairle once journeyed there to find her, but she had refused, through shame, to let him bring her home. Where she was now, living or dead, no one knew, though Beathag maintained she had long since sold her soul to someone more treacherous even than a Campbell. It was all chaff dispersed in an ancient wind, just another of the hundreds of tiny tragedies Angus had witnessed down the decades. It was best to stay within the world you knew, to keep with your own kind. Beathag had licked whatever wounds she carried and retreated with the child to her hovel on the hillside. She spent most days there now, crouched over her spinning wheel, casting mischief through her half blind eye, delighting in the fear she could waken in the children, and more than a few of the adults. As for her daughter, Meg's mother, there had been no further word. She had been a bonny enough creature, Angus remembered. Dead, likely, he imagined, of whore's disease or the pox.

Inverness was a wicked and stinking place, sinful and proud, a fitting destination for daughters of devils and lovers of Campbells.

But Beathag was almost upon him. She squinted into his face through the last of the sun's rays.

"It is long since you went to the shielings, Beathag," he observed dryly in greeting, for he remembered there had been a time when she had laughed and danced and sang just as they did now on the slopes high above. The old woman spat contemptuously towards the loch. Angus narrowed his eyes until only a pale lizard-like slit glinted. There was no one but Beathag to hear his words. "Or is it that you aspire to go further? You, or one close to you in blood?"

This time it was the turn of Beathag's eye to sparkle.

"I did not devise the foretelling, Angus Ban."

Angus let out a long sigh. "The time grows close when none will know it. Euan MacMichael was the last man permitted to hear the words. They are forbidden to his son."

Beathag's wicked eye still shone. "His son will hear the *Faisneachd.*"

Angus shook his head. "Not while MacSomhairle lives." They moved together now like conspirators. John Stewart was far from their minds. Ancient messages from old ghosts spoke louder.

"MacSomhairle will not live forever." Beathag gave a sudden cackle. "Unlike you, Angus Ban, who we can all see has supped with the devil himself."

"From the same spoon as yourself. When it had a longer handle," Angus countered. He had almost forgotten how enjoyable a tussle with the old witch could be.

"We will all need its nourishment one day," she answered. "For it begins to seem the words speak also of you."

Angus let his eyes stray upward to the silhouetted slopes and his ears caught again the drifting snatches of song.

"It is strange that you say so," he answered. "For the same idea has been growing in my own mind. Perhaps we should mention it no more."

"Mention it or hold your tongue," she hissed. "It will make no difference."

As her words died it seemed to Angus that he heard another pulse behind the music on the mountain, a low throbbing such as he had never known before, a rhythmic, insistent pounding, as if of far off drums.

* * *

Soon after his visit to Cairnill MacSomhairle summoned his lawyer and old friend, Gavin MacVey, from Edinburgh. They had exchanged several letters on the subject of Donald's future and Gavin could see no advantage in re-treading old ground, especially in the light of the worrying changes the past two years had wrought on the chieftain. Gavin let his shrewd eyes linger on his old friend, noticing how sparse and grey the once chestnut hair had become, how pale and sunken the cheeks and, most worrying of all, how vague the expression creeping over MacSomhairle's eyes.

"I do not wish to dwell on the subject of your health, John, but in my opinion you have delayed this moment long enough."

"A sick old man's selfishness?" John Stewart replied, and then he sighed. "I know it. I know it, Gavin. The boy must learn. He must experience a wider world."

"He must become a man," stated the lawyer simply. "For no-one would wish him to inherit responsibilities for which he was not equipped." Again he waited, in some trepidation for his old friend's response. MacSomhairle might have a reputation for sound common sense, but scratch a highlander ….

Today, however, MacSomhairle was not inclined to rise to any bait, real or inferred. "Donald will do his best always, Gavin," he said simply. "Why can you not share my faith in him?"

Gavin looked away and steeled himself for the task he had come north for. It was not to prevaricate. "There is a wildness in him which must be of concern."

"And is that wildness not in us all? Even in you, despite your years in the city? Surely something of our birthright remains?"

"I am reminded in him at times of your brother," Gavin went on, pressing home his advantage. "And you know how little your glen benefited under his stewardship. I wonder also what notions the scribe of Ardallan has implanted in his no doubt impressionable mind."

"So you have abandoned more than your heritage, Gavin," John Stewart acknowledged sadly.

The lawyer inclined his head and averted his eyes. "It is true that I would no longer lend my support to King James." He lowered his voice. "That I would even go so far as advise my friends to do likewise."

"Yet beliefs of the heart lie too deep for change," MacSomhairle sighed, before his tone grew more practical. "Oh, I cannot altogether blame you, Gavin. The world is altered and you are wise to adapt with it. But it is with my blessing that the scribe of Ardallan teaches my sons the politics of our age. I would be sorely disappointed if, were the time to come again, they would not be among the first to lay their swords at the feet of the true king."

"But meanwhile," replied the lawyer dryly, "Donald must mix with those of other persuasions, and perhaps see for himself the state of affairs in an exiled court. It is long since you ventured beyond the sea, MacSomhairle, but no doubt your old friend Allomore could paint a truer picture, were his mind not still blinded by dreams long dead. You plot only for your own ruin, and I am afraid that is the truth of it."

John Stewart sighed again. "We have argued these lines so often, Gavin, that we should have learned their fruitlessness long ago. There is merit, perhaps, in what you say and especially of Allomore. But has he been wrong to sacrifice his life for his dream? He has been more faithful to the cause than any of us, and thoughts of him still have the power to shame me."

"He alone can answer for the sacrifices he had made. But I wonder how his children will see fit to honour him, for King James has cheated them of their inheritance. Will the tattered pride of a life spent in exile be compensation enough for that loss? Would Donald recognise this as part of the dream you lay upon his heart? For all the loyalty you profess for him I would be surprised if he would accept the life Allomore has chosen."

John Stewart lowered his gaze and turned away. It was harder for him to put his heart into words than it was for the practised lawyer to speak his mind. But despite their differences he could take comfort from having at least one good friend in the city to keep a watchful eye on his son.

Three weeks later Donald buckled down the saddle girth, slapped his stallion and turned to look full into the face of his oldest friend.

"I will not pass a happy hour until I return," he stated simply.

Fraser tried to hide his own heavy heart behind a pawky grin.

"Ach!" he snorted. "And how would you ken when you've never stayed in another place long enough to see the half of it? How many times have I telt you, you canna fully love your home before you ken what it is to miss it."

Donald had said all his goodbyes. He had wandered through the clachan all of the day before and would not take that route from the glen. Iain MacCombie would ride with him to Cranachferry and return with the horses. Donald would take a fresh mare to Fort William and from there, thanks to General Wade, the roads would enable him swift safe passage by coach. He would be in the capital inside two days. The knowledge brought a dry sob to his throat.

Fraser patted his shoulder, then, overcome himself, clasped him tightly to his chest.

"God speed," he muttered.

Donald gave the groom a fierce and final hug before he threw himself over his horse and galloped through the gate without another backward glance.

At the edge of the clachan Meg MacLeay and Euan MacMichael turned their eyes from the direction they knew he was taking.

"He will always be ours," Euan hissed savagely. "It is here he belongs, not in a strange city, not across the sea."

Meg let her fingers gently brush his arm, for it was so much harder for Euan. She at least could accept that her special time with the son of their chieftain was over, that she had lain in the heather with Domhnull MacSomhairle for the very last time. But Euan would always be his brother, his protector, and a city held many dangers.

"Remember he is born to other things," she said softly. "And other things will draw him. For a time they might possess him."

As Euan turned his bleak gaze over the lochan Meg found her attention drawn in a different direction. From somewhere inside the small valley that split the green lower slopes of the Giant's Mountain came the sound of the pipes, the haunting notes of an unfamiliar pibroch. Strangely it did not sound at all like a lament, and as Meg listened she found it impossible not to smile. Kenneth Mhor could put feelings into his tunes that no words could express; yet she understood them. She had understood them for as long as she could remember. The notes reached deep inside her, right to the core of the new life she had already begun to sense stirring.

* * *

Alison Bothwell peered down from her drawing room casement onto the Lawnmarket below. It was market day in Edinburgh and the stalls straggled nearly the length of the High Street. Sedan chairs borne by cursing porters squeezed past stray dogs and grasping beggars. Haughty gentlewomen manoeuvred their hooped petticoats around squabbling urchins and toppling merchandise, while vendors of vegetables, herbs, satins and lace, candy-men and fishwives all vied raucously for the public's attention. Yet despite the spirited scene below her Alison's attention seemed preoccupied with the young man who first hurried, then deliberately loitered behind a scissor-grinder's stall.

"Now, I just wonder ..." she murmured to herself.

Kirsty, her maid of all duties, turned from her less than absorbing task of setting places for the taking of tea.

"What might you be wondering, Mistress Bothwell?" she replied in the pert tone she sometimes slipped into when answering her mistress's requests.

"I was not addressing you, directly, Kirsty, as it happens," Alison explained with a pained show of patience. She turned a peevish glance towards the table. As usual the setting was anything but satisfactory, and it would not do for her nephew to be given a second rate welcome.

"Did I not request the silver tea spoons?"

Kirsty scowled, considered a retort, but caught the expression in her mistress's eye. She moved to the dresser and reached for the velvet-lined box containing the spoons in question. As she opened it her glance fell on the face of the handsome, bewigged young man depicted in the oil miniature propped in the corner. She tossed her auburn curls at the pouting red lips and mournful brown eyes, then for good measure stuck out her tongue. The portrait stood defiantly between two engraved glasses, their twisting stems supporting delicate goblets, which bore the inscription "Jacobus III". An intricate design of roses was engraved on the front and back of each one. Neatly folded beside them was a lace handkerchief, placed there by Alison who had been assured on the best authority it was the very one which caught her monarch's tears before he took ship at Montrose, bidding a sad and hopefully temporary farewell to his homeland. Not a night passed without Alison ending her prayers with a fervent entreaty for him to return at the earliest opportunity.

Loyalty to the Royal House of Stuart was one of the few things she had ever had in common with her family by marriage. Her sister had been contracted to John Stewart while he was a hard working student in the city. Their father, unwisely as it turned out, had decided that an ancient lineage with its links, however tenuous, to the royal house, would provide suitable security for either of his daughters. John Stewart had been offered his choice and had taken Janet, the younger and undeniably prettier, if not the more robust. Scarcely had Janet made the daunting journey north when she found herself faced with the spectre of the Old Pretender and his raised standard, enticing her

53

new husband from her side to his. Abandoned and horribly homesick, the new bride had laboured to establish herself in a society as foreign to her as the tribes of Africa, while struggling with the even greater demands of a debilitating pregnancy. Not surprisingly she had quickly became immune to the glories of her surroundings and sent desperately for her older sister to provide some much needed support.

Alison had arrived in Glenshellich to find Janet a sad shadow of her vivacious self. And little wonder. Alison shuddered to remember the mists and the rains, the snows that crept up and down the Giant's Mountain through the long dark months that separated the hunter's moon and the summer solstice. She had dutifully remained in Glenshellich until her ailing infant nephew died and Janet sailed for France to present her husband with his ultimatum. When John Stewart had returned from exile Alison had resumed her duties in the Lawnmarket with relief, the whole experience banishing any regrets that might have lingered over his choice of bride. She had been more than content to tend to the needs of her invalid father who could fend off with a clear conscience any remaining offers of matrimony. In time Alison had found her niche as the guiding light of Edinburgh's formidable and notorious band of Jacobite ladies, and if ever she harboured an old maid's regrets that the years had passed her by, she had only to cast her mind back to her sister and her premature death in that God-forsaken land.

Yet despite everything she had never held her brother in law entirely to blame. Perhaps she had been fonder of him than she was prepared to acknowledge, or perhaps hindsight had simply made her grateful for the choice he had made. Alison had been afforded the luxury of constructing a life that suited her to perfection. If it lacked romance on a personal level there was more than adequate compensation in observing, assessing and passing on Edinburgh's endless scandals and intrigues. Watching the comings and goings of her fellow citizens was Alison's greatest entertainment, and her apartment window, five stories high, afforded a unique insight into most of them.

In pursuit of today's best vantage point she was forced to stretch her neck awkwardly and, she feared, unbecomingly. The young man below had disappeared inside her own close, but Alison was striving for a better look at an elegant young woman picking a delicate and careful path through the debris underneath her high-heeled shoes.

"Just fancy…," she breathed before she withdrew her head abruptly on hearing the click of the drawing room door. Smiling triumphantly she stood back to allow the young man from the street his share of the view. "Am I correct, Mr Fettes? Can that vision be the girl from Bella Galbraith's …..?"

As the young man leaned past her shoulder Alison could detect, despite the early hour, the distinctive bouquet of claret. But she would not judge her young lodger too harshly. Hugh Fettes was a gentleman from a thriving Whig family near Pitlochry and it was hardly incumbent on his landlady to object to his activities, especially since his political leanings were far closer to her own than his father's. Besides, Alison had a natural indulgence towards the young and hot blooded. Hugh had just passed his twentieth birthday and cut a fine figure. Short and sturdy with fair unpowdered hair, he took dainty pride in his fine French brocade and velvet swagger. His ruddy complexion might have owed more to hours spent in the city's taverns than to his native Perthshire air, but he was a cheery and likable fellow who filled a comfortable niche in his landlady's heart. His blue eyes twinkled back at her as he let out a long and undeniably appreciative breath.

"Jean Petrie as ever was." A hint of wickedness lay behind the twinkle. "She has been transformed. Could it be by love?"

"By canny grooming and silver, more like," Alison snorted, before adding darkly, "but once a whore always a whore."

Hugh threw his landlady a knowing glance, while keeping his sceptical eye on the street below.

"None the less," he declared. "I'll wager there's no shortage of fellows who wish they'd set their eyes on her before Kilclath came to his *arrangement*."

Alison snorted more loudly, and the object of her speculation glanced momentarily upwards as she passed under the window, almost as if she were excusing the lapse of refinement. A small smile played around the corners of her mouth and her head inclined very slightly in subtle acknowledgement of their attention.

"The hussy," Alison breathed.

Hugh continued to study the young lady's progress while Kirsty clattered more plates behind him. He turned to her with a grin.

"Not to mention the fellows who'd cast their bonnets in your direction, eh, Kirsty my sweet," he smiled. "If you were not already spoken for by me!"

Kirsty suppressed a giggle of delight.

"Oh, Mr Fettes….." she simpered.

"And do not for one moment consider," he went on, "transferring your affections to Mistress Bothwell's nephew when he arrives. For we have all heard the tales of those wild highlanders and the wicked ways they have with city servant girls."

"Away with you," Alison chided. "The poor creature never knows when you are serious."

Meanwhile the young woman below them had paused to examine some linen cloth. So intense was her scrutiny that she did not notice a figure, in a gown of dazzling vulgarity, approach her quietly from behind. For some moments Jean remained unaware of the older woman's strangely affectionate gaze. When she did turn around a broad grin spread across her perfectly formed features.

"Bella!" she exclaimed, wrapping the old whore in an intuitive hug and noticing that it was not as easy as it once had been to pass her arms around her waistline. "Please don't be thinking I've not been asking how you've all been."

Bella raised her painted eyebrows. "My, he's worked his spells quicker than even I imagined. "Please don't be thinking I've not been asking how you've all been." Jean's cheeks flushed at Bella's mockery. "And what did he say, the bold master?" she demanded. "No need to concern yourself with the likes of her any more?"" She took a step backwards and waited for Jean's reaction.

"Indeed he did not! It's only that he's not wanting me to….." her voice faded, for she was still very anxious not to give offence.

"…..have too much to do with any of your old acquaintances? For fear that some of their coarseness might rub off," Bella finished for her. But seeing Jean's expression of dismay her own face softened and she cupped the girl's chin, smiling almost gently as she gazed into the beautiful face. "And who could blame him? Or yoursel'. All of us in the Chapel Land would understand that, hen. There's no' a single one of them wouldna give their eye teeth to be standing in your shoes." Then she leaned closer and held her face next to the girl's. "Jean Petrie rose out of the gutter just like I promised her mother. I hope the angels were watching."

Jean tried not to recoil from the stale gin on Bella's breath. As well as her widening girth the old whore mistress's complexion was showing signs of its age and usage.   It had been many a year since she had serviced any of her clients personally but few would deny that in her day Bella Galbraith had been the best. She had more than earned her honourable discharge from the bedchambers of the great, the good and the not so worthy. Now she need simply collect the dues from her girls and her boys. She had taught them well, for Bella had familiarised half the city's judges and professors with parts of the female anatomy even their own wives might have remained in ignorance of.   But none owed her a greater debt than Jean Petrie. It was Bella who had schooled the Master of the Stones in the dark and light arts of seduction, and Bella who had introduced him to her.

Donald swung his bundle out of their way and glanced up at the casements that seemed to reach out to touch each other above his head. He had walked the colourful length from the Canongate, pausing frequently to glance into the disorientating mysteries of steep closes and shady wynds. He was a good head taller than most of the passers by who seemed readier to make way for him than for each other. His plaid was a further statement, and the oak leaf in his bonnet pronounced his identity to all who could read it. Many could, for the streets of the city had more than their share of highlanders, sturdy cattleman with straggling hair, canny shopkeepers and stall merchants, and most of all the gentry, famous names from ancient lines, Lawyer Mackenzie, Judge Fraser, Professor Menteith, Advocate Campbell. There was no shortage of dignified doors bearing the latter surname, the clan of common sense, the office bearers, the agents of government.

"I am sorry!" Donald exclaimed, as his bundle struck hard against Bella Galbraith's shoulder. Without thinking he brushed her arm where the rough sacking had scraped, hardly noticing the younger woman beside her. "I am truly sorry."

Bella stood back. Behind her benevolent expression Jean had no doubt that a professional assessment was taking place.

"Never heed, sir," Bella assured him, taking blatant advantage of the opportunity for closer scrutiny. "Never heed. My! Newly down from the north, would it be?"

Donald doffed his cap politely and Jean hid a small smile.

"I am on my way to my aunt's house," he told them. "Her name in Mistress Alison Bothwell." His eyes looked helplessly about him. "It is so long since I was here, I have quite forgot the way."

"Mistress Alison Bothwell!" echoed Bella. "Well you'll no' be long in finding her, for that's the house just there," and she pointed to the tenement opposite. All three looked up and all three received the fleeting impression of two shapes shrinking out of sight.

"And a grand panorama she commands!" observed Bella, who knew the exact identity of least one of them.

Donald looked up at the toppling tenement with a mixture of fascination and dismay. He swallowed and turned again to the ladies who continued to regard him with expectant smiles.

"Her apartment is past halfway," Bella directed him. "In between the Laird of Drumcairn and Dalgleish the tailor. There's a family of mutes on the landing below – you'll likely meet the eldest out with her begging bowl, though I hear tell they're well enough supported by their kin in Newhaven."

Donald blinked at the mass of information and doffed his bonnet again.

"I cannot but thank you, ladies," he stammered politely, and noticed for the first time just how beautiful the younger of them was. But he backed away, unsure quite how to deal with the amused expressions neither of them could keep from their faces as they watched him lower his head towards the gloom of his aunt's close.

All manner of families shared the steep and narrow stair, from the sweep and caddies in the cellars to the poor mechanics in the garrets. In between could be found such worthies as the octogenarian Doctor Bethune and William Carcudden, dancing master, renowned for his dainty feet and fleeter fingers. All of their apartments were reached by sloping and slippery stone steps and Donald soon abandoned any attempts at politeness as he squeezed through the human traffic of Alison's neighbours. By the time he reached her door he was quite out of breath on account of the smell forcing him to hold it.

He dragged the iron risp on its notches until the door was slowly pulled open by a red headed, barefooted, wide-eyed maidservant. She gawped at him until he heard a reassuringly familiar voice from inside.

"For the love of God, Kirsty, if that's my nephew show him in this minute."

Donald reached her side at the window in less than six paces. He made no attempt to stand on ceremony but swept her into his arms, catching her distinctive smell of musk and lavender.

"My!" she gasped when he eventually released her. "What a broad fine chiel you've grown!" Then she turned to Hugh. "And here's the fellow you'll be sharing my roof with. Mr Fettes has volunteered to take it upon himself to introduce you to the delights of our city."

Hugh twinkled mischievously back at him. "Beginning as soon as you feel fit," he offered.

Alison threw her lodger a glance that was only fractionally disapproving. "He is a gallant enough young gentleman," she went on pointedly. "Despite his father's politics he's here because his mother is

59

a tried and trusted friend. I daresay the two of you will manage to find some common ground."

Donald found little difficulty in summoning a smile. The vow he had made on his journey south, the determination not to waste his opportunities by being miserable, was already proving easier to keep than he had imagined. Despite its superficial squalor, there was something about the city that stirred a corner of his heart. If he was to make it his temporary home he could see no reason not to make the most, as well as the best, of it.

* * *

The old man's head slumped on the pillow and he allowed the Signora to draw the cool sheet over his frail shoulders. The lime washed walls were too bright in the dazzle of the afternoon sun. It must rain soon. If only he could catch again that sweet sound, the rattle on the shutters, the drumming on the rooftops, the rush of the streams…. But there were no streams in the city, at least no streams like the ones he remembered: only a slow wide river that had once sent its sailors to colonise the world. He was dreaming again and he felt the breath spill from his body, rushing faster than the foaming waters that carved their memory on sparkling granite. He would stem the flow this time, but he knew the day was not far off when the surge would overwhelm him.

"Signor, I must fetch her."

His pale eyes implored weakly. "I will not have her distressed."

Signora Valotti let out a deep and disapproving sigh. Her gentleman was stubborn. Even in these extremes of his affliction he would accept no advice, from her or from anyone. For months now she had watched him struggle with his debilitating weariness, determined his son and his daughter should return from their labours to a smiling face. It was his pride, she supposed, the strange emotion that kept his head high even when his stomach was empty, his eyes bright when his heart was broken.

Signora Valotti was not a rich woman. Her house in Rome had been handed down from her husband's family who had since fallen on hard times. Now a widow, the rent she received from her gentleman was enough to allow her to keep the property, but where his money came from she had no idea. The son and daughter earned barely enough to keep them in food. Sometimes Signora Valotti heard him talking softly when she knew he was alone. Sometimes she heard him pleading with an invisible companion: for what she had no idea, though gossip on the street whispered he had once been rich and honoured, a man fallen on hard times through his own misjudgement.

Signora Valotti did not believe the whispers. Her gentleman was kind and mild-mannered, if increasingly frail. She had taken it upon herself to provide the family with extra sustenance: soups rich with vegetables and light fresh bread passed beneath the door in the long days when he sat alone, gazing from the window out onto the busy passage of the Via Fallone. Somehow Signora Valotti did not think his view was the same as hers. She had the strange fancy that he saw another world through the shutters: the Seven Hills magnified into other mountains, their vineyards swelling to vast forests, the streets thronging with half remembered faces.

She watched his eyes flutter and close as he drifted at last into his private world. The fit had passed once more, but Signora Valotti knew that one day there would be no wakening, no bright smile from his golden haired daughter, no quiet greeting from the son whose heart carried so heavy a weight. Signora Valotti crossed herself and gave thanks to the Blessed Virgin for delivering her gentleman from this latest and worst seizure.

She did not allow herself to wonder how soon would come the next.

* * *

"My dear Helen," wrote Andrew, and heaved a long sigh. He balanced his quill in its inkwell and stared out at the shadows the clouds made as they drifted over the Giant's Mountain. Before he picked up his pen again he knew he must try to shape his thoughts into a less resentful pattern.

"My dear Helen," he repeated softly and sighed again. But why should he be accusing himself of disloyalty? After all, she had written to him first. What possible harm could there be in letters exchanged between friends? But he could not pretend he did not know the answer. It was the reason he remained at such pains to conceal the correspondence from his father.

He shook the ink gently from the pen's fine point. "I am happy to hear that you are in good spirits, and that the same is true for your family. We fare reasonably in Glenshellich, despite our growing anxiety over our father's health…..

Donald…….." His hand paused again and his eyes narrowed. Best get mention of him over and done with first. By all accounts his brother was giving Helen small consideration in his new life. His studies appeared to be of equal insignificance. Donald's letters to his father might describe the classes he was attending, but to his brother he wrote only of card games and whorehouses and a companion by the name of Hugh Fettes who was obviously intimately acquainted with both.

"…. Donald is more contented in Edinburgh than any of us believed possible. It is hard to believe he has been gone for nearly half a year…….." Though not, he reflected grimly, if you caught sight of the belly of Meg MacLeay. Andrew sighed again. "… even though the seasons pass more noticeably here in Glenshellich, as they will also in the Glen of the Black Cattle." He paused and scribbled quickly, "But I will be very surprised if he does not find time soon to send you a letter."

And enough of Donald, he decided.

"As for myself, I have finally shaken the dust from every single one of the medical books on the study shelves. They may be antiquated, but nevertheless contain much that is of interest and relevance. My apprenticeship to our healer, Euan, continues, though Euan's own health is far from good. He was injured, as your father will remember, at the Battle of Sheriffmuir and has carried the bullet in his chest these last twenty-five years. Still, he is ever cheerful and concerned for my future as a man of medicine, insisting that I should not yet abandon those dreams...."

Though better for my own sanity if I did, he reflected grimly. Donald's excesses were making it increasingly unlikely that there would be any capital left over for his education. Andrew did not know if he would have been so easily enticed from his responsibilities in Donald's place, but it was almost impossible not to feel bitterness at his brother's squandering of precious funds, funds that in more considerate hands might have given them both the chance of an education.

"We are all greatly looking forward to your visit," he continued at last. "Spring is pushing the snow to the highest corries of the Giant's Mountain. The purple saxifrage defies the frosts with its exquisite flowers and the eagles are already tending their nests. I believe this is my favourite of all the seasons, the pale sunshine and soft mists so full of promise. Yesterday on the shore I glimpsed the first pink petals of the sea daisy....."

If only I could be the one to share Glenshellich's beauty with you, he thought, and indulged himself for a brief moment in his fantasy. But Andrew knew such dreams were not for him and never could be.

He had not been born first.

* * *

Nestling a few yards down a narrow wynd in the shadow of the Castle's garrisoned walls was The Ensign, a tavern of wide and favourable repute. Its clients were cheerful and its fare was cheap: minced collops, rizared haddocks, tripe, a fluke or roasted skate and onions could be chased on their way with brimming pints of French wine or Scots ale. Many a business bargain, honest or shady, had been "wet" within its panelled walls, many a hanging arranged, many a minister carried senseless from its dusty corners into the anonymity of night.

For some it had the added advantage of being a tavern where men could discreetly raise their glasses to King James and exchange eagerly sought news from his exiled court in Rome. For others it had the more enticing benefit of being joined by a short passageway to Bella Galbraith's court of more colourful notoriety. Both attributes had made the tavern a favourite destination for the young Hugh Fettes of Ballingry and it had not taken long for Donald Stewart of Glenshellich to become equally at home there.

Some of The Ensign's patrons had spoken with their king over the water, and been promised rich rewards for their continuing loyalty. It was Hugh's intention to make the pilgrimage to Rome himself, and he could be heard boasting of his plans on many a brandy-fuelled night.

"Discretion, Mr Fettes," warned Lowrie, the landlord, one evening, after an exceptionally fine claret had fired Hugh's political passion. "The panels have ears," and he nodded towards the farthest corner, where a cloaked figure hugged the shadows.

Donald had been late in joining the company and was therefore the most sober. It struck him as odd that anyone should choose so convivial a place as The Ensign to drink alone. He studied the stranger more closely.

"Allomore's man," Lowrie warned softly in his ear. "Tell your friend to be careful of bringing himself to that gentleman's notice. He is avid in his search for enemies of the state."

"Allomore!" Donald exclaimed.

"The present incumbent," explained the landlord, spitting to emphasise his contempt. "Not the true old gentleman you or I would honour with the title."

"Why should I be discreet?" blustered Hugh. "If I cannot profess my true loyalties here, Mr Lowrie......"

Donald laid a restraining hand on his arm. Fortunately Hugh was as good-natured in his cups as he was sober and raised no objection when Donald led him out onto the street.

"What say we make our next destination Sullivan's?" he pronounced. "The place for all honourable gentlemen."

"But wealthier ones than you and I," Donald smiled, sounding an uncharacteristic note of caution.

"Then we will set about making ourselves wealthy," Hugh laughed. "In worldly goods as well as in humour and high spirits. Come."

Across the wynd the public door of Bella Galbraith's yawned and disgorged the shapely figure of Beth Niven, a particular favourite, temptingly plying her trade. Donald left Hugh to stumble down the street in pursuit of his fortune and followed her inside. When eventually he found his way back onto the street it had grown quiet and the stars were winking from the narrow strip of sky above the tenements. He had lost all track of time in Beth's company, but he felt sure the ten o'clock drum would not be beating yet awhile. He set off in pursuit of his friend.

Hugh was not to be found in any of his regular haunts and Donald hesitated as he passed under the wooden faced gable half way down the Canongate which he recognised as the discreet frontage for the hazard tables of William James Sullivan, renowned adventurer and socialite. He did not honestly believe Hugh would have carried out his threat to seek admission to that exclusive establishment. He was about to turn and retrace his steps when the man he had seen earlier in the Ensign emerged from the doorway. If he recognised Donald he showed no sign of it as he hunched his shoulders, drew his cloak close and proceeded down the cobbles in the direction of the old Palace of Holyrood. The door swung open behind him for just long enough to let Donald place his toe inside and peer through into the stark and empty marble floored hallway.

Three doors led from it, but only one was ajar. A bright light shone from inside, as if from several chandeliers, and a sudden murmur rose and fell into silence. Still unnoticed, Donald crept towards it and saw twenty or so of Edinburgh's most affluent citizens standing around a card table. As he edged closer a group stepped aside and with a sinking heart Donald found himself face to face with his quarry. The combination of excitement at his rare good fortune and a reckless consumption of port had brought a deep glow to Hugh's features. Donald elbowed his way closer and stared around the growing audience. He did not much like the atmosphere developing at the table where only two figures remained seated.

"A gentleman must ensure his fellow players have the opportunity to make good their losses," proclaimed Hugh blithely. He caught sight of Donald and winked. Barely able to keep the glee from his voice, he added, "I would not wish to deny Mr Hamilton his."

Hugh spoke the name with unmistakable scorn and Donald could feel the tension simmering between his friend and his middle-aged opponent. On the evidence of his upper half he judged the man to be several inches above average height, slender, delicate as bone china, with a subtle eyes set in a pale pinched face. The emotion Mr Hamilton was fighting so hard to control seemed very akin to rage, while Hugh beamed happily and quickly gathered up the cards.

But before the hand was dealt the room fell silent. Someone else, tall and imposing, had positioned himself at Mr Hamilton's shoulder and when Donald raised his eyes to the man's face he felt his heart lurch. It had been more than ten years since he had laid eyes on George Campbell of Kilclath, yet he knew him instantly. His legs felt suddenly weak as he stared into the face of the man he still held responsible for his father's failing health and strength. Gone now was the self-conscious youth who had struggled to redeem his honour on that bleak evening in the House of Glenshellich. This man radiated authority, yet did so carelessly, as if by right, as one by one the spectators moved respectfully aside.

The game continued and Hugh won again.

Kilclath bent his head close to Mr Hamilton's and Donald read a quiet warning on his lips before he spoke for all the room to hear.

"Come, Allomore. Enough is enough."

Donald continued to stare. Allomore. Mr Hamilton. Finally he understood the reason for Hugh's excitement. This was the scoundrel who had inherited the estates of his father's oldest and best friend, the man whose reputation now rested on his ability to identify and condemn those who still professed their old loyalties. All through his life Donald had heard enough about this usurper, this opportunist, who sought to style himself MacIain Mhor, to understand only too well how universally despised he was.

Allomore showed no inclination to heed Kilclath's advice.

"I suspect," he almost hissed, "that this young gentleman's run of luck cannot be entirely attributed to good fortune." His face shone hard under the bright light. Another silence fell and, although victory and port still kept Hugh convivial, a shadow slipped behind his eyes.

"I hope I misunderstand you, sir," he replied, his tone deceptively cordial.

"I suspect that you do not."

Kilclath frowned. He cast his eyes around the company and Donald could see that the attention of all those present was on him. "Perhaps it would be sensible to discontinue the game," he suggested again.

But Allomore again ignored the advice. He was a poor loser and a spiteful one, as his next remark proved. "Perhaps we should examine this gentlemen's credentials for entering a respectable establishment."

Hugh gazed around with wide, innocent eyes. The uneasy expressions on the faces of the spectators masked a mounting interest. Few failed to understand the dispute's potential. Hugh Fettes belonged to a long line of wealthy tenant farmers who leased their estates from the Laird of Allomore. He smiled again.

"This fellow has on two occasions now placed doubt on my good name, gentlemen," he announced. "You have all watched our hands. I say he is a liar." His voice unleashed an uncharacteristic and chilling harshness as he added. "And I say he is unworthy of the noble name he bears."

A deeper, more ominous hush spread across the room. All eyes and ears were on Allomore, whose face was now a livid white.

"I will tolerate no insults from upstart pups."

Kilclath leaned over him again, and although his words were directed at Allomore they were intended for the whole room.

"It would be prudent to let this pass, Allomore. You and I can take our leave together."

But Hugh's outburst had incensed Allomore beyond reason.

"I repeat," he hissed again. "I will not accept insults from upstart pups."

"And I repeat," Hugh retorted, his eyes hard as flint, "That you are unworthy of the title you bear." He drew a breath and turned his head away in a gesture of deliberate contempt before meeting Allomore once more squarely in the eye. "But you borrow it only."

Allomore's eyes, small and sly as a snake's, darted back at him. "I will settle this affair with you, Hugh Fettes of Ballingry. I know who you are and what you are. You would be wise to mark your movements in future."

Donald had heard enough. "And you, sir, would be wise not to threaten my friend."

Allomore rose slowly and stood beside the Master of the Stones. They were an arresting pair, both reaching head and shoulders above every other man in the room.

"And who might you be, to interfere in affairs so plainly not your own?" Allomore demanded.

Donald met his pale stare with defiance. "I am Donald Stewart of Glenshellich," he replied proudly, unable to prevent his eyes flashing to the face of Kilclath. The features of the Master of the Stones tightened only slightly as he turned his attention briefly from Hugh, but in the strained silence the two older men exchanged glances.

"Then allow me to suggest, Donald Stewart," and the note of gentle mockery in Kilclath's voice seemed to lack any trace of hostility. "That you and your friend take your leave also." He turned to Hugh. "I am sure that Allomore would not wish his intentions to be misinterpreted. He is simply unaccustomed to losing at cards."

Donald took hold of his friend's arm and began to propel him towards the door. Uncharacteristic prudence, or perhaps a sense of self-preservation, told him that their honour remained intact, that Hugh would emerge from the encounter unscathed, if he proceeded no further. Apparently sharing his instinct, Hugh finally complied.

Later, as they relaxed at Alison's fireside, Donald looked seriously at his friend.

"What do you know of those men?" he asked.

"Mostly that they are dangerous fellows to fall foul of - and especially dangerous to those of our persuasion. Allomore...." Hugh's face filled with contempt, "....... as you must have deduced, trades information. And most of that information passes through the offices of Kilclath."

Donald's expression grew as dark as his friend's.

"A man I have hated from the day he sent a bullet through my father's chest."

"To hate Allomore is one thing, to hate Kilclath quite another. He is not a man it would be wise to make an enemy of." Hugh gave a sudden grin. "In fact, most in this city fall over themselves to achieve the opposite." He grinned again. "And there is certainly no shortage of ladies seeking to make a husband of him."

Donald made a dismissive gesture. The incident had left him unsettled, irritable and unsatisfied.

"Though anyone wishing to become his wife would have some daunting competition," Hugh went on, lowering his voice, "that I'd wager few could overcome."

"What do you mean?"

"It's common enough knowledge. Kilclath has plucked the most exquisite bloom from Bella Galbraith's House of Delights, and turned her into a fine beauty to keep for his sole pleasure." Hugh grinned again. "Apparently he is too proud even to share his whores."

With the image of Jean Petrie before them Hugh closed his eyes and drifted into a pleasurable sleep. But Donald found it impossible to contain his whirling thoughts. He moved to the window and breathed in the night air, hearing the drum's sharp tattoo finally echo from the end of the High Street. It had been many weeks since he had felt the pull of Glenshellich, but now a longing for it wrenched at his heart. He found himself craving the silent darkness of his land, the silhouetted mountains, the lapping water of the lochan. However determinedly he had locked its memory away, however eagerly he might have seized the pleasures of his new life, he knew that the yearning for his home would never leave him. On the street below the last of the beggars and revellers stumbled towards whatever shelter they could find, but Donald was scarcely aware of them as his thoughts spun further, drawn beyond the boundaries of his own glen eastwards to where the twin Mountains of the Eagles towered above the clouds like brooding sentinels guarding the stark pass of Kilclath. He shuddered at the prospect of their shadows stretching even to the darkest and most secret wynds of Edinburgh itself.

"Kilclath would brush you and I aside like two flies," Hugh had warned him when they left the gaming house. As he turned from the window Donald had the sudden sharp sense, more vivid than a memory, of the old Master's sweetly treacherous breath against his cheek.

It had been the first time he had known what it was to fear another human being. Until tonight it had also been the last.

* * *

A chill north wind swept from the slopes of the Giant's Mountain and sliced against the walls of Euan MacMichael's cottage. Inside all was uncannily still as the healer and his son hunched silently together by the hearth, alert to every sound that came from the bed in the dark alcove behind them.

Catriona's charges had been dismissed early, but they had not removed themselves far from their schoolroom. Little knots of inquisitive figures ranged along the foreshore and behind the outbuildings. They were all waiting as anxiously as the two men inside to hear a very particular sound.

Down beside the water Angus Ban finished tying together the strands of his net. It was unlikely that the tear would have let a single herring escape, but mending it was Angus' excuse to linger in a place where he had no particular or immediate business. His grandson had no need of any such pretext. MacSomhairle's piper paced a well-worn path along the shoreline, back and forward, then back and forward again, keeping his head bent, but constantly casting his lowered eyes in the direction of the healer's cottage.

"Why should you trust him for this of all birthings?" Euan Mac-Michael had asked his father when the witch's granddaughter arrived at the cottage and he had been sent to summon the son of their chieftain.

"It will be the first of many," Euan had answered seriously. "And a fitting initiation."

They waited now together in silence, until at last they heard the small gasps, struggling to an insistent cry. Smiles that spoke much louder flashed between them.

Down on the shore Angus looked up from his net. "No quieter than its father," he muttered.

Kenneth turned eyes full of wonder towards the healer's house. His pacing ceased and he sat down, quite spent, on the jetty rock, while Angus, as if by instinct, raised his glance higher, to the half-hidden cottage on the first slopes of Ben Feodag. From the shadows inside her doorway Beathag squinted down at the clachan, but not even Angus could have divined what emotions stirred in her heart.

Catriona removed the baby from Andrew's arms and began to rock him gently. She gazed down at his tiny features, her expression an exquisite mixture of joy and pain, and then she slowly crossed herself.

"What would you wish for him, Catriona?" whispered Andrew.

"Happiness," she breathed, at last. "Happiness, good health, loyal friends and a long life."

Andrew took Meg's hand and stroked it with his long fingers.

"He will have them all," he said softly, and smoothed the strands of black hair from her damp forehead. She smiled weakly up at him. He held out his arms and took the baby briefly again from Catriona before returning him to his mother. Only Meg heard the words he whispered next, so close to her ear, though only she would have understood them. "Will he not?"

Then Andrew rose to his feet and moved to the tiny window. The bright winter sun dazzled his eyes, but he could make out the figures on the shore: the old man pretending to mend his nets and the piper gazing over the lochan. There would be a new pibroch tomorrow, of that they could be certain.

Only the son of the healer was awkward, almost embarrassed. He and Meg had been friends for so long but now he feared all that would change. When she called him he hesitated.

"He is a special gift, Eochain," she whispered to reassure him. "He belongs to us all."

Finally Euan crept close and gazed down. "He has your black hair, your blue eyes," he breathed.

"All babies have blue eyes," she answered with a smile.

He swallowed and looked across to where Andrew remained, his back straight and still, staring over the water. Catriona passed the window.

"She has gone to take the news to the clachan," he said. Meg closed her eyes contentedly with his next words. "I think she will first speak with the piper."

But whatever melody formed itself around the heart of Kenneth Mhor that winter morning, in his grandfather's head throbbed the once strange but now familiar drumbeat, less distant now than ever before. As he squinted up to where Beathag crouched against her doorway, there was no doubt in his mind that she would be hearing it too.

* * *

Hugh and Donald might have been anxious to put the incident in Sullivan's behind them, but it seemed that city gossip was not prepared to let it rest. Caddies whispered of it on street corners, ladies raised their eyebrows over teacups, while those in Bella's employ, who possibly knew the Laird of Allomore best of all, roared with delight and threw back raucous toasts to his humiliation at the hands of the bold young Ballingry.

On the street outside Parliament Close Gavin MacVey found himself face to face with George Campbell of Kilclath.

"Your kinsman is much in the news," he remarked dryly.

"An increasingly troublesome connection," replied the Master. "You will understand my preference for confining our dealings to matters of business."

"Your preference may signify not one whit," Gavin replied mischievously.

Kilclath's expression remained troubled. "He draws altogether too much attention."

"Perhaps an adjournment to his estates would be advantageous for the time being," suggested the older lawyer.

"That has already been my advice," Kilclath replied grimly. "But knowing him as we both do, is it likely he will avail himself of it?"

Gavin smiled again and moved on. He had some concerns of his own over the affair, but was reassured by Kilclath's attitude. If any man had influence over the improbably styled MacIain Mhor it was the Master of the Stones, a man himself never far from the agenda of the city's energetic tongues.

Alison Bothwell watched Kilclath's handsome figure pass under her casement, and gave a little smile of satisfaction. Kirsty continued to hover at her shoulder.

"Thank you, Kirsty," Alison announced pointedly and turned her attention back to her guests.

The maid showed no sign of leaving the three ladies to the enjoyment of their tea and tittle-tattle. She might have lacked the status to indulge her natural curiosity, but it was on a par with any of those present. She simply stretched her neck to admire Kilclath's noble progress for as long as possible.

Alison cleared her throat and remarked more pointedly still, "The Master of the Stones cuts a fine dash this afternoon."

Kirsty finally condescended to heed the steel in her mistress's tone. She turned with a toss of auburn curls and flounced from the room while the elder of Alison's guests, the Dowager Countess of Dalvey, picked up the more significant hint in Alison's remark.

"On any afternoon," she retorted, with a sharp chuckle and a sly glance in the direction of the third member of the party, a matron perched as daintily as her substantial form would permit on the chair beside her hostess's bed.

"Indeed," that lady agreed. The flush spreading across her plain features belied her casual tone and Alison and the Countess exchanged slyer looks.

"So you've nothing to confide to your old friends, Henrietta?" Alison cajoled. "You surely canna doubt our discretion."

But Henrietta still refused to be drawn. She simply inclined her head in the manner of one who knows more than she can possibly divulge.

"Rumour does have it," murmured the Countess, "that he is considering several alternatives…"

"… And in no great hurry to pursue a single one of them," went on Alison, peeved at being denied such vital information from so impeccable a source. "Of course," she continued, in the vain hope that flattery might provoke a better response, "Margaret canna be short of admirers of her own."

Henrietta took a delicate sip from her tiny cup and wiped a linen napkin across her sealed lips.

"She is not," she agreed at last. "But what of events in your own household, Alison? Mr Fettes has been acquiring something of a reputation for himself, I hear."

"So I believe," snapped Alison, her annoyance increased at being outmanoeuvred by an inferior strategist. "But nothing we canna attribute to youthful high spirits."

"Allomore should not be trifled with," observed the Countess. "He had a lucky advancement but he still kens fine the opinion of most good folk – especially those in the old country."

"A traitor from the day he drew breath."

"A wary man from the moment he stole a title," the Countess murmured sagely. She herself had been born in the year the Great Fire swept London and had already seen out six reigns. While she might draw the line at bending her knee to German Geordie she could not remember life being a whit more comfortable when the Scottish Stewarts had occupied the throne.

"But it's one thing for harmless old women to wear their sentiments on their sleeves," she went on. "Quite another for hot blooded young gentlemen. A man who jumps at shadows will lurk in them himsel'. Your young Mr Fettes would do well to keep an eye ahint him from here on in."

"It's Allomore's poor wife I feel for…" murmured Henrietta, again veering the conversation in another direction. Alison threw her an even more irate glance.

"She'll need to pray like the rest of us he'll get his comeuppance one of these fine days."

"Even though the climate's shown little improvement these last twenty years," Henrietta retorted. "No matter how much some folk might pray for it."

To Alison this was treason indeed, but treason of an informative kind. If the Menteiths were aiming for an alliance with Kilclath their politics would certainly require a reversal. She took some small consolation in the thought of Jean Petrie. There would be more wives than Allomore's to sympathise with if Margaret Menteith became Mistress of the Stones. A time might well come when Henrietta would be less inclined to sing so dumb to her old acquaintances.

But before she could draw breath to retort Kirsty made an agitated re-appearance.

"There are more guests, ma'am," she announced with an impudent smirk. "A gentleman by the name of MacLean, and his daughter."

Alison's mouth gaped in dismay.

"Would that be Hector MacLean, Laird of Cairnill?" enquired the Countess, with a wicked twinkle.

"MacLean of Cairnill," Kirsty repeated smugly. "And his daughter."

Alison gulped. "An unexpected pleasure indeed," she declared at last. "Show them into the drawing room then, Kirsty, without delay."

The Countess of Dalvey looked meaningfully at Henrietta, then struggled to her feet and held out her arm.

"Then we'll take our leave rejoicing, Alison," she announced. "No doubt we'll be seeing you at Professor Baird's soiree the morn's night."

Distracted, Alison summoned Kirsty to escort the two ladies onto the street. Henrietta bestowed a small and patronising bow at the bedchamber door and Alison made a fist behind her back. Then, smoothing her skirts, she stepped forward with as much dignity as she could muster for an altogether more daunting engagement.

Alison had met Cairnill at occasional gatherings over the years but was most familiar with him by reputation. Her nephew's prospective father in law was the archetypal Highland chieftain, a man whose very entry to a room could command it to silence, and as Alison stepped into her own drawing room she almost felt herself to be the guest. Cairnill took her hand and very charmingly raised it to his lips. Alison inclined her head and wondered fleetingly if a curtsey might be more appropriate.

The chieftain was not tall in stature, but his figure radiated authority from the crowberry on his embroidered bonnet to the buckles of his gleaming brogues. He wore his plaid belted over a blue velvet jacket hung about with an uncompromising armoury of broadsword, dirk and for good measure a matching pair of jewelled pistols. Only when he turned to present his daughter did his austere features show any sign of softening. Helen MacLean was at great pains to remain composed, but Alison could not fail to feel how her hand trembled.

"Mistress Bothwell," she began, her eyes too betraying her anxiety. "I hope you do not consider us presumptuous, but I could not allow our visit to the city to pass without calling on you."

Cairnill's expression grew more sceptical. "In two days time we return north," he added pointedly, "and we have as yet received no communication from your nephew."

Alison let her eyes drop. Her exasperation with Donald knew no bounds. She motioned helplessly in the direction of the breathless Kirsty whose feet appeared nailed to the floorboards in the doorway.

"Perhaps Kirsty should run to the university and see if he can be found," she suggested, hoping against hope that the maid would for one time in her life be able to take a hint. Kirsty gaped back in blatant incomprehension.

"The university....?" she echoed, with an expression on her face to indicate a belief that her mistress had entirely taken leave of her senses.

"Or thereabouts," Alison elaborated through clenched teeth. Somehow she did not think the Laird of Cairnill was deceived.

He cleared his throat tactfully.

"We have no wish to inconvenience him."

Alison clasped her hands together in order to resist the urge to wring them.

"He has been much occupied with his studies," she assured them, and hoped it was not a snort she heard as Kirsty eventually picked up her message.

The maid found Donald at her first attempt, in The Ensign, in the centre of an unruly gathering. When he finally grasped the reason for her agitation he lost no time in straightening his clothes and casting the boisterous whore from his knee. Wishing it would be as simple to rid himself of the claret fuelled muddle inside his head he followed after Kirsty down the High Street.

Back in her apartment Alison was fast running out of subjects for small talk. Politics was not an option as Cairnill's were a closed book, and he was unlikely to give much credence to hers. Neither could he be expected to divulge details of any transactions that had brought him to Edinburgh's law courts. Alison encouraged Helen's descriptions of the gowns she had ordered from her dressmaker in the Grassmarket, while noticing her anxiety intensify with every minute that passed.

"Perhaps a time could be arranged for your nephew to call on us at our lodging house," Cairnill suggested irritably, but relented once more under Helen's beseeching gaze.

Alison strained her ears hopefully at another set of footsteps on the stair, until she recognised them as the quick tread of Davie, younger son of Dalgleish the tailor. She looked helplessly at her guests. Cairnill had apparently reached the end of his patience, but as he began to rise to his feet Alison heard an altogether more promising sound.

"I believe that might be Donald at last," she said, jumping up herself so as to arrive on the other side of the door before her nephew. Closing it behind her she came face to face with him as he stood smoothing his clothes and drawing deep and pungent breaths.

"My head is bursting like a drum," he muttered. "Cairnill will be wondering why I have not been to call on them. Damn it, aunt, what am I to do?"

"Keep your distance," she muttered. And serve you right, she thought, as she re-entered the room. "The wanderer returns," she announced.

Donald stepped forward with a sheepish grin. He saw immediately that he was forgiven, by Helen at least, as he quickly bent and kissed her hand. He took two steps backwards before he spoke.

"Forgive me. It was only yesterday that I received your note,"

Charming as his smile might have appeared to his intended, Alison could see that it cut no ice whatsoever with her father.

Donald himself felt the familiar stab from his conscience. As on every meeting with the girl who had been chosen for him he was struck anew by her beauty. And as on every meeting the exquisite features, the gleaming hair, the eyes brimming with unmistakable emotion, left him reprehensibly unmoved.

"I had been intending to call after my afternoon lecture," he went on, ignoring Kirsty's petulant clattering from the pantry and Alison's poor imitation of a smile. The relief in Helen's eyes told him that he was forgiven and arrangements were quickly made for him to spend the evening in their lodgings in the Canongate.

"That girl deserves better," Alison sighed as she leaned over the casement and watched the chieftain and his daughter pick their delicate way around Bannie MacFee's begging bairns. "You arrive here fresh from the whorehouse …" She ignored Donald's feeble attempt to deny it. "And steal away her heart without a shred of shame."

Donald was suddenly angry. "Why must I be condemned for everything I do?" he complained. "Am I expected to live the life of a monk? You never see fit to lecture Hugh on his behaviour."

"Hugh Fettes is not my sister's son."

Alison watched him wrestle with his resentment. It was time he began to shoulder some responsibility. She sometimes felt the soul of him slowly slipping away.

"Do you ever think of your mother?" she asked more gently.

His lowered eyes provided the answer. And what would Janet have made of him? Alison wondered. What would she think of this son she had brought into the world but known so briefly? There was little point in dwelling on it. Janet had left the care of both her sons to others, and whether they had made a proper enough job was something that remained to be seen. But she was not about to shirk her own share of responsibility.

"You've never had to accept the slightest criticism," she went on, warming to her subject. "You've been raised to think you can do no wrong, that you'll be forgiven every mistake. Your mother wouldna have allowed that to happen. She may have turned a miserable lost cratur in the shadow of that mountain, but she was never afraid to speak her mind. Janet had no time for moonshine or fools."

"So you are calling me a fool now?"

Alison tried not to smile at his outraged expression, but her voice remained serious. "I sometimes fear you'll begin to care less and less for others. Blind devotion works to no-one's advantage. That poor girl canna mean much to you."

Donald found it hard to meet her eyes. "I have agreed that she is beautiful and virtuous," he snapped, ignoring Alison's contemptuous snort. "As my father has foreseen, I could not ask for a better wife."

"You might ask for one you were in love with."

"There will be time enough for me to fall in love with Helen."

Alison was sorely disappointed. But what right, she asked herself, had she to lecture him on the subject of love? She who had only read of it in books and watched it work its spell on other people's hearts. Nevertheless, she felt entitled to the last word.

"I may be a confirmed old maid," she declared, "but I know this much. A love that can be felt to order is no love at all."

* * *

The Master of the Stones strode past the church of Saint Giles. He glanced neither to his left nor his right, for Hughie McIvor did all the glancing, with eyes that were never still. The Master paid not the slightest attention to the appreciative stares his imposing figure drew from a group of ladies on the pavement. Perhaps he did not notice them. He increased his pace and Hughie did the same, a dog at heel, watching and guarding. Hughie curled his lip at the fine highland gentleman making his way towards them and leered at the beautiful girl at his side. He had seen the same gentleman only days before in his master's chambers and had easily guessed his business.

"Kilclath!" the chieftain called in greeting.

The Master of the Stones swung round instantly and gave a smile of pleasure. "Cairnill! So the attractions of our city continue to detain you."

The two men slowed to stand together on the kerb. Helen took a delicate sideways step to distance herself from the sour smell wafting from the folds of the ghillie's plaid.

"I trust your son's transaction went according to plan."

But as the Master of the Stones spoke his eyes were on Cairnill's daughter. The chieftain ushered her gently and subtly forward.

"With the benefit of your assistance, I believe," he answered smoothly. "The title deeds were as you suggested and we purchased them most reasonably."

"Excellent," beamed Kilclath, still gazing approvingly at Helen. "And this must be your daughter."

"It is indeed. My reward from the Almighty for siring four sons."

Helen smiled slightly uncomfortably into Kilclath's penetrating eyes.

"I am charmed," he replied, taking her hand and raising it fleetingly to his lips.Helen blushed. Hughie spat into the gutter.

"I hope we will have the opportunity of doing business again," the Master said, and bowed once more before continuing in the direction of the Castle.

"The Master of the Stones," breathed Cairnill gazing after him. "What power rests in those hands, my child."

Helen kept her eyes on the broad back, the upright gait, and the proud angle of Kilclath's head as he shouldered through crowds that seemed to part naturally in his wake. But her father's next words, soft though they were, sent a strange ripple of unease down her spine.

"Who is to say they might not hold the key to all our futures."

* * *

Jean Petrie dipped her spoon into the bubbling pot of soup, raised it to her lips and blew on it gently. The dour faced servant woman blinked three times as she watched for a reaction. Jean supped slowly, narrowed her own eyes and gave an approving nod. A smile spread over the servant woman's face, transforming it completely, like a flicker of sunlight on dark water.

"Delicious," Jean breathed.

The servant woman looked away. Perhaps she was embarrassed at the compliment. Jean knew that she understood it perfectly, for despite the fact that English remained a foreign language to her Jean was increasingly convinced Mhairi was more familiar with it than she

81

was prepared to admit. It was something other than ignorance that kept a curb on her tongue.

"And will you promise to put a slug in Mistress Menteith's slice of mutton pie tonight?"

Mhairi giggled. Fine she understood, thought Jean, grinning broadly back at her. Not that words were the currency of their relationship. Their bond was the Master, the man who had taken a girl destined to whore on the streets and a woman born to the poverty of a hostile glen and transported them to the comfort of his apartments, the protection of his house. Jean and Mhairi, together with the savagely devoted Hughie, knew more than the world knew of the Master of the Stones, but what they had glimpsed beneath his casually assumed cloak of authority remained unmentioned, a secret shared. Sometimes in the fire-lit winter nights Mhairi would croon her old songs, and Jean would recognise in her eyes the same longing she had seen in the Master's. He had promised one day to take her to his glen. He had described how the twin mountains soared as high as their namesakes and carved their outlines on every colour of sky. She would never let him suspect that the very thought of Kilclath cast a darkness over her heart, an impression etched deeper than Hughie's scowl of shadows best undisturbed.

Jean's debt to the Master went far beyond gratitude. The contract between them had been precisely defined from the moment she had crossed his doorstep on a dazzling July evening two years past. That night his voice had been kinder, his face less stern than she remembered from their meetings under Bella's roof, and until that night he had not laid so much as a finger on her, only his troubled, distant eyes. They had sat together as dusk fell, sipping cold glasses of champagne, and she had listened to his terms.

"You are not a whore," he had said softly. "You will come to me willingly or not at all. And if a time comes when our arrangement ceases to please you, you are entirely free to end it."

Overwhelmed by this result of Bella's rare benevolence Jean had nodded her agreement, and from that moment a curtain had opened onto a world she could have imagined only in her wildest dreams. Jean knew there was but one circumstance that would bring her arrangement with the Master of the Stones to an end, yet matrimony was an option that the most eligible bachelor in the city appeared to grow increasingly reluctant to pursue.

In the two years they had been together Jean could count on the fingers of her hands the number of nights she had chosen to sleep alone. It was her delight to undress quickly in her own small room next to Mhairi's in the eaves of the Master's apartments and slip down the narrow candlelit stairs to his wide four poster bed. There she would take off her robe and slide naked beneath the satin sheets, savouring their freshness, smiling secretly as she caught the sounds of the society below her, the muffled voices of Edinburgh matrons, pompous men of law and business, politicians famed throughout the land. For when they had taken their leave the Master of the Stones would return to her, whore's daughter from the Chapel Land, and they would combine in ecstasy long into the night.

He had released her from a world of misery: frantic couplings in stinking recesses, the scuttling of rats, vicious wretches screaming ugly threats. Worst of all was the memory of her mother, beaten and abused, lurching drunkenly to an untimely grave with eyes beseeching Jean not to follow. There were those who maintained that theirs was a profession you were born to, but Bella Galbraith, whose veins throbbed with the blood of generations of whores, had saved Jean from her birthright. She had kept her intact for the man who could promise her body would be the property of no one in the world but herself. Yet not even Bella could have appreciated the true nature of the union she had engineered. Only the whore's daughter and the Master of the Stones understood that in their moments together there was no place for pain, recrimination or shame. There was no bitterness, anger or regret, no demands or expectations, no responsibilities: only a pure and exquisite pleasure that in many a quarter might easily have passed as love.

* * *

Allomore found it prudent to heed Kilclath's advice. He occupied himself with the affairs of his estates and returned to Edinburgh only briefly and occasionally, though each visit added fuel to the increasing speculation that his gambling habit had turned to an addiction. Donald glimpsed his darkly cloaked figure early one evening, slipping through the knots of customers spilling from one of the Grassmarket's less respectable gaming houses. He hid himself quickly inside the doorway of a bookseller's and watched the older man stoop down the well-trodden narrow close that led to the Chapel Land. Donald grinned and was about to follow, when he came face to face with his old friend Beth Niven emerging from the very same close.

"My, oh my! It's my bold Heilandman," she teased. "I've been missing you for many a night."

Donald searched his mind for a response. He could not admit that he was becoming tired of the frantic debauchery of establishments like Bella's. There were more exclusive brothels in the city and he had visited them all in the hope of reviving his enthusiasm. But instead he had found his thoughts drawn back to his times with Meg MacLeay on the slopes of Ben Feodag. He had not ventured home since their son had been born and had not dared to ask himself why.

Beth pawed at his arm. "And where might Mr Fettes be tonight?"

"I am on my way to discover. Or I was," he added, "Until I caught sight of the gentleman who has just slipped down your close." He gave her a sly nudge. "Perhaps you could tell me which of Bella's ladies he favours."

Beth grinned so impishly that her bright eyes disappeared into slits.

"Indeed I could not. You know fine well Mistress Galbraith's ladies do not discuss their customers."

"Come, Beth. You must have come face to face." He nudged her again. "His name is Mr Hamilton."

"Mr Hamilton," she echoed slowly, making a meal of every syllable as her finger traced the outline of Donald's lips. "I know of no Mr Hamilton...." she went on slyly. "The gentleman I came face to face with was Mr Macdonald. And he takes the back stair to the attic room – where there are no ladies to entertain him."

"Now, Beth," Donald chastised her playfully. "What way is that to speak of your fellow comrades of the night?"

This time mischief made Beth's eyes wider than globes.

"But I meant no offence!" she protested. "Mr Macdonald hasna the least interest in Bella's ladies." She paused again and ran her hand downwards from his waist as he continued to gaze at her expectantly. Her hand began to do its work, but Donald's response clearly disappointed her. She shrugged and stepped back. "The attic is Martin's territory."

Donald stared at her with dawning comprehension. "Mr Macdonald!" he breathed, and a smile of delight spread across his features.

When Beth had taken her own trick with him he made his way across to The Ensign where Hugh was finishing his supper. Soon the two were sniggering down the close to the Chapel Land where they hid themselves in the shadows, watching the rising tide of humanity flow in and out of Bella's doorway.

At last Allomore reappeared, swinging his way into the close and wrapping his cloak tighter, more to cover his identity than to fend off the April chill.

"Mr Hamilton!" called Hugh lightly, and shrank back into the shadows beside Donald.

Allomore turned sharply but hesitated for only a moment before continuing on his way.

"Mr Hamilton!" repeated Hugh, and Allomore's shoulders stiffened. This time he was unquestionably alert.

"Or perhaps I should say, Macdonald," Hugh went on. "A fine Highland name to be sure. So how did you find the fair Martin tonight?"

Allomore whipped to face them, eyes glinting in the pale lamplight. They pierced Hugh's clownish face like rapiers. Donald found himself instinctively recoiling as the tall figure took two steps towards them. The rage trembling on his lips was the more threatening for being contained.

For seconds Allomore held his pose, then his voice slithered through the darkness.

"I will meet you for this, Hugh Fettes of Ballingry. Find me at the Prince Regent tomorrow morning at ten, where we can decide upon a time and a place."

Donald stared after the black figure as it faded into the tenements' shadows, then turned to face his accomplice. Hugh seemed almost jubilant.

"So," he exclaimed, "the stakes grow interesting."

* * *

Two days later, in his aunt's drawing room, Donald stared down at a letter in his hand bearing the seal of his father's lawyer. He cursed softly. Gavin MacVey needed no excuse to demonstrate his disapproval of Donald's activities, but to summon him to the offices of George Campbell of Kilclath for discussion of "this ill-conceived duel" was an instruction barely to be tolerated. Nonetheless, in the hours since the arrangement had been made Donald had learned considerably more of Allomore's reputation as a swordsman. The information did not auger well for Hugh whose experience in such matters, despite his bravado was limited to say the least. Yet Donald could understand his friend's excitement. To challenge an upstart such as Allomore would be to strike a blow for his rightful landlord, and by implication, for his rightful king.

But he was less confident when he found himself raising his fist to rap on the substantial front door of Kilclath's chambers. A sallow manservant held it ajar but as he entered Donald's glance barely flickered in his direction. Instead his attention was drawn to two figures lurking at the entrance to the outer office. One was a highlander, clad from shoulder to knee in uncompromising plaid. The other was a woman, middle-aged, a kitchen servant by her appearance, with wide and strangely lit eyes. They stood, side by side, silent and staring, and Donald felt a shiver run through him. The man was like a wolf, mangy and lean, the predator's snarl a whisker's width from his eyes and mouth. The woman was dark and secret. She wrapped her shawl closer and took a short step backwards into the man's shadow.

Then the door opened, and Kilclath stepped into the hallway. With only a cursory glance in Donald's direction, he spoke quickly and angrily in their native tongue.

"Hughie! What did I tell you? Take her back to her quarter."

Hughie appeared undaunted by the roughness of the Master's tone. His lip curled as he took a last unhurried measure of MacSomhairle's heir. But the woman's disconcerting stare sent the coldness through Donald again before she lowered her head, turned and slipped out of sight.

Only when he was satisfied they had gone did the Master usher Donald inside his office, a comfortable chamber with chairs of plush velvet, book-lined walls and a desk of polished mahogany. The scents of leather and fresh flowers banished the less attractive smells that threatened from beyond the open window. Gavin MacVey struggled to raise himself in greeting and Donald had the unsettling impression that his father's old friend was quite at home in the surroundings.

Determined to make his attitude clear from the outset he chose to ignore Kilclath's extended hand and declined the offer of a seat. "I fail to see what concern the affair can be to either of you gentlemen," he began.

Gavin shook his head slowly and apparently with regret. "You are my concern, Donald. I made a promise to your father to safeguard your welfare. I fear I have been negligent in that duty."

Donald held his gaze steadily. "I am not a child to require your supervision, Mr MacVey," he replied, and condescended to throw a glance, albeit a contemptuous one, in the direction of the Master of the Stones. "And you, sir, are presumably acting in the interests of your associate."

Even seated as he now was Kilclath remained commanding. He seemed distant, scarcely concerned, and Donald realised he was at a greater disadvantage than he had feared.

"I have no associates in the matter," Kilclath replied coolly. "I merely act on some affairs of business for Allomore."

"What we are saying, Donald," Gavin broke in, "is that Mr Fettes will surely come to harm."

"And what I am saying is that Hugh's honour is at stake."

Kilclath gave a weary sigh. "I scarcely imagine honour to be involved at all. What I can assure you is that - despite all appearances to the contrary - Allomore is an expert swordsman." He leaned back into his chair and made a casual gesture with his hand to invite Gavin to take up the story.

"We have drawn up two letters of apology, one from each of the gentlemen concerned," Gavin declared, passing them across the table for Donald to read. "The wording of both should be acceptable to reasonable men....."

Donald cast his eyes over the pages. Even he could not deny that the proposal made sound sense, yet he was reluctant to capitulate too easily on Hugh's behalf.

"We believe that with good luck, and good influence," Gavin stressed, "the whole affair could be discreetly and harmlessly concluded."

Donald appeared to give the matter serious consideration, then sighed. "So, gentlemen," he said at last. "You are asking me to deceive my friend and to stand aside while he sacrifices his reputation?"

"You might well be preventing him from sacrificing his life," countered Kilclath, with a glance at Gavin.

"There is no doubt, Donald," the old lawyer advised in soothing tones, "that the most sensible course here is for us three to join together. I can assure you our suggestion will best serve the interests of your friend."

"Nevertheless, I do not believe that Hugh would thank me for my part in the scheme," Donald replied.

"There is no reason for him to be aware of it."

Looking between them again, Donald realised how much more skilled than himself they were in the art of deception.

"Very well," he agreed at last. "But only for the sake of the love I have for Hugh. It grieves me to find myself joining with my enemy against my friend."

For a moment Kilclath let his eyes drop while Gavin drew a disapproving breath.

"I greatly regret your opinion of me, Mr Stewart," murmured the Master of the Stones at last. "Though I can understand it." He paused again. "How does your father?"

Donald met his eyes defiantly. "He has not done well these past ten years."

"I am sorry to hear it," Kilclath said softly, then stood up. Ever the tactician, his parting words were uttered in a different tone. "The times grow increasingly unsettled. Such times require reasonable men. I hope we take leave of each other on cordial terms."

Donald's only response was a brusque lowering of the head. He had no intention of meeting Kilclath's eyes again. Gavin followed him to the door with a backward glance of apology.

"Not gracious, Donald," muttered the old lawyer as they passed out onto the street.

"Indeed? I believe I was reason itself under the circumstances."

"I doubt your father would think so. He bears Kilclath no ill will."

"My father would share our contempt for the man who stole his best friend's name."

"Allomore – the Allomore you recognise – chose his own path."

"An unquestionably honourable one."

"Indeed it was. But most of us would prefer not to be dependent on men possessed of too much honour. Life very often requires trimming."

Donald narrowed his eyes, but in view of what he had just put his own name to he did not feel justified in arguing.

From behind the mottled glass of Kilclath's kitchen basement Jean Petrie craned her delicate neck to gaze upwards along the street, unaware that the gesture was a mirror image – though in an up rather than down direction – of Alison Bothwell's regular endeavours to extend her view across the Lawnmarket. Jean watched the two pairs of buckled brogues and tartan trews cross the road and disappear into Martin's Inn opposite just as her ears caught the distant chime of the eleven thirty bells from the church of Saint Giles. It seemed to her that she recognised the young man her companions had been so anxious for a glimpse of, but where she had seen him before she could not for the life of her remember.

"He looks a handsome enough fellow," she commented as she pulled her head back inside. The remark was directed at Mhairi who only shook herself and returned her attention to the pot of stew, muttering indistinguishably in Gaelic.

Undaunted, Jean teased, "Would the two of you not agree?"

Hughie turned one of his darker scowls in her direction and the servant woman wiped the grease from her hands onto her apron. Jean cocked her head expectantly and studied Mhairi's expression. A spiteful glimmer stirred behind her eyes. Jean waited for an answer, her own eyes dancing with mischief.

"Handsome or no," Mhairi ventured at last, "he will be Glenshellich's last chieftain."

Jean gave an exaggerated shudder but resisted the temptation to make another teasing reply. As her fondness for Mhairi had grown she had become less inclined to mock her morose mutterings and peculiar ways. Hughie's lip twisted into a sneer. Now he was a different kettle of fish, treacherous as mountain mist to all but his master. She understood that the two of them shared a unique bond, the fierce highland devotion that bound chieftain and clansman, the unfathomable union that no distance, time or misuse could ever break. He snorted his contempt at Mhairi's prediction, so to pay him back him Jean feigned an admiring gasp.

"My, Mhairi, you'd make a braw penny on the High Street telling fortunes."

But Mhairi's attention, ever fickle, had returned to the pot.

Jean shrugged. "Well, I daresay he'll attract his fair share of ladies," she concluded, and gave Hughie an impudent poke in the region of his ribs. "Though just like you, Mr Misery, there can only be one man in the whole world for me."

Mhairi glanced at her slyly and giggled. Jean turned her face again to the reassuring bustle of the street, though she knew that Hughie was still watching her, with the peculiar hooded expression that made her suspect he might be able to read her mind every bit as easily as he could the Master's.

* * *

"My Dear Helen," wrote Andrew, and paused, as he always did, to swallow the almost physical pain that struck him each time he took up his pen. My Dear Helen, he wanted to say, I note that my brother has still not replied to your last letter, as he has not answered any of ours. He prefers to squander his days and nights, along with any hope of my advancement, in the stews of whatever city his whim dictates.

But he wrote:

"I am sorry that Donald has not found time to answer your letter. Perhaps he did not receive it, for he has been these past few weeks in Paris. We are assured that he is well and nearing the completion of his studies. It will not be long now until he returns home to Glenshellich."

For finally there was no money left. Andrew sighed. What was there for Donald to return to? A disillusioned brother and a feeble old man? Friends he had outgrown even as he forgot them? With a heavy heart he continued.

"Thank you also for your kind wishes towards our father. I am sorry I can only report that his health grows weaker. He has become an old man, plagued with the pain of past wounds, his mind too often falling into confusion. There is sad news, too, for your father of Euan MacMichael. I have mentioned him so many times in my letters that you must feel you know him also, so you will share our grief at his

91

death. When I turned from his graveside my spirits were heavier than I have ever felt them. It is still impossible for any of us here to think of the clachan without him. ....."

Andrew paused again, his eyes moist as he recalled the notes of Kenneth's poignant lament. It struck him that only now, in writing to Helen, had he been able shed healing tears for his mentor. He did not believe Catriona had shed them yet and he pictured her standing at Euan's grave, lonely yet proud, searching the horizon with her tragic eyes. Her son had climbed to the giant's cave in the mountainside where he had remained for two days and nights. John Stewart had raised his head to where the eagles soared against Beinn Feodag and watched the mating pair disappear eastward. They had all paid more than respect, but Donald had not come.

Andrew had tried to convince himself that his brother had received word and mourned somewhere in silence. He hoped so with all his heart, for while the clachan stood silent in the heather even Beathag, who gave honour to no one, had crept from her doorway and crossed herself. But Donald had not come and Andrew saw how much the want of him added to the grief of Catriona MacMichael and her son.

"I hope you will forgive me for pouring out my heart so freely to you," he wrote on. "In all the years of our correspondence I have come to look upon you as my most valued friend. I sometimes believe you can sense things in me I do not always understand myself....." save one, he hoped bitterly before continuing. "But I must own that I fear too soon we must make another farewell. And as the old order passes what will the future hold for those of us who remain? You have urged me not to abandon my dreams, and I will not, though they grow fainter with each passing year. I remain forever grateful for all that Euan has shown me and can only hope that although I lack his special gifts, he might have instilled in me some small part of his skill....."

* * *

Archie Fraser scuttled along the path to the clachan. He did not pause to admire the freshness of the morning, for his thoughts were preoccupied with more uncertain matters. MacSomhairle, much as his old servant hated to admit it, was not in full control of his mind. Euan had known it. Eilidh of the red face knew it, and so certainly did Catriona. What Andrew's views on the matter were he had no idea, but the time had surely come to take them into account. Fraser was convinced that the day could not be far off when Glenshellich must feel a different hand at its helm.

Catriona was waiting for him at the door of her cottage. There was no need for comment as he bustled inside. She knew why he had come. The absence of the healer seemed to have emptied the house of its very soul, but Fraser would not remark on that to the one who must feel it so very much more.

"I've counted more than three hundred guineas in my metal chest," he grunted as he lowered himself onto the wooden bench at the fireside.

"And there are fifty seven cattle in Euan's herd," she replied. "Two calves were born today. Together you have done him proud."

"So now's the time?"

"I am sure of it."

"I would be too," Fraser murmured thoughtfully. "Were it no' for the matter of MacSomhairle's health." He looked up at her sadly. "He'll no' agree."

"Then we must insist."

"He needs the boy more than ever."

"Donald must return."

Fraser gave a dismissive snort, but she knew it came from his own injured feelings.

"Do not be so ready to lose faith," she soothed. "I held him to my breast with my own son. There is much for him yet to learn, far for us still to travel together."

But Fraser could not hide his resentment at Donald's neglect. "I mind his fine words to me when he took the road south. In six years how often's he been back to the home it broke his heart to leave?"

"Now is not the time to judge him," she urged, and then hesitated, for still something hung unspoken between them. "Or is it that you believe," she went on, "those ancient words already have found the power to darken his life?"

Fraser sighed. Old whisperings around firesides might have been forbidden, but he had sat where Catriona had not, where no woman was permitted.

"They're powerful words," he answered. "More powerful than ever I thought to admit."

Catriona rose and moved to the window. For a long time she looked out, until her eyes finally came to rest on the cottage by the shore, the cottage of Angus Ban where the peat embers glowed night and day.

"I have heard what Angus tells at his fire."

Fraser stared at her.

"Euan kept no secrets from me." She stretched her hand towards him and for the first time in nearly thirty years he let his eyes linger on the angry scar. "When you and I first came to the clachan how could he deny there was no welcome for us? How else could he explain why they shunned you with your strange tongue, and me with the mark of the knife?"

Fraser's face twisted. "Angus is forbidden to speak of it," he breathed, but his words sounded feeble even to his own ears.

Catriona's expression was full of tenderness. "Do not be fooled by what Angus tells his chieftain," she went on. "He believes himself to be the true descendent of the seer. Eochain is the man of this house now and not even his own father would have sought to keep him from his destiny. He will hear the words. Donald will hear the words." She saw the dismay on the old man's face, and tried to reassure him. "Their promises are vague and their interpretation may be beyond us. But they will not be denied."

Fraser continued to stare at her. Why had it never occurred to him that there might be others, besides Angus Ban, prepared to ignore the orders of their chieftain? But to be defied by his own foster brother was almost beyond the old groom's belief. He shook his head helplessly. He would never understand these people. Gazing into Catriona's calm face he was struck by the thought that she looked scarcely a day older than when he had first set eyes on her all those years ago. And why had he not realised before that with her teaching of their children she was already bringing a new kind of future to the glen?

"And will you tell him your own story?" he asked at last.

She shook her head. For a long time she gazed into the pale glow in her hearth and Fraser could have no doubt what she saw there.

"Soon there will be none left who know it," she whispered at last. "And for that I thank God."

As she spoke Fraser's eyes strayed to the open doorway. Outside on the stony path to the jetty Meg's son was running to greet the piper's boat. Fraser saw Kenneth's face break into a broad smile. He stretched out his arms and the boy hurled himself into them.

"And there's someone else no' feart to take a chance with his heart," Fraser observed dryly. He smiled and added, "Let's hope it goes as well with him."

Standing together on the slopes above, Meg and Andrew also watched as Kenneth swept the boy into the air and swung him high above his head. Domhnull squealed and giggled with delight.

"The piper would make a fine father," murmured Andrew.

Meg threw him a sharp look. "Especially to children of his own," she retorted. "And they are what he deserves."

"But perhaps not what he most desires."

They continued to gaze down to the shore. Domhnull was sturdy and brave. He started to help Kenneth pull in the nets. They worked comfortably together, like old friends, and Meg's eyes grew tender as she watched them. Andrew cast her a sideways glance and smiled mischievously before he added, "Or what you desire yourself? Remember I can read your heart."

"I doubt it would take your special powers to do that." Then with a smile she added, "But perhaps I should tell you, since you bring my heart into it - that Kenneth Mhor has almost convinced me to follow it."

* * *

The old man turned from the window and picked up his pen. So it had all been for nothing, the stubborn clinging to hope, the entreaties to a God who had indeed abandoned him. There was no justice left in this tarnished world, no regard for sacrifice, no reward for honour. Now his children must pay the price of his constancy, destitute when they might have been wealthy, pitied in a foreign land when they should have been feted in their own.

His hand shook so that he could scarcely scratch the quill across the rough parchment. Signora Valotti clasped his wrist and tried to guide him. But it was no use. He must dictate the words, even though she could not scribe in an English hand. He would have to leave the translation to fortune, for there was not a single soul in Rome he could trust with so important a message – his last testament to his lost homeland.

* * *

The Giant's Mountain was invisible in the darkness. Not a single lamp glowed from the silent cottages and the moon had disappeared behind the one remaining cloud. The only sounds were the lapping of waves and the occasional knocking of the fishing boats as they nudged each other against the jetty. Euan MacMichael was the only human presence out of doors. He stumbled, but not because he mistook his footing. Euan could have found his way through Glenshellich blind-fold. At his front door he steadied himself, listening to the hollow sound that was his own breathing. He waited and listened again. The last thing he wanted was to waken his mother.

Euan had no idea how long he had sat with the old men beside the reeking peat embers of Angus' fire. Time had drifted and stretched, turned itself inside out, turned him inside out with it. The whisky made his head throb but whisky had nothing to do with the torment in his heart. He did not believe he would know another peaceful hour as long as he lived.

The door creaked under the slow pressure of his hand. He raised his head and straightened his shoulders. The embers in his own hearth had almost disappeared, but as he closed the door behind him a sudden tiny flame danced on the wall and conjured shadows that briefly came and went. He closed the door softly against the blackness of the night and began to creep towards his bed. But before he reached it he heard her say his name.

"Eochain."

With that one word he knew beyond any doubt that she understood and shared his suffering.

"Come sit with me," she whispered. "Let me find comfort for you."

She had found him comfort all her life. How could he tell her there could be none for him now, in any place or from anyone? Even so, he found himself inching towards her, like an old man, a man as old as Angus Ban who had only hours ago destroyed what was left of his world.

But his mother reached out and gripped his hand with a defiant strength.

"Look then, my son," she urged. "Look again on the mark of the knife."

Another tiny flame darted from the embers and left its fragile spiral of smoke twisting between them. Euan had many times watched from the shadows as his father caressed that hand. He could remember how the healer had raised the maimed fingers to his lips and run his own touch tenderly over the smooth red scar, tracing and banishing a secret sorrow. Euan had none of his father's gifts, yet he found himself taking Catriona's hand and almost by instinct repeating the gesture.

"You are a good man, Eochain," Catriona whispered. "The best of all God's gifts to me. You must not bear this burden alone."

"I am his brother," he breathed at last.

"Yes, you are his brother."

"And I, I who love him above all men, must be the one to...."

"To rip his heart more savagely than a hundred dirks."

He stared at her in disbelief. It was not possible that a woman should have heard those forbidden words. Yet even as the thought came to him another one replaced it. For if their glen was to empty of its men, who else would there be but a woman left to repeat them?

"Your father could not leave me in ignorance," she went on, "to wonder why it was the clachan shunned me, and gasped and shrank away when I passed them by."

"So what is there left for me?" he cried

"You are a man of your clan," she answered softly as a pale hint of dawn began to creep across the mountain towards the cottage window. "There would be no purpose in me pretending as your chieftain has done." She held the silence for a long time and Euan still clung to her hand. "You are not his only brother."

"It is of me the words speak."

Catriona sighed and her eyes drew distant. "Andrew will soon go to the city."

She let his hand fall and he felt his hopelessness return.

"I will drive a dirk through my own heart, before the day comes of which they speak," he hissed.

He could not know that all his life his mother had dreaded this moment. Yet though she had been prepared she still hesitated before she took his hand again.

"I cannot see into the mists of time and tell what will be," she whispered. "But I do believe I can see into your heart, Eochain, and into Donald's. There is nothing there to bring this fate about, nothing in either of your hearts. I know that as you love Donald so he loves you. You are bonded in more than just the ancient way."

"If I died now it would spare his grief."

"And that would not make him grieve all the days of his life?"

Euan turned away again. "There is no way, then. Angus Ban spoke true."

"Angus is an old man who gives voice to dead words. MacSomhairle has forbidden them, and rightly. Such stories bring nothing but misery and fear."

"It is hard to find the strength to combat the words of the seers."

Catriona drew another deep breath. "I have found the strength, and you must do the same. You will do the same. Put this superstition from your mind, Eochain."

He let go of her hand but still gazed into her grey eyes and for the first time sensed in her something that lay buried far beyond the reach of any healing.

Outside the sky grew paler as he whispered, "It was my first thought, to take my life."

She showed no surprise, but only brushed her hand across his cheek.

"One day," she told him, "if it pleases God you will be brought to look again into your father's eyes. You would not wish a mortal sin on your conscience." She paused and seemed at last to make up her mind. "There was once a time when I had nothing to hope for but death. And that was when God brought me your father. We must always look for the light ahead, Eochain, for it is always there."

He reached out and drew her close to him, feeling the strength that came from her stillness. He would do as she said, but he did not believe the words of the seers could be ignored. Euan was an elder himself now, privy to his clan's secrets, in touch with powers that lay unspoken, barely even sensed. There was nothing for him to do but wait for his destiny and accept it when it came.

* * *

Hugh Fettes reached casually for a fresh bottle of claret. The fading drumbeat and distant snatches of song had long ago signalled the last revellers on their unsteady way home but in Hugh's mind the night was still young.

"Why so pensive, my friend?" he murmured. "This melancholy does not become you and completely baffles me." He grinned suddenly. "You are sought after by the choicest whores in the city, and possess the devotion of the most beautiful woman I have laid eyes on. Well, the most beautiful save one," he corrected himself, the wine sending his reflections hazily in the direction of Jean Petrie.

But Donald's thoughts still dwelt his own inadequacy. He had made his arrangements to return to Glenshellich, yet here he was, postponing the moment again, and even trying to deceive himself that his delay might somehow strengthen his father's tenuous grip on life. But he could not deny that his fear was the future, creeping inevitably closer, with its relentless demands and expectations.

"Perhaps I have never given proper thought to the subject of love," he murmured, and then tried to bring a lighter note to his voice. " I do not believe I know what love is, Hugh, other than the passion I feel in my heart for my glen. Should it not be an overwhelming and desperate thing, whose object you cannot live without, or even bear to think of being without? Yet I could bear the thought of losing Helen where I could not bear the thought of losing Glenshellich."

Studying his expression Hugh decided against a flippant response. Donald was undoubtedly in earnest. He leaned back in his chair and endeavoured to look solemn.

"Perhaps we should leave love to the poets and storytellers. A gentleman should take his pleasure where he will and marry for advancement, exactly as you propose. A little more advantageously than most," he added. "I doubt you will regret leaving the whores to the rest of us when you get that beauty under your bedcovers."

Yet as ever Donald retreated from the prospect. Instead an image of Meg MacLeay rose in his mind. He had been home just once since the birth of their child. Shame had kept him away. But Meg had not been ashamed. Neither had she concerned herself with foolish talk of love. She had understood better than he that theirs was a passion that would not be returned to.

So shame had kept him from his glen ever since: shame and the fear that his father would think less of him, that Catriona would discover his unworthiness, that Euan would condemn him for abandoning them in their time of need. For it seemed to Donald that he had betrayed them all. He was ashamed and afraid to acknowledge how Andrew's dreams had been snatched by his own extravagance, how Fraser's trust in him must have withered and died. And so he had hidden in his unworthy places, knowing that the city was eating his soul, destroying his heart, turning him into a debauched shadow of the boy he had been. He took another miserable draught of claret.

"Your responsibilities are overwhelming," Hugh agreed gently, recognising the mixture of passion and despair in Donald's eyes. "And you do not believe you are equipped to bear them. But you are wrong, Donald." His next words died on his lips and he looked away. He had been going to say that his friend had in him the makings of a hero. But he remembered there were many kinds of hero, and a shadow seemed to drift over his heart. "I prefer to take a simpler path in such matters," he went on with forced lightness. "I suspect," he admitted with a smile, "that may be because I love myself too much." Still he studied Donald's face in the last glow of the firelight. "You will not share my ways for much longer, Donald. I suspect you have already begun to tire of them. One day you will take your place as chieftain, prouder even than Cairnill, strutting among us lesser mortals like a peacock in your ancient glory." He smiled again, but his eyes did not lose their trace of sadness. "And I hope you will not forget your old friend whose pleasures you once shared. For I will be one of the shabby, red faced gentlemen at the card tables, raising my head from the game only to call for more wine or to leer at the ladies. I am born to follow, I fear, even if that must be my own instincts down an unfortunate road, while you …. you are born to another destiny. And I have no doubt that you will acquire the wisdom to find it."

Donald gazed at him, surprisingly touched by his words. He reached across the hearth and grasped Hugh's hand.

"You are a true friend, indeed, Hugh Fettes," he said.

"And proud to be so as long as I live and breathe," Hugh replied.

* * *

Further down towards the Canongate, in the shadows of Milne's Wynd, a cat wailed and a voice responded with a curse. The commotion woke Jean Petrie. She lay for a while, breathing in the hint of stale claret that escaped from the Master's lips until a low moan escaped with it. Jean reached out and ran her hand softly over the features of his face: the long, straight nose, the lean cheeks, the smooth but trembling lips. She stroked the dampness breaking across his forehead.

"Hush! Hush!" she soothed. Sometimes she found she could banish the dream without even wakening him. But not this time. His startled eyes opened wide and he cried out. Making light of it, Jean sniffed disapprovingly. "A fine night, then?"

She watched as he struggled to regain his composure. Finally he gave a small smile. "Perhaps I have indulged myself more than I should." His eyes narrowed. He was once more in control. "But if so, it was because I heard distressing news."

She bent her head over his, and with her finger delicately traced a line that ran from his nostril to the corner of his mouth. He gazed up into her face and his features relaxed.

"Disturbing news?" she echoed.

He sighed. "Of my neighbour, MacSomhairle, chieftain of Glenshellich. It appears he is not long for this world."

Jean had no particular interest in the chieftain of Glenshellich, but any news disturbing to Kilclath required her full attention.

"I once ..." he went on, but his voice faded and a shadow seemed to cross his eyes. Then he pulled himself together. "I once did him a great injury. If I could be offered an event in my entire life to live again and change I believe it would be that moment." He seemed to drift with his thoughts. "Yet he and my father were … if not exactly enemies, far from being friends."

Jean ran her hand over the delicate white skin of his shoulder. She propped herself onto an elbow and gazed seriously down at him.

"Savage Highlandmen?" she whispered.

He smiled. "Quite the opposite. They were both men of peace – though perhaps in different ways and for different reasons. I have tried to follow my father's example in that at least," he paused thoughtfully, "although I am not sure the same could be said of MacSomhairle's son."

For a moment Jean looked puzzled, then she remembered. "What is MacSomhairle's son to Mhairi?" she asked quickly, and was surprised to see his eyes register alarm.

"To Mhairi?"

Jean was not fooled. She studied his expression, but it had become guarded once more, inscrutable, wearing the lawyer's look, the politician's disguise.

"It doesn't matter," she said softly, and meant it. Whatever MacSomhairle might have been to Mhairi belonged to the Master's other world, the world her influence was making more distant every day. The city was his home now, the courts and drawing rooms, the inns and gaming houses. Kilclath's mountains and glens might still pull his heart and direct his dreams, but Jean remained dedicated to her mission. It was to lead him into the light.

He picked up a loose strand of her hair and held it to his lips.

"It doesn't matter," he agreed. "In a hundred years it will matter still less. In a thousand not at all. What matters now . . . ."

But she did not let him finish. They both knew what mattered now.

* * *

Andrew jumped from old Angus' boat onto the loose shingle. His feet crunched through it as he hauled the net from the sighing waves.

"I promised to stay only until the wedding," he said, gripping the edge of the stern and heaving another heavy net across the shingle. "For I am anxious to begin my studies."

Angus squinted past him into sunlight he could scarcely see, but made no reply.

"I love my home, Angus," Andrew went on. "I love our people. But I cannot stagnate in Glenshellich forever. Now my chance has come I must seize it."

Angus remained silent, but turned his eyes towards the eager face of his chieftain's younger son. When he finally spoke his voice was high-pitched and trembling.

"You will return but twice. And each returning will break your heart."

Andrew looked at him with a mixture of affection and frustration.

"So you have said. But I cannot base all my decisions on your signs and portents."

"You know the power of The Sight."

"Enough to believe there is more than one possibility ahead of us. Surely what we think we glimpse of the future is only part of it, something which might take place, but just as easily might not. ..."

He was certainly not going to admit to Angus how many times he had paced this shingle trying to summon his gift. If only he could have reached into the future, even once, to catch a glimpse of Helen as mistress of his glen. But the power of The Sight came in its own time and of its own choosing. Never once had it spoken to Andrew of the matter closest to his heart and he had begun to suspect – almost to hope – that the gift had deserted him altogether. He shrugged his shoulders. Whatever the future held, he had long ago accepted that his own happiness must come from work and service. He would do no woman the injustice of taking second place in his heart.

Angus was still regarding him with the same strange expression.

"I suppose what I mean, Angus," he went on, "is that no prediction should deny us the opportunity of choice."

But Angus only shook his head. Choice, he thought, to himself. What could the sons of MacSomhairle know of choice? For them it had all been decided long ago. His gaze lingered slyly on the boy. He was as foolish as his own grandson, believing they could change the world. But let them have the comfort of their dreams while they could. Angus watched the ripples spread across the water. Like himself it seemed they went on forever, growing slowly weaker, carried by a force they were powerless to oppose, until finally and silently they slipped out of sight of the shore.

* * *

Two letters were waiting for Helen MacLean when she returned from her walk, one addressed in a familiar hand and the other in one less recognisable. But that was the one she snatched from her father's desk and carried upstairs, without for one moment believing there was anything unseemly in her haste. She tore apart the seal and as she began to read a warm smile spread across her face.

Her father gazed after her and frowned. He remembered the admiration he had seen in the eyes of the Master of the Stones and wished, not for the first time, that hindsight did not shine such an unfavourable light on past promises. He sighed. Soon his own lands might rival Kilclath in prosperity and his daughter might have had her pick of suitors far richer and more influential than the one whose long overdue letter brought such brightness to her eyes.

A shadow crossed his own eyes. Kilclath and Glenshellich, he thought to himself, so close yet so distant, so different yet so entwined. The old story would have many more chapters, of that he was certain, and the fate of his daughter must now be written into them. Cairnill was not a man to betray his word but he would have sacrificed much of his newfound wealth to return to an April day in the rain. Like the Master of the Stones he knew he would have given MacSomhairle a very different reception.

In a rare lucid moment John Stewart reached for his younger son's hand.

"Donald will be too late," he whispered. "You will tell him – how he was in my thoughts."

Andrew tried to swallow the tightness in his throat, but suddenly his father sat upright. His eyes searched wildly ahead. There was something else, something he had almost forgotten. "Fraser!" he gasped.

The old groom stepped out of the shadows. "Hush, hush, now," he soothed.

John Stewart fell back on his pillow. They were growing more distant, while he was drifting down the road, unevenly, dragging himself by ropes on either side. Not a road, but a gangplank, the gangplank to a ship, and Fraser was trying to reach him, swimming through the water, swimming but not moving. It was himself who was moving and leaving them behind. But he would be too late, and Donald still had no sons. A cold sweat gripped him, for his work was not done. Donald must have sons. He turned to pull himself back, but the tide surged against him. Cairnill's figure was there, fading into the distance. Was that a smile of parting, of triumph, or of contempt on his face? They would be his blood too, their seed united, their alliance sealed down the generations. But Cairnill was disappearing also. It was Allomore who waited on the shore ahead, Allomore with his sad eyes: his dead eyes.

"No!" MacSomhairle gasped, and felt the soothing hand of Catriona MacMichael on his brow. "Catriona!" he pleaded desperately, panicking now. But her soft glance faded as a huge shadow rose at Allomore's shoulder.

"Catriona!" he gasped again, but this time his voice was spent. He had reached that other shore and Euan was there waiting. The healer smiled. John Stewart sighed. Peace was there with them. If God had forgiven his foster brother then surely he must forgive him also.

"Catriona," he whispered. But when he opened his eyes she was gone. The gangplank was raised and the ship was returning home.

* * *

Donald galloped through the fading light, skirting the Valley of Stones, spurring his stallion into the sinking mist. Soon the dark mass of Beinn Feodag rose above the cloud and he could make out the Watcher's Stone against the dull orange sky. He pressed his heels into the horse's flank and above its hoof-beats heard the familiar roar of the waters cleaving and churning as they tumbled in spate to the lochan.

All the while the same prayer repeated itself in his mind like a drumming incantation.

It was a prayer that would not be answered.

* * *

Two days later brought Gavin MacVey. In the house of Glenshellich Euan MacMichael lurked at the door, ashen faced, deliberately apart. Donald had seated himself uncomfortably at his father's desk while Fraser gently removed the tray with its brandy glasses from Eilidh's trembling hands. Catriona and Andrew stood silently beside the chimneypiece.

"It was an arrangement – a reciprocal arrangement as it happens - made many years ago, in less settled times," the lawyer went on. Catriona continued to stare at him, and Andrew continued to stare at Catriona. He had not seen such a light in her eyes for many a day. Fraser edged imperceptibly closer to her.

"Where did my father expect to find the resources for this?" Donald demanded.

"MacSomhairle put honour above resources, loyalty above convenience," rebuked Gavin. Then his tone softened. Donald was in no frame of mind to be rational and the news had clearly come as a shock. He decided to approach the situation from a different angle. "You know as well as I do, Donald, that the lands of Allomore are among the most favoured in the country." He lowered his voice. "And who knows, might even yet be restored."

Andrew frowned. "So do you imply that this... undertaking.... might have been another canny move on our father's part?"

"The fact your father had not made you aware of it makes me suspect it was not."

Catriona stepped forward, hesitantly. "When did Mac Iain Mhor die?" she asked.

The old lawyer had no need to ask to whom she referred. "Two weeks past," he answered.

"Two weeks!" Donald echoed.

"No word reached us," Fraser stated firmly.

Donald looked around their faces. "Catriona?"

Catriona was giving the subject careful thought and did not answer immediately. "I do not believe your father could have known of it," she said at last. "But even if he had...."

Andrew turned away. They had all, save perhaps Donald, been aware of the frailty of MacSomhairle's mind, but Andrew was the only one present who sensed what lay behind Catriona's concern. Something was happening in this room. He felt the walls creeping closer, tightening around them. It was not because of his father's death that Glenshellich would change forever. It would change because of this moment.

"They are in Inverness," Gavin added briskly, anxious to relieve himself of the information for fear of being held responsible for it. "And preparing to make their way west. MacSomhairle, to his credit, was in the habit of sending regular sums of money to Rome. He was not alone in his benevolence, although of course the family was still forced to survive in desperately reduced circumstances."

Donald let out a long breath. He continued to stare helplessly at Gavin. "This could not have happened at a worse time."

"I agree."

"And how many dependents am I so suddenly to answer for?"

Gavin scratched his nose. "I believe they are a boy and girl, who we must consider to be completely alone in the world."

Catriona reached out for Fraser's hand. "While we are alive they will never be alone," she breathed.

"A finer gentleman than James Hamilton never walked this earth," he agreed stoutly. "And half the nation would vouch for it."

Donald was still struggling to come to terms with the situation. "That is not in dispute," he snapped. "Any more than that a worse scoundrel than his successor never breathed."

"What would you know of his successor, Domhnull?" Catriona asked sharply.

The old lawyer threw her an equally sharp look. "We are all aware of the shortcomings of the present incumbent," he interrupted impatiently. "But the fact remains that he is in command and will not lightly be set aside."

"Unless…." Donald began.

The lawyer made another dismissive gesture.

"In the future," added Andrew, "if and when the wind changes…."

"The wind blows in one direction and one direction alone in that matter," Gavin answered with finality.

Donald forced his attention back to his own situation. With his father not yet in his grave this was a truly unwelcome complication.

Gavin drew another deep breath and continued. "Their mother was of the Delarange line, minor French nobility, considerably younger than Allomore and like himself unsuited to adversity. The marriage was by all accounts an unhappy one and I believe she died giving birth to a third child, who also did not survive."

"MacSomhairle never breathed a word of it," muttered Fraser.

"Possibly with a view to their own safety."

Catriona was looking closely at Donald. He was clearly far from happy at this unlooked for piece of news. He moved to the window and gazed out, deep in thought. Catriona beckoned the others to follow her from the room and closed the door behind them.

Donald poured more brandy and motioned Gavin to one of the seats at the fireside. "I know you have little reason to feel confidence in my abilities," he began. "But I intend to continue my father's work, to care for the clan as he did, to invest as much as he did in improving their lives."

"Then you intend some changes in your own habits," the old lawyer commented dryly.

Donald let the criticism pass. "I will be content to remain in my glen, as my father was," he continued seriously. "Glenshellich has always been more to my liking than any place in the world."

"Fine sentiments, if somewhat unexpected ones," Gavin returned. Then he cleared his throat and lowered his voice. "On the subject of your father's arrangement with The Plotter, you must be aware that there will be more than a few interested parties."

"I have hardly had opportunity to consider it."

"Or perhaps sufficient information at your disposal." Gavin relaxed into his chair. "You know, of course that Allomore has no heir – and is unlikely to produce one."

"So you think that this boy….?"

"Will be in an intriguing position, to say the least." Gavin drew another long breath. "It may be a dangerous one or it may not," he went on. "Who knows what will fall out in these uncertain times?" As an afterthought he added, "I hear the Pretender's son has been in dialogue with the French."

"The French have been constantly loyal in their support for our cause."

Gavin did not look convinced as Donald refilled their glasses.

"Well, well, what matter any of it," the old lawyer sighed. He too was beginning to feel his age and the passing of so many of his contemporaries was a further weight on his spirits. " What will be will be. The old order may or may not return. I can only suggest that you make your new dependents as welcome as your grief permits - until such time as fuller consideration might be given to their future."

Donald nodded but his mind was already digesting Gavin's information. Allomore. The Plotter. He had in truth given little thought to any of them since Hugh's unfortunate encounter with the Laird in Edinburgh. His father's old friend had been scarcely more to him than a figment of fantasy, a minor character in a far off adventure, but now his ignorance began to trouble him. It was indeed a sad thing that the children of a man who had not only devoted his life but sacrificed his birthright for a cause so close to all their hearts, should be facing so grudging a welcome. He swallowed down his brandy and vowed to do everything possible to make amends.

* * *

The next morning he and Fraser were saddling two stallions and two of the sturdier garrons.

"I have seldom embarked on a journey with more trepidation," he murmured. "I fear that Euan and I will prove very inadequate guardians. And what if they are unable to ride the garrons?"

Fraser narrowed his eyes and patted his favourite pony's rump.

"They'll no have muckle choice since the two of you have as much chance of getting a cart through Kilclath as you'd have of sprouting wings and flying ower it. If they're their father's bairns they'll no be feart of pony rides."

Donald stood back and looked seriously at his old friend.

"I wish their riding skills were all I had to worry about. We are in no condition to receive them as my father would have wished." His eyes searched the jagged summit of the giant's mountain. "Especially as I am far from sure that I want them here at all."

"They deserve the best of all welcomes," Fraser replied stoutly, then, as his eyes fell on the track from the clachan and the burly figure of Euan MacMichael lumbering towards them, he added grimly, "And one look at him would be enough to set them winging all the way back to Italy."

Donald sighed again as he watched Euan's hostile approach. The two of them had spoken but briefly since his return, and never alone, but Donald had recognised at once how things had changed between them. Euan's expression remained thunderous as he took his horse's reins.

"I am not late, I hope," he muttered brusquely.

Donald ignored his tone. "It is I who am early. Through anxiety," he added, with a wry glance at Fraser who stepped back and smiled. "This is my first real duty as chieftain."

"And what duty could be more fitting?" Fraser exclaimed. "If nothing else it'll do the house a power of good to hear the sound of bairns' voices again."

* * *

"My dear Helen," wrote Andrew. "My last note was from necessity brief, but I can write at length today, with so many hours to occupy while Donald and Euan journey to Cranachferry to collect the children of our fathers' old comrade in arms, Allomore. Our information regarding them is scant to say the least, but it appears that my father made an agreement several years ago to safeguard their futures if need be. Perhaps he mentioned the arrangement to us at a time when we were not interested enough to take heed, but it has certainly come as a surprise to everyone, and at the most inopportune of times. ...." Andrew stared ahead and swallowed the sudden sourness that had risen in his throat. His father had been much given to making arrangements on other people's behalf. "However, by the end of this day Glenshellich House will be transformed from the sombre dwelling it has become to something more like a family home ..."

His mind wandered again. The house had indeed lost much of the warmth he remembered. Perhaps mostly because of their father's declining health, but Andrew knew that his own disappointment and frustration had played its part. Now Donald had returned to take his rightful place and seemed finally inclined to put duty before pleasure. The reflection brought another pang. With that duty came other promises to fulfil.

"I know," he wrote, or I imagine, he thought miserably, "that Donald will be writing to you as soon as he has an opportunity...."

* * *

"We have become men too quickly, Eochain," Donald said softly. "Perhaps you are better prepared for it than me, in spite of my so called education."

For the first time since they had left the house Euan let his horse draw level with Donald's. The garrons for Allomore's children trotted calmly behind on their long reins, but Euan had left Donald to lead them in a single line along the track. Around them the day seemed set fair as the early mist spread in the thin sunshine above the lochan to drift and disperse in trails across the lower slopes of Beinn Feodag. Yet the morning's promise was lost on Euan MacMichael. He had been thinking of another journey, one he had not personally taken. He was remembering a day in the rain when he and Donald had waited for so many hours at the end of this same route. He shook himself back to the moment. MacSomhairle had spoken and was waiting for a reply.

"It was a sorry day that I became one," Euan muttered bitterly, "and sat at the fires of the old men."

Donald turned the full force of his gaze upon his foster brother and let out a slow breath. "You once wished for nothing more," he recalled, with more than a trace of awe, "save that the day would only come when you were the master of your own house. Well we are both that now, Eochain. So what is it about their tales of the past that so disturbs you?"

He looked sideways at Euan who seemed to be concentrating on keeping his own gaze fixed rigidly ahead. But he did not need an answer. They could be talking of nothing other than the tale he had been forbidden; the one he knew was of him.

"It is not their tales of the past that concern me."

"In God's name!" Donald breathed. "You have heard the *Fais-neachd*!" Did my father not say it went ill with all who listened?" Yet he could not ignore the sudden rush of his own curiosity. "Tell me then, Eochain," he urged. "If you are man enough then so am I."

"No-one is man enough to hear of their fate."

"So you believe it."

"I do not."

Donald's horse stumbled and he pulled carelessly on the reins. Euan was absorbing all his attention.

"You have shown too well what you believe." Donald's voice became petulant. "It is not fitting to keep this from me. Or is it too terrible for you to even mention?"

Euan turned on him suddenly and jerked his horse to a halt, stunning Donald by the passion in his voice. "In my mind, no, I do not believe it. But it is not always my mind that speaks to me. It was my heart that heard those words at Angus Ban's fireside and it is my heart that feels their burden." Then, embarrassed, he added," It is a burden for me though and not for you."

Donald laid an arm across his shoulder. For the first time he sensed there was a chance that Euan might return to him. "And how could any burden of yours not be mine?" His eyes took on a beseeching expression. "Tell me the words, Eochain, for they loom too large between us. Do you think I could bear to lose you as well as my father?"

Euan drew himself tight within himself and it was a long time before he answered.

"It is the story of the second son, Domhnull, and they say that is you. The second son of the second son, and because on the night you were born it was as if the lochan caught fire. The *Faisneachd* tells sad things for our glen, sad things for all the glens and people…" Euan stopped himself suddenly, forcing his eyes back to the road ahead. He was saying too much, but Donald had always been able to read his mind. Euan urged himself to draw a veil and be silent. It was not his place to discuss ancient mysteries with his chieftain, still less to dare feel resentment towards him. But Donald was also his brother. That was Euan's pride, and that was his torment.

"So must I go to the clachan myself and sit at the old men's fires?" Donald challenged.

"There would be no purpose. You will not hear it from Angus Ban. Your father made him swear on the iron."

"Then I must hear it from you."

But Euan shook his head and it was Donald's turn to fall silent as he remembered his father's scorn for superstition. He had promised himself there was not a single one of his father's wishes he would not make it his duty to fulfil.

"Very well," he said at last. "We will speak of it no more, for it causes nothing but discord between us. And I would as soon be cast from my glen as be estranged from you."

Euan attempted a smile, for Donald's sake, but it faded on his lips. He had his own memories of the reeking hut, the grim faces, the thin voice of the descendent of the seer. Yet he knew it was his duty to serve his chieftain as a foster brother should, as his own father had once done so honourably. And if the day should come of which the words spoke then it must come, he told himself. Until then he would not let his fear of it come between them.

The sun was at its height when they reached the little coaching station tended by old Colin Chisholm of the Clan of the Cats. Colin lived alone but he was never lonely for he was never without entertainment. Travellers from the furthest ends of the country and beyond broke their journey at his table and shared their news. Few of them departed without feeling a touch of envy. The old man was always interested and impeccably informed. Although Donald had seen him only days before they still found much to discuss and Donald found some relief in being able to delay, however slightly, his meeting with Allomore's children.

"And I was telling the lassie it would be yourself who would come," Colin went on. "The news of your father was a great shock to her, MacSomhairle, a great shock and sorrow, as it was to us all."

Euan edged closer to the door of the shelter but Donald was still reluctant to follow him inside. Every word of his well-rehearsed speech had left him and he was combing his mind for it when Euan suddenly reappeared, lurching against the wall and clutching its rough stones. Gazing in alarm beyond him into the gloom, Donald could distinguish no cause for his reaction other than two vague outlines, taller than he had imagined, one sinking backwards, the other moving forward into the light. Euan raised his arm, as if to shield his eyes from the brightness of the sun, as Donald shrugged him roughly aside and strode through the doorway.

CHRISTIE

Donald stood for a moment, angry and ashamed, letting his own eyes accustom themselves to the shadows. What sort of welcome was this for the orphans of their father's oldest friend? Gradually the two figures fell into focus.

"You have had a weary journey," he said simply and stretched out his hand. "I am Donald who they must now call MacSomhairle. My foster brother and myself are here to take you home."

"Home," the girl echoed wistfully. She turned towards her brother with questioning eyes, then added in a voice so soft Donald wondered if he had imagined it. "Thank you."

Again he hesitated. These were no pathetic waifs who stood before him, and no children. The angle of the sun cut shafts of light through the vents in the shutters, shafts that struck the girl's golden hair, absorbing and reflecting its brightness. A dusty travelling bag lay at her feet. Her shoes were stained and tattered and she wore a creased cloak of blue velvet, yet she faced Donald with a profound and unexpected dignity. Her brother remained silent, but he too held his head high. It was clear that Allomore had kept enough of his pride to bequeath to his children. Donald was thankful for it.

"We were so very sorry to hear the news of your father," the girl continued simply. "What a strange fate has brought us together at such a time."

Donald struggled for a reply as he continued to gaze into her face. Christie Hamilton was not unaccustomed to such reactions. She smiled.

"The other gentleman...." she began.

"Euan MacMichael," Donald muttered. "My foster brother. He was not polite."

He lifted their light bags and swung them towards the doorway. Christie turned to her brother. "And you are not polite, either, James. This cannot be easy for him."

His reply was another sullen glare.

She sighed. "Do you feel nothing to be in our own country at last?"

"Your father renounced any right we might have had to call this our country," he muttered darkly, and his lip curled as if the word itself had a bitter taste. "We have no country. You would once have been less eager to accept charity. Or does it have a different name when the benefactor is handsome and speaks of a home we can never share?"

Christie looked at him sadly. If she had been warmed by Donald's words it was for neither of her brother's reasons. It was because the sound of his voice had brought her father's old stories alive. He was the son of John Stewart, of MacSomhairle who had returned to his glen. And who could wonder at it? Now that Christie had seen at first hand the land that might have been theirs she understood the enormity of her father's choice. The mountains they had travelled beneath had stirred unfamiliar feelings, strange longings and dreams that made her heart quicken.

She followed Donald out into the sunlight and touched Colin's arm. "Thank you for making us welcome," she said softly.

"It has been my pleasure," Colin replied.

Euan was pacing beside the horses, leaving Donald to fasten the baggage. Christie saw them exchange an angry glance and some rough words. She looked uncomfortably at her brother, but James was equally morose. Once mounted the little party proceeded in silence. Euan led the way, his eyes trained on the road before them, and he remained ominously silent as Donald drew level.

It did not take long for Christie to realise that although her garron might carry her unusually close to the ground she could trust him to pick his way over the roughest terrain. Freed from the concern of staying in the saddle she gazed around her, although she noticed that her brother appeared immune to the spectacle of the mountains rising around them, the lush green of the hill pastures, the sharp pink outcrops, the brilliant blue sky.

Ahead of them Donald was finally moved to speak.

"And what is the cause of this latest ill humour?" he muttered gruffly in their native tongue.

"It is an ill-omened day," Euan replied blackly. "And you tell me to forget the words of the seers. It is a day you will regret, MacSomhairle, for grief will come to you through that girl. I have seen the sun in her eyes."

Angrier than ever, Donald made a fierce gesture of frustration. "Ach!" he almost spat. "You are too greatly changed, Euan. You have made this breach between us and you make it wider it with every word you utter. It is through you that all my pain comes, and I am heart-sick crawling on my knees to make peace."

Euan fell into an even more dejected silence. When he finally spoke his words seemed intended mostly for himself. "Then perhaps we are all powerless now."

It was a comment too far for Donald. "My fate is my own," he spat. "And not for you or Angus Ban to spread out before me. You are obsessed, Euan, and you prove with each hour the wisdom of my father's words. You have been rude to our guests and you have shamed his memory. It would go ill with Catriona were she to hear of your manners today, for she knew and honoured their father well."

Euan hung his head. For a long time he said nothing, but the mention of his mother seemed to have calmed him. He turned to look back at Allomore's children and his cheeks flushed with shame.

"Forgive me then, MacSomhairle," he whispered, "for it I who must crawl to you. I cannot bear to be the cause of your anger."

Listening, Christie felt as if a shadow crossed her heart, even as it warmed to the clansman Euan, hunching so wretchedly now in his saddle. She leaned forward. "I am sorry," she interrupted softly, "But please do not speak of matters private to you in that tongue, for I have had it all my life, and have no wish to intrude into what is not intended for my ears."

A flush to match his foster brother's spread over Donald's features. Such rudeness was unforgivable: to speak of a matter that excluded his guests in a language they could not be expected to understand. Euan might have shown grave discourtesy, but he had done far, far worse. He could find no excuse, least of all to answer this girl's apology to him. Surprisingly it was Euan who came to his rescue.

"Indeed," he said simply, "I am thinking it is not yourself who should be making the apology. I have given you too much cause for unease already. I deserve a thrashing, as a man would once have had, for speaking so."

"Surely not!" the girl exclaimed, and it seemed to Donald that her smile mocked them, though it did not seem so to Euan who appeared to have no trouble in responding with one of his own.

"I might once have been thrashed for less," he said with a glance at Donald, realising that his foster brother would not have been averse to carrying out that very punishment there and then.

"In those old lawless days our father used to speak of?"

Recognising that this was an opportunity to make amends Euan still spoke in Gaelic. "In the days when we made our own laws. Each clan has its stories, its heroes, its ghosts."

He had waited for her to draw level and they paused together to let Donald and James ride ahead. Her eyes were a dazzling blue and Euan found it impossible not to fall under their spell.

"Please tell me of them," she breathed.

Euan smiled. He knew tales enough to entertain her all the way home. His head was full of tales: of history and beyond, true tales and the legends that sprang from a land where fairies once danced and giants cast their shadows, where in the moonlight the stealthy might catch a glimpse of a sea horse or hear the selkies swim singing from the sea.

"I could tell of the selkie princess," his gentle voice went on, "who was born deep in the sea kingdom in the days before men came onto the earth. She was more beautiful than any woman who lives today, but her beauty made the sea witch jealous. One night when the moon shone on the water the sea witch cast a wicked spell...."

As Euan warmed to his task their two horses fell into regular step together. From time to time Donald glanced behind him at his foster brother and the captivated girl from Rome, but he remained silent, as did the boy who rode dejectedly beside him. Euan's increasingly infuriating voice continued, interrupted from time to time by a sudden question or a soft peal of laughter. James fell back alone to bring up the rear of the small procession as above their heads the afternoon sky grew radiant and the sun shone with a fierce intensity. Only as they approached the borders of Kilclath did the clouds creep overhead, though they remained too high to obscure the massive peaks of the twin Mountains, sharper edged than swords against the cobalt sky.

* * *

The same image rose in Hughie McIvor's mind as he slunk behind his master down the seething Canongate. Edinburgh was not to the ghillie's liking at any time of year, but especially not in high summer when the stench in the gutters heralded new outbreaks of disease and the air hung rank and suffocating over sunless wynds. Yet Hughie knew the city increasingly suited his master, so much so that he had chosen to postpone yet again his visit to the Valley of Stones.

Kilclath turned sharply into his chambers and casually dismissed Hughie to the servants' quarters. Hughie ignored him and continued to lurk in the hallway. His master did not bother to repeat the command. His attention had already shifted to the note on his desk and his face grew dark. Why could Allomore not keep himself occupied on his own estates? Why did he not have the foresight to stay out of the public's increasingly censorious eye? Not that his whereabouts were the Master's affair, any more than was the information his note contained. He had already received prior notice of its contents from other sources.

Hughie appeared in the doorway, his expression darker still, and Kilclath's heart sank as he heard the high-pitched tones of complaint from the hallway. Within seconds Hughie's swarthy presence was replaced by one taller and considerably more elegant.

"I took the liberty of letting my own self in," Allomore announced, throwing an arrogant glance of contempt behind and before. Kilclath did not appreciate such glances falling in his direction. He scowled almost as darkly as his servant. His hand barely touched the corner of the parchment, which he indicated with the slightest of head movements.

"They have gone to Glenshellich."

Kilclath eyed him coldly. "So I believe," he answered. "It is of small significance."

"Small significance!" Allomore echoed.

"In fact," went on Kilclath calmly, "it might appear almost timely. Do you intend to make contact?"

"Have you taken leave of your senses?"

Hughie stiffened. He had cause to hold Allomore in even more contempt than did his master.

"My senses and I are perfectly united," Kilclath replied. "And in their opinion some gesture on your part might be appropriate. After all, Glenshellich commands limited resources, while Allomore...."

The older man's face grew whiter, emphasising the outrage glittering in his eyes. It occurred to Kilclath that he was becoming as viper-like in appearance as he was in nature. Hughie's fingers tightened on the handle of his dirk.

"Their father gave up any entitlement they may have had from my estates."

"My estates," Kilclath echoed softly, ironically, but nodded with apparent deliberation. Hughie gathered some saliva into his mouth but forbore to expel it.

"Yet we live in complex – and changing – times," the Master continued. "Should you not also bear in mind….." He paused significantly. "…..the future?"

"I am hardly in my dotage."

Kilclath sighed. Why should he concern himself with Allomore, the man or his lands? He had enough concerns of his own. Yet that old story, that old injustice, continued to nag at him, an unhealed scar on the conscience of his house. But perhaps this was not the time. He glanced again at the man across his desk. Kilclath knew well enough how many in Allomore would be happy to see the old order restored. The present Laird knew even better. His note had already conveyed the extent of his anxiety.

The Master drew a deeper breath. "I will set a watch on the situation. If it changes you will be the first to know."

"I have your word on that?"

The Master threw a small warning glance in Hughie's direction but the ghillie's face had become an impenetrable mask.

"You have my word."

* * *

"I believe," Christie breathed, her voice full of awe, "That of all the places we have seen on our journey so far, this glen is the most impressive – so huge, so lonely."

Euan shifted uncomfortably in his saddle, but Donald found himself at last moved to speak.

"It is Kilclath we have entered into, a bitter place of ill omen for our clan," he growled.

Christie continued to gaze around her. The sun scattered sharp shadows over the corries surrounding the twin peaks and she thought she saw far above them a soaring speck that hung, then dropped, sudden as a stone, behind them. The pass they were entering was dark, must always be dark, she thought, save perhaps for a brief space when the sun crossed from one summit to the other. That moment had passed for the day and the sun was with the eagle on the other side. The little group rode on in silence broken only by the clatter of the horses' hooves as they scraped for a hold on the gleaming rocks.

Donald instinctively looked towards Euan whose eyes were trained on the screeline. It must have been here, he thought, just about this very spot. Donald cleared his throat as he allowed them to draw level.

"It was in this place," he began bitterly, "that my father received the wound that finally took his life. It was here that he was shot in cold blood by the scoundrel who now sits at the head the Clan of Eagles – when he is not behind his desk in the city trading in the lives of honest men."

Christie was taken aback. "I am sorry," she said at last. "I had no idea . . ."

James fixed his scowl on the track ahead. He had still not uttered a single word and Donald too resumed his silence.

"We are almost home," Euan said softly. "It is unfortunate that the light is fading, for soon I believe you will not think the Valley of Stones so fair a place."

"You love your own land, Euan," Christie replied, and Donald's face grew darker still. His anger was now as much directed against this girl as Euan. She showed little modesty to speak with a stranger in so familiar a way, and even worse, Euan had greatly changed his tune and gave no sign of objecting to her forwardness. Donald's respect for himself had been deeply wounded. He desired only to reach Glenshellich quickly, where others could relieve some of his responsibility.

The sun had disappeared behind the Giant's Mountain when they passed the Watcher's Stone, but they could clearly distinguish Fraser's figure, hobbling down the track to greet them, his moon-like face beaming in the glow from the lamp.

"What the devil kept you?" he chided, squinting to distinguish the features of their guests. "Aye," he went on. "Bonnier craturs than your father, that's for sure." He held out a knobbly hand. Christie took it and smiled. She had heard a great deal about Archie Fraser.

When they reached the stables he was there to help her from the garron.

"No' the best choice, then," he muttered. "For either the pair of you."

James eased himself stiffly from the saddle and briefly took Fraser's extended hand, while Donald clapped the old groom's shoulder and gave him a desperate look.

"They're gey weary looking," Fraser remarked under his breath, referring to the horses. "Children?" he muttered, referring to their guests. He raised his eyes to the mountain and gave a grim chuckle. "Children!"

* * *

The servant woman was uncommunicative, though not unfriendly, and as she followed her along the narrow corridor at the top of the staircase Christie wondered if the enormous birthmark flaming half her face might explain her dour manner. She was too tired to notice many other details of her surroundings, though in her imagination she heard again the hushed tones of her father's voice.

"John Stewart will keep an honourable house." He had paused. "Of principled men." And those had been the very last words he had uttered before slipping into his final unconsciousness.

Well, thought Christie, she had met two principled men already, at least she supposed Donald to be one. His moodiness on their journey had suggested he might be every bit as temperamental as her own brother, whose company she was entirely glad to be relieved of.

"Thank you," she said, taking the lamp from the servant woman. "I'm sorry, I don't believe I caught your name."

The woman looked at her with an odd expression in her green eyes. Christie smiled and repeated her question in Gaelic. Eilidh seemed satisfied with the gesture yet replied in English nevertheless, before she hurried away.

The room they had given her was simple, fresh and clean, and Christie sank onto the big bed with a final overwhelming weariness. Outside she could hear nothing but the distant rush of the stream tumbling to the waiting waters of the lochan. She thought back to the sounds of Rome: the bickering of neighbours, the scuffling street fights, her father's thin breathing through the humid nights. Here the air was cool and smelt of nothing at all. She tried to grasp her feelings before she drifted into sleep, though they seemed more confused than ever and escaped her yet again. But she could not ignore the spirit that stirred inside her, nor the unfamiliar sense of peace that had been her father's last and perhaps most precious legacy.

She did not know if it was the sunlight streaming through the window that woke her or the faint knocking on the door. For a moment she was confused, oddly still after so many days of travelling, her mind slow to emerge from the deep sleep she had fallen into.

"Yes?" she called.

"It is Euan's mother Catriona," came the voice from the hall. "May I come in?"

Christie sat up and rubbed her eyes. In the bright daylight the oak panels seemed to glow. The linen on the bed was cool and smooth against her skin. Once more she was aware of breathing in odourless air.

"Yes," she answered. "Yes, of course."

Catriona's graceful figure slipped inside. She was holding a bowl of crimson roses and smiling warmly. "I had intended to leave these for

126

you when you arrived," she said. "But they are fresher with the early dew."

Christie was struck by the richness of her voice.

"Thank you," she breathed. "They are beautiful." But as Catriona reached out to put the bowl beside the bed, she gave a gasp and instinctively recoiled, as if she had been struck a blow by the sight of the drawn and mutilated fingers.

"Your hand!" she exclaimed in dismay.

Catriona smiled, as if to reassure her. "It is an old wound," she said softly. "Indeed I have grown so accustomed to it, like everyone else, that I have almost forgotten how it should be, how it once was. Do not be distressed. It has been so since long before you were born."

"What happened?" Christie breathed.

Catriona looked away, then gave another sad smile.

"War brings many kinds of wounds, Allomore's daughter," she said softly. "And this is but one of them. Your father's wounds were not so visible."

"No," Christie agreed, and hesitated again. "I am sorry. I should not have mentioned it."

"But I am not sorry in the least. And now you will not need to mention it again, or look on it either if you do not wish to."

But Christie did not avert the direction of her eyes. She stretched out her own hand and gently ran her fingers over the scar. "I will not *remark* on it again," she said.

The two women studied each other. "I see much of your father in you," Catriona said at last. "He would be content to know you are here with us." She stood up, ready to leave, but at the door she turned. "Try not to judge Donald too harshly. He tells me he believes he gave you a poor welcome yesterday. He has much on his mind. Sometimes he expects too much of himself."

She closed the door gently behind her and Christie slipped on her gown, rose and pulled open her curtains. Behind the outbuildings the mass of the Giant's Mountain caught the shadows of the drifting clouds. The air was so clear she could distinguish each amber fissure in its sheer face. She drew her robe around her, opened the shutters and gazed out. If she leaned forward she could see the track down which they had travelled in the dusk the night before, and she could hear again the tumbling little waterfalls the spring rains had spawned. Then she saw her brother striding along the track towards the house, his eyes fixed downwards and straight ahead, unaware of the two men who emerged from the stables and studied him. One was Fraser. The other was a younger man with an open face and smiling eyes.

The young man approached James immediately with his hand outstretched. But James only nodded brusquely and turned back to the house, his shoulders set and his body stiff. What would they think of him? wondered Christie. She might have found some sympathy for her brother's black moods, but she could not expect others to excuse his rudeness and self-absorption, especially when their own hearts must still hold so much grief. But the young man and Fraser exchanged a look not lacking in compassion, and only watched with solemn faces as James disappeared from sight.

Christie waited for her brother to come to her room, and they made their way downstairs together. The door of the study was ajar and Donald was seated at the desk, with a clear view to the staircase. He stood up immediately he saw them and motioned them inside.

"I trust you have both slept well," he began formally, feeling a flush spread over his face.

"As well as I have done for many a night," Christie answered, nudging James who said nothing.

"I must admit I slept badly," Donald confessed. "My behaviour yesterday was ungracious. I am resolved to explain it in the hope you might find some excuse. Your own highland blood may make it easier to provide one."

Christie let her eyes linger on his face, sensing the tension behind his lean features. Again she was uncomfortable in his presence. One minute he seemed kind, the next aloof and distant, and she had no desire to bring the dark scowl back to his expression. She remained silent, as did James, so Donald went on, gradually easing into his explanation.

"There is a tale – I have not heard it myself – which some believe to be some kind of prophecy, one which refers to me. It was that which caused the quarrel between Euan and myself yesterday. You may think it a trifling matter to make us so forget our good manners...." His voice faded as he watched for their reaction. Then he drew a deep breath. "You will perhaps hear talk of this from the people in the clachan. They all seem to know of it. If you do, I trust you will regard it as idle nonsense, for it has already proved itself to cause nothing but harm."

Christie looked at her brother and was disappointed to see only scorn in his expression. He turned his eyes to the view outside.

"You make too much of it," Christie assured Donald. "But since apologies are the order of the morning I believe we should make one to you." She raised her eyebrows in her brother's direction. "James?"

James scowled back at her before flashing another glance of contempt in Donald's direction.

"Indeed, Mr Stewart" he said, at last, and Christie was as shocked at the address as at the scathing tone in which it was made. "We must offer our humble apologies for throwing ourselves on your charity at this very inconvenient time. I can only hope I will soon find the means of providing for my sister. The beggar's part sits comfortably with neither of us."

"James!" Christie gasped, horrified, although she recognised his words as hopeless bravado.

For a long space Donald said nothing, but traces of several emotions passed over his features. Christie stared at him with anxious eyes as she awaited his judgement. When he finally found his voice his words surprised her.

"No," he agreed quietly. "That is no man's wish, Allomore's son, and I know that were our roles reversed I would feel as you do. Poverty and dependence must be bitter pills for anyone of your birth to swallow. But there are times when a man must look to his friends. I may be obliged to offer you my support, my charity as you call it, but my friendship can only come from the heart. It is a small gift, I know, but a sincere one."

James' expression lost none of its defiance and Christie held her breath as she looked from one to the other. James was the first to turn away. "I must be grateful for your charity for now," he said. "But that is all I will accept."

Donald's face darkened and he drew a harsh breath. It was not in his nature, Christie was sure, to tolerate such snubs. She had not expected such hostility from her brother, such bitter disregard for their father's efforts to provide for them.

"Very well," Donald answered at last. "Your way of thinking saddens me, but it would be wisest to discuss your future immediately and set you on a course that can give you the independence you seek. Have you embarked on any career?"

James threw him another look of contempt. "I have had many," he retorted. "As a child I ran errands for the garrison. I have served at table. Before my father's death I was apprenticed to a watchmaker near the Spanish Steps. My sister sewed clothes for The Pretender's court. What career can you suggest? Service in your stables?"

Donald looked away. Somehow the thought of the girl whose eyes held the sun crouched low over her needlework brought with it a stab of pain. He cast the image from his mind.

"There is the army," he suggested. "My cousin holds a commission under the Marshal De Saxe. I have no doubt he could exert some influence."

"The army of France!" James almost spat out the words. "You would have me serve that power? I would rather sweep the streets."

Donald was struggling to keep his temper under control. "It is a noble enough profession," he argued. "One that I might have considered myself had I not had cause to return to Glenshellich. And when the time comes we would be well placed."

"What time?" James' voice grew more scathing still. "When the king comes into his own? What fool's dreams you men have. Do you not know that time will never be? How many good men must become old and broken before you see the truth? He is finished, that king you have who wastes men's lives and fortunes."

This was too much to bear. Donald's eyes flared. His hand flew to his dirk.

"If I believed you knew what you said I would order you from this house!"

"*I* know?" cried James. "What do *you* know? What have you seen of the pretence, the corruption of that place? You know nothing, wrapped here in your blind loyalty...."

"That is enough, James! You have said enough!" Christie's voice was harsh as she turned to Donald. She took deep breaths to calm herself "My brother and I are not Jacobites," she said at last. "I do not know how much politics means to you, or how our sentiments will affect our position in this house, but we have seen too much and suffered too much to follow that way."

Donald was stunned into silence. They had lived in the shadow of the court. They must have seen and spoken with the king all their lives, and yet this girl could stand here and calmly denounce the creed to which she had been raised. It was incredible to him, abhorrent, that Allomore's children should so betray their father and the cause for which he had sacrificed everything. He could only search his heart for his own father's reaction, and he finally pictured his father as he should have been, standing behind the desk, facing their cool defiance with compassion in his eyes. And they were John Stewart's words he spoke next, for he could find none of his own.

"We will not mention this again. It is distressing for me to know your feelings, but I hope they will not cause discord between us."

Christie looked again her brother. His face was ashen. Donald had turned his back to them and seemed to be staring through the window. Then she heard a sound at the door and the young man she had watched earlier appeared.

"Donald," he announced. "You are keeping our guests to yourself instead of allowing me to introduce them to the clachan. That is to say, after I have been introduced to them myself."

Donald made no move. For a moment Andrew looked puzzled then sensed the need to assume control.

"I am Donald's brother," he went on, stepping forward. "Andrew Stewart. And it will be my pleasure to show you Glenshellich."

* * *

As they rounded the final curve of the track and into the clachan what had appeared to Christie so attractive from a distance was less so at close quarters. There were twenty or so cottages clustered around the edge of the lochan, some little more than huts, others larger with rough stone outbuildings tumbling behind them. They all stood low to the ground, their roofs covered with heathery divots on which grew weeds and grass. From all of them issued thin brown trails of pungent smoke.

At least two inhabitants emerged from each building and regarded the visitors with polite curiosity. James surveyed the scene with an expression bordering on disgust, but Christie's eyes widened with fascination. Then came a childish giggle and the sound of running feet. She took a pace backwards as a small boy rushed from behind one of the larger cottages and launched himself into Andrew's arms. Andrew swung him in the air and held him suspended against the sky. Behind him appeared a dark, wild haired woman. Both child and man were unaware of her and only Christie saw the dazzling smile that spread over her face.

But at last Andrew turned around. "Meg!" he cried. "So you have not gone to prepare the shielings!"

"I have waited..." the woman began hesitantly.

"Ahh," Andrew sighed. "To see our guests." He finished her sentence for her, replaced the boy's feet on the ground and stepped back. "Who now stand before you."

He moved aside and Meg came closer, drawing Christie by the strange fire flashing from her dark eyes. Then Meg turned to Andrew.

"It is well," she said briefly, in Gaelic.

Andrew let out a different sigh and took Christie's hand. "Domh-null! A lady and gentleman to see you, all the way from Rome."

"From the king?" breathed the boy.

"You see we have him well taught already," joked Andrew. "He knows that the king is in Rome and the Elector is in London – until his father and all his uncles can put that to rights." Then, seeing the alarm on Christie's face, he added, "I speak in jest. We do not judge men or women by their politics here. Is that not so, Meg?"

Meg was gazing quizzically at Andrew. She threw another look at Christie and James, who seemed to have sunk deeper into his hostile mood. Andrew turned and made a gesture to include all present.

"The son and daughter of the Laird of Allomore. They are come to share our home." He lowered his voice and almost whispered into Christie's ear. "Do not mind their stares. They only wish to welcome you."

No one moved, but the dark faces continued to gaze keenly, intense faces swept by unkempt locks of hair, men with rough beards straggling from weathered cheeks, children with dirty arms and thin legs. An old man stepped forward. His bright blue eyes stared dimly from a face the texture of leather, and he stretched out a trembling hand towards Christie. James sprang protectively to her side but the old man ignored him and let his hand linger in the air above Christie's head, somewhere, it seemed, between a blessing and a curse.

Then Catriona's voice broke the strange spell. "Angus!" she cried. "Will you scare the poor girl half out of her wits?"

Angus gave a sly grin and turned his eyes to the first slope of the mountain. He could not see Beathag, but he knew she was there, watching in satisfaction, savouring the moment. Meg's eyes took the same direction and she saw the shadow drift between the doorposts of her grandmother's hut.

But Catriona MacMichael's eyes were on Allomore's son. "Now that you are here I hope you will come to my house," she said.

"We would love to," Christie answered.

"Speak for yourself," James muttered as they followed her. "I have seen more than enough of this God-forsaken place."

"You are growing tedious."

"They are savages, these people," he hissed. "I have condemned our father often enough, God knows, but never more than for despatching us here."

Christie turned away from him. Behind her she saw Meg and Andrew, heads bent close, and following them, careful to keep a respectful distance, came the boy. Christie stopped and so did he, gazing with shy uncertain eyes. She smiled and called out to him. He approached her timidly as James made another impatient noise and continued on his way.

"What is your name?" she asked him in Gaelic.

"Domhnull MacCombie."

"And how old are you, Domhnull MacCombie?" Christie asked him.

"Soon I will be seven years."

"And what do you do with yourself all day?"

He screwed up his face. "Many things," he replied. "I go to my lessons with Catriona. I help my father with the cattle and now I am learning some of his tunes. One day I will play the pipes for MacSomhairle."

"Domhnull talks too much," interrupted his mother with a smile. "And dreams too much."

"How can he dream too much?" Christie asked. "What would our lives be without dreams?"

"What indeed?" agreed Andrew drawing alongside them. "And I am proof that if we hold to our dreams for long enough they can come true."

Domhnull gazed up into his face and Andrew took his hand.

"Andrew is to become a doctor of medicine," explained Meg. "He is already a healer and a seer."

"Not a healer," Andrew corrected her. "I have seen a healer at work and my gifts do not come close. I am an apprentice, and will be a practitioner at best. I will become proficient with training. Though I was not trained when I brought this young man into the world," he added, letting Domhnull slip from his arm and follow after James, who had wandered away from them and was idly throwing pebbles into the water. Domhnull stood a little distant from him and began to do the same. Meg gave a peal of laughter. Christie looked uneasy, but Andrew grinned.

"Watch," he said.

Domhnull edged closer to James and picked up a handful stones. No word passed between them, but it was soon clear that a contest was developing and that although James was already a man Domhnull looked the likely winner. As well as possessing a lithe strength, a natural grace of movement and an instinctive skill, he knew exactly how to flex his body and arm to achieve the maximum effect. James watched and was unable to keep the admiration from his expression. He studied Domhnull's technique and began to copy it. Domhnull slowed his movements to make the demonstration clearer and James began to grasp the idea. His movements soon mirrored the boy's. Domhnull's pebble soared high in the air and landed in sparkling circles almost at the centre of the lochan. James threw another, finally able to use his extra height and strength to full effect. His stone landed feet beyond the ripples continuing to spread from Domhnull's.

Meg clapped her hands and laughed again. Christie looked at her in surprise but then caught sight of the expression on James' face. He had turned to the boy and he was smiling. Not a grudging smile, nor a smile of victory, but an expression of genuine pleasure. Christie could not remember when she had last seen her brother smile like that. Above them a light mist swirled from the peak of the Giant's Mountain and over the scattered streams dancing down its rocks. From higher yet drifted the lonely cry of a distant bird. Christie was suddenly filled with a sense of wonder that was almost painful. It was as if she had stood here always, as if she belonged here as much as the boulders scattered over the higher passes, as if she had never known a different life and would never need to know another.

* * *

As the days and weeks passed Christie grew familiar with the scents of the bracken and the ferns, the sweetness of the heather on the hill. She grew to know by name each herdsman tending his cattle, each woman gossiping in the clachan, and to recognise the smiles of the children who flocked to Catriona's cottage for their daily lessons. And in return the people of the glen took her to their hearts, drawn by her beauty and the warmth of her spirit. They smiled when they saw her, though smiles did not come readily to their faces, and amongst themselves they knew her as the golden one, the one they had whispered of and expected for so long.

Glenshellich was setting free in her all that had been shackled by the poverty of exile. Christie had lived with the emptiness of others for so long: struggling to ease her father's black depressions, fighting to combat her brother's fits of blind despair. Her role had made her old before her time. Now, under the Giant's Mountain, she felt her youth flooding back. Sometimes she lay gazing up at the fantastic patterns the loose rocks and boulders made, pointing their obscure pathways to the ragged summit, imagining that the giants of old were still there, looking down on their land. She would row out into the lochan with the fishermen and help them with their catch, or wander on cattle tracks over the foothills, listening to the cries of the birds through the silence. And she felt herself at one with the timelessness of the land.

Once, when the damp air pressed down on the loch and a thick mist hid the mountain, she climbed the lower foothills until she completely lost her way. Suddenly, and without warning, she came upon a figure that might have sprung from the very earth. Her heart racing, she looked helplessly around for a means of escape, but as the spectre loomed closer she saw it was nothing more sinister than an old woman, covered from head to foot in a soiled and tattered plaid. The exposed strip of face was criss-crossed with deep wrinkles and one bright eye darted into the swirling mist. But as the eye drilled her Christie's relief was replaced by a sense of unease. The old woman muttered something and gave a soft chuckle. But just as suddenly she turned, startled herself, as another figure appeared from the blanket of fog. Christie saw with some relief that it was Donald. The old woman's eye glinted briefly before she turned and shrank away into the bracken, as rapidly as she had appeared. Christie stared after her while Donald strode closer, his face full of concern.

"I hope Beathag did not alarm you." Seeing that his hope was in vain he continued with a smile, "she is not as harmful as she would have everyone believe."

Christie tried to force a smile in return, but she was still shaking. He took her arm and led her to a large boulder, which she leaned against, feeling her legs absurdly weak.

"Beathag is her own worst enemy," he continued, studying Christie anxiously and deciding it would be best to keep talking. "My father felt some affection for her, perhaps because she is so absurd, a weird relic from days of old." Seeing that Christie was still trembling he decided to make the old witch into a story. "My father never blamed her when crops failed or cattle fell sick," he went on, "though many in the clachan did, and still do. She likes to think she keeps her evil eye on Glenshellich, but the mischief she does is human and comes only from her own nature. Her hut is inside the mist, just above the Watcher's Stone, where she weaves all her spells and prophecies of doom." He paused. Christie's breath was still uneven. He watched as her breast rose and fell, her lips parted, half in anxiety, half in interest. He wanted to put her mind at ease, but even more he wanted to hold her attention, to stay so close to her that he could define each bead of mist shimmering in her hair and breathe in all the sweetness that seemed to come from it. He felt his own breath grow less steady as he continued. "And in truth she has had a sad life. Even her grand-daughter does not visit her these days." He smiled suddenly. "Domhnull is her great-grandson. Sometime he sits at her fire and she tells him the old tales of the glen. He has no fear of devils, that boy." It was impossible for him to keep the pride from his voice. "And if Beathag feels affection for anyone in this world it is for him."

Christie was still gazing at him and he pulled away, needing to break the spell, for he knew it was cast on them both. He drew another breath and changed the subject.

"I hope it is wise for you to wander here so freely. There are many dangers we tend to forget. Sometimes rocks slip from the high reaches, and the falls can be treacherous in spate. Even on these small slopes you could stumble and injure yourself."

"Thank you for your concern," she smiled, "But now that you have explained the story of Beathag," she added, "I do not expect to be so alarmed again."

He wondered if she was laughing at him but was surprised to find how little he cared. As long as he could look at her and talk to her, he was happy.

"I was watching out for hare before the mist came down," he went on. "I think I might return by way of the clachan. Will you join me?"

They fell into step together. Donald paused often to guide her over a rough patch of ground, and she did not draw back from his strong arm beneath her elbow.

"I am sorry," he cried suddenly, as she stumbled and he caught her. "I have warned you of the risks and is I who am going too fast."

"You travel at a hunter's pace," she remarked.

"Yes," he agreed. "We have hunted this hill all our lives, Euan, Andrew and myself. We are familiar with every rock, every clump of heather."

"And you are glad to be home from all your travelling."

He did not reply, and it seemed that he had become distant again. She hoped she had not overstepped a line, but still she said, "Catriona has told me that no matter where you went you would always long for Glenshellich."

He pulled his attention back to her and smiled. "By choice I would never have left Glenshellich," he admitted. "But perhaps my father was wise to insist I should have experience of a wider world. The son of a chieftain must learn its ways...." He paused. He had almost mentioned her father's cousin and was glad he had stopped himself. "But I am more than content now to be home. I can pursue my father's dreams, to keep our people healthy and safe, to try to bring them some knowledge of what lies beyond their glen. We may be primitive in some ways, but we have a wealth here I have encountered nowhere else. For my part it is a wealth I have sworn to guard and preserve." He flushed suddenly. "Though perhaps to you and your brother that might appear simply foolish, at best sentimental."

"It appears to me neither of those things," she answered softly. Though she knew she could not say the same for her brother. To James Glenshellich remained a bleak and dismal place, a remote wildness too miserably evocative of his father's misfortunes, a place from which the only course of action was to escape.

* * *

He might have been heartened by a conversation in the capital, where Gavin MacVey was enjoying a tumbler of claret within the mahogany walls of Kilclath's elegant inner sanctum. Gavin took an appreciative sip and cast his eyes approvingly around the art on display, remembering the sparser days when the old master held court, days when the currency of respectability had been the shady deal, the careless betrayal, the signing away of lives. Some hinted there might be more of the Old Fox in his son than met the general eye, but Gavin had yet to see evidence of it.

"I realise that the young MacSomhairle would not at all approve of this conversation," Gavin admitted, before adding quickly, "though he would be wise to recognise the advantage of it."

Kilclath's eyes were distant. "How old did you say the boy was?" he asked quietly.

"Eighteen." Gavin paused. Although he knew what Donald's reaction would be to the pronouncement he was about to make he had had more than a passing acquaintance with The Plotter. He did not think he would be satisfied with his epitaph, or too unwilling for those with more flexible allegiances to promote his son's interests. Gavin drew a slow breath and assumed a deliberately knowing expression before adding, "He is apparently not of his father's persuasion."

Kilclath's only visible response was a slight inclination of the head. Then his dark eyebrows crept together into a reflective frown. "So I have heard," he mused. "And how would you expect that information to be received by his father's," he paused only slightly before finding the word, "successor?"

Gavin smiled slyly. "I imagine you might be better placed to know what goes on in that gentleman's head."

Kilclath gave a snort. "It would be difficult to determine much of what goes on his head, beyond his own depravity," he retorted, then added darkly, "which grows more disturbing by the day."

"Making the prospect of a natural successor increasingly unlikely...." Gavin dared to venture. He was beginning to enjoy this collaboration. It was gratifying to be consulted by someone of such indisputable influence. The two men of law held each other's eyes.

"His wife does not enjoy good health," went on Kilclath, "thanks in no small measure to his own activities." He paused again and leaned back in his chair. He appeared to be giving the matter serious thought. "I suppose I might offer the boy a position," he suggested.

"Donald would not hear of it."

"He would not hear of the boy's advancement?"

"He would not object to the boy's advancement, only by that particular route."

Kilclath nodded again but Gavin saw a flicker at the corner of his mouth.

"Donald has a long memory and an unforgiving nature," he went on, then a sudden idea made him add, "Of course he may not object to a placement within my chambers."

The notion had clearly not occurred to Kilclath. "Then suggest that to him," he answered quickly. Too quickly, perhaps, thought Gavin, eying him shrewdly.

"There may be some who would consider your own connection to be of relevance," he murmured, surprised once more at his own temerity. But Kilclath showed no inclination to rise to the bait. Gavin was aware that the Master was already a powerful force in Allomore. Perhaps that was the extent of his personal ambition. Certainly he showed no urgency in providing an heir for his own estates. Not that Gavin blamed him for any reluctance to alter his domestic arrangements. He himself still made his regular visits to Bella Galbraith's fourth storey, and the prospect of having a personal provider under his own roof, especially one with the indisputable charms of Jean Petrie, was a delicious one. He heaved a reflective sigh before casting his thoughts back to the more immediate subject of the Hamiltons.

"Perhaps Allomore could be persuaded to make some small allowance..."

"I think not." Kilclath's answer was abrupt. "He will not welcome this situation at all. Best let your plan take shape in Glenshellich for now. There must already be pressure enough on MacSomhairle's limited resources."

Gavin shuffled in his seat. "And the prospect of more to come." he added.

Kilclath rose to his feet. "There are always rumours," he observed. "But Allomore's son is certainly wise not to pin his faith on any forlorn hopes surrounding the exiled House of Stuart."

* * *

"I hear Lochiel has ordered enough tartan cloth to fit out an army," the Countess of Dalvey announced. She took a small sip from her teacup and looked meaningfully at Alison Bothwell.

"His patriotism was aye beyond question," Alison replied.

"I was referring less to his patriotism than his timing. What has your nephew to say on the subject?"

The clang of a dropped tray startled them both.

"Kirsty!" Alison reproached. "Can you not be more careful?" But her tone was tolerant. Kirsty backed from the room apologetically and the Countess regarded her with raised eyebrows.

"She is in love," Alison explained. "I can scarce believe the change in her. Her every task is designed to impress…"

"Not yourself, surely, after all this time?"

"She'll need to impress me to cut any ice with my nephew."

"Ahh!" breathed the Countess. "I hear he is a very personable young man. And more diligent in his studies than was his brother."

"There's certainly no doubting that."

"Though he's been spared the influence of any distraction."

"Mr Fettes has returned to Perthshire."

"With more than he arrived with, if rumour is to be believed."

The Countess was determinedly tapping a vital source, but Alison sensed the need to be discreet. "I couldn't say," she murmured. "Although I know his health has not been what it was."

Mischief gleamed from the Countess's eye. She clapped her hands and chuckled. "So enough of Mr Fettes. What are you saying to the news of Henry?"

She had caught Alison off guard. "Henry?" she echoed.

"So you've not heard of your old suitor's good fortune?"

Alison remained at a loss.

"Henry Matheson." The Countess enunciated the name slowly. "Soon to become Mr Justice Matheson."

"Oh, Henry Matheson!" Alison exclaimed. "Hardly a suitor," she added, although perhaps, thinking back, he might have been. She had been called to her sister's side in Glenshellich early in her acquaintance with Henry, an experience that had taken away all notion of matrimony. Henry had departed southwards to join a law firm in London. He had been good humoured and conscientious, Alison remembered, and no doubt deserved his belated success.

"Politics not withstanding – or perhaps true politics withheld," continued the countess slyly. "I believe he was enquiring after you."

"I'm flattered he minds me after all this time."

"Once met never forgotten, Alison. They say he's planning a visit north to see his sister. Perhaps you should expect a call."

* * *

"Mhairi!"

The voice came from the doorway opposite, a hoarse croak, feeble but urgent. Kilclath's servant woman turned, wondering if it had been her imagination. She so seldom ventured abroad that few in the city could know her name. She glanced towards the shadowed wynd that twisted from the main thoroughfare and thought she saw a tiny movement.

"Mhairi!"

"Who's there?" She did not know why, but she asked the question in English.

Very slowly a hunched figure emerged onto the pavement. Mhairi's heart began to beat a little more quickly.

"D'ye no' ken me?"

At first Mhairi did not. The old woman before her was scarce more than a ruckle of bones gathered into a tattered and filthy plaid. It was impossible to tell her age, or even her height, so bent was her back. Then she raised her face, pallid beneath its rash of angry sores, and Mhairi looked into eyes that had not changed at all. She gasped and drew back.

"Hannah?"

"It's a while since Inverness, Mhairi," the old woman continued, "when fortune went your way."

Mhairi's face drained of its own colour. The old woman made an impatient gesture.

"Dinna worry. It's Jean I'm here about."

"Jean?"

"Aye, my wee bonnie bairn I nursed for so long, a' that time when her mammie lost the will. Tell her I've come to say goodbye. She'll find me if she wants to in Branwell Wynd." She paused and her eye gleamed sharply as she added, "Will you mind that, Mhairi?" It was more of a threat than an appeal. With another sudden gleam from her eye Hannah turned and scuttled away, not up the Canongate but into the warren of dark closes that would eventually take her to the address she had mentioned. It was not an address that Mhairi was familiar with, but she would remember it.

She stepped back towards the entrance to the Master's chambers. At that moment Jean was not the person she most needed to find.

* * *

Donald and Christie had fallen into a habit of spending the first and last hours of each day poring over Glenshellich's old volumes and genealogies. To begin with they had searched for any mention of the lands and the men from Allomore, but Christie soon came to learn as much about the tales and legends of Glenshellich. And the more she discovered about Donald and his dreams the more she came to puzzle over what lay at the heart of a man who could love and hate with such intensity, could so readily be moved to laughter yet be so quick to take offence.

She spent long hours too with Catriona and grew especially close to Fraser. She loved to talk with him of the past and hear his old stories of Edinburgh and its port, the ships and their cargoes. But they always seemed to return to the subject closest to both their hearts.

"It seems to me – and it did from the first -" he told her as they sat one evening in the fading sunlight outside the stables, "that there's something in this land reaches out and draws a body to it, never to let go."

"That is because you have a romantic soul, Fraser," she laughed. "Although not everyone would detect it." Then, becoming serious, she added in scarcely a whisper, "I feel it too."

He looked away. Of course she felt it. She belonged here, perhaps more than any of them.

"Yet you've never set eyes on your own land," he murmured.

144

Her face tightened and her eyes grew distant. "I have no wish to set eyes on it. Allomore is not my land. It was no longer my father's. It will never be my brother's. We are as dispossessed as the Pretender."

Fraser frowned, remembering her father and his deep empty eyes. "What destiny could have been greater than the one he threw away?" he asked. "Yet they all sought it. They seek it still."

Christie clasped her knees in her hands and leaned back against the rough stable wall. She could see dark clouds rolling in from the east, an unusual direction for the weather's approach. "That foreign court," she sighed. "The flatterers, the spies, the painted women, the uncrowned king. What could be further removed from these mountains and their people?"

"To you and me, nothing. But there's those too willing to let dogma blind them."

"And what," she went on, still intent on her own thoughts, "what if that web should spin out again? It is woven with so many dangerous strands of intrigue. The fear of it makes my heart grow cold."

Fraser did not reply. Whether he agreed or not, they would make no difference. They could only hope and perhaps pray that the world had learned and moved on. He heard the gate swing behind them and over his shoulder saw Donald, followed by the boy they liked to pretend was the piper's son.

"You see," Christie went on, unaware of their approach. "They are brought up to grandeur and glory because it is all around them from the day they are born. They draw their stature from their lands but equate it with a past that has betrayed them again and again. And some, like my father, are so blind that they cannot see the truth." She paused. "And some are so stubborn that they will not."

Blind or stubborn, thought Fraser to himself, it would all end the same. Unless. He let his eyes linger on the boy, so like the man he knew only as his chieftain. The boy left Donald's side and ran to Christie.

Unless . . . . .

Back in the clachan Catriona MacMichael spread Euan's plaid over the cottage wall to dry. As her fingers smoothed the damp wool she thought she heard the distant chime of jangling metal. She stood for a moment, listening intently, before her face broke into a wide smile and she turned to hurry down the path in the direction the sound was coming from.

"Hallo, there! Hallo!"

The clanking grew louder and out of the clear evening sunshine a remarkable sight came into view. In reality it was nothing more than a man and a horse and cart, but Andra' MacAslan had left many miles and many settlements behind him and was not known for travelling light. The weight of the pack on his back would have defeated most men, but Andra' had honed every muscle of his wiry frame, not to mention that of his garron, a native of this very glen, and utilised every last inch of space on his cart.

"Ribbons and lace from the finest milliner between here and Aberdeen," he announced as he drew up before Catriona's cottage. His cart's contents shuddered to a standstill in their appointed order. The last to be still were the copper pans, which kept up a soft ringing that echoed gently across the water.

"A devout gentlewoman from Nairn," he added, looking furtively all around him as if the information was about to be seized upon and used against him. "Who minded my special order, though she's more than enough to keep her fingers active night and day."

"Hats are in fashion, then?" Catriona challenged dryly, for Andra was as welcome for his gossip as for his merchandise.

"No' so much the hats side o' things." Andra's eyes grew sly again and he tapped the side of his nose for added effect. "No' so much the hats."

"So what side of things?" Catriona obliged.

"Ribbons. White ribbons," he repeated, stressing each word. "White as rose petals." He nodded slowly and significantly. "If you'll understand my meaning."

Catriona did not immediately.

146

"All the way from ahint Banff there's been rumblings and grumblings," Andra explained. "And folk o' the opinion it'll no' be long before a certain person might be looking for a frigate back to Hanover."

"Ohh!" Catriona let out a slow gasp of understanding. "To Hanover? Do you think so, Andra'? After all this time?"

"It's no' so much me that thinks so. But those with an eye to the future can set about preparing for it."

Catriona smiled. "Like your milliner from Nairn."

"A lady of shrewd business sense."

"But you obtained your ribbons."

"A man in my line must keep his customers happy or lose his livelihood."

"And who in Glenshellich might be ordering ribbons and lace?"

But even as she asked her question she saw Kenneth hurrying towards them from the shore. Andra stepped back and waited. Catriona's eyes softened.

"I'm happy to say there's a market everywhere for romance," he said.

"We can all be happy for that."

"Though I'd a lean passage through Kilclath." He paused. "Yet again."

"The House of the Eagle still lies empty?"

"While the Master's away there's no heart in it – no heart at all," he observed. "And no coin for fripperies."

"No market for romance?"

"I hear tell the Master'll no' be back till he brings a bride. Which could be long enough since another thing I hear's he likes best the company of whores." He paused and gave Catriona a sly wink. "Like the Old Fox before him."

Catriona's eyes had been turned eastwards towards the distant twin peaks of Kilclath, but she transferred their gaze to Kenneth who was almost upon them.

"Then I am sorry for it," she said softly.

"No more than I," Andra winked back. "For there's a wheen o' travelling for no gain and still the garrons to feed and water. If it wasna for the thought of a blether with yourself and a good bit trade up at the house…."

* * *

The younger son of Dalgleish the tailor pushed his way down Alison Bothwell's tenement stair and out into the bustling Lawnmarket. He slipped silently through the mid morning crowd and into the unsavoury wynds of the Cowgate, his fingers tightening instinctively on the guinea in his pocket. It would have another one for company if he completed his mission. He took out a handkerchief and held it to his nose as he stepped over a whimpering beggar gazing up at him through the holes he had for eyes.

"No change," he muttered as he hurried on. Young Davie Dalgleish had no intention of letting his life ever slide into such dismal straits, but neither had he designs on following his father's trade. Davie had lain awake through many nights planning his future and his schemes were already bearing fruit. He was to become a caddie, one of the growing band of informal authorities on the city's thoroughfares and those who walked them: or crawled through them, he thought to himself, as in the case of the object of his present assignment.

"Hannah Bain!" he hissed into the ear of a pockmarked pimp lurching against the crumbling wall of Branwell Wynd. There was no name to indicate the locality, but Davie had spent most of his fifteen years watching and listening. The streets of Edinburgh were laid out like a gazetteer in his head.

"Who's asking?"

"Just mysel' for now," Davie intimated, stepping closer, but not close enough to suffer the full impact of the man's foul breath.

The man sniffed and shrugged and spat at Davie's feet.

"Try the cellars," he coughed. "If it's vermin you're after."

Davie swallowed. He would have preferred to have been pointed in a different direction. There could be no worse den in the whole city, and the cellars the worst reaches of it. But two guineas was not a sum to be spurned. He stepped over a heap of bodies he hoped were just sleeping and over the broken-down threshold that led from the street. Crumbling steps spewed only feet from the doorway and descended darker than night. Davie had brought neither torch nor candle. The thought struck him that those who dwelt in this basement would have little need of daylight. Darkness would have been a blessing. He heard faint sounds of coughing and retching from below, and what could have been the whimper of a child.

"Hannah Bain?" he called, hearing the trepidation in his voice as it faltered around the name: too low for any to hear. "Hannah Bain!" he repeated with feigned courage, reminding himself that he was young and healthy and had a sharp knife in his belt.

"Who wants her?" came a croaking reply.

"A friend," he stuttered.

The only response was a chilling cackle.

"Hannah. Here's a friend come for you. Must have come for your bones."

Davie crept closer. The smell made him feel like vomiting himself. There were folk here, how many he could not say. It was putting him in mind of an etching he had once seen of the furthest reaches of Hell. A claw-like hand reached out and grabbed his wrist.

"I've no friends, son, no friends left," a feeble voice whispered.

"Aye you have," replied Davie as cheerfully as he could. There was nothing to be gained from letting them sniff his fear. "And they'll be for you before this night's out, now I've found you. Mark my words, Mistress Bain. Your friends will be."

Then Davie turned and scampered up the steps and past the drunk on the corner, past the beggar and out into the High Street. He turned his face from the castle rock and elbowed his way through the jostling passers by, ducking and dodging and gasping for his breath. He did not stop until he reached the Canongate and raised a trembling hand to rap on Kilclath's apartment door.

* * *

Christie pressed herself against the side of the Giant's Mountain. Mortified at the extent of her exhaustion and terror, she grappled for a hold beyond the overhanging lip. She knew she had only herself to blame. She had been the one to insist she would be able to reach the giant's cave. Donald had done nothing but take her at her word. She pushed harder into the rock, tears of frustration and panic starting from her eyes, but the mountain's solid indifference defeated her. Donald had explained exactly how to overcome this final hurdle. She knew it took a simple swing of knee and hip, an action that, once mastered, became as effortless as breathing. But although it might have been second nature to him it was too big a step for her. He leaned over her, repeating his instruction, encouraging, but showing not the slightest inclination to stretch out a hand to hoist her up beside him. But of course it was a matter of honour. Only by ascending to it alone did a person earn the right of entry to Feodag's cave. The sharp rocks scraped her knees and grazed her palms. She pressed her chest into the cliff wall and tried to grip the bulge in the rock face with her thighs. Resentment of him swelled inside her and escaped in frantic gasps. She could not bear to look down, yet looking up was more terrifying still. Then, as if by magic, her feet found the tiny hold he had described and she understood exactly what his instruction had meant. She could swing herself from this position, springing with her feet and pressing with her shoulders and for a split second letting go her grip until she could grasp the next hold. She knew and felt exactly what she had to do. She only had to find the courage to do it. She gasped again with effort and concentration, closed her eyes, and swung.

When she dared to open them she found herself sprawled on the ledge beside him. It was at least two yards wide, growing wider still as it became a line of tumbled boulders. Her breath was ragged and her hands were throbbing. A red weal disappeared from her exposed shoulder into the line of her bodice. Her whole body shuddered with a mixture of exhaustion, relief and exhilaration. She looked down the dizzying drop to the clachan below, then her eyes spun back to gaze into Donald's face, disturbingly close to her own, so close that she could feel the warmth of his breath on her cheek. His gaze was fixed on her shoulder. He took his finger and ran it gently down the edge of the scratch. A different kind of trembling seized her as he drew back, stood up and held out his hand. She did not take it, but followed him around the rocks that guarded the mouth of the cave. It was there that he pulled her close. Her arms reached around his neck and the trembling grew stronger still as her body melted into his. His hands passed firmly and gently over her breasts and between her legs. She heard herself moan as below them the whole glen turned and spun. Their lips and bodies fused and she let her legs yield and part. There was nothing she could do to stop what was about to happen. He gazed into her face and she closed her eyes, waiting to feel his lips again on hers. But instead she felt his body grow tense.

"Don't," she whispered. "Don't stop."

But she could tell he was fighting to control the passion she had already abandoned herself to. When she opened her eyes she saw the anguish on his face before he turned it from her, wrenching his body behind it. Only then was she aware of their separate gasping breaths. At last his hand reached out and gently touched her cheek. She forced her head away. She could not look at him. She had acted shamelessly and he had been the one with the power to resist. He turned from her and she felt a sob rise in her throat. Then he stepped back, reached behind him and clumsily, blindly, grabbed for her hand.

"I am sorry, Christie." His voice was a hoarse whisper.

She had no words to answer him. Her body had said everything. He kept his face turned from her but he still gripped her hand. She knew he would neither let go nor look around until she had recovered at least a trace of her composure.

She could not imagine when that would be.

151

* * *

Out on the lochan Meg MacCombie dangled one hand over the edge of the boat and dragged it along the surface of the waves. Her other hand played lightly with the ribbon in her hair and she stared dreamily into the face of her husband. Although he appeared unmoved, she smiled, knowing her smile would warm him into a response. Exercising her power to make the piper happy was the greatest pleasure of her life.

"MacSomhairle has gone to the giant's cave," she said mischievously. "He has not gone alone."

Kenneth turned his slow brown eyes towards her. She smiled again and he found it impossible to look away. "And what would that be to you?" he asked at last.

"It is like living in an old story. A story we are part of."

Kenneth had never become completely comfortable with the more fanciful workings of his wife's mind.

"Everyone is part of their own story," he said patiently. "And all stories are important, the old and the new."

"You are always so sensible," she murmured, then paused and looked up again at the place under the summit where the cave lay. She remembered only too well the urgency of Donald's passion.

"Have you climbed to the giant's cave?" she asked.

He screwed his eyes against the sun. "Once or twice. Not since I was a boy."

Meg sighed, but not sadly. "I will never go there. I have seen twenty five summers and I have not even explored my own glen."

"None of us have done that. There would not be days enough in even my grandfather's life."

"And in twenty five summers I have never left Glenshellich."

"Is that such a bad thing?"

Her eyes grew dreamy again. "I hope that Domhnull will see more of his world."

Kenneth studied her seriously. Her body may never have left the glen but he knew that her mind and spirit had travelled further than anyone in the clachan. Not that it was his place to make reference to her gift. From him she needed only the security of his devotion. He gave a slow and reassuring smile. "You are still young. I am not so very old. Who is to say we will not see more of the world together?"

He watched her expression drift again. As usual her answer was something entirely unexpected.

"I dreamed my mother was in America."

"America!"

"I would like to believe it." She gave a half embarrassed smile. "Or is that just foolishness?"

Kenneth was afraid that it was. He had no reason to believe that Meg's mother would still be anywhere at all in the world. His expression softened. He had heard nothing but ill of the woman who had given birth to his wife, yet without her his own life would be unthinkable. "You have never mentioned your mother to me," he said softly, "before today."

"That does not mean I never think of her. If you can think of someone you have no picture of." She smiled suddenly. "But then, I can make her anyone at all. I can weave a hundred stories around her. I will never be angry with her, or disappointed, or ashamed."

"And neither will I," Kenneth answered stoutly. "I will only be thankful for her, and hope that wherever she is she is as content as she has made me."

Meg took her hand from the water and flicked her fingers playfully at his face. The droplets sparkled like tiny diamonds across the sky between them.

"I love you, Kenneth MacCombie," she said.

"I know," the piper answered.

"Each time I look at you now I will feel only shame."

But Christie did not look at him, even as she whispered the words.

"It is I who must bear the shame," Donald muttered darkly as he searched for words to comfort her, knowing that what lay behind any words could only condemn him in her eyes forever. "For you must understand I am one of those too weak to resist his passion." He was sick to hear himself. But if he had come to his senses too late it was not too late to restore Christie's honour. "I have lived a life of dissipation," he went on, feeling his soul shrivel with each word. Soon it would disappear altogether, and he would be a chieftain none could honour, worse even than the lowest beggar. "And now..." He heard his voice tremble. "I find myself here, in the most special place in the world to me, with ......but we will not speak of this again. Only know that my punishment is your power."

* * *

Bella Galbraith opened the back door of her apartments and pulled the frayed grey shawl around her shoulders. She was confident in her disguise, but the stare of the caddie, or possibly her own conscience, unnerved her. She stepped delicately over the gutter and nodded towards him. Clutching his inch of candle he led her through the back wynds to the closes behind the Cowgate. She followed him, but she knew the way well. It was a way she had devoted her life to avoiding.

Davie's heart thumped against his ribs. He had no wish to repeat his earlier visit but he had been given no choice, since the second guinea had been conditional after all. He led Bella to the broken doorway and nodded towards the stair. She hesitated and he studied her shrewdly in the flickering light. Without the paint on her face she was nothing special. Underneath her disguise she was just like them all, except a little older now than most. Since embarking on his career Davie's observations of his fellow citizens had grown more astute. It occurred to him that this might be another event worth storing in his capacious memory.

Bella raised her handkerchief to her face and took Davie's arm as together they crept down the crumbling stair. Davie clutched the damp wall but it offered treacherous support. Below them the basement was silent, the atmosphere eerily still. He hoped they had not arrived too late.

"Hannah!"

There was no reply.

"Hannah!"

Then they heard her voice, less than a whisper.

"Bella!"

"Aye, Hannah. Here no' before time if what I hear's true."

"Is Jean . . .?"

"Jean's fine, Hannah, just fine. She doesna' ken. We've come to take you back. Jean'll see you in the eyrie."

Davie heard the old crone let out a cracked sigh, but whether it was of relief or despair he could not tell. He hunkered down beside her and felt his stomach churn as the stench rose in his nostrils.

"The caddy'll help you, Hannah. Let him lift you."

Davie tried not to retch as the skeletal arms groped around his neck. The smell grew fouler still as Hannah turned her face into his chest. He knew she would be able to feel his heart pumping like a piston.

"I wasna' told this," he muttered to Bella.

"Feart you'll catch it, son?" she sneered.

Davie was not fooled. Afraid as he might be, he was not as afraid as her. Bella's desperation to be gone from the basement was palpable. She took the candle and held it high, until its wavering trickle of light led them back into the dingy passageways of Branwell Wynd.

Hannah might have been a filthy bundle of rags for all the substance there was to her, yet Davie had the sense that her spirit was a weightier matter. "Who's Jean?" he asked Bella, as he tried to keep up with her hobbling haste.

"A mutual friend," she spat back over her shoulder.

"No' Kilclath's whore then?"

Bella turned on him with spiteful eyes. "There's risks in poking snouts in troughs."

"My snout's been in filth enough for the time being, thank you very much," Davie retorted, at the same time deciding it might be wise to keep it clear of Bella at least in the immediate future. It was easy seen how she had put the fear of God in so many. She led him past The Ensign and through the back entrance of her property. This time their steps went up instead of down. Davie had never before set foot inside Bella Galbraith's, though he had reason to believe his father was fairly familiar with the premises. He could hear the muffled sounds of a variety of copulations coming from behind hidden doors on either side of the seemingly never-ending stair. Halfway up, one of them flew open and a girl emerged.

"Bella?" she gasped.

The girl was bold and bright, dazzlingly full of life, the opposite extreme of the wretch he held in his arms. Davie gaped at her full breasts and bright eyes and tried not to think about her prospects.

"Another one for the eyrie, Beth," Bella announced grimly. "I've set the pallet ready. If you're no' too busy you could fetch her up a cup of broth. She's maybe past the state for it, but we can aye try."

The girl leaned closer, pulled back the shawl and gave a little gasp. Davie had the brief warm sensation of her breath on his cheek. But his arms were aching. He was anxious to be free of his burden.

"Aye, it's her." Bella muttered. "Hannah Bain."

"Then Jean . . ?"

The unfinished question hung on the air.

"Dinna worry. Jean'll see her." Bella paused and gave Davie a threatening grin. "But only when her tongue's beyond doing anyone any harm"

* * *

Alison Bothwell had never experienced a week like it. First there had been Henry the magistrate, fresh and bursting with his promotion in the London courts, appearing on her doorstep and squiring her to destinations never before dreamed of: then there had been the arrival of Hugh Fettes, apparently free of his syphilis and ready for a fortnight's revelry of the traditional kind. Alison was not displeased to discover that her younger nephew was less inclined towards Hugh's pursuits than his brother, despite having been persuaded to accompany him on several of his more traditional jaunts.

But the undoubted highlight of Henry's visit was dinner at the MacVey's, where Alison found herself seated beside no lesser personage than The Master of the Stones. She realised immediately that her casement window had framed a very inadequate image of the man. Alison did not believe she had laid eyes on a handsomer face or figure, and she cast a sly eye across the table at her old sparring partner, Henrietta Menteith.

"I'm surprised Margaret isna with you tonight, Henrietta," she remarked slyly.

"She had a previous engagement," Henrietta simpered, and could not prevent her own glance fluttering towards Kilclath.

Alison could hardly keep the smirk from her face. "A most attractive girl," she added, with blatant insincerity. "Would you no' agree, Kilclath?"

It was the first time she had dared address him directly, but she noticed the corners of his mouth twitch as he turned to her. "I would indeed, Mistress Bothwell."

Gavin MacVey, seated beside Henrietta, saw his opportunity. "And how is your nephew finding life in our city?" he asked.

"Very agreeable I believe, Mr MacVey," Alison replied. "He occupies himself greatly with his studies."

"I daresay," Gavin agreed. "And how do they fare in Glenshellich?"

Alison felt the slightest stiffening in the arm that rested against her shoulder, but put it down to the Master raising his fork to his lips.

"They fare well, by all accounts."

"The young Hamiltons . . . ? Have any plans been made . . . ?"

"None that I know of."

"I was considering offering the boy a position," Gavin went on. "Perhaps you would have some idea whether such a gesture would be appreciated."

Alison was aware that Kilclath's attention was now entirely on their conversation.

"Well, I believe it might," she replied. "Though resources might prove a difficulty."

"As you know I, too, was once close to their father," Gavin continued. "I could offer the boy a fair salary."

"Then perhaps you should do so."

"As for accommodation . . . " Gavin murmured, well aware that Alison had never been averse to the company of young gentlemen.

"I daresay I could take care of that."

Henrietta cleared her throat and fixed Henry Matheson with a pointed look, but Henry was too far down his second bottle of claret to notice. Gavin observed Kilclath hide another small smile.

"Then perhaps we could present the possibility to the young Mac-Somhairle," he suggested.

"Perhaps we could," she agreed.

* * *

Christie stared at her reflection in the glass. The shame of her encounter with Donald was fading, though the memory of their passion was not. She slowly placed around her neck her one precious piece of jewellery, the diamond collar that had been her father's wedding gift to her mother, and raised a hand to her hair to push a strand from her cheek. The girl gazing back gave a little provocative smile.

"Christie!"

The hoarse whisper of her name from the shadows startled her. "James!" she exclaimed, horrified at the sight of him. Straw, dust and the pungent smell of the stables clung to his clothes. "Have you forgotten there are guests tonight?"

He edged along the wall until he could lean against the doorframe of her room.

"I will not be dining with you."

She turned to stare at him in dismay.

"Will you not, indeed?"

The question had not come from Christie. It was spoken in a sharper voice from the top of the stair, a voice that cut powerfully through the shadows as Catriona MacMichael emerged from them into the lamp's dim light.

James swung himself around to confront her. "What business are my decisions of yours?"

Catriona took two steps forward. Her face was hidden and for a moment Christie felt almost afraid.

"I have stood aside long enough while James Hamilton's son behaves like a spoiled child." Catriona drew herself up inches from his face and stared accusingly into his eyes. "You are your father's rightful successor." There could be no mistaking the passion in her voice. "And you are a disgrace to his memory. I have watched you, Allomore's son, and said nothing. But I can hold my tongue no longer."

James was determined to stand his ground. "How dare you address me in this way?"

Steel lay behind Catriona's stare. She turned to Christie. "Go downstairs," she instructed. "Your brother will join you presently."

Christie felt no inclination to argue. Catriona waited until she was out of earshot, never taking her eyes from James' face. "You have the pride, MacIain Mhor," she said at last. "But it has turned to bitterness inside you. It grieves me more than you can know to see your heart so twisted, for you are the last hope of those in your lands." Her voice grew softer, yet somehow more insistent. "They wait for your return."

James stared at her in helpless misery. Hot tears pricked behind his eyes.

"How can you believe that?" The break in his voice was deeper than a sob. "I have never dared to. I am a penniless beggar, forced to accept charity from those I despise."

"But who knows what might lie ahead for you," she paused again and looked at him strangely, "MacIain Mhor…"

He felt his heart stir again at the natural way she bestowed upon him his father's old patronym. *You are the last hope of those in your lands.* Yet he had believed his father had been forgotten. He saw that Catriona's stare was no longer angry, but held a mixture of sorrow and affection.

"Perhaps you will not accept Donald as your friend," she went on. "But you would do well to accept his support. The wheel turns. It is customary for the House of Allomore to provide, not to take. One day the wheel will turn your way."

And gazing back at her James no longer saw the maimed clanswoman he had scarcely before spared a glance. She now seemed wise beyond his telling, someone who could look into his heart and read all that lay there.

"How do you know all this?" he breathed at last.

"Because you are my chieftain." She waited for the impact of her words to reach him. "As your father was. Because I understand how those in Allomore detest the man who is now their master. You can deny your birthright no more than I can escape mine."

And with a final penetrating stare she turned to descend the stairs. The subject was closed, for now and perhaps forever. Slowly James returned to his room and saw his own clothes, neatly arranged on the counterpane, and knew that she had done it. He had declined Donald's offer of a suit, but this woman had understood. She had brushed and laid out his doublet with its patched elbows, the threadbare breeches and frayed shirt. He was touched despite himself. He would not reject her service.

As Christie entered the drawing room below Ardshiel rose to his feet. He was a tall man, fine in the bone and his lips were smooth and soft as they brushed her hand. Over his head she saw Donald watching them, beautiful in the firelight, resplendent in velvet doublet, white lace gleaming at his throat. She saw how he forced himself to turn away and she felt a tiny, guilty pleasure at her own power.

And then, to her delight, her brother appeared in the doorway. By contrast James was shabby and slight, yet it seemed that he had found a new confidence. He had only time to give her the briefest of smiles before the distant drone of the pibroch reached their ears. A hush fell over the company as Christie pulled back the drape and saw Kenneth and his pipes outlined between the stables and the sky. At his side were Fraser and Domhnull, small shadows listening in the torchlight. As the notes soared it seemed to Christie that Kenneth had distilled the very essence of his land into this pibroch, the stillness and glory, the strength and the magic. Donald drifted to her shoulder and gazed out with her, but while she could sense how the music moved him too she could have no idea of the darkness settling over his heart.

Throughout their dinner he wrestled with his melancholy thoughts. Christie sparkled and amused the guests with her tales of the exiled court in Rome. Even James joined in with his mocking descriptions of the petty jealousies and intrigues that had once formed the background to their lives. But before the meal had drawn to its close Ardshiel had grown impatient. This was more than just a social visit.

When he and Donald were finally alone he looked shrewdly across the table.

"You rise well to your new position, MacSomhairle. Tell me, how are your relations with your neighbour?"

"Why do you ask?"

"I was speaking to Gavin MacVey, who believes Kilclath has an interest in the welfare of your wards."

Donald scowled. "An interest in the welfare of their kinsman, most like."

"I am not convinced of it. Neither do I think Kilclath bears any ill will towards yourself."

"I, on the other hand, bear nothing but ill will towards him."

"That is regrettable."

"So you propose I should forgive the man who brought my father's life to its premature end?"

Ardshiel shrugged. "All our lives come to a premature end, one way or another," he observed. Realising there was little to be gained in trying to persuade Donald out of his opinion he sought a way to steer the conversation towards his other purpose. "Perhaps I should say most of our lives. Possibly Allomore's unhappy exile dragged out longer than he might have wished." He lowered his voice. "What fate has brought his children to your house at this time, when the rumblings across the channel grow louder. What support his son could muster."

Donald paused before answering. "He is not of our conviction," he said at last. "And I do not consider it my duty to try to change his mind. I have accepted a responsibility for Allomore's family which does not include tampering with their beliefs."

"Well, well," sighed Ardshiel, disappointed now on two counts. This last pronouncement did not sound at all like the Donald he was familiar with. "The matter is not immediate," he conceded. "But you should be aware there are those who might be more – perhaps I should say less - concerned about his welfare."

"Which is why Glenshellich might well be the safest place for them at present."

"Though some might consider Allomore's daughter too bright a jewel to hide from admiring eyes. Glenshellich must seem a lonely place to a beautiful young woman on the brink of life."

Later that night, Ardshiel's words still fresh in his mind, Donald found himself outside the door of Christie's room. He knocked and she answered. She was still dressed and had been sitting gazing into the embers of her fire. He lowered himself onto the chair on the other side of the fireplace.

"Had things taken their rightful course, you would be far richer than we," he began. "In your brother's position I do not think I would forget that."

Christie was disappointed to find herself trembling again at his closeness. She tried to keep her voice even. "Our fate was our father's choice."

Donald turned away. All their fates would be different without the choices of their fathers. But he dismissed the thought as unworthy. "Our guests were intrigued by your accounts of Rome." He had not come to make polite conversation, but was not yet ready to broach the real purpose of his visit.

"I did not want them to think our lives were so unhappy," she answered. "We knew nothing else. There was warmth and colour – and friendship. There was no need for either of us to dwell on what might have been, though that was not the case, of course, for our father."

"I cannot envisage what it would be to lose my home. If your father felt for Allomore just a part of what I do for Glenshellich then his exile must have broken his heart."

"I believe his heart was broken, yes," she agreed softly. "He felt great guilt, great conflict, great grief."

"Yet his final act was to send you back." Donald tried to keep the eagerness from his voice. "Did he perhaps begin to hope that what had been lost might be regained?"

At last Christie sensed what lay behind his words. "Please do not speak of that – least of all to James. It is too painful for him. He has learned what madness it is to pin hopes on dreams."

"Not dreams, Christie, if what I hear from France is true. There could be great hope!"

Christie turned her head away in exasperation. The clouds were about to gather again and she was certain the result would be no different than before.

"There is no hope, Donald," she sighed. "If only I could convince you of that, for you have so much here to lose."

He turned away in despair. His longing for her grew stronger and harder to deny with each day that passed. He dug his nails deep into his palms until he felt them sticky and damp. His head spun with the urge to take her into his arms. But that was not what he had come to do. He had come to tell her of his forthcoming marriage, and once again the words had disappeared, running through his brain like grains of sand through a child's fingers. He shuddered and stood up, and Christie only knew that another moment had come and gone.

But at the door he turned back. He must end this deception. He cleared his throat. "Christie ..."

She knew at once that his words would be unwelcome. When they came they flowed so quickly she scarcely grasped their meaning.

"I should not keep from you any longer that I am to be married. And very soon." She stared at him, but he looked away, and she knew it would be the same as before. She knew that he would not look back at her until she had time to compose herself, to wipe the distress and bewilderment from her face. He continued, his voice dull and formal. "Many years ago my father entered into a contract with Hector MacLean of Cairnill. As you know he was a long standing ally of both my father and yours. It was a marriage contract between Cairnill's daughter and myself." It could so easily have been a contract with Allomore, he reflected miserably. But it had not been, and the words continued to fall through the hollow space in his heart: pretend words, words like himself, without substance, without soul. "I intend the marriage to take place very soon. And I am sorry," he added, "to have kept it from you for so long."

Christie felt entitled to a little longer to regain her composure. It was another, even worse, humiliation, yet it would have been unthinkable for her to pretend, as he appeared to be doing, that nothing had occurred between them. She wondered if she would ever be able to bear to look into his eyes again.

"I wish that you had not," she said quietly at last, "kept it from me."

Still their backs were to each other.

"I wish it too."

Another silence fell.

"This will not at all alter your position in this house..." he went on, but he knew his words were simply foolish. He understood her fury at them.

"Do not play polite games with me," she retorted. "Or try to discuss my future - when it has taken you so long to arrange for your own."

* * *

The atmosphere in The Ensign was beginning to simmer and Andrew Stewart no longer had any desire to remain a part of it. The debauched scene before his eyes grew increasingly unsavoury. Hugh Fettes and a couple of his more disreputable associates had one of Bella's girls stretched across their knees. Hugh had removed her bodice while the others were setting about her skirts. She was screaming, with forced laughter, and as the sound grew more hysterical Andrew rose quietly to his feet and began to back away. It was unlikely that Hugh would notice his absence, and equally unlikely that the landlord would allow his best customer to come to harm. It would not be the first time Hugh had been found a bed in The Ensign. But as Andrew was about to raise the door handle the laughter stopped and the room fell silent.

A young woman was standing beside the landlord. She must have entered from the back close, otherwise she would have passed him, yet she did not look at all to Andrew like any of the whores who commonly took that route. Her cool gaze took in the room, but he noticed that her breast rose and fell quickly beneath her cloak. She was more agitated than she would like them to believe. He also had the strong suspicion that he was the only man in the room who was unaware of her identity.

"I need a doctor," she said at last, turning to the landlord. "I thought there might be a chance of finding one here."

Andrew cast his eyes around the assembled crew of inebriates. Doctors there may have been, but none in any condition to put their profession into practice.

He took a step forward. "I am a student of medicine. If there is anything I can do…?"

She looked around her again, and Andrew recognised contempt in her expression. Several of the company had the grace to lower their heads.

"Thank you," she said briefly and waited as he made his way back towards her. The landlord threw her a quizzical sidelong glance.

"It's Hannah," she muttered. "Hannah Bain."

He drew a long breath. "Then I doubt she's past any help this gentleman," he stressed the word, "can offer."

Andrew was studying the young woman more closely. Her plain garments did nothing to hide her arresting beauty. "Perhaps we should allow the lady to explain," he suggested.

"For your own safety, Jean," the landlord hissed. "You're a fool to be tending to her."

She turned on him angrily. "Who else will do it? You've a short memory, Mr Lowrie, if you canna recall the times she came down here to beg on my behalf – the times you gave her soup and meal when I struggled for my last breath?"

"A man will stir himself for the sake of a child."

"But no' for a dying whore – even if she's sat times beyond reckoning at these tables and kept your customers sweet and spending."

"And dosed them with the pox, forby." The landlord turned to Andrew who was listening with increasing alarm. "An old whore of Bella's," he explained. "Given a room to die in, but beyond anyone's aid if I ken anything of this world. Beyond yours," he warned the girl who stared defiantly back. "And beyond any doctor's – qualified or no'." He looked sternly from one to the other. "And if you ken what's best for you, Jean Petrie, you'll get back to your master quicker than Hannah's hand could once slip inside an honest man's pocket."

Jean cast another scathing look around the room.

"Present company would be safe enough then," she countered. Andrew took another two steps towards her and Hugh raised his head to squint over his tankard.

166

"What the…." he began. "Where the…?" His face lit up like a man beholding a vision, but Jean barely spared him a second glance.

"Are you still willing to help?" she challenged Andrew.

He continued to look from her to the landlord and back again, then finally reached above her head and pushed the door.

"Dinna say you werena warned," was Mr Lowrie's parting shot.

Andrew followed the young woman through the narrow close that led direct to Bella's back door. From inside he could hear snatches of the same amusements they had left behind, interrupted by more sinister sounds, cries, and the sound of a lash. Jean glanced behind as if in doubt that he would still be following, then with a brief nod grabbed a candle and took out a key. They climbed and climbed, into reaches few of Bella's clients would even have imagined existed. The stair grew narrower and blacker than the night. A rat scuttled under Jean's skirts and over Andrew's feet, its passage rank and warm. He drew a breath and into his mind came a picture of spring sunshine spreading over the water of his lochan, Feodag's stones raising their glittering heads above the tide. His closed eyes made him stumble and the girl turned quickly again.

"Having second thoughts?"

Andrew swallowed, righted himself and returned to reality. He watched her fit her key into the lock of the very last door of what must have been the highest garret in the whole brooding city. Even before it creaked ajar the foul stench of decay almost choked him. In the far corner pale candlelight licked the edges of a splintered pallet raised from the floor by bricks. A threadbare blanket was carelessly strewn across it and as Jean crept closer the blanket stirred, a shadow inside a shadow. Andrew remained in the doorway, watching in horror as she gently pulled it back to reveal a sunken grey face. Her hand briefly stroked the thin strands of hair and a surge of compassion banished the sickness rising in Andrew's throat. Death could be hours at the most away for this poor wretch.

"Mr Lowrie spoke true," he whispered through dry lips. "I fear there is nothing any doctor can do."

"I feared the same," breathed Jean. "But at least now I can be certain."

Andrew drew as close as he dared. "This is a truly foul place."

"But a quiet one. And sheltered from the street." Jean rested her smooth hand on the damp forehead. "Hannah!" she whispered. "Hannah, it's Jean back. I'll no' leave you again. The doctor's here with me. He'll give you something to make you sleep."

She reached under her cloak, brought out a flask and passed it to Andrew. He sniffed the contents, brandy laced with laudanum. He nodded and waited while she raised Hannah's head, then he tipped the flask gently against the cracked lips. For a second he saw a strange brightness in her eye and wondered if she was really as old as she seemed. In this nether world where whores were schooled from childhood the pox could steal years and juggle lifespans. He instinctively placed his own hand against the sunken cheek and felt it like a soft leather mask.

"Hannah," he whispered. She opened her eyes and the light seemed to spring from them again. Jean leaned behind him.

"Doctor!" Hannah whispered and gave a feeble cackle. "Doctor!"

"See what I can do for you, Hannah," Jean smiled. "Miracles." Her voice dropped to become less than a whisper. "The same as you once did for me."

Andrew turned to gaze up at her. He saw steel as well as tenderness behind the clear eyes, and something else, something unexpectedly familiar.

"Close your eyes, Hannah," he whispered. "And take hold of Jean's hand."

Hannah did as he asked.

"Do you feel any pain?" he went on.

"No pain," she breathed, and her eyes closed. Andrew moved one hand softly over her scaly head and held the other above Jean's.

"Put your hand on her forehead," he whispered. "For there is no doctor alive can dispense your medicine."

At first Jean looked puzzled, then suspicious.

"She does not need me. She needs your hand," Andrew insisted.

Jean did as he instructed and a silence fell.

At last Hannah opened her eyes. "Are the angels come for me?"

Jean tried to smile. "I think so."

"And your mother…? Is she with them?"

A tear dropped from Jean's chin and fell onto the filthy blanket. "Yes. My mother too."

As if that was all she needed to hear Hannah smiled back at her. Her eyelids dropped and her breathing grew calmer. Jean sat for a long time gazing down, and then looked up at Andrew. "What did you mean, my medicine?"

"Your hands have medicine. They are healer's hands."

Jean's eyes opened wide. She shook her head and smiled in astonishment, continuing to study her hands. They looked to her much the same and just as ordinary as ever, though beneath them Hannah slept on almost contentedly, waiting for the angels or the old whores to spirit her away to a place with better prospects.

"You see," Andrew whispered. "Though I am to be a doctor and will learn ways through medicine to make folk well, there are some who can do much more with just a touch."

Jean did not look up, but whispered, "Will you stay with us?"

"If that is what you want."

She seemed relieved. Andrew sat down on the edge of the pallet.

"I remember the nights my mother lay beside her," Jean went on. "For comfort, I think, in lives which had precious little."

"So why has she come to such a place as this when she has you?"

She seemed surprised at his question. "We all come to this room to die."

"We?"

"Bella's ladies and gentlemen canna' take their tricks forever. Sooner or later the pox, or something, brings us back. Hannah lasted longer than most, by begging and picking pockets. But Bella saves this room for us to die quietly. With no fuss and no complaint."

Andrew stared at her in dismay. Yet even as he stared he felt something shift inside him. His breath grew ragged. He knew what was about to happen.

"You are not a whore," he gasped.

A flash of mischief lit her eyes. "And you are not the first to tell me so."

He had almost begun to believe, to hope, this feeling would never come again. But he could do nothing. It had come and as always he was in its power.

"You are not a whore," he repeated. "But the next time we meet you will be the mistress of whores."

Her eyes grew wide with amazement. Andrew was amazed himself. Something uncanny had brought them to this eyrie at the top of the city, this garret where angels drifted and flesh decayed, where the past and the future were one, and an unschooled girl had more power in the touch of one hand than he could achieve from a lifetime's learning. The Sight had returned to him with terrifying intensity. It swept him to a strange and dazzling landscape where out of a merciless sky crawled a bear, huge and grizzled, a brown mangy monster that loomed over the body of a child. And Andrew knew he must kill the bear to save the child, but its fangs dripped and foamed, its claws were hooked and razor sharp. He could hear his heart pounding above the child's whimpers. He could taste the fear in his throat and feel its cold numbing his spine. Then something else swept from the blazing sky: an eagle, but an eagle that bore no resemblance to the majestic golden bird that soared above the giant's mountain. This was its poor relation, ragged, with dusty black and white feathers, yet Andrew knew that the eagle would tame the bear, even as he knew that this whore-mistress would tame the eagle and he would save her child.

The light faded. He looked down on her again. It amazed him what he knew.

"Your mother died in this room." It was not a question.

"She's here now," Jean whispered and it was not an answer. Her hand moved gently on Hannah's brow. "Come at last to set Hannah free."

For a long time after Hannah had left them they sat together in silence. And to Andrew it seemed as if he had always known this girl and this old woman, as if between them they might somehow finally summon the power to stem the tide of his terrible gift.

"What of her body?" he whispered at last.

"She'll have a decent burial."

He was about to offer to help again, but she was already slipping away.

"Thank you," she said. "We helped her home together. I think it was you who called the angels."

Andrew turned his eyes to the corner. There were no angels now, no bears, no eagles, golden or black, only the stale remnants of untouched food scattered around a ragged corpse.

Hannah Bain was silent at last, and would be for all eternity.

* * *

Donald picked up his quill for the tenth time. It had been reprehensible enough to anticipate his union with Helen without the commitment or the enthusiasm she deserved, but far worse now to enter into the contract with another woman filling his heart.

"My dear Helen," he began. "For many years we have had an understanding...."

He stood up and dashed his fist against the wall. Outside in the morning sunshine he saw Christie and Fraser laughing together. How could she laugh while he suffered such anguish? The sun glinted in her hair and lit her eyes with a brightness that pierced his heart.

"...and now would seem the time to set the seal on an arrangement which I have long looked forward to....."

He groaned and let his head fall into his hands. A letter would not do. If he wanted to make Helen his bride he must go to the Glen of the Black Cattle himself.

* * *

Jean watched the broth bubble gently in the pot and listened for a phrase she might recognise. But the three tongues raced so quickly that their words seemed to merge into one. There could be no doubt that whatever they were discussing was a matter of great urgency. Theirs was a language of emotion, and the passions of master and servants were running high. Even Jean shrank from the fire in Kilclath's eyes, while Hughie slumped petulantly into the ingle corner like one cowering from a blow.

Mhairi was the only one undaunted by Kilclath's wrath. Jean had never heard her say so much. She was angrier than either of them and her voice was insistent and shrill. Jean was as certain as she could be they were still talking about Hannah. Mhairi let loose a final fierce outburst and Hughie's hackles rose dangerously. He made a quick, cutting gesture. At once the atmosphere changed and it was Mhairi's turn to shrink back. The Master took two strides towards Hughie and grabbed his throat. Hughie shrank back, but Jean saw that his eyes did not submit and she felt a cold stab of fear.

"Stop it!" she cried.

All three of them spun their attention onto her.

"What was Hannah to you?" This time her words were directed at Kilclath. He stared at her, but she stood her ground. Finally, as it always did, her gaze caused his anger to ebb away.

"She was nothing to me," he answered at last. There was no emotion left in his voice. "Nor to Hughie, nor even much to Mhairi," he sighed. "She was something to my father a long time ago. It is not my secret, Jean, and I could not reveal it, even if I wished to." He paused and frowned what could have been a warning in Hughie's direction. "Like many of our stories, it is best left untold."

Jean did not doubt it. She was only relieved to have him in control of himself again. He touched her cheek gently. "You should not have gone to Bella's without telling us."

"You would have kept me here."

His anger had left him completely. He almost smiled. "You are right. And in doing so denied an old soul her peace – though only through concern for your safety."

"Why should I be in danger in the place I was born and raised?"

He did not answer, but another shadow crossed his face, and she knew her words had caused it. Jean might have been dragged up through gutters but she had no fear of her past. She could return to it, step in and out of it like an old suit of familiar clothes. His was locked away in the dark closet of his memory. Mhairi and Hughie trained anxious eyes on him. Whatever the story was, they knew it, as Hannah had known it, and the knowledge was treacherous, as the Master had warned, best left untold.

Jean sighed and thought again of the student doctor whose name she had not even asked. She remembered his careful hands and troubled eyes but most of all she remembered his odd and alarming prediction. Much as she had warmed to him she sincerely hoped it would be a very long time before they met again.

* * *

Andrew was breaking his fast when Hugh arrived, dishevelled and still tipsy.

"You sly devil!" he slurred. "A night with Jean Petrie! A night to savour, I'll be bound!"

Andrew did not reply. It had been a night he would be more comfortable to forget, especially with the knowledge he now had as to Jean's identity.

Kirsty shuffled beside him and he gave her a kind smile. He was pinning his hopes on her transferring her affections to James when he arrived later in the week to take up his position in Gavin MacVey's chambers. She removed his plate and accidentally brushed his shoulder.

"Whether you want to or not, perhaps," Hugh added cunningly. "I assume you kept well clear of the patient."

Andrew folded his napkin with the reassuring thought that Hugh's bags would be packed before the day was out.

"And will keep clearer of Kilclath for the next while." Hugh slapped him on the back. "For you can be sure he'll have the whole story by now."

* * *

Christie took a mouthful of whisky and felt her throat burn as she forced herself to swallow it. Outside Catriona's cottage a steady drizzle fed the falls and hid the lochan. It was a dreary day to match the dreariness that hung over their spirits. Catriona leaned forward and pressed Christie's fingers around her glass.

"Drink it all. It will calm you."

"We have never in our lives been parted." A sob rose in Christie's throat.

"Your brother's destiny is not in Glenshellich," Catriona told her. "And he knows he must seek it."

Catriona's sons had ridden eastwards too. From Kilclath they would go their separate ways, Euan and Donald north to the Glen of the Black Cattle, and James south to the capital. Catriona could picture them galloping through the mists below the Mountains of the Eagles, skirting the empty house that pined for its master. She drew a deep breath that passed her lips as a sigh.

"You have been such a joy here, Christie," she went on. "A joy to all in the clachan. In their hearts they have wished for something they knew could not be." She turned away and moved to the window to look out across the lochan. Christie sat silently staring into the weakly glowing embers.

"You must listen to me now and listen well," Catriona told her. "For I do not intend to speak of this to you again. I should not speak of it now, but it is your right to hear the truth." She drew another sigh and turned back to face Christie, her expression tight with compassion. "This marriage that Donald goes to seek was John Stewart's dream, the dream of a man who wished to make a better world for his children. For Donald he wanted a wife who was perfect, for he believed such women were to be found. It was his dream to strengthen his bond with Cairnill to a union of blood. He had seen that Cairnill's daughter, child though she was, was beautiful and kind and good. In John Stewart's eyes there could be no union more fitting. So he told Donald of his hopes and Donald was happy to agree. Neither considered that Donald would give his heart elsewhere." She paused again. Christie was listening intently. "The love between Donald and his father was at the very heart of Donald's life. He is ashamed he did not do more to make his father proud, but he can at least fulfil his greatest wish for the future. Perhaps it is a mistake, but in his mind he does it for the right reasons and he will not be persuaded differently. I pray you will understand this, Christie, for you will have no choice but to suffer with him."

Christie kept her eyes on the smoking peat. She did not answer immediately, letting everything Catriona had said take its place in her mind. "I am used to disappointment," she said finally. "But not to humiliation. I wish at least I could have kept some pride."

Catriona held out her arms and drew her close. "You have lost no pride, Allomore's daughter," she whispered. "Hold your head high, for the blood of great men and women runs in your veins. You have already proved yourself worthy of them."

* * *

The lands of Cairnill were vast and fertile, a thriving testimony to their chieftain's acumen. Donald and Euan rode among the black cattle grazing peacefully on the shore of Loch Laggan, letting their eyes absorb the rolling pastures and neat crofts.

"Would a herd like this one suit you?" Donald asked with a grin.

"I am minded for one like it. Some day," Euan answered quietly. "Glenshellich is not so favoured."

"It could be made so." Euan needed no encouragement to warm to his favourite subject. "For instance, the furrow to Beathag's cottage would fill with seaweed. In time we could squeeze some crops along the channel and graze over the whole slope." He pointed to the first incline beyond a sturdy dry stone wall. "Like Cairnill has done there."

"We could bury Beathag with it," Donald joked.

"Beathag's bones would make poor corn."

But Euan knew it was not wise to mock Beathag, even from this safe distance.

"Your son is of her blood," he warned. "And do not think she forgets it."

"Though perhaps this is not the best of times to remind me."

As they rounded the last curve of the shore Cairnerrich House fell into vision, a sight as far removed from the spectre of Beathag's blood or bones as any could imagine. It stood solid and sharp, rising from its own parkland, oak and silver birch behind it and lawns stretching before, large enough for all of Cairnill's sons and fitting in its stateliness for his one treasured daughter. A ghillie began to stumble down the slope towards them and another appeared from behind the stables.

Euan narrowed his eyes and Donald sensed his suspicion.

"Is something amiss?"

Euan did not reply. He looked behind him on the track and was sure he saw a figure disappear behind the outcrop they had just ridden past. He could not help wondering why the Glen of Black Cattle should be so well guarded against friends.

But someone else was coming to meet them, someone running lightly down the path that led from the front door, the silk of her dress rustling and the bright tartan plaid streaming behind her. Donald dismounted and handed the reins to Euan who took them in silence.

Then Donald too began to run, determined to make the best impression he could. He met Helen just inside the carved granite gateway where she fell breathlessly into his arms. When she raised her face to look at him there could be no mistaking the love in her eyes. In that moment he vowed he would never betray her again.

"Have you guessed my reason for coming?" he asked.

"I can think of two reasons," she said softly. "I hope I am right in the one I prefer."

"And that would be?"

She blushed. "Come, Donald, that is not fair."

"No," he agreed with a smile. "It is not. I am here because I wish to make you my wife and soon." He kept his eyes on hers and swallowed down his sense of shame. "We have been betrothed almost all our lives, but I have never formally asked for your hand. So will you, Helen, become mistress of Glenshellich?"

How quickly and easily it was said, the question that had for so long troubled his dreams. Euan leaned forward in his saddle and ran his hand down his horse's mane, thankful that no woman had discovered a route into his heart.

"Oh Donald!" Helen breathed.

Donald touched her glowing face and drew her close. For a long time they clung together as he gently stroked her smooth hair and told himself that he did love her. He had always loved her. He held her tighter and closed his eyes to shut out the picture of Christie that smiled before them. From now on the pain, the guilt and the longing would be his own secret, a wrong he had done this gentle girl in his arms and must do her for the rest of the days of his life.

She drew away and led him through the front door and across the corridor to her father's study. She did not knock but when she burst inside it was clear that their arrival was expected. Cairnill held out his arms, but as he hugged his daughter he raised his eyes above her head to search the face of the man who would take her away. And Donald had a sinister sense of a shadow, a suspicion that Cairnill had seen into his heart. But the shadow passed and the old man extended his hand.

"I have long anticipated this day, Donald. You must be aware of my answer." He gripped Donald's hand, but the shadow still drifted with him as he nodded to Helen and indicated the door. He needed her to leave them alone.

"I will do everything in my power to make her happy," Donald assured him as the door closed behind her.

"I do not doubt it," Cairnill agreed. "And although I will miss her more than words could express, I would not dream of keeping her here forever."

"She will be among friends in Glenshellich." Donald paused before adding. "And we wish for the wedding to be soon."

The old man regarded him shrewdly. "Though you have delayed longer than I would have expected – or Helen might have desired…." He did his best to keep the note of misgiving from his next words. "Does your present haste have anything at all to do with the arrival of the son and daughter of Allomore?"

Donald felt the eyes drilling him again and was aware of a rush of blood to his face. "Not directly…" he began. "More to do with tidings from France."

"I see," Cairnill interrupted, nodding slowly. "That might give rise to a different perspective."

Donald studied him more closely. The old chieftain had grown cautious, wary, protective of his empire in ways he had not been thirty years before. But then he had so much more of an empire to protect. He had acquired enough for his sons to become powerful landlords in their own right.

"Let us be frank with each other," Cairnill continued smoothly and Donald found it hard not to look away. "I have one issue at stake here and that is my daughter and her happiness. Do you come here now with this desire for a hasty marriage because you sense greater changes ahead?"

"We have every reason to hope," exclaimed Donald. "You must know that the glens are alive with stories. The time may well be ripe.

France will lend troops; they say the prince is ready and restless. There is every chance he will come soon."

The old man's face darkened. "And you will be ready, too, Donald? To sacrifice your home, your freedom, your family?"

"Of course," Donald cried, his eyes shining. "As you were. As my father was."

"A man can learn wisdom with the passing years."

"A man's loyalty cannot change."

"Can it not?" Cairnill's voice was harsh. "You do not know what your father's advice would be to you today. I have searched my heart on this matter since they came to me." He paused briefly at the sight of Donald's puzzled stare. "For they have been here, the priest and Doctor Cameron. I made no pledge, no promise, but I have an answer for them now. I would not give my support to the prince, Donald. I have too much to lose. And I would urge you to do the same, and for the same reason."

Donald gazed at him in disbelief. "You say this to test me."

"You are young, Donald, and have a young man's dreams. Your father and I were once the same." Cairnill shook his head sadly. "But I am all that remains of our fellowship, and for me wisdom has replaced dreams, wisdom and the acceptance of what must be. Young men may think they are the masters of fate. Old men know better."

"But these are traitor's words!" Donald exclaimed in dismay.

Cairnill was not prepared to let such an insult pass. "They are my words and you will guard the looseness of your tongue!" His voice rang sharper still. "I have called men out for less."

"My father once risked everything. He would do so again."

Cairnill heaved another long sigh. "Perhaps you are correct, Donald. Perhaps he would still risk all."

"I know only what my heart tells me," Donald insisted. "The rightness of our cause lies in men's hearts. It is not a belief that words can dissuade me of. Words have too often been the weapons of traitors."

Cairnill's anger had subsided. He regarded his future son in law with an expression bordering on regret, but when he spoke his words

179

were sincere. "It grieves me to be speaking thus with the son of my greatest friend, my daughter's future husband. And God forbid that I should try to dissuade any man from doing what is right. I wish only to be sure you understand what it is you will lose, especially since Helen will share your fate." His pale eyes grew distant, trawling troubled memories. "Do not forget I was once forced from my home, compelled to sit impotent in a foreign land while all I loved was lost to me. Sometimes that is what it takes for a man to be acquainted with his heart, to discover it might not be as he imagined. It is the small things you miss: the cry of the gulls in the morning, the soft voices in the clachan, the lowing of cattle at sunset, the fires in the chill winter nights, the smoke in the huts that fills your lungs and sets you coughing and sick, even that, perhaps that most of all, you miss. Can you not see I am too old to risk it all again? And I fear for her that I love."

"Then you would not rise if the time comes?"

"No. No, Donald, I would not."

"Then on whom can he rely?"

"There are many, and more like me who wish him well. But the die is cast in the Glen of Black Cattle. I ask only that you will consider your decision as carefully."

"I do not need to consider. There can be but one way for me to follow. And if Helen becomes my wife it must be her way too."

He turned away, but his mind was more troubled than before. Had there been such a shadow over his father's eyes in his later years? He brushed the question aside with a final challenge. "I wonder what your old friend Allomore's view would be."

He had no way of knowing that his father had once asked the very same question in the very same room. The old chief inclined his head. It was an argument that could not be countered.

"He would say as you do," he answered quietly. "Allomore remained truest of all to the cause, and for that his memory demands the greatest honour. Is that what it receives, I wonder, from those he left behind?"

* * *

180

"If we adhere to the natural line of succession," Kilclath stated, "Then your claim would be indisputable. The present Laird arrived at his title through a very indirect route."

"I am very well aware of it," James Hamilton answered. "My great grandfather had one son, my grandfather two, but the younger died, and this man is descended from a daughter of my great grandfather."

"Through the noble lines of Fraser and Chisholm," Kilclath added. He was of necessity an authority on the complexities of Highland dynasties. It was the expertise his father had built an empire upon. He drew a businesslike breath. "However, that is beside the point. In these changing times a person's persuasion is of more consequence." He cleared his throat. "And since the situation remains that Allomore has no legitimate heir this would seem an opportune time to consider where you belong in the equation. The old line will always be favoured in Allomore, but Gavin and myself are both of the opinion that we should approach with caution. That is why we have suggested your new identity."

"James Bothwell," James murmured. The name did not displease him.

"Your connection with Glenshellich might still prove an obstacle," Kilclath went on, " but Gavin was close to your father. He did not always agree with his politics but he will do all that he can to further your interests and, of course, those of your sister."

"MacSomhairle also has your best interests at heart," Gavin broke in quickly, anxious not to widen the rift between this young man and his guardian any further. "But, it has to be said, less influence."

James looked from one man of law to the other, unsure quite how to interpret their interest in him. Although he had long been familiar with the petty machinations of an exiled court he suspected that its manoeuvrings were amateurish in comparison. Allomore's lands were prosperous and well favoured: its tenants were shrewd and influential and ready to seize whatever political opportunity might present itself. Inexperienced as he was, James could not fail to be aware that lines were once more being drawn in Scotland, sides were again being taken.

"So …?" Still he hesitated.

Gavin looked at him with intent.

"So, in my opinion, you would be well advised to accept the offer the Master of the Stones is about to make."

* * *

"My father has a gun in his thatch," announced Domhnull Mac-Combie. His eyes shone. "He says that all the men do, Euan and Iain and Martin. And MacSomhairle has many in his house. My father says it is maybe time to take the guns out and give them a dusting down."

"Is your father thinking of going to war then, Domhnull, with his gun?" breathed Callum MacMichael.

"He will go if MacSomhairle calls him," Domhnull stated with pride. "He is ready, just as his own father was ready to play the pipes before. He will go with MacSomhairle and one day I will go with MacSomhairle's sons."

"MacSomhairle will have no sons."

Angus stopped himself too late and Domhnull turned on him fiercely.

"What is that you say, Angus MacLeay?"

Angus dropped his eyes and mumbled an incoherent excuse.

"What is it you say, Angus?" Domhnull repeated, a quiet but unmistakable threat in his voice.

"I say only what I heard my father say," stammered Angus. "My mother told him that MacSomhairle had gone to find a wife and my father said it would be no good to the glen. Wife or no wife, MacSomhairle would have no sons, and what would become of us then, he said, and who would you play your pibroch for, Domhnull?"

Domhnull stared at him in astonishment. Then he smiled at Angus's ignorance.

"He is not gone for a wife," he explained patiently. "He is gone for news of the war."

"He is gone for a wife, Domhnull," Callum assured him. "All the clachan knows it."

Domhnull continued to stare. All the clachan! How would all the clachan know what he did not, he who was always first to be told what was in MacSomhairle's mind? And how could he be going to find a wife when the golden one was in the glen. He stared his challenge back into the faces of his friends, but they could only look away.

At last Domhnull turned his back on them and ran in the direction of the lochan. There was someone he needed to see.

Christie was not reading as she often was but gazing across the shining surface of the water into the glinting ripples that spread from his great-grandfather's boat. Domhnull approached quietly and sat down beside her. She turned to him, smiled and held her hands apart.

"You will see I have no stories today."

He shrugged his shoulders and remained silent. She noticed that his expression was troubled and said no more, waiting for him to speak in his own time.

"Where is MacSomhairle?" he asked at last.

"He has gone to the Glen of Black Cattle," she answered softly.

"Why has he gone there?"

"He has business. I do not always know his reasons." She was aware that the boy was studying her closely. "Why do you ask, Domhnull?"

"Och, for no real reason." But she could see that his casual manner was feigned. "They were telling me it might be to do with the war that is coming."

"Then perhaps that is your answer."

He continued to gaze with a furrowed brow across the water.

"What is it that troubles you, Domhnull?" Christie asked gently.

He turned almost fiercely to face her. "What do the old men talk about around the fires?"

She made an attempt at a light laugh. "And how would I be knowing that? Do I have a grey beard and a bent back like your grandfather?"

But Domhnull could not be diverted by flippancy. She was not making him feel better. She was making him feel very much worse. He changed his tactic. "Will you ever leave the glen?" His eyes were still fixed on the other side of the water.

Christie felt a sadness creep over her heart. She had no idea how to answer him, so instead she asked a question of her own. "How can any of us know what will happen even tomorrow?"

"Angus MacLeay thinks that he does. And the old men at the fires, they believe they know."

Christie cupped his chin with her hand and turned his head to face her. She recognised the fear in his eyes. "But they do not know, Domhnull. The future is a mystery to all of us. Perhaps there are some who think they have the sight – your own great-grandfather for one – but there are few true seers, and even they are most times proved wrong." She paused. He was still staring at her. If anyone was entitled to the best explanation she could give it was Domhnull. She sighed again. "There is some story here," she went on, "in this glen, that they whisper. MacSomhairle spoke to me of it not long after I arrived. He also told me it was nonsense and not to be heeded, and he was right to say so, Domhnull, for these tales make fear creep into men's minds and push out their sense. Such tales are dangerous and can only do harm."

Another silence fell while he digested her words. Then all his left him in a sudden rush. "MacSomhairle has told me that one day I will play the pibroch for his sons. It is all that I could wish for – to be a maker of tunes for my chieftain. Now Angus MacLeay tells me that MacSomhairle will have no sons, that he heard his father say so and it is true."

Christie felt a chill run through her. Yet she was not prepared to let Domhnull see her distress. She made another determined effort to keep her voice calm. "Perhaps that is not what he said, nor what his father meant. Why should MacSomhairle not have sons?"

"If he went to war and did not come back he would not have them," Domhnull answered with perfect logic.

Christie laid her hand on his shoulder. "I will tell you something," she said. "All my life there has been talk of this war. Men who planned it have grown old and died and still it has not come."

But Domhnull had his answer. "There are always wars. There will be one for MacSomhairle and there will be one for me."

Christie gazed at him sadly. His eyes were keen and bright. He was a member of a tribe and all tribes went to war, no matter what Catriona might have taught them or what she might believe. Christie had an unpleasant suspicion that Domhnull's version of the future might have more chance of coming to pass than her own.

"And you think that is the correct way – for us, now, in these times?" she asked him gently. "Oh, you do not need to answer. If that is what you think then you must accept that death and war walk hand in hand. There is fear in someone's heart for every man who ventures down that path. And for you that fear is for MacSomhairle. But now is not the time and I am telling you to put it from your mind."

"You have not answered my other question."

She ran her hand gently across his head and pulled him close to her. His small body grew tense and then relaxed. She could see Donald in his face more and more plainly as the weeks went on. How could she tell him that his own existence was the answer he sought? Because that knowledge brought another, more awful dread.

"Only some of our questions can be answered," she said softly.

* * *

James Hamilton, or Bothwell as he was now to be known, had declined his invitation to return for MacSomhairle's wedding celebrations. His sister might have considered it ingratitude, and perhaps it was, for Alison and Andrew would have welcomed his company on the journey north, and Gavin MacVey was himself preparing to attend. In truth, James was less resentful of Glenshellich's charity now that he was no longer dependent on it, but if he was to ally himself with Kilclath, as seemed increasingly likely, relationships must change.

There was also the matter of his sister. Now that they were to be reunited in the city James was looking to his responsibilities for her future. Their prospects no longer seemed so gloomy, especially in the light of the trip of his own he was preparing, a trip made easier by the lack of prying eyes in Alison's household.

He heard the sound of the risp at exactly the arranged time. Kirsty answered it almost straight away.

"Ah, Davie," James greeted the cheery young arrival. "Are they despatched?"

"On the coach for Stirling as arranged."

"And the ferry and horses ready for ourselves?"

"The Master assures me of it."

Davie grinned and stepped back while the young gentleman gathered his cloak. It was an adventure indeed to be leaving the familiar confines of the city on such an errand.

"Well then," James announced, patting his doublet where the letter was neatly tucked away. "Let us waste no more time. I believe I have waited long enough to make my way home."

* * *

Even Cairnill's horse was a statement of his wealth, Fraser reflected, as he slapped the black stallion's rippling haunch. The House of Hanover had made him rich recompense for his guarantees of neutrality. Fraser's spirits were depressingly low on this eve of Donald's wedding for it had become impossible for him to imagine the house without Allomore's daughter, so deeply had she embedded herself into Glenshellich and his heart. Yet he knew he could not expect her to change her mind. It would be impossible for her to remain in the house when it had a mistress.

As he ran the brush once more down the stallion's gleaming back Christie slipped behind him and into the stall. "No songs today, Fraser," she remarked sadly.

"Do you wonder at it?"

"Don't be thinking I'll forget them. Folk can still sing in Edinburgh, can they not?" She touched his shoulder lightly. "And I'll pay a visit to that old warehouse and remind them of the chandler who saved the rebels and swam away to an enchanted life. You're all the evidence I need that a change can often be for the better."

He ran his hand across his eyes and sniffed. She reached hers across the horse's back and he grasped it tightly.

Donald and Helen were returning from their walk and paused at the gateway. Christie watched him bend his head and whisper something into her ear.

"She is beautiful," Christie murmured. It had come as a surprise that seeing the two of them together did not upset her more, but like everyone else she had found it impossible to harbour a single unkind thought towards Helen.

"She is that," Fraser agreed, the beautiful embodiment of an old chieftain's misjudgement, he thought to himself before he heaved a deep sigh. What was done was done. And perhaps Donald had made the only decision possible.

The two of them were able to smile the next day, all through the wedding ceremony, all through the banquet, and all though the frenzied reels that followed it. Christie was only sorry that her father could not have been a part of the celebrations. It was the extravagant coming to life of his old dream: resplendent chiefs with their sparkling women, laughing and spinning to the skirl of pipes and fiddles. And above them all towered Donald, the host and the hero, touchingly protective of the beautiful bride who clung to his arm.

Then the music calmed and she felt a soft pressure on her arm.

"Will you and I take the floor?" asked Andrew.

Christie smiled up at him. "Why, thank you, sir."

He slipped his hand under her elbow and led her to join the dancers. The cheerful smile never left his lips or reached his eyes as he muttered, "We can be partners in pretence."

Christie followed his gaze to where Helen stood beside Donald, laughing up into the face of Ardshiel. Her beauty was breathtaking, captivating, and immediately she understood.

"I am so sorry," she whispered.

"We are all sorry," he murmured as they took the first light steps together. "But there is one thing for which we can be grateful. Helen is happy in her innocence. I have never seen her so happy." Christie's throat grew tight as he went on. "I have loved her from the moment I laid eyes on her, when she was little more than a child. But she was marked out for Donald even then. I have always played the part of a brother. It is a part I must be content to play forever."

"And will you play it for me also?" Christie asked softly.

He held her slightly from him and looked seriously into her eyes. "A brother, a friend, a soul-mate," he answered. "Would that it had been you and I who had fallen in love."

As Christie looked around she could see that the same thought was in many minds. She and Andrew danced elegantly and effortlessly together, a couple almost as remarkable as the bride and groom, hiding their broken hearts in perfect rhythm beneath the sparkling chandelier. And if Donald's face darkened as he watched them it was only for a moment, for he was an old master of the game of deceit while they were still novices.

Eilidh of the scarlet face leaned on the banister and looked on wistfully. The music soared from Kenneth MacCombie's pipes and settled around her soul, even as she watched his wife bring more trays of meats to the table. Meg raised a goblet to her lips and swallowed deeply. Only she would have the impudence to do a thing like that under the very nose of MacSomhairle. But as he passed her by he grinned and slipped a fleeting hand around her waist. Eilidh had her own memories of love gone by, and no dreams of it ever returning, but she knew in that she was not alone. The old aunt was smiling to herself. Eilidh remembered her less fondly, descending on Glenshellich with her fancy southern ideas and clipped commands. Eilidh heaved a long sigh. She was growing older. Wrinkles were spreading around her eyes and her mouth, puckering the red birthmark that, along with Meg MacLeay, had kept her an old maid. Meg was at the piper's side now, with her boy, whirling and twisting and the healer's widow was smiling at them. Eilidh let her eyes linger on the scene, knowing no one would notice her taking her ease. Dancers flashed past, their feet drumming on the flagstones. The house was alive as she had not known it for many a year. Her own feet began to beat a rhythm and her head started to sway. Kenneth's cousin, daft Iain MacCombie, slid up beside her, but it was MacSomhairle himself who took hold of her arm. He swung her onto the floor and the clapping from many hands cheered them on their way. Eilidh saw Kenneth's warm eyes on her and Meg's delighted grin, and then MacSomhairle was gone, swirling out of sight and she was in Iain's arms, as the breathless bright world whirled by.

Old Angus Ban took a deep draught of whisky. To him the scene was nothing but the hazy passing of a distant dream. He remembered better than any the last time, when the old MacSomhairle had danced with his bride from the south. No, he corrected himself: that had been the time before.

This was the last time.

* * *

The raucous squabbling of herring gulls screeched over James's head as he and Davie stumbled from the pitching ferryboat and onto the northern shingles of the firth. Their horses were waiting, delivered by a scowling ferrier who accepted his payment with a dour nod. Davie was far from being a skilled rider, but did his best to disguise it as he drew his mount alongside James.

"See the furthest hill on the horizon?"

James squinted towards it.

"Allomore," Davie pronounced. He hesitated before adding, "Mr Bothwell."

James shot him a sharp glance.

"There's good reason for my assumed name, Davie," he said.

"Aye," Davie agreed, his voice still heavy with emphasis. "But that's mebbe all you should assume when dealing with a certain gentleman."

"What do you mean?"

"I've seen him strutting up the Cowgate by day and slinking down it by night. There's no a stone he'll leave unturned to cover his slimy tracks, nor a throat he'll leave uncut if what I hear's true."

"So why would Kilclath . .? " James was unsure of how to finish, but Davie was ahead of him.

"Middens must be raked to ken as much as he must ken." Davie paused ingenuously. "Seems that this time he's passed the job on to you and me."

James fell silent, but his attention was soon diverted by the magnificence of the scenery that opened up around them. No countryside could have appeared less like a midden as they cantered through neat settlements and bright cornfields, until at last they turned the corner of a deceptively low foothill and the Vale of Allomore spread itself out before their eyes. Instinctively they both drew their horses to a standstill.

"In the name…!" breathed Davie.

James said nothing. He had no words to describe what he felt as he gazed down on the stately stone extension of an ancient keep reflected in the still waters of the lake. In those dark waters must dart the descendents of the pike and trout his father had netted as a boy. The cedars, horse chestnuts and broad-leaved laburnums, the ash brushing the lake's surface and the oaks spreading around it must be the very ones that he had climbed. Northwards the purple mountains merged into the misty horizon, and behind them, James knew, were more of their territories, stretching to the next firth and beyond. This had been his father's valley and with his first sight of it James vowed that one day it would be his.

"So this is what he's squandering at the tables," muttered Davie.

"Squandering?"

"They say he's gambled away half his fortune. And maybe that's what our friend's so feart of."

"Our friend," James echoed. "You say that in a strange way, Davie."

"A finger in every pie. A foot under every table."

"And you find that suspicious?"

Davie's expression was ingenuous. "What's it to me? I've never been any the worse for doing the Master's bidding. Play your cards right and neither will you."

* * *

"So are you sleeping any easier in your bed?"

Bella pursed her painted lips, opening a network of tiny pathways across the powder that plastered her cheeks. Since Kilclath did not reply, she added, "I hope Hannah was the last of them - apart from the one you keep sweet under your own roof." But her sentence ended in a splutter. With a look of alarm he handed her a cloth and she coughed for a solid minute. When she passed the cloth back to him it was more red than white.

"Bella! Bella!" he sighed. "You must take more care."

"Dinna go thinking I'm ready for the final cough quite yet!" Her eyes glinted. "And you'll aye have Jean. Though I've warned you, Geordie, and I've warned you well." She lowered her voice. "You need a son and there's no good looking to any more whores. In the name o' God can you no' just decide on one of the brood mares that swish their petticoats everywhere you go?"

"Where is the urgency?"

She snorted, bringing on another fit of coughing. When she recovered she managed to splutter, "Does he need to come back from the grave to remind you?"

His eyes flashed back at her. "His vices have stalked me from the day I was born. Secrecy was my inheritance, and deceit will be my son's. Do you wonder at my delay?"

"Did he give a damn for his whore when he sired you?" She knew how to whip up his rage just as she had known how to manipulate his father's. Her voice rasped on. "The Old Fox risked it all for him, Geordie. No' for you. For the son you must sire."

"And Jean?"

"Ah ha." Her own eyes were slyer than a vixen's "I promised her mother and I'm a woman of my word. I'm no' saying you won't be willing to provide, but …." Her voice fell to a sinister whisper. "None o' us ken what might be lying at the foot o' the next wynd. I've made sure all that's mine will be hers - and what's more she'll never have to raise so much as a skirt for it. The papers are safe with Mr MacVey, all signed and sealed and one of these fine days delivered. That's what we've done for Madge Petrie between us, Geordie." She paused and fixed him with her steely eye. "I think she'd be well enough pleased, don't you?"

* * *

James and Davie's boots rang hollow across the empty hallway. The servant held out his hand in a surly warning to proceed no further, then retreated through a doorway and disappeared. Although the March day was warm it was hung with dampness, and the chill in the air seemed to complement the niggling odour of neglect. James raised his eyes along the line of portraits climbing the wide marble staircase. The Hamiltons were a handsome and haughty breed. Vain too, judging by the extravagance of their costumes, and all with lean, fine-boned faces and defiant eyes.

He felt the weight of Davie's scrutiny. The caddie gave him a nudge and a wink and muttered, "Let's hope he doesna recognise you."

"Do you think there's a chance of it?" James breathed, his eyes shining. He took several steps forwards, careless that he was breaching the servant's line of demarcation. The portrait nearest him gazed condescendingly down: John Alexander Hamilton, tenth Earl of Allomore.

"My great-grandfather," he whispered, and stared back, unable to wrench his eyes away even as he heard a door close at the other side of the hallway. Davie cleared his throat significantly.

"I believe you are come from Kilclath." It was a woman's voice. When he turned to face its owner it occurred to James that he had seldom seen an unhappier looking figure. She came closer, advancing with a weary tread, her expression displaying complete indifference both to themselves and their purpose. Yet James found it oddly difficult to take his eyes from her face. It seemed to him that the portraits on the wall displayed more animation.

"With a message for the Laird," Davie broke in sharply. "In the form of a letter," and he nodded with even more significance in James' direction. James finally managed to pull himself together. He reached inside his waistcoat.

"To be delivered into no other hand but his own," he declared, seeing her outstretched arm, "I am very sorry your ladyship."

"Do not be ridiculous," she retorted. "Kilclath knows full well that I am privy to every aspect of my husband's affairs."

"I am sorry," James repeated.

Allomore's wife gazed at him with an expression bordering on contempt. Davie shot him an anxious glance and wondered whether he should intervene again.

"What is your name?" Her question was curt.

"James Bothwell, your ladyship."

"And your position?"

"I am in the process of moving chambers to become the Master's clerk."

"Moving from which chambers?"

"From lawyer MacVey, your ladyship."

Her eyes grew suspicious. "My husband is indisposed and unable to receive visitors at present. Why has Kilclath sent you and not his usual messenger?"

Davie stepped forward quickly. "We have another errand in Stirling, your ladyship and Hughie has not the English for it."

She half closed her eyes, nodded slowly, and turned away as if coming to decision. Davie cocked his head in anticipation while James continued to take in the flawed grandeur of their surroundings.

"Then please wait here," she said, and crossed the hall to the third doorway. She disappeared and James and Davie exchanged uneasy glances as a different servant appeared from the back quarters and regarded them with a cold and hostile stare. Almost straight away Allomore's wife returned.

"Please follow me," she instructed and held open the door.

James hoped she did not notice his hesitation. He felt the pressure of Davie's hand at the base of his spine, a little shove to help him on his way, as they followed her into the drawing room where James finally came face to face with his father's successor.

Allomore made no attempt to rise from his chair beside the magnificent stone chimneypiece. Above it their family arms were entwined with the arms of the Royal House of Stuart while bright tapestries alive with classical scenes hung on three walls. The entire back wall housed the library, row upon row and column upon column of ancient tomes and manuscripts. Beyond the velvet draped window James could see the second courtyard, half enclosed and half open onto the green and yellow sweep of lawns patched with daffodils. The impression caught his breath and a little gasp escaped his lips before he turned his attention towards his kinsman.

He was drunk, of that there could be no question. The reek of stale brandy oozed from his every pore and the focus of his bloodshot eyes skewed from his wife to Davie to himself without showing a single sign of recognition. James reached inside his waistcoat and took out Kilclath's letter. He handed it to Allomore who had the presence of mind to examine the seal before casting it down onto the floor beside him.

"Satisfied?" he hissed.

"I apologise if you have been inconvenienced, sir," James told him, backing away from his malice. "But we have our instructions."

An even more alarming leer sprang to Allomore's eyes and James backed still further. "Then tell the Master that I have people still to see." Allomore hissed. For a moment it looked as if he might get up but clearly the effort was too great. James could see that beneath his stained trews his legs were spindles.

"Would we tell him which people?" Davie ventured.

"He'll find that out soon enough."

Allomore reached for the brandy bottle and took up his glass with a shaking hand. He fumbled to fill it, but his aim and strength were insufficient. James watched in dismay as his wife took the bottle and performed the operation for him. Allomore snatched the glass from her without a word of gratitude, not that she seemed to expect one. She turned back to James and Davie.

"Well gentlemen, your mission is accomplished. Will that be all?"

James and Davie backed towards the door, which was now held ajar by the same servant who had admitted them. Something made James turn for a final look at his kinsman. He had slumped back in his chair and was gazing dully into the fire's embers. Beside him his wife crouched and grappled beneath his foot for the letter.

* * *

Far into the night that shone silver through her window Christie lay remembering her times with Donald MacSomhairle, knowing she would neither forget nor deny what they had shared. The pain would become just another part of her, to add to all the other disappointments and heartaches, and her life would move on in yet another unknown direction. Deciding that sleep was impossible, she threw a wrap around her shoulders and crept from her room, stepping over clansmen with half closed eyes sprawled in their stupors on the staircase. She tiptoed across the shadowed hallway, in a silence somehow deepened by the memory of the day's excitement.

In the cool night air she slipped down the track to where the mountain ash and willows stretched their arms across the grey streaks in the night sky, scarcely feeling the chill beneath her thin nightclothes as she gazed for the last time out over the lochan, shining and rippling in the moonlight beneath the awesome mass of Beinn Feodag.

It was some time before she realised she was not alone.

"The moon is in your hair tonight," Andrew said softly. He gathered a strand of it and held it against the silver light. Then he eased her around to face him. "You have seen the glen in all its moods. All save this one."

"The time for goodbye," she whispered.

His voice was still gentle. "I do not believe it is goodbye."

Christie tried to smile. "We still have each other. And James and I will be together again."

Andrew fell silent, remembering the words of Old Angus Ban. "You will return but twice. And each returning will break your heart." He did not feel that his heart was any more broken with this return. And how could a person return to a place he had never truly left? He forced a smile of his own and shrugged his shoulders. What were Angus's predictions anyway but the rantings of a senile old man? He could not actually remember a single one of them that had come true.

* * *

Donald looked down at Helen's sleeping face. A smile still lurked around the corners of her mouth as she nestled her head against the cool linen of her pillow. He imagined he must be the only man left in Glenshellich with a sober head, but he had needed one to be sure of being gentle with her. Now they were truly man and wife, and there had been beauty in their coming together. The moonlight bathed her features with its silver sheen and he drew down the cover to let it spread across her firm breasts and smooth hips. For a moment he imagined Hugh's voice.

"I doubt you will regret leaving the whores to the rest of us when you get that beauty under your bedcovers."

Hugh was in Rome, but when he returned Donald would tell him he had been right. He was so much more fortunate than he deserved.

196

He ran his fingers lightly from Helen's nipple to the dark triangle of hair between her legs. Immediately she stirred. He eased his arms under her back and gazed into her face.

"I have the most beautiful wife a man could wish for," he whispered, and prayed that she would never glimpse the emptiness that had taken the place of his heart.

CHARLIE

In the early days of July eight men gathered in the French town of Nantes. One had dressed himself as a student of the Parisian Scots College. He was between twenty and thirty years old, tall and well built, with a thin face, clear complexion and newly sprung beard. His name, he said, was Douglas and he had endured eighteen frustrating months in France, restless and confused by broken promises and conflicting intelligence. Now he found himself in possession of two ships: the privateer *Du Teilly* and the *Elisabeth*, a sixty-eight-gun frigate.

His intuition told him they might be all he needed to sail to his destiny.

* * *

Dusk fell across Edinburgh. The tenements reared on either side of the Lawnmarket as its citizens spilled and mingled under the pillared piazzas. Andrew Stewart and Christie "Bothwell", handkerchief to her face, elbowed through them as best they could. After two months the smell of the street still caused Christie's eyes to water, but she had been reassured to find that she could still be enticed by a city's vitality. Although there was little in the architecture of Edinburgh to remind her of Rome its inhabitants were not so different and Christie was fast becoming as riveted by Auld Reekie's comings and goings as her landlady. Only occasionally did she let herself remember the soft voices of Catriona and Domhnull, the notes of Kenneth's pibrochs and Fraser's tuneless ballads, the sunset over the Giant's Mountain. Never did she allow herself to think of Donald.

"Companion to the Countess of Dalvey," Andrew grinned as they turned into Alison's close. "It seems you will be baited and hooked before long, one way or another."

"As Miss Bothwell or Miss Hamilton?"

"I daresay Miss Hamilton would be the better long term prospect." Then he paused and added seriously. "I suppose we both must think of making new lives."

"Lives based on deceit?"

"Not necessarily."

"I will choose a particularly vain and insensitive husband," she declared. "One who prefers his whores and leaves me to my own devices, whatever I decide they will be. I will demand his indulgence, but not his curiosity. I will raise our children to be honourable citizens of whatever king is on the throne. And I will be content."

"You will not."

"I can persuade myself into anything. I have no expectations, no illusions, no interest whatsoever in romance. I will be resolute and practical, as I have been for most of my life."

"I will not attach myself to a wife," Andrew vowed. "Ever."

Christie was suddenly serious. "Then that would be a shocking waste. Any woman would be fortunate to have you. Why should we imagine love to be essential for a successful marriage?"

* * *

Christie could not know that an identical thought was at the very same moment crossing the mind of the Master of the Stones as he gazed into the dusk descending outside the Menteiths' drawing room window.   He heard the rustle of his hostess's hooped gown behind him and turned reluctantly, for the stars and the darkness were more appropriate to his mood than the glittering soiree she had arranged in his honour.

"You are pensive tonight, Kilclath," she murmured.

A flicker of irritation stirred inside him.   Gatherings such as this grew increasingly tiresome, essential no longer to someone of his established rank and reputation.

"I am contemplating the heavens," he sighed.   "An awe-inspiring prospect, even from our less than celestial surroundings."

She simpered, then flashed him a knowing smile.   "Could it be that you are hankering after your glen? Much stirs in the north, I hear."

"Much that is no concern of mine."   His tone was deceptively casual as he looked across the room at her daughter's carefully powdered ringlets, her embroidered silk gown, the dull white skin stretched over fleshy breasts.   Could he bear to share a bed with Margaret Menteith?   For all her attributes he did not believe he could.   But could he bear to share a bed with anyone after Jean?

Yet the matter of Kilclath and its succession grew more pressing.   He must secure it sooner rather than later.   He knew he need only say the word to Margaret.   Her eager eyes even now devoured him from across the room.   The Lady of the Stones, he reflected darkly.   There had been a vacancy for too long, a vacancy that left a chasm not even a hundred Margaret Menteiths could a quarter fill.   Perhaps not even a hundred Jeans.

"Will we adjourn for dancing?" Margaret suggested, the predatory gleam still shining from her eye.   Kilclath drew a resigned breath and offered her his arm.

He thought it unlikely that he would be offering her anything more.

* * *

"A fine gentleman, the Master of the Stones," Alison remarked. "He was speaking most highly of you, Christie. I wouldna be the slightest bit surprised if that wasna the reason he called this afternoon."

Andrew winked across at Christie. "Now would that not be the perfect match for you?"

Alison snorted. "More caps in this city have been set at George Campbell than lifted to the governor. However," she went on, "he has left an invitation for yourself and myself to dine with him the evening after next." She could barely contain her glee. "What with you become companion to the Countess, and your brother safe set up as Kilclath's clerk, your family fortunes would seem to be on the right road at long last."

Andrew pushed the thought of his own brother from his mind. He did not dare to imagine Donald's reaction to this latest association. Andrew had misgivings of his own about Kilclath's interest in the Hamiltons, yet the Master of the Stones was in an undeniably better position than anyone in Glenshellich to help their advancement.

"If only we were able to acknowledge our family," Christie said softly, then added hastily, "grateful as we are of course for the loan of your name, Alison."

"Who's to ken what might be getting acknowledged before too long," Alison observed. "If any store's to be set by what rumour would have us believe."

* * *

The young man leaned on the ship's rail and trained his eyes on the eastern horizon. The vague humps of the Outer Hebrides beckoned silently through the mist, as The *Du Teillay* drew closer to the island of Barra. Above it an eagle hovered and drifted among the clouds.

"The king of the birds is come to welcome your royal highness upon your arrival in Scotland," observed the frail Marquis of Tullibardine, trying to suppress the quickening of own his heart at the thought of his own lost title. But their second ship, the *Elisabeth*, with its men and supplies had been engaged and forced to return to Brest; another of the misfortunes that seemed to dog them at every turn.

He wondered if there had ever been a worse prepared venture to reclaim a kingdom.

* * *

For the first time in his life James Hamilton could feel almost satisfied with his lot. His employment in the offices of Kilclath had finally made him a person to be reckoned with. The Master of the Stones not only consulted him on matters of importance, but seemed to set great store by his opinions. James had the sense that there was very little Kilclath's patronage could not achieve and the prospect brought a new jauntiness to his step as he made his way towards his sister's lodgings.

"My!" Alison cried when she saw him. "It's a fine gentleman you are tonight!"

"My week's wages were the down payment," he admitted with a wink. "But when I accompany such elegant ladies to dine the least I can do is to look my best."

"And do we come up to your standard?" Christie challenged, with a twirl of fine silk from the Countess's own wardrobe.

"We will be the best rigged trio in the city tonight," James boasted.

Andrew suppressed a twinge of apprehension as Christie gave a gracious smile and held out her arm.

"My wrap, then, sir, and we will step out."

"With the greatest of pleasure," James replied, and presented an arm to each lady.

Alone now but for Kirsty, Andrew reached uncharacteristically for the brandy bottle. He had intended to begin his overdue letter to Helen, but for once she was not foremost in his mind. His uneasy thoughts had dragged him back to Bella Galbraith's secret attic where he imagined himself staring down once more at the wooden pallet covered with its threadbare blanket. Only this time he did not dare pull back the corner to reveal what lay beneath it. He was too afraid of whose face he might see.

* * *

Mhairi flung a plate of stew onto the kitchen table in front of Hughie. At the same time she cast an almost gloating eye in Jean's direction. The jarring of the metal accorded well with Jean's mood. It was painful enough to have lost her strongest link with her past, without having to face the long dreaded prospect of returning to it. But all the same she was determined not to give these two an insight into her anxiety. She had always known this day would come. It was not so much the thought of the Master abandoning her, for she did not believe he ever would, but the possibility of him falling in love that she found impossible to bear.

Hughie scowled, first into his meal and then at Mhairi. He and Jean were not often allies, but her instinct told her that tonight they shared the same impulse to wipe the smug expression from the servant woman's face.

Mhairi darted to the window as soon as they heard the creak of the sedan chair, then stepped back to afford Jean a better view. James Bothwell extended his hand and Jean watched his sister slowly emerge onto the sidewalk. As they stepped closer a sinking sense of change settled over her spirits. Hughie swallowed and belched into his tankard. He did not move to the window but he knew as well as Jean that this was indeed the moment she had dreaded. This girl with her anxious yet defiant eyes, her unconscious dignity, and her natural beauty was without shadow of doubt someone who had the power to steal the Master's heart.

* * *

In the drawing room Kilclath rose to greet his guests. He took Alison's hand and bent over it charmingly, but his dark eyes held Christie's for seconds longer than convention required.

"This is a pleasure long overdue," he said simply.

"You are very kind," Christie answered. "In every way."

Kilclath smiled. "Your brother is becoming a valuable asset. He has a talent for anecdote and an admirable memory."

Gavin MacVey cleared his throat and apologised for the absence of his wife who was suffering one of her frequent fainting spells. The evening proceeded pleasantly and without mention of either Glenshellich or Allomore. It was Christie who first made reference to their highland connections.

"I have twice now passed through the Valley of Stones," she told Kilclath. "It must have been an awe-inspiring place to have been raised." She waited for his reaction, but he remained silent. "James and I have spoken this evening only of ourselves," she went on. "While you have told us next to nothing of your own life."

For the first time she noticed the heavy-eyed servant woman quietly rearranging the plates on the dresser beside the door. Kilclath also flickered a glance in her direction.

"I am pleased that you found Kilclath impressive," he answered, and turned towards Alison with a wry smile. "And not oppressive, as so many have judged."

"My opinion of your mountains and glens is common enough kent," she retorted. "Though no-one's ever heard me say yours is any more oppressive than your neighbour's."

The ring of a spoon falling from the dresser made Christie turn suddenly. The servant woman bent hastily to pick it up, and then appeared to preoccupy herself with carefully returning it to its set.

"I have not set foot in Kilclath for a year or more," the Master answered, ignoring the interruption. "In truth there has been too much to occupy me in the city." He chose also to ignore the less than subtle glance exchanged between Alison and Gavin. In the brief silence that followed the servant woman began to make a slow but purposeful way towards the table. Christie noticed that she did not for one moment take her eyes from her master's face. She wondered if it was her imagination that his voice grew tighter. "But I will return before the summer is over."

"The Valley of Stones!" Christie sighed. The servant woman's calloused hand seemed to tremble as it lifted the plate from her place and Kilclath kept his eyes trained on her face. "They say your father was a man of great influence," Christie went on blithely.

This time there could be no mistaking the servant woman's nervousness. The plate fell from her hand and in an incongruous but strangely touching gesture Kilclath reached out and gently covered her wrist.

"He was indeed, Christie," he answered smoothly, before letting his fingers slide back onto the tablecloth. "In the north he was known as The Fox, for he was quick and sly." He sighed. Alison and Gavin looked at each other again, yet Kilclath's next words seemed to surprise them. "You speak of your own father with affection, though he was never judged a success in the world's eyes. Many reckoned my father great, but few could feel much warmth towards him. I am afraid he inspired fear rather than respect." He was looking at Christie, yet strangely she did not believe his words were directed at her. Yet who else could they be intended for? She looked uneasily at Alison who gazed innocently back. Kilclath smiled almost sadly as he continued. "To us that may seem a sad epitaph. Yet I do not believe it is one which would cause him any regret."

"And your mother?" Christie continued. "What of her? Was she known as The Lady of the Stones?"

She realised immediately that this was a question too far. The servant woman backed quickly from the table, in her haste sending a vase of flowers clattering from the corner of the dresser to spill across the floor. A shadow seemed to pass over Kilclath's face as he stared at it. His fingers gripped the stem of his wine glass and his knuckles gleamed in the candlelight. James shot him an anxious glance.

"Christie has an unfortunate habit of prying into other people's business," he remarked, trying to make his voice sound casual. His sister picked up the warning.

"I am sorry," she faltered. "I had no wish to..."

But Kilclath had already regained any composure he might have lost.

"Of course you did not wish to pry." The wine clung thickly to the sides of his glass. Both he and Christie continued to gaze at it while Gavin and Alison kept their eyes fixed on the tablecloth. "It is true that I seldom speak of my mother," Kilclath went on with a short sigh. "I am afraid I remember little of her. As I believe was the case with both of you, I lost her when I was very young." Again the glass twisted in his hand and its contents swirled crimson in the candlelight. Christie glanced across the room, but there was no attendant now at the dresser: the servant woman had not returned.

Down in the kitchen Jean was sewing beside the fireplace. She lifted her head as the door swung open, but Mhairi did not spare her a glance. Her focus was entirely on Hughie. They spoke in their own tongue, and Jean could make sense of only the occasional word.

"She asks about the Old Fox."

"What business it of hers?"

"She is forward, a hussy."

"She must be kept away." Hughie's head jerked grudgingly in Jean's direction. "Better with her."

Once again Mhairi appeared to dismiss Jean entirely.

"He will not keep her away. And it will be the same as before."

Hughie sprang to his feet and pulled out his dirk. Jean gathered up her sewing in alarm and shrank back into the fire's recess. But Mhairi was undaunted. Her unprecedented elevation to the dining room had added massively to her stature.

"She is from Glenshellich."

Jean recognised that name at least. Why were they so interested in Glenshellich?

"She is from Rome."

That was what Jean had believed. She jumped up and forced herself between them.

"What is it?" she demanded, and heard the edge that fear had given to her voice.

Hughie turned away with a scowl, but Mhairi moved closer, her breath warm against Jean's cheek. This time she spoke in English.

"It is for you to keep him from her," she urged. "And make him want only you."

"How can I?" Jean cried. "He needs a lady, not a ...." She stopped herself. Both of them were staring at her, challenging her, daring her: Mhairi with a new intensity and Hughie with his old dark menace. Then his lip curled in scorn. He knew as well as she did how powerless she was. She might not have been a whore, but even the Master could never make her into a lady: least of all the Lady of the Stones.

* * *

Fresh flounders hissed and spat over a bare fire inside the cottage of Angus MacDonald on the tiny island of Eriskay. The young abbe had been guided there for shelter, and now he stood in the doorway deciding which discomfort was preferable: the choking smoke inside or the irritating cloud of midge that hung on the evening air. He had sent a message proclaiming his true identity across the two-mile stretch of water separating Eriskay from the seat of Alexander MacDonald of Boisdale on the island of South Uist. Boisdale had already guaranteed his support. The young man returned to his seat at the fireside, for it was easy to ignore smarting eyes when a heart held so much hope.

* * *

"My dear Helen," wrote Andrew. "We are delighted to hear how happily you are settling into your new life as Mistress of Glenshellich. I do not need to write that we think of you often, and with a great deal of envy on occasions like today when the heat makes the city air almost intolerable. Yet despite our small discomforts we are well and considerably occupied. Christie has become an indispensable asset to the Countess who will scarcely hold a gathering without her, though I at least would prefer it if she had been allowed to create less of a stir. Questions have been asked as to her exact relationship with Alison and we have had to invent a connection going back at least four generations. Their other kinsman has fortunately kept to his estates and been fed the story by their new benefactor that they have found patronage south of the border. In fact . ...." Andrew paused and wondered just what he should include in his letter on the subject of that gentleman. There seemed little doubt that he was taking more than a friendly interest in Christie, and why that should continue to make him uneasy Andrew had no idea. He bore Kilclath no grudges and had no reason, Jean Petrie notwithstanding, to consider him as anything other than a man of honour. And yet ... He gave a long sigh and decided to mention the Master of the Stones only on account of his part in the advancement of Christie's brother. "James has begun his legal studies and has taken to them with great enthusiasm. We can only conclude that his patron has some scheme of his own for James's advancement, but any dealings with the scoundrel on whom that would depend must be treated with the utmost distrust. I hope I make my meaning clear. Alison grows increasingly convinced that the fortunes of our entire country are about to change. She has been insisting on this, of course, ever since I have known her, but it does appear that at present more than just the usual rumours are in the wind ...."

* * *

Much might have been expected of MacDonald of Boisdale, yet he had brought the young man nothing but more bad tidings. Neither he nor his kinsman in Sleat, not to mention his old allies MacLeod of MacLeod or MacLean of Cairnill, were prepared to join a campaign so lacking in support from the French king. Now the young man and his companions were moving southwards, trekking to the seaweed shore of Loch Moidart and to the house of another MacDonald, this time of Kinlochmoidart. And as word of them spread so did the doubts and the warnings. Surely no rational leader could foresee the slightest prospect of the young man succeeding? Most advised him to return to France and await a more auspicious day. But the young man had waited long enough. He had come to claim and win the crown of his ancestors or perish in the attempt. To prove to them the strength of his resolve he sent the *Du Teilly*, his last link with the continent, back home to France.

* * *

Henrietta Menteith glowered across the room at the beautiful girl who sat between the Countess of Dalvey and Alison Bothwell. She was furious to observe that Alison's cheeks had acquired a rosy bloom and that her eyes displayed an irritating sparkle.

"I hear Margaret has been receiving particular attention from your husband's young assistant," Alison murmured. "She is fairly spoilt for choice these days, yet still no commitment."

"And I hear," Henrietta countered, "that your Mr Fettes has galloped away from his father's estate and off to the west."

"Did you now, Henrietta." This was news to Alison, though she did not intend Henrietta to know it. "I wonder what can have enticed him in that direction."

"I wonder that you need to ask."

"Now ladies," the Countess interrupted. "I daresay we all ken fine well what we're alluding to." She paused thoughtfully. "Though this time it does seem the stories might be worth heeding ".

Almost as the words were leaving her lips Hugh Fettes was gazing glumly down the line of sweeping hills that bordered the dark waters of Loch Shiel. Three glens met at the spot the Prince had chosen for his rallying point, but as the sun began its descent there was no sign of the hoped for support. A few hundred men and some cattle drovers would not be enough to seize a throne, even men with the stout hearts and true dedication of these, whose company Hugh had shared for almost a week.

Then, faintly in the distance, he heard the sound of pipes, a thin skirl growing steadily stronger and closer as over the mountain appeared the bright plaids of the Camerons, following their chieftain Lochiel down a crooked path to the shore. On they came in their hundreds, striding rank upon rank, cheering as loudly as those who had waited for them, until the hollow where they stood seemed full to overflowing.

"This is truly the time!" breathed Hugh to the man of Clanranald who towered proudly beside him. It had come at last, the day they had dreamed of for so long. Before him, framed by the cloud-capped mountains stretching down the horizon was his prince, regal, dazzling and home at last. Hugh's heart swelled to know that he had been one of the first to kiss his hand. He followed as King James' standard was carried across the river to be blessed by Bishop Hugh MacDonald and his bonnet soared higher than any Cameron's as they watched the red silk with its inset square of white spread defiantly in the wind. Even before the evening saw hundreds more of Keppoch's men flock to the standard all of those present recognised the swell of excitement spreading throughout the land.

* * *

Kenneth MacCombie closed the door of his grandfather's house without looking behind him. He did not believe in omens, but Angus's life was entirely governed by them and Kenneth had no wish to leave for battle with an unlucky backward glance. He told himself he must remember that when he made his farewells to Meg and Domhnull, though he doubted if it would be possible to resist a final look at them from the far side of the Watcher's Stone. He shifted the pipes on his shoulder. He had not yet devised the tune that would accompany his clan to its prince, but he was confident those notes would be given him when the moment arrived.

Sunset was at least an hour away. Kenneth paused on the shore of the lochan and gazed into the silver framed clouds that stretched across the water. He must have seen ten thousand sunsets, each one unique and extraordinary. He wondered how many had found their way into his pibrochs. More than he might imagine, perhaps, yet he could summon to mind none but this, just as he could keep but the one pibroch in his head at a time. He smiled at the notion. Perhaps that was all life required of a person: the one moment, the one sunset, the one tune.

By the time he reached his cottage the evening had already altered. The silver light had flooded the clouds and edged them with shining pink. Soon the sun would grow heavy and its red light would carve a place for the giant's mountain against the darkening sky. He gazed across the lochan for one final moment before he stooped inside the door of his cottage.

Meg was already in their bed, waiting for him, naked beneath the thin summer blanket. He laid the pipes beside her, lifted the blanket and gazed down at her body's smooth beauty. Kenneth would willingly have traded a future without her for one night in her arms. He had won her astonishingly and she had brought him delight beyond imagining. She was a miracle he gave thanks for every day.

He kicked off his brogues, unwrapped his plaid and lay down beside her.

"I heard tell," she said softly, "that the old McCrimmon pipers did not take arms in battle."

He smiled. "Then your ears deceived you. You should know as well as I do there is always the moment when we throw down the pipes and take up the broadsword."

"Do not you take up a broadsword, Kenneth Mhor. I need you to come back to me."

"And what if I were to promise that this will not be our last night together?"

"You promised to take me to America."

"That was not a promise exactly."

"To see my mother."

He sighed, but saw that her eyes were twinkling. Sometimes it was impossible to separate her laughter from her tears. He took a strand of her black hair and held it to his face. As he recalled her mother's hair had been a light shade of brown.

"That is supposing she is there. Which I doubt. And I hear tell that America is a very large place."

"You are right. You did not promise," she smiled. "Anyway, you cannot leave MacSomhairle and he will not leave his glen. And I will not leave you."

"Are you sure it is me you would not leave?"

She studied him for a long time. He did not believe there could be such beauty anywhere in the world. Then she took her finger and ran it gently over his face, down the straight bridge of his nose and over the lines that had begun to etch themselves around his lips. Unable to take his eyes from hers he whispered, "I have seen forty winters."

"And you have taken something special from each one," she whispered. "There are those in this glen could see a hundred winters and be no wiser." She paused, never taking her eyes from him. He was enraptured, enchanted by her. "I hope MacSomhairle will not be one of them."

He drew in his breath sharply. She should not dare to criticise her chieftain, even if she might be better placed to do so than most.

"I never loved Donald MacSomhairle," she whispered. "I did not understand what love was when I lay with him. I understood it only when I came to you."

The disclosure was unsought and almost impossible to believe but Kenneth felt his heart swell inside him. MacSomhairle was handsome and tall and proud. He was young while Kenneth was grown weathered and wiry. As if she could read his mind she said. "It was not the same thing at all. With MacSomhairle it was a game for children. Yet I have not given you your own son, Kenneth Mhor."

Kenneth could have told her that Domhnull was more than a son. He and his mother were so much more than a man could dream of.

"He is my son in every way but one," he said softly.

She put her arms around him and they lay together, still and silent. The sun's last rays threw the curves of her body into light and shadow and as he ran his hands over the cool flesh he felt his spirit lift and soar. For a strange moment he felt part of another world, a world where so many had gone before. If he were to die in this war it would not be the end, of that he was certain.

"Then if I do not return you will not let him forget me," was all he said.

She rolled over and stretched her body down the length of Kenneth's own.

"How could he forget you? He has your music in his soul."

* * *

Donald's eyes were prepared for a deeper darkness than this crimson dying of the day. He turned off the track before he reached the clachan and took the less obvious way to the last hut before the mountain began its steep ascent. The evening had been fine and he had explained to Helen that he might be late in coming to her side. He had last minute business to attend to in the clachan, final arrangements to make before the next day's march.

He could not let her guess he was on secret business, business that she more than any must not suspect. It was bad enough that old ghosts, one in particular, were watching and judging a mission of which they could not fail to disapprove.

The door of Beathag's hut was unlatched, making him wonder if the old witch had been expecting him. He had not ventured across her threshold for many a year, but the familiar smell immediately assaulted his nostrils, the noxious mixture of smoke, effluent and rancid meat, the suggestion of vermin decaying in spaces only they could find. He did not sense a human presence but he knew she was there. The fancy took him that she might be fading to a wraith herself, slowly preparing to disappear into the mountain mists.

"So Domhnull MacSomhairle," she hissed from the shadows. "You have come to bid me goodbye."

He was almost relieved to hear her voice as strong as ever.

"Will it be goodbye?" he asked, as she stepped forward, her body stooped and so twisted that her head barely reached his waist. He crouched beside her until their eyes were level and he wondered if the stinging smoke wove its own spell, giving mortal eyes the power to penetrate the hut's darkness.

Beathag craned her head until their faces were only inches apart.

"Tell me!" he whispered.

"I cannot."

"It was my father's order. My father is dead."

"Your father is watching me. They are all watching me. I cannot tell you, Domhnull MacSomhairle."

"Even though the blood of us both runs through my sons veins."

She gave a sudden cackle and fell back, as if the smoking embers of her fire were drawing her inside them. She crouched, watching him, then she laughed again, not a malicious cackle this time, but a chortle of genuine amusement.

"One day you will understand the joke, Domhnull MacSomhairle, even if you will not find it so funny." Her voice turned to a shrill command. "Go back to your wife. There is but one person who will hear the *Faisneachd* from my lips."

Donald fought back his fury. He was the chieftain, with power of life and death, especially over malevolent old hags like her. She had been spared the wrath of the clachan too often, and repaid kindness with spite, tolerance with malice. He gripped her bony wrist, but its vigour so shocked him that he let go at once. Surely such strength in so frail a body could have no other than a supernatural source. Or was he slowly going mad himself? She laughed again and the sound chilled his soul.

"So you have come on a wasted journey, on this precious night," she scorned. "For it is I, the lowest of the clachan, and not you, our chieftain, who must do your father's bidding."

"Your chieftain can command you, Beathag. On pain of death."

"There is higher chief than you, Domhnull MacSomhairle."

Her breath rasped behind broken teeth and Donald choked back the stench rising in his nostrils.

"There are no shadows in the glen tonight," she went on. "But there are shadows in your heart. There will be another such night, and you will remember my words."

He stood up and swept her aside, sending her sprawling across the room. But she only twisted to face him again.

"Do not leave Glenshellich in anger," she urged. "For be sure that if you do it will never receive back your soul."

* * *

Euan MacMichael gently laid aside the tools of his father's healing. He had picked them up and examined them one by one as if to gain strength from the knowledge that his father had used them. There was no healer now in the clachan. It was a huge source of regret to Euan that he had not been blessed with his father's gifts. He did not think he had been blessed with any gifts at all, not his mother's wisdom or cleverness. Not any of it.

Catriona moved behind him and stroked his shoulder.

"Your time has come, Eochain, my son. And you must stay strong, stay far from the heat of battle, for much will depend on you in the days ahead."

"Do you think …?" he began, before his will failed, for they had not spoken of the *Faisneachd* since the night he had heard it. But she knew what question had died on his lips.

"There may be many wars ahead, or there may be none. It will not be easy for you to go from your glen, Eochain."

"I have no business with kings and governments."

"Maybe that is not why you are called."

"I am called to serve and protect MacSomhairle."

216

She gazed at him sadly. "MacSomhairle is not my chieftain," she whispered, "and although I love him more than many mothers love their own sons, I love you more. You are more special to me than anyone in the world."

He reached out and took her hand. He believed her, but he knew that her words made her sad, sad in a way he could sense but not understand.

"One day, Eochain," she breathed, "when this war is over, I promise I will have a special story to tell you."

* * *

Donald stumbled past their cottage and along the shore of the lochan. On this, the eve of the day he had dreamed of all his life, he was closer to despair than ever he could remember. He was not worthy to lead his clan like those legendary warriors who had gone before him. He had not grown into the man he had imagined in his childhood dreams, only a poor impersonator, a man of no integrity, unworthy of trust. For who could trust a man who had so betrayed himself and those he loved? Even a half-crazed wretch like Beathag was his superior in God's eyes.

But if death were to be his destiny he was ready to embrace it. He would become a soldier with one aim and one intention. He could lay down his life for his prince.

"Where have you been, Donald," Helen asked as he slipped beneath the covers of their bed. She stroked the lines that framed the pain in his eyes and he took her hand. Tomorrow she would be alone, in a bed too big for only one.

"How can I hide my feelings and my fears?" he cried and heard his voice choke on a sob. He loved her. He knew he loved her. For many husbands these tender feelings would be more than enough.

"Promise me this, then, Donald," she whispered, "now while we are alone together."

"What is that?"

"Promise that whatever happens you will come home to me."

He stared down into her face, so filled with love for him that he thought his heart would break, and knew he could promise her nothing.

* * *

Domhnull MacSomhairle, chieftain of Glenshellich, led his clansmen to join the Prince in the brilliant sunshine of a late August morning. Twenty-seven of them rounded the track under the shadow of the giant's mountain while the woman and children stood silently watching them go. Beathag slunk from her doorway as the company passed below her cottage. She might not have been laughing in the light of this bright morning but she was not sad and she was not angry. Her eyes were not on her chieftain but on his piper and the boy who scampered at his side. Beathag knew it was not the past but the future that was marching with them, and whether she witnessed it or not she was guaranteed her place. Watching from the glistening shoreline Angus Ban shared her conviction as he strained his ears for the last fading notes from his grandson's pipes and wiped away the tear that trickled from his marbled eye.

Euan turned his eyes to the hillside and called out impudently, "Make a spell for us to be victorious and send The Elector back to his German den, Beathag. Send us good weather and good luck and a happy result."

"Be not so proud, Euan MacMichael" she called back, and muttered to herself, "For there will be little pride at the end of your road."

Catriona looked up anxiously and placed her arm over Meg's shoulders. Together they watched as the men from Glenshellich strode behind their piper and chief into the distance, leaving the small boy who had halted at the Watcher's Stone to stare after them.

Euan looked back and tried to smile but his spirits could not be lifted, even by Kenneth's stirring pibroch. An older message clouded his heart. "*The river will run red but will not quench the flames. Their smoke will shroud Beinn Feodag for a hundred years.*"

* * *

Christie slipped determinedly through the morning crowd. Her steps gathered pace as she wove her way down the Canongate to Kilclath's chambers. Usually the Master did not hide his pleasure at her visits, but today he frowned, it seemed as much at her appearance as at the information she had come to seek.

"The rumours are quite correct," he replied. "This crazy army continues to advance. It is believed they will be banging on the city gates before the month's end."

Christie felt a reprehensible quickening of her heart. "Do you think -" she ventured, but stopped herself and turned away from Kilclath's dark scrutiny. "Alison and her friends are jubilant," she went on. "At times I am almost caught up in their excitement. And then there is Andrew..." Her voice faded. She could not admit that the thought of the Prince's army marching towards the city filled her with a strange exhilaration. Was it her father's spirit speaking to her, whispering that old dreams could come true after all? Was this the outcome that might even yet make all his years of disappointment worthwhile? Or was it simply that Alison's enthusiasm was dangerously infectious?

Kilclath sighed and flicked a speck of dust from his velvet cuff, as casually as he might have brushed aside an upstart prince. "The streets and my ears are resounding - extremely disagreeably - with their excitement."

Christie could not resist a mischievous smile. "They do all seem to wish the rebels well"

"No doubt they can be excused the attraction of a young and handsome adventurer marching with his loyal clans. It would be a picture to stir most hearts were it a true one. However, while I cannot guess the extent to which this intrepid force will proceed, it will certainly not reach the steps of the British throne."

"And your own position?"

He sighed again. "Those of my name have done their best to bring this country peace. We have acted with sound judgement and an eye to the future, yet to the MacDonalds, the Camerons... the Stewarts...... we are condemned as self-seeking traitors. Of course I have concerns when the world still places such value on the rash and the passionate."

She understood, but her divided loyalties were written plainly on her face.

Her brother snapped a rebuke. "I had not expected you to be so impressionable - after everything we have been through."

Christie sighed. "Perhaps all those years of listening to our father have affected me more than I imagined."

"Or your months in Glenshellich," James countered bitterly.

She turned away. Donald would be with the Prince, marching south with Euan and the men from the clachan to the sound of Kenneth MacCombie's pipes, staking their lives and futures as they had so long dreamed. She could picture them even now, their strides demolishing the miles to the capital, men born to the sword at last obeying its call.

"Suppose they succeed..." she ventured in a voice so quiet that she barely heard it herself. But the Master of the Stones was in no doubt of his answer.

"Impossible."

"They could take our city."

His eyes narrowed. That was a prospect he could not altogether discount. "Then in that unlikely event I would be compelled to take arms myself."

Christie stared at him in amazement. She found it impossible to imagine him as a soldier. He smiled at her reaction.

"Do not forget that I too am highlander and we are a martial race. I have my place in the Argyll militia. I would not hesitate to stand with them."

"And I would stand with you," James vowed stoutly.

Both stared at him, equally alarmed.

"James!" Christie breathed.

Kilclath looked from one to the other and the expression on his face would have been difficult to define. At last he drew a deep breath.

"Let us hope that neither of us will be called upon," he concluded and with a brief nod took himself to his inner office and closed the door behind him.

* * *

The bulk of the Hanoverian Army approached Dalwhinnie in the dying days of August. Close by the roads parted, one leading north-eastwards to Inverness, the other north-west over the Grey Wolf Mountains to Fort Augustus. Fourteen years earlier General Wade had identified the Corrieyairack Saddle as the only passable route for his road through this volcanic barrier. Thank God for him, thought Andra' MacAslan, not for the first time but more fervently than ever. He had precious little else to thank his maker for as he steered his empty cart over the last of the pass's precipitous traverses.

"As mean a chiel for a future monarch as ever I laid eyes on," he muttered to his leading garron. "Name my price! Daylight robbery and no question, and us left to take the long empty way back to Inverness."

Andra' had every right to his indignation. He had expected better, especially from the so-called prince's officers. Had he not travelled these routes since long before their last futile attempt to seize the British throne, bringing them their orders and their gossip? Yet still they had stripped him of his wares in less time than it would once have taken to haggle over the price of a yard of brocade.

And now they had set him on the road to meet the British Army head on. It was not long before his ears caught the low, regular drumming of the advancing red and white column. He swore softly into the distant dust it raised. This was indeed bad fortune. At least among the highlanders there had been the chance that some would recognise him and show mercy - for his life if not his merchandise. With a leaden heart he drew his garron to a halt and prepared himself for the inevitable.

General Cope, the column's commander, was a man with an unenviable decision to make. He knew that the road to Fort Augustus was swarming at the Pass with hostile highlanders, men accustomed to wild terrain, appearing and disappearing from the heather at will, men who had the advantage of numbers as well as surprise. Cope's soldiers were weary and dispirited, fearing an ambush behind every rock. Yet a retreat to Stirling would imply weakness and disrespect for those still loyal in the north-east highlands. His leading officer pulled up at the sight of the dishevelled peddlar perched dejectedly on his creaking cart.

"What is your business?" the officer demanded.

"A good question, your lordship, a very apt question indeed," Andra' began. General Cope heaved a weary sigh and drew impatiently on his reins. "My business was a fair and honest day's trade, but as you see the rebels have left me without so much as a candle to light me through tonight."

"Though you may be thankful to have escaped with your life," the officer observed.

"As might your own good selves," Andra' assured him. "For take my word there's ambushes set up all the way before and beyond the pass. And a plan to cut off the route at the Slochd Mhor."

This was exactly what General Cope had feared. A massacre was the likeliest outcome if he chose to lead his men that way.

"Then you may take your chances with us if you wish," he offered irritably.

Andra' appeared to consult with his three garrons. Each one nodded wisely back at him. "I am forever in your debt, sir."

The column passed quickly on and Andra' fell in gratefully behind.

So while General Cope retired with his men to Inverness the clans took the Pass of Corrieyairack and the road to Edinburgh, gathering recruits daily. On they came, through Blair Atholl to Perth and on again through Tullibardine, Bannockburn, Linlithgow, to the very borders of Scotland's capital.

Alison could scarcely contain her delight. James considered offering his services to the volunteer force the city elders were recruiting but received no encouragement from Kilclath who remained of the opinion that Edinburgh's panic was unnecessary. After all, the city guard was employed for the city's defence and as a force were surely better trained and equipped than the likes of James. Yet Kilclath had a more realistic concept of wild highlanders on the rampage than the hysterical citizens whose panic was soon approaching fever pitch.

"They don't know what to do!" cried Alison in glee as she returned from one of her frequent forays into the street. "There's a band formed in the College Yards thinking to oppose the Prince!" She snorted her contempt. "Fresh faced students against the might of the clans! They're coming, Christie! They're on their way! God be praised!" and she hung herself from the window to wave out at the swimming street. The clamour reached a crescendo as Christie moved to her side, only to see the band of unlikely volunteers marching clumsily up the Lawnmarket.

"Would you just take a look at them," Alison continued. "A sad bunch of ill fitted galoots as ever I saw," and she thrust her head out further and began to jeer louder than anyone.

"Alison!" cried Christie, half in amusement but mostly in alarm at the prospect of the Prince's most fervent supporter joining them more dramatically than she might intend.

"You'll not stop him!" Alison continued to yell. "Edinburgh belongs to the Prince. Long live King James!"

Caught up in the panic below Jean Petrie tried to elbow her way to a better position, but the task proved beyond even her resources. She caught a glimpse of many familiar faces from the Chapel Land, though not Bella's, and recognised Davie Dalgleish as he wriggled under an apothecary's armpit and out into the centre of the street. For a moment Jean caught his eye and he grinned upwards to where Alison continued to harangue a company of dragoons passing beneath her, bound in the direction of Colt Bridge. Helpless to dampen any of Alison's excitement, Christie left her and hurried out in the hope of finding her brother, while citizens further afield in the Lang Dykes watched Colonel Gardiner's dragoons canter eastwards to meet up with General Cope's tired forces who had finally taken ship for Leith. In the event their destination was to be Prestonpans and when Christie returned with James some hours later Alison could scarcely contain herself. "They've run! They've run!" she cried. "The city is open to the Prince. What a day this is! What a day!"

The next day was even more of one for it brought the Prince's summons. As Kilclath made his irritable way to the city chambers he encountered a flustered Gavin MacVey on the same mission.

"I daresay you will not be too downhearted at this turn of events," he remarked dryly.

The old lawyer shook his head. "The well being of the city is my main concern at present. The Prince has apparently promised that if he meets with no resistance he will ensure it, so I have urged agreement to his demands. I can see no other solution."

"No more can I at present," agreed the Master of the Stones. "It appears the only course to take when the defenders of our city turn their tails on it. The whole affair grows increasingly embarrassing."

"At any rate, the provost hopes to gain more time by conceding. Apparently Cope has landed at Dunbar, though it's becoming my considered opinion that little faith can be put in the British Army. There's a deputation gone to the Prince at Slateford."

Kilclath made another gesture of irritation. "So we've little choice but to grit our teeth and thole the situation," he muttered, and then added grimly, "in the hope that the Pretender's son will not wish to linger too long in his ancestor's old haunts."

In the event Edinburgh's capitulation turned out to be a much simpler affair. The deputies' coach, returning for stabling in the Canongate, required the opening of the Netherbow Port. Lochiel's highlanders passed through with it and Edinburgh was in the Prince's hands.

"Praise be to God!" cried Alison, turning to Christie in delight.

"A confounded nuisance!" muttered Kilclath as he scowled out onto a street already bright with the plaids of the new masters.

King James was duly proclaimed at the Market Cross, Scotland's pride was restored, and the city gave itself up to the Prince's followers. On the same cloudy September afternoon Donald Stewart of Glenshellich called upon his aunt.

Kirsty let out a gasp of delight when she opened the door. Donald wrapped her in a spontaneous hug and stepped inside. The next person he saw was Christie. She turned away from his shining eyes, hating the pounding of her heart and the rushing of the blood in her head. She could not bring herself to look at him again until Alison had released him from her own tearful embrace. Andrew and Hugh were still with the crowds on the street, thousands cheering and pumping their hands, offering a welcome beyond any they could have dreamed of. When Christie did dare to look at Donald she saw that he was different: relaxed and, to her amazement, almost happy.

"Christie," he said softly, with only the slightest trace of uncertainty.

"I am an impartial observer," she answered, summoning a smile, determined to show no weakening in her own defences.

"I had not expected to see you so soon," he muttered.

"I had hoped the same."

Try as she might to persuade herself what had passed between them had been in another world his eyes told her otherwise. He took both her hands and gazed earnestly into her face.

"All will be well, Christie. I promise."

Deciding that the time had come to intervene Alison bustled forward. "And when can we expect a visit from Mr Fettes?"

"He will be here presently," Donald declared. "It is only that I was too impatient..."

Christie turned to look out of the window. He had sent her into a completely different confusion. When Kirsty ushered in Andrew and Hugh it was impossible not to become part of their celebration. When all the greetings were over she tried to bring herself back to earth.

"I am still afraid," she told them. "It has all happened so quickly. I cannot believe you will go unopposed."

"Speed is of the essence, the only way to succeed," declared Hugh, his eyes wide with instant admiration. He lowered his voice and spoke close to her ear. "And you of all people should be rejoicing today!"

His florid complacency was mildly irritating. "And why might that be?" she retorted.

"Your father's faith justified."

Christie heaved another helpless sigh. "Why am I so torn?" she cried. "Your King James has defined my life. We were born in exile because of him. We have no home .." She deliberately avoided Donald's eyes, ".. because of him. I never followed or believed in his cause, but now here you are, with your army and your hopes and….." her voice faded. She had been going to say, in my heart I am with you. It would have been an impossible admission, but true. None of them were allowing her a life of her own. After only three months, not nearly long enough for her to adjust to losing him, Donald was back. He could never be hers, yet he still held her, with eyes eager as a child's that she might finally share this passion that now consumed him, the passion she had once believed was the only issue dividing them.

Andrew cleared his throat. "Perhaps we should not absent ourselves too long from the camp."

Hugh opened his mouth to disagree, but Donald seemed grateful for the excuse. Christie stood with Alison at the window watching as they joined the other tartan-clad warriors swaggering down the High Street.

"Damn them!" she breathed. "Damn them and damn you too, Charles Edward Stuart."

* * *

But far from being damned the prince and his followers were making the most of their bloodless conquest of the capital. They also occupied themselves sensibly in gathering and organising ammunition and supplies. General Cope was not far away and anxious to redeem himself for his earlier embarrassing failures of command. When the highland army marched from the King's Park to re-assemble at Duddingston the Prince made a stirring announcement.

"Gentlemen, I have flung away the scabbard: with God's help I will make you a free and happy people!"

His men cheered loud enough to raise the sky, and marched at full speed behind him towards Mussleburgh.

Cope saw them in the afternoon from his fine position between Prestonpans, Cockenzie and the sea, crossing the grassy mound of Falside Hill. He turned his forces around in readiness and, determined not to be out-manoeuvred again, posted guards at every approach to his lines: all save one. Fatefully he failed to guard the way the clans were to take, the little travelled, little known, path through the marshland. In the hours before dawn, led by a local farmer's son, they filed northwards in a grey column through the track that ran past Riggonhead Farm, emerging like a line of stunted bushes in the half-light. They formed their ranks before the sun climbed towards the horizon and too late Cope recognised the threat. The charge when it came was devastating. Lochiel's Camerons surged on the left wing and Ardshiel's men tore to the right of them, their savage screams chilling the hearts of the disorientated redcoats.

At his shoulder Donald heard the cry of his foster brother, wilder in this southern air than ever it had sounded under the giant's mountain. Kenneth's pipes rose above the clamour and Donald saw on all their faces the madness of their first charge, the careless frenzy as they tore towards the enemy. At first their progress was shaken by artillery, but only briefly until they came again, running and firing their muskets. Soon they were close enough to stab and lunge into the ranks and lash through the drifting veils of mist and smoke and terrified white faces. Andrew watched his brother shoulder his way to the midst of them and knew the very moment when Donald would pull the dagger from his stocking and grip it with the hand that still bore its childhood scar. A terrified dragoon turning to flee froze before him as Donald reached down his leg. Andrew watched him advance, lips drawn back in an ugly snarl. He watched him spear the dragoon with his broadsword, hold the twitching body against his before thrusting the tiny blade into the soldier's throat. With another fierce cry he disappeared into the smoke after Ardshiel and his clan in pursuit of more victims.

Andrew took a step backwards. Already the sounds of battle were fading. He did not need to follow his clan. His place was here with the struggling wounded. On the other side of the field he could see the MacDonalds set about unleashing their unique brand of fury. The field was littered with bodies in red coats, horribly mutilated by the savagery of claymore and scythe, and even as others pursued the terrified fleeing red coats he saw clansmen scuttle and crouch among the dead like scavenging crows.

"Return to your ranks!" he roared, passing angrily among them. "This is work for the surgeons."

To his relief his order was sanctioned. He set about his duty and fell into his tent long after the others of his regiment had begun their celebrations.

Alison looked out onto the swarming Lawnmarket just in time to see a fleeing band of soldiers gallop up the High Street, heedless of whom they might trample in their rush for the safety of the Castle. She heard the clang of the gates behind them and rubbed her hands in unadulterated glee.

Further down the Royal Mile Kilclath slammed the door of his own stronghold.

"It is totally beyond belief," he exclaimed, as James looked up in alarm, "that this rabble is able to cause such havoc!" He threw the papers in his hand onto the table and watched them spread before he swept them to the floor. "The British Army ran this morning," he announced with scorn. "They ran like rabbits and we are left to suffer the consequences." He paused and his expression darkened. "It would appear the time has come for us to take this whole desperate adventure somewhat more seriously."

* * *

Donald had declined the offer of accommodation at Alison's and remained with his men in their billets at Duddingston. The narrow streets of the capital were jaunty with the plaids of the highlanders: the inns and taverns and brothels bulged with them while the citizens went about their business much as before, some enjoying the excitement of the events that had so suddenly overtaken them, others hoping for an end of it and a return to the security of a routine, however predictable.

Davie Dalgleish was not one of them. His patch of the city might have been under siege, but the new opportunities by far outweighed the dangers. He successfully dodged any stray bullets from the castle as he carried messages and arranged assignations between the Highland Guard in the Lawnmarket and the growing band of Bella's employees in the Chapel Land.

"My, Mr Dalgliesh," Bella herself exclaimed as she stepped delicately across the overburdened gutter, "you're quite the man of the moment, I hear."

"Oh?" replied Davie casually. "Just keeping mysel' busy."

"But no more commissions from your old patron?"

"They tell me he's lying low for the time being."

Bella closed one eye and kept the other firmly fixed on his face. But Davie had learned enough from their last encounter to be immune to intimidation.

"I see your own business is thriving," he observed slyly.

Bella had not crossed the road to engage in small talk. "We take it while we can," she retorted briefly and moved on to her more serious concern. "I was wondering what you could tell me about the lassie downstairs from you – Mistress Bothwell's distant cousin or suchlike."

Davie disguised his sharp intake of breath as a cough. "I ken fine who you mean," he spluttered eventually. "But I ken next to nothing about her. Was there a reason for you asking?"

"Which side of the fence would she be perched on, do you think?"

Davie stared back innocently. At least he could give that question a truthful answer. "No idea," he told her. "No idea at all."

Bella clicked her tongue. It made little odds whether she believed him or not. It was clearly as much information as she was going to get.

"We've taken a few rooms in the Canongate for the time being," she announced with another penetrating one-eyed glare. "So if you're giving directions – "

"I'll recommend your new premises," Davie finished her sentence for her with a wink. He was thinking up a suitable wisecrack when the sound of a scuffle spun him around. Bella skipped surprisingly nimbly back underneath the shelter of the piazza just as the first shot rang from the castle. Temporarily stranded himself Davie saw Kirsty, the Bothwell's maid, clutching a pail of water and firmly rooted to the spot. He opened his mouth to cry out a warning, but the world seemed to be slowing to a silent standstill.

"Watch yourself!" he finally heard himself yell as he launched himself across the space that yawned between them. But Kirsty seemed incapable of watching anything. Her mouth hung open in frozen dis-belief.

"The bastards be damned!" cried Bella from the safety of a saddler's booth as Kirsty, with Davie on top of her, collapsed across the gutter at the blast of the sentry's shot. She did not dare to step back into the castle's range, but held her breath and watched and waited.

Alison Bothwell swung back in horror from her casement viewpoint. She closed her eyes tight and clutched at the drape for support.

"Kirsty!" she gasped.

"Kirsty!" breathed Davie, his heart pounding louder than the canon that had hurled their casual spite down on the city for days. Then he felt the pain sear his shoulder and heard vague voices above him.

"Is he alive? Did he save the lassie?"

Davie raised his head and looked down at Kirsty's motionless figure stretched across the pavement.

"Kirsty?" he whispered, remembering her pert smile, her petulance, her lovesick sighs. "Kirsty?"

Still she made no move. Her pale face was turned into the pavement and her red hair tangled with the filth of the gutter. Then she opened her eyes. He gripped her shoulders and bundled his hands down her arms shaking her out of her dead faint as the crowd finally ventured closer.

"Is the lassie alive?"

"Davie Dalgleish took the bullet." That was Bella's voice and no mistake. "Get the laddie a doctor."

The castle was quiet again, stark against the autumn sky. Davie said nothing. His weakening concentration was focused on shaking Kirsty back to life, but all it succeeded in doing was slowly spinning him into an unconsciousness of his own.

* * *

The foothills of Beinn Feodag were fading from purple to amber and a thin mist drifted in and out of the hollows around Beathag's cottage. It studded tiny beads of moisture in her great-grandson's hair as he bent in concentration over the trap he was baiting. Beathag herself was nowhere to be seen, but her dog watched Domhnull steadily, ready to play its own part when the hare came too close.

From inside the house of Glenshellich Eilidh of the scarlet face looked sadly down towards the shore. Her mistress spent too many lonely hours there gazing across the dark water, but Eilidh could understand why. She felt a grief of her own at the strange emptiness their men-folk had left behind. Fraser stepped from the stables and shook his head gloomily as he also caught sight of Helen's frail figure. Better by far if she'd returned to the Glen of the Black Cattle and the comfort of her father's house. She had proved more stubborn than any of them could have guessed, preferring the simplicity of her new home to the luxury of her old, or at least professing to. Fraser sighed. That was love, he supposed. He watched Angus' boat start to sail out from the jetty but then, almost instantly, veer about and turn again for the shore. Curious to discover the reason Fraser secured the stable gate and headed for the clachan.

Meg MacCombie had been the first to hear the news. She had seen Andra' MacAslan steering his garrons past the Watcher's Stone and had run to meet him. By the time they reached the clachan she had already learned of his adventures in the Grey Wolf Mountains. The other information he had was little more than a rumour, but Andra' had heard of a great battle outside Edinburgh, a battle that had left his old protector General Cope in a very sorry situation indeed. Andra' had lamented the General's fate in Kilclath, but now he had crossed into Glenshellich he gave hearty thanks for it. He cast his crafty eyes around the eager faces and elaborated some more. He had heard that MacSomhairle's men played a brave and honourable part. Meg toyed with the ribbons in her hair and her eyes grew thoughtful. She shot a sideways look at Helen who seemed suddenly short of breath, then cast a slyer glance at Catriona.

"Are you sure they've taken Edinburgh?" she demanded.

"As sure as a man can be that's travelled the road from Inverness. There's soldiers there grown very wary, that I can promise, with more and more flocking to the cause the whole road to Aberdeen."

"And will they stop at Edinburgh?" It was Catriona who asked the question.

"Who's to say? Would you?"

Angus Ban let out a long breath. Domhnull had arrived at his mother's side and was staring anxiously up into her face.

"Meg . ." The warning died on Catriona's lips. Who was she, she reminded herself, to try to dissuade the piper's wife from the plan that was so clearly forming in her mind?

"How long would it take us to reach Edinburgh?"

"I could be there in three days," Andra' boasted.

"Then we could be there in less. Couldn't we, Fraser?"

He knew what was coming. "Could we?" he countered. But it was too late. He had seen the excitement shining from Helen's eyes and the determination in Meg's. The saltwater tang of the dockside was more than a memory in his nostrils, the creaking of masts more than an echo in his ears. It seemed he was destined to sing another song in the city after all.

* * *

"Davie! Davie Dalgleish!"

Andrew stepped back from the boy who lay peacefully now across Alison Bothwell's own bed. He had remembered the last occasion he watched a bullet removed. His hands had followed where Euan Mac-Michael's had led all those years before, and once again, because of Glenshellich's healer, another patient would live to fight another day.

Alison shook her fist in the direction of the window, not at Bella Galbraith who sat delicately sipping tea in the Countess's favourite chair, but at the castle garrison who continued to rain their bullets down on the Lawnmarket's inhabitants. Bella chose not to observe that the neighbourhood had been peaceful for decades; nor did she allow her eyes to linger with too much interest on the golden haired girl who smoothed Davie Dalgliesh's brow. But as she sat back and savoured her brief and unprecedented social elevation she did silently congratulate George Campbell on his choice.

Kirsty, completely recovered from her ordeal and bearing not so much as a scratch, bustled in to replenish Bella's cup, then lingered by the bedside to gaze into Davie's pale face.

"A worthy hero," Andrew murmured with a smile, and Kirsty could only nod her head and agree.

* * *

Donald had a new and pressing priority: the campaign and the fitness of his men for war. He spent hours with Ardshiel discussing future tactics and possibilities, more hours training their men into a keen fighting force, organising supplies, and making himself an indispensable cog in the giant wheel of the Prince's army. His mind was preoccupied with one goal, one ambition, for he had discovered how easily the concerns of a soldier could swamp the desires of a man.

Hugh, however, was less diligent in his soldier's role and found his attentions increasingly fixed on Christie. He had done his utmost to obtain an invitation back to his old quarter, but Alison's better judgement had prevailed and Hugh was lodged to no great disadvantage in an anteroom of The Ensign. He still seized on any excuse to visit Alison's apartments, leaving little doubt as to his intentions.

"Perhaps it is unkind of me to say it," Christie complained one afternoon to her brother and Kilclath, "but I do appreciate the opportunity to escape the attentions of Mr Fettes."

"Surely not Mr Fettes of Ballingry?" Kilclath exclaimed.

"The very one."

"But the fellow is a buffoon!"

She laughed. "He means well enough, I daresay. It is just that the whole city is becoming so crowded. I sometimes feel I have no room to breathe."

"Then we must find you a means of escape." Kilclath spoke with genuine concern. "Why not ride out over the hills with me tomorrow." He narrowed his eyes. "I promise not to burden you with unwelcome conversation or attention."

She was surprised and intrigued by his offer. The prospect of galloping out in the freedom of the fresh open air was almost irresistible.

"Then thank you, sir," she replied with a grin. "I will be delighted."

* * *

Catriona ran her hand softly over Domhnull's head.

"You must be the man here now," she whispered.

He sniffed and shook his shoulders. He would not ask again why they had not taken him to see his father and MacSomhairle and the golden one. All those he loved would soon be there in the city, save Catriona and his great grandmother, and they were only pretending to need his protection. Domhnull knew perfectly well they were fit enough to protect themselves.

Fraser looked back over his shoulder as they rounded the Watcher's Stone and gave a small shiver. He could still feel the clutch of Beathag's bony fingers on his wrist, still hear the whispered urgency of her plea, but what she had asked of him had come as no surprise. It was Catriona's request that had set the shiver in his spine, for he did not believe he would have the courage to fulfil it.

* * *

Jean Petrie was only pretending to be asleep. She had heard the Master tiptoe into the room and could almost picture the expression on his face as he sat on the edge of the bed looking down at her. Jean had no intention of making his task any easier. She stretched sleepily, sensuously, a cat slowly wakening.

"I am wondering if it will be possible for me to live without you," he whispered.

Her heart lurched from despair to hope, though her tone was flippant when she answered. "And how would you hide me from a wife? Especially one who is at least as clever as I am myself."

"Why would I hide you? I would not be the first to keep a mistress and a wife."

"In the same house?"

He ran his hand very lightly over her cheek and let his long fingers cup her chin. "There are alternatives," he said softly.

"You could find me a husband," she smiled. She could afford to smile now that she had glimpsed his predicament. He wondered if it would be possible to live without her. She tensed and flexed the muscles of her legs under the covers and curled her toes. Her arms were raised above her head and he gently touched the tips of her fingers before stroking his hands slowly down her body.

"Would you have a candidate in mind?" he murmured.

"Your young clerk looks warmly at me."

"You are ambitious, Jean. My young clerk may one day be Laird of Allomore."

"Then we would be related in more ways than one."

He turned onto his back beside her and let out a long sigh. "I do not intend to play our sort of games with them."

"Our sort of games?"

"They are young and they are pure in heart. That is not a luxury that has been afforded us."

"Ambition must know the world's darker side. Even if only to reject it."

He rolled over to face her. "Where do you find such notions, Jean?"

"In all sorts of places. Mostly in the nights I lie waiting for you." She leaned onto her elbow and stared into his solemn face. Then she let her own hand slip lower. "How many saw us as an affront to God? But look what we've become."

"Yes," he agreed softly. "We have become what no-one would have imagined."

"Your son must have a mother of rank." She smiled gently. "Of rank and beauty." She smiled again. "But you do not think you could live without me."

He had already started to make love to her. Jean entangled her fingers in his smooth black hair and arched her hips against his. Yet even as he cried out in his ecstasy her fears came creeping back. For Jean knew only too well that in time all loveliness must fade. Whatever he might tell her, she was still far from convinced she had it in her to compete with the kind of beauty that rested in Christie Hamilton's soul.

* * *

Since Helen had arrived in Edinburgh Donald had been attentive, but his priority had been the campaign. Meg had moved with Kenneth to a tent on their camp, much to the amusement of the rest of the clan, who had no use for such womanish shelter and preferred to do as they always had, which was wrap themselves in their plaids and sleep under the stars. Having Meg beside him more than compensated Kenneth for their teasing and the two of them found ample time to explore the wynds and closes and thoroughfares of the city together.

Helen had been delighted to be reunited with Donald and had entered wholeheartedly into the spirit of excitement that had flooded the city, attending the soirees and gatherings, tea parties and balls that had become such a feature of the Prince's occupation. On many nights Donald joined her in the anteroom Alison had set aside for them, where they made love far into the night. It was a strangely unreal world they had come to inhabit, a temporary world of moments to be seized.

* * *

The chandlery on Leith's dockside had scarcely changed since Archie Fraser had last contemplated its tidy shuttered frontage. He studied it now not so much with nostalgia as with relief. He was enjoying his sojourn in the city more than he had expected, but much of that was due to his companion. He watched her peer into the shop's dusty interior with unconcealed fascination, blinking to accustom her eyes to the dim light. A couple of sailors loitered at the counter and Fraser edged towards them, straining to catch their words and brushing his hand across the rough wood. There were some new notches on it to be sure, but he recognised the old ones, and could remember more than a few of the hands that had hacked their bargains in the tallow light. The familiar aromas of port and brandy, sour citrus and sweet molasses wafted among the earthy essences of ropes and tar and human sweat. Fraser listened as the swarthy Spaniard haggled for a cart to take him and his barrels of wine to the camp at Duddingston. Business was good just now, with the city's population so swelled. At the wharfside the hammers of the shipwrights kept up their steady beat and beyond them sailed the regular traffic, the whalers and the West Indian traders, the vessels bound for the Baltic and the Americas, the Berwick Smacks plying their cargo, passengers and news to England's uneasy capital. Deals by the dozen were sealed and shaken on all along the quay, and Fraser guided Christie to a bollard at the water's edge in preparation to instigate his own. But she was thirty years behind him, gazing through the swaying masts with eyes held spellbound.

"Don't tell me, Fraser," she breathed, her eyes sparkling, "that this is the very place!"

He had indeed taken his fateful leap alongside the steps that crumbled below them. The Petit Dauphin had drifted out to sea with her father on deck, ready to watch his homeland fade to a memory. What would he say to them now? Fraser wondered. Would he endorse the entreaties of an old mad woman?

"The very place," he echoed. Then he added quietly, "Beathag sends you a message."

"Beathag!" Christie exclaimed.

"She wants you to return with us to Glenshellich."

Christie smiled in disbelief. "And live with her in her hut on the mountainside?"

"She didna offer accommodation," he muttered dryly.

Christie was still astounded. "But why?"

"Because it's where you belong." He waited for the impact of his words to take effect. "And because she says you're no' safe here."

"Not safe!"

Fraser shrugged his shoulders. He was afraid to say too much, afraid to betray his own desperation to have her back in Glenshellich. He could not believe the city held any real danger for her. For her brother, maybe, if word escaped of his true identity, but she was surely safe enough under the protection of Alison and the Countess: at least Fraser had no reason to believe otherwise. Yet Beathag had been uncannily determined and Fraser did not relish his own prospects if he returned without her.

"We all miss you," was all he said.

"Helen does not miss me," she answered softly. "Nor Eilidh, I must believe. And as it is their home more than mine I think you must tell Beathag that I am sorry," she said. "I appreciate her concerns for me, I truly do. But you and I both know I cannot go back to Glenshellich."

Even so, Beathag's message would not leave Christie's mind. It still lingered there as she spurred her horse after the Master of Stones over the first slopes of the Pentland Hills. The wind blew golden strands of hair across her eyes and she turned to look back at the city, surely as safe as it had ever been. When Kilclath reined his horse to a standstill they sat together in silence for some moments before she murmured, "Mr Fettes does not approve of our diversion."

He smiled. "And MacSomhairle? Does he still consider you his responsibility?"

She was not sure how to answer. "He may consider me to be," she said at last.

Kilclath looked seriously into her eyes. "I would be honoured, Christie, if you would agree to become my responsibility." His voice came so softly that she wondered if she had imagined the words. He turned his head away from her and she gazed at his fine dark profile outlined against the pale sky.

"I do not understand my feelings for you," she whispered at last.

He looked at her with a strange tenderness. "It is enough to know you have feelings for me."

She was afraid to meet his eyes, knowing that her own would show too clearly the depth of her confusion. Kilclath reached out his hand and gently gripped her reins. "We will not speak of it again - until you are ready with an answer," he reassured her.

She nodded silently and turned her head from the contrasting images that rushed to her mind: the sombre grandeur of the Valley of Stones, the sculpted splendour of Glenshellich, so close yet so irrevocably divided. She had no idea why she should find herself trapped and torn between them. She shivered suddenly, but not with the cold.

Kilclath tugged on his stallion's rein, turning its head towards the city. There was careless pride in the gesture, a natural confidence and authority, yet Christie had a sudden sense of unease, the same disquiet she had felt as she sat at his dinner table. However much of his feelings the Master of the Stones might chose reveal she had the chilling certainty that the essence of him might forever be beyond her reach.

* * *

Hughie McIvor seldom forgot a face, and never if its owner had come within a whisker of harming one of his clan. He watched the squat, ruddy complexioned fellow limp down the Lawnmarket and hid himself the shadows of the old church of St Giles, a good vantage point. The man was in no hurry and had a cheery word and pawky smile for the poorest beggar and haughtiest gentlewoman alike. All seemed familiar yet at the same time unexpected as he peered into the murky depths of wynds and closes. He had the look of a man revisiting his own past, or perhaps his old self, a situation he had in common with Hughie McIvor who squinted through the dusty stonework, feeling himself no longer trapped in an alien city but tall in his saddle on the rain drenched foothills of Kilclath. Hughie breathed a low curse and flexed his fingers on the handle of his dirk as he slipped in behind his quarry who was by now wandering among the market stalls.

"Hughie!"

Hughie cursed again.

"My!" Jean went on playfully. "It's no' like you to be shopping for finery."

Hughie scowled into her mischievous eyes as she picked up a lace edged handkerchief and pretended to examine it. "Now that would do Mhairi very nicely," she went on. "And what a gesture it would be, Hughie, a wee gift from her old friend and admirer."

Hughie let loose a stream of invective which Jean was happy enough not to understand. She rumbled through her purse and pulled out a coin. "Allow me."

His eyes darted past her and into the crowd. Where was the brown suited fellow? The last time he had been wrapped in a plaid, with oak leaves pinned to his bonnet. But whatever his outfit the next time Hughie would know him. Patience was the essence of Hughie's world: the longer the stalk the surer the kill. Sometimes retribution took generations, but somehow he had a quiet confidence that he would encounter this quarry again in his own lifetime.

"Since you are here," went on Jean, "you could come with me round to Bella's. The Master wants to find out just exactly what happened to Davie the caddie." Jokingly she held out her arm. Hughie took a pace backwards and motioned for her to lead the way. She did not see the look of contempt he threw at the back of her head as he followed her. Waiting on whores was another duty he knew well. Mostly he chose to avoid their eyes, but of all the faces imprinted on his memory theirs were the ones that would remain the longest.

One in particular, he knew, would haunt him until his dying day.

* * *

October was drawing to its close when the tenacious Hugh finally succeeded in persuading Christie to accompany him to one of the Prince's balls. Still no closer to arriving at an answer for Kilclath, she decided to put aside all thoughts of his proposal and make up the party setting out for the Palace of Holyrood. Alison and Helen had spoken of little else for days, but Christie was not deceived into believing that a ball was Helen's priority. The Prince's council remained divided, but it seemed that his own views would prevail and that his army might soon be planning an assault on the English border.

She had dressed herself with care in deep blue silk trimmed with lace, cut low at the breast. For the occasion she had powdered her hair and piled it high, leaving a few curls to stray around her throat. Hugh's eyes did not leave her as they jolted together down the High Street.

"We might have been neighbours," he murmured wistfully. "I might have known you all my life."

"Indeed you might," she agreed. "But as it was you had your estates and I my room in a Roman pensione. Where will we be this time next year, I wonder."

Seeing Hugh's downcast expression she wished the words unsaid. It gave her no pleasure to have such power over his feelings, but being Hugh he quickly recovered his good humour. "Dancing in White-hall?" he countered.

As he led her into the Assembly Rooms she gazed around the bright plaids, the velvets, the silks, and found it impossible not to be caught up in the excitement. The atmosphere sparkled under the candela-bras, bustled with anticipation, buzzed with promises. Her eyes found Donald close to the entrance, intent on his conversation with Lord George Murray and Ardshiel, and her heart lurched as their eyes briefly met. Hugh began to steer her towards the company that contained Alison and Helen but before they arrived a sudden hush descended and Christie turned to see the Prince making his stately way down the aisle his subjects had created for him. She could not help smiling as she saw the way he drew the eyes of the ladies. How well, she thought, he fitted this new role he had found for himself. How ready they all were to admire, even to worship him. Tearlach, the highlanders called the boy she had known all her life as Charles Edward, and she could not grudge him his moment of glory in the house of his ancestors.

"Christie!" he exclaimed as his brown eyes fell on her and became instantly warm. He reached out his hand as one old friend to another, and Hugh stepped back in amazement as she extended her own hand in a gesture that exactly mirrored it.

"Your Highness," she smiled at him, her eyes dancing with mis-chief. Then she lowered her voice. "We have come a long way. You furthest of all."

His eyes were earnest in return. "And would you wish to see me go further?"

"How could I wish otherwise?" she whispered, and in the silence that had fallen all ears strained to catch the conversation between their prince and this beautiful girl he had singled out.

"How well you look," he continued, but his time he spoke in Italian. "Why have I not seen you here before? And how is your brother?"

Donald also gazed at these two who had come to so dominate his heart. He had not understood just how well they had been acquainted.

"I hope he does not still resent us," the prince went on. "It will give me my greatest pleasure to restore to your family what has been sacrificed."

She drew a deep breath. "God go with you," she breathed, and meant it, for she understood him, despite her fears for all those he took with him on his quest. Her father had lost an estate. His had lost a kingdom, but at least he had discovered what it was to have it restored.

Alison had managed to squeeze her way to Christie's side. As the prince continued on his way she could not keep the wonderment from her voice. "What an honour!"

"Shared exile must be a greater bond than I realised," Christie answered softly, then smiled again. "His charm has increased in proportion to his good fortune."

Hugh had reached Donald and drawn him aside. "What a girl that is!" he exclaimed in wonder. "What would I not do to have her." He did not notice how Donald's face darkened. "I will be coming to you after this campaign for support in my suit."

"I do not believe your attentions will be welcome," Donald muttered.

Hugh was taken aback. Several emotions crossed his face, but he decided to make light of it. "Am I so bad a proposition?"

"I will support no suit from you, Hugh."

Hugh stared at him, suddenly angry. "Then whose will you support?" he retorted. "The Master of the Stones'?" He laughed maliciously at the fury on Donald's face. "For she spends much of her time with that gentleman, and even rides alone with him over the Pentland Hills."

Donald turned away, struggling to control his emotion. He took a deep breath and reminded himself why he was here. The army was prepared and hungry for the next step towards destiny, and he and Hugh were part of it together. Donald had already put aside his old preoccupations, or believed that he had. He took his wife in his arms and they danced as if there were no such day as tomorrow.

* * *

Not so many yards from them, in Kilclath's Canongate apartments, Jean Petrie poked the fire into sudden life. The flames leapt quickly and threw her features into stunning shadows and light as she leaned closer, listening intently to the voices rise and fall behind her. As usual she could only decipher the occasional word, but the tone told her they were arguing again. Hughie was attacking a loaf of bread with the vicious little knife he kept in his stocking. He sounded disgruntled, almost petulant, while Mhairi's voice was cunningly persuasive.

"Such men as MacIolair do not die," she hissed. "They live on in those who remember them. They eat away at their hearts."

"He has a duty."

"If he has a son with her …" Mhairi did not finish her sentence. Jean stole a glance over her shoulder.

"It will be the same as before." He bit off a crust and chewed it savagely. "I will kill her first."

Mhairi spat in contempt. "MacIolair supped at the table of power but his belly would never fill. A son with the daughter of the Plotter would be more than even he could dream."

Hughie nodded dourly in Jean's direction. "And a son with her?"

"Another dead whore for a grandmother?"

He snarled and tipped his flask to his lips.

"Though a dead whore has her uses," Mhairi added slyly. She drew back, as if expecting a blow. Jean held her breath, but Hughie resisted the bait, though his brow was drawn like thunder. He turned his back sulkily and took another mouthful of whisky. Mhairi made a contemptuous gesture and began a new tirade. Jean noticed that this time the same word occurred time after time, a word she had no trouble in recognising.

It was the name Glenshellich.

* * *

Donald helped his aunt and Helen into the sedan chair, stepped back and watched it sway into the night. Hugh, by now more than a little unsteady on his feet, followed with Christie and Andrew.

"See him back to his quarter," Donald muttered.

Andrew looked surprised, but was in no doubt that his brother intended his order to be obeyed.

"And yourselves?"

"I will ensure that Christie returns safely." Realising that Andrew was not at all happy with the arrangement he added. "There is nothing to fear, Andrew. You have my word."

Hugh was already beyond the stage of making any serious objection, though he did remember that Bella had set up a new establishment almost on the Palace's doorstep. He bowed theatrically to Christie and disappeared unsteadily into the night, with Andrew close on his heels.

"Hugh is a good fellow," Donald said. "But he would not make a good husband."

"I have no intention of making him mine," she answered with a smile, "or anyone else I think," she added thoughtfully. "The times are too uncertain."

"I have heard...." he began, but his voice faded as she continued to look levelly into his eyes. "...a rumour concerning the Master of the Stones," he ended feebly.

"He has been a good friend to James. We owe a great deal to him."

"Perhaps your brother should have changed his name to Campbell."

She could see that he immediately regretted his words but she answered sharply nevertheless. "I will discuss neither one of them, Donald. I am sorry."

He turned away and they stood together in silence under the moonlight, beneath the shadow of an ancient palace in a city they had both come to know so well, yet the same place filled both their hearts.

"I have something to ask of you, Christie," he whispered. "In case…" His voice broke and he turned away. "If I do not return from this campaign then please remember that Glenshellich is your home. I would like to think you would always be safe there."

Christie pulled her wrap tighter against the chill night breeze and thought how much simpler her life had been when it had offered no choices. Now every road ahead seemed dark and uncertain. The spectre of her father rose in her mind. Was he reminding her that she was bound every bit as firmly as he had been to the desperate cause of the Stuarts, a cause whose brief fire had only ever succeeded in reducing dreams to ashes?

"And if you do return?" she asked softly.

He did not answer, for he could not explain the conviction that tightened its grip on his heart with every passing day. He would not tell her he was certain he had taken leave of Glenshellich for the last time, that the answer to his fate lay in those old forbidden words, the prophecy that had clouded his life from the moment he was born.

"If you do return?" she repeated.

He drew a sharp breath and the moon showed her the pain in his eyes. He did not need to answer. There was no answer: for either one of them.

* * *

Meg MacCombie blew softly into the rough hair that sprouted from the piper's chest. "Promise me something?" she asked.

He smiled. "There can be no going to America until we have seized a kingdom."

"What has America to do with it?"

Outside the tent Kenneth heard the familiar night-time sounds: the whinny of horses, the rattle of tins, the distant drone of pipes, fractured peals of women's laughter. He had been glad to have his woman in the city with him, glad that because of him she had seen a little more of her world.

"Then what will I promise?"

"The same as before."

He thought of the miles that lay ahead, the battles they must face before they met whatever fate awaited them. Some of the women were marching alongside their menfolk, but he would not have that for Meg. Much as he would miss her he would rather picture her safe in Glenshellich, with Domhnull, with Catriona, even with Beathag who he knew would protect her kin with her dying breath. He had many pibrochs to play before he would find his way home, but he did not believe he was raising false hopes when he whispered, "I promise this is not the last time you will lie in my arms."

Outside his chieftain's tent Euan MacMichael gazed up at the stars and also imagined the days ahead. It was hard not to feel a stirring of excitement, despite his fears. Euan had had more than enough of the city. He had sampled most of its temptations and found them seriously over-rated. It disappointed him that MacSomhairle had once found the place, and the women, so much to his taste. And England would be worse, of that he was certain. It would fall to himself and the piper to keep the men's spirits high, even if their own hearts were heavy. The night air was crisp and still. Euan watched the thin trails of his breath disappear into the darkness and dreamed of Glenshellich.

* * *

As early morning spread over the city Hughie McIvor leaned against the chestnut mare's flank, his hand cupped ready to receive the booted foot of the Plotter's daughter. Hughie remembered the Plotter well, and what he had done, but it had not been required of him to bring retribution. The old fool had finally and conveniently seen to that for himself. Hughie found the vitality, the spirit, which flowed from this daughter almost an affront. He kept his eyes firmly averted from her face. It would have been a simple enough task to tamper with the girth, a small cut here, a loose buckle there, but Hughie had resisted the temptation. The Master would look no further than himself in the event of an accident. Best bide his time.

As he watched the two of them ride slowly towards the King's Park he heard the rustling of silk behind him and turned to see the Master's whore at his shoulder. She leaned forward earnestly. She and Hughie shared the same interest. Surely they should be allies.

"Hughie," she asked softly. "Why are you afraid?"

He responded with his usual snarl but Jean was resolute. She moved closer and kept her gaze steadily on his shifting face. Her patience eventually drew a response.

"Bad," he muttered in his piping English. "With her is bad."

Jean felt her breath trembling to escape. She let it go slowly. "What is bad with her, Hughie?" she breathed.

Hughie seemed to be struggling with an invisible demon. "MacIolair," he gasped, and Jean had an unpleasant suspicion he was addressing the demon rather than herself. She fixed him with a stare every bit as fierce as his own, as if to prove that she was a match for any force, human or inhuman, when it came to protecting her protector.

"Remember I love him too, Hughie," she whispered.

He squinted back at her and for the very first time it seemed that they might be speaking the same language.

The Master of the Stones and Christie Hamilton rode quietly at first, their horses gradually gathering speed as tenements and cobblestones gave way to grassy tracks and ploughed fields. Soon they were galloping over the first heathery slopes of the Pentland Hills. There was still some summer warmth in the late October sun and their faces were flushed when they finally drew rein, dismounted and began to walk towards the shelter of a small outcrop. The grass at their feet was still green and thick and the horses began to quietly graze. The Master did not look at Christie, but simply waited for her to speak. She wondered if he had already anticipated what she was going to say.

"I am sorry," she breathed.

His expression was tight, perhaps with regret, or perhaps with relief. "A union between ourselves may indeed have been ill-advised," he sighed, "at risk from too many conflicting interests." He reached out his gloved hand and gently ran a finger down her cheek.

To her complete amazement a fire surged through her body at his touch, a fire every bit as fierce as the one that had disorientated her outside Feodag's cave. She stared into his face. This time she was on no-one else's territory, not even his, though his eyes seemed to seek out her very core. Standing so close he was taller even than she had realised. She saw that he scarcely seemed to be breathing. It was her own breath she was conscious of, quick and uneven, keeping time with the drumming of the blood in her veins.

"No," she heard herself murmur in hopeless protest as her lips parted and she leaned back against the bank. He leaned with her and she did not even try to push him away. Slowly he began to remove his gloves and belt, never once taking his eyes from her face. Her own eyes were held captive by them as he unhooked her cloak and delicately loosened her bodice. She let out a sigh as she felt his cool hands run lightly over her breast. The mounting passion seemed all hers. Kilclath simply studied her with a detached interest as he carefully removed garment after garment, until she stood naked and quivering before him. In that moment she knew she was not capable of resisting his power. She wondered if any woman would have been. He knelt, resting his face between her thighs as he ran his hands from her ankles upwards until he could follow his hands with his mouth. She felt his tongue licking the hot moistness between her legs and penetrating smooth and deep inside her. She gasped with the intensity, incredible beyond anything she had ever dreamed of. Then he stood up, took her hand and pushed it over his rising hardness. Christie was disorientated by her desire. She had no idea if she was standing, or lying or tumbling upside down in the heather. All she was conscious of was the sensation he gave her, and a tiny pain with the pleasure as he throbbed inside her, moving gently, slowly, expertly, working her body as skilfully as he worked his own. She heard her gasps grow louder as she moved with him, in him and around him, while all the time he took her higher and deeper into her own unbearable pleasure. Every inch of her body sang and cried out as it soared and soared again. He knew exactly his effect on her: angel or devil, he was in complete control, claiming her senses, ensuring that now he would always be a part of her. At last she became aware of the low whinny of one of the horses above the soft rhythm of his breathing. Her own breath had subsided to gentle gasps. They lay with their heads touching, facing upwards to the bright blue sky. It occurred to her that they would have to ride together all the way back to the city. What would they talk about? What could she ever find to say to him again?

He leaned on his elbow and smiled down at her. "I hope you will not refuse every offer of marriage so graciously," he whispered.

He might be the devil himself, she thought, but she did not care. "Then perhaps you should ask me again." The grass was sweet against her nakedness. She wished for nothing but to abandon herself to him entirely.

"I can repeat my question until the sky is full of stars," he told her, "if you will continue to give me the same answer."

As it was the sun had only begun to sink behind the soft outline of the hills when they finally remounted their horses. Christie had no idea what might happen when next they met. What she was certain of was that not even Donald could ever have the power to raise such passion in her. Riding beside The Master of the Stones in silence towards the darkening city, her emotions torn between exhilaration and shame, she blushed to remember how Alison had first defined his reputation. He might have made himself notorious for turning a whore into a lady, but in the day they had spent together he had proved himself every bit as capable of accomplishing the reverse.

* * *

The Prince's army was almost ready to march. Scotland was in Jacobite hands, but a richer prize beckoned. In the camp at Duddingston the clans prepared to make their farewells.

Meg MacCombie gazed out over the city's horizon with an inexplicable sense of longing. She stretched her hand towards the sky, pale now with the approaching shades of winter, but let her arm fall weakly back to her side. What she sought was not within her grasp. Perhaps it had never been, though oddly she felt closer to the missing part of herself here than she had ever done in Glenshellich.

"Meg."

She turned to see MacSomhairle and gave him a wistful smile. He came closer and took her hand.

"You and our son are so much a part of my memories of home," he whispered. "I know you will raise him to be strong and true."

"And never to go to war."

"Perhaps this will be the last war."

She looked at him shrewdly. "Why does this feel like a farewell, Domhnull MacSomhairle?"

"There is every chance it may be." He lowered his voice further and kept his eyes fixed on her face. "But I promise I will do everything in my power to keep my piper safe."

She let out a little sigh. Her heart was heavy, as if the strange cloud she had seen through the night hovering over the groups of sleeping men had settled there. But she would tell no one of that. This was a day for only good omens.

* * *

Kilclath's servant woman had not ventured onto the streets since the Prince's army had arrived in the city. Now there seemed definite word of their leaving Jean noticed that Mhairi's head was held higher, her eyes were returning to life. Jean closed the kitchen door behind her and folded her arms.

"So there is to be no marriage," she said, her tone deceptively light.

Mhairi tossed back her hair. "It was a fool she was to spurn him," she muttered at last. "He will not forget."

This was not what Jean had wanted to hear, though she knew that Mhairi was only confirming her own suspicions. When the Master had returned the night before he had spoken to no one, not even Hughie, and for the very first time he had dismissed Jean from his bed.

"What do you mean," she whispered, "he will not forget?"

Mhairi saw no need to answer. They both understood the Master well enough. Whatever he had felt for the daughter of the Plotter would be consigned to the secret places of his heart, buried, perhaps, but not forgotten.

"She was the one," Jean breathed.

Mhairi simply nodded and looked away.

"Why?"

This time the servant woman was ready to give her an answer. It took a few moments for her to translate it into words that Jean could understand, moments during which Jean wondered if Mhairi was looking back into a pain of her own. When she spoke her voice was low and her eyes were heavy.

"She carries with her what has already broken his heart."

* * *

Donald lowered his head and ducked into the Netherbow apartment belonging to the Countess of Dalvey. The Countess stepped forward to greet him, fixed him with a rapier like gaze and came characteristically straight to the point.

"Have you discussed your intentions with your wife?"

"Of course."

The Countess frowned. She was in two minds as to the advantages of young Glenshellich's proposal, but something had happened to greatly distress her young companion. The Countess had lived long enough to understand the impermanence of decisions reached in uncertain times. She drew a resigned sigh.

"Just to let you ken that whatever she decides she'll aye be welcome under this roof." She paused and felt a tear prick at the back of her eye. "But there's no' a shadow o' doubt in my mind where her heart lies." She sighed again, a throaty rattle from the depths of her brittle frame. "What will be will be, and I can only wish you well in your dealings ower the border. I daresay she'll be as safe in Glenshellich as she would anywhere for the time being." She struggled slowly to her feet and began to hobble across the room. "I'll tell her you're here."

Donald paced the cluttered room. The longer he was left to wait the more his words ran from his mind like water from a leaking pail. Outside the window he could hear a rising clamour: shouts, sharp orders, the pounding of horses' hooves. He was anxious now to be part of it, free of these burdens of love and guilt and regret. But before that was possible he had one final task to fulfil.

Christie crept around the doorway and stayed almost hidden in the room's shadows. He looked in her direction and heard his voice falter.

"Have you decided?"

"You mean whether to return to Glenshellich?"

"It is much to ask, I know."

"You are not the only one to ask me."

He stepped closer, but she shrank back and turned her head from him.

"We all wish it," was all he said.

Still she could not bring herself to look at him. "It seems I must," she whispered. Whether she returned to Glenshellich or not, one thing was certain: she could not remain in Edinburgh, not with her brother growing more dependent by the day on Kilclath. She did not dare take the risk of falling again under that dangerous and irresistible spell.

His body grew less tense. "Then let there be no more pretence between us, Christie," he breathed, as he slowly bent down and drew a tiny jewelled knife from his stocking. "I have one more request to make of you."

Still she could not bring herself to meet his eyes. When it came to pretence she easily outshone him now. He was holding the knife delicately between his fingers.

"This has been carried by MacSomhairle's son over many generations," he began, almost reverently. "It is an old tradition. And when it has done its work it must be passed on." Even as he spoke the blade seemed to tremble, as if already anxious to free itself from his hand.

"Its work?" she echoed.

"Its work in battle."

"You mean killing."

"That is one duty." He paused again. "But I fear I may not have the opportunity to fulfil the other." He took her hand in his and then gently pressed the handle of the skean dhu into her palm. "There must be a chance that Helen could be with child."

At last Christie could bring herself to look fully into his face. Seeing the pain in his eyes she felt a fierce tenderness fill her. There was no room now in her heart for resentment. At last she understood they had never been destined to be together, even before Kilclath made doubly certain of it. She understood also that the prospect of death had become Donald's solution, his escape, perhaps even his salvation.

"And if Helen has no son...." she answered quietly as her fingers closed over the handle. He opened his mouth to speak, but her words had not been the start of a question. "Then I will give it to Domhnull McCombie, the son of the piper."

She did not go to see the Prince's army start their long march south. Some watched them leave with relief and some with regret; some waved handkerchiefs with hope in their hearts, while others crossed themselves and offered up uneasy prayers. Few who saw the dust that was their leaving rise in the distance would have dared to predict just where their journey might end.

"The citizens are merry today," James quipped. "Edinburgh will soon be theirs once more."

For a moment Kilclath's eyes grew distant, and James felt a twinge of unease. Something was amiss and he was certain it concerned his sister.

"Did she tell you of her latest insanity?" he added

"I have received a note." Kilclath turned away. "Your sister and I may meet again, or we may not. Either way, our," he hesitated only slightly, "friendship, will not be in question."

"I cannot understand her at all," James went on blithely. "I have tried to forge a life for us here, most of which we have owed to you. Yet she has rejected it all to go back to Glenshellich. She might have accepted a proposal from MacSomhairle," he added carelessly, "had he not been wise enough to ally himself to wealth."

Kilclath turned his back quickly and James threw a worried glance in his direction. He hoped he had not gone too far. It was some time before Kilclath spoke again, but when he did his voice was measured. "Well, we must wait and see where it all leads. I believe we can anticipate stronger resistance to this makeshift army from south of the border. Meanwhile -." He did not finish his sentence, but simply disappeared into his inner sanctum and closed the door firmly behind him.

* * *

The lonely land seemed empty of more than its men-folk. In the clachan they listened to the sad cry of the swooping gulls, the feeble lowing of the cattle and the thin notes that faltered from Domhnull MacCombie's pipes. At the house the fragments of song drifting from the stables were half-hearted, the barking of the dogs at every new footfall no longer expectant. The winter began harshly, its frosted silences, bitter snows and driving sleets dragging out the long hours of darkness. But there was always a fire in the cottage of Catriona MacMichael where Christie found herself drawn most often. In the big house it was clear that Eilidh and Helen had established a bond that left no room for her. Eilidh had finally found the mistress she had sought all her life: the last thing she wanted was to encourage the one who had almost robbed her of that chance.

In late November Christie had her monthly bleeding though Helen did not. Both gave heartfelt thanks, but while Christie remained haunted by shame and regret Helen seemed to sail through her days in a dream.

"In my last letter to Donald I told him I have reason to believe," Helen wrote to Andrew, "that I might be with child. I hope that by now he has received it and that you will also have heard the news. Eilidh has told me it is a good omen that you are all gone to war, since she seems to believe any child conceived under such circumstances will grow up with a fierce fighting spirit. I do not take this too seriously, and have a sense it may be tempting providence to make too many plans, though I cannot always contain my dreams. I mostly remain quietly around the house, with Eilidh, sewing and reading and remembering. But I must own I sometimes have uneasy feelings. One is that Beathag is watching me every time I venture to the clachan. Donald has told me, and you have too, I know, that she is harmless, yet I cannot help the coldness the sight of her sends through me and prefer to avoid her if at all possible!

My father was unable to extend his stay beyond last week, but promises to return early in the New Year. I suspect he intends to try again to persuade me back to Cairnill with him, but Glenshellich is my home and I must wait here for my husband. My father avoids all mention of politics and the Prince, though I know that my brother Ranald is keen to raise men in readiness to add his support. If I know my father he will choose the path of least risk and most advantage!

We have not seen Andra' MacAslan since before you left, and we miss Iain MacCombie greatly to take our messages. Thankfully we do still have Murdo Ban, who travels constantly between here and the Glen of the Black Cattle and I know I can rely on him to find a reliable hand to reach you.

I must seal this now ready for when Murdo comes, assuring you as always of your place in my thoughts and my heart, and trusting it will soon be God's will that we are together.

Your loving sister and friend, Helen.

* * *

Kilclath frowned down at the paper in his hand, his fingers drumming on the leather of his desk. James shot him an anxious glance, but decided not to enquire as to the note's contents. Hughie had not seen fit to leave the room after presenting it, but shuffled at the door picking at his teeth with his grimy fingernails.

"Allomore is upon us," Kilclath announced, "and anxious for advice. I will see him." He turned to James. "You may remain if you wish and pretend to occupy yourself with papers."

James felt a quickening of his heart and an unpleasant prickling up and down his spine. He was not sure that he did wish to remain. The few minutes he had previously spent in his kinsman's company had been uncomfortable enough. Judging by Allomore's reaction when he swept inside it appeared the feeling might be mutual. He threw James a look of utter contempt before focusing his irritable attention on Kilclath.

"Is it not enough to have to have your highland vagabond privy to my every word?" he complained.

"To those he understands. But Mr Bothwell will take no part in our conversation," soothed Kilclath. "He has other matters requiring his attention. However, if you would care to speak in the other office...."

Allomore made an impatient gesture and James looked across at him slyly. He was better turned out than the last time, quite the dandy in fact with his velvet doublet and sweeping cloak. There were more people to impress in the city, or more to deceive, but James noticed that his hand still trembled and the pulse in his neck still throbbed. He pretended to immerse himself in his own documents.

"So will you raise your clan?"

"It seems likely. I am making arrangements to travel to Kilclath."

"And light a fiery cross?" Allomore's voice was snide, but Kilclath responded quite calmly.

"The days for that are long past."

"Long past?" He emphasised the first word.

Kilclath made his own gesture of irritation.

"I only mention it," went on Allomore, "since I remember the last time your father sent out the rallying call."

"You may remember. I do not."

James tried to keep his head low over his papers. More seemed at stake here than might be immediately obvious. Hughie sniffed and flexed his fingers. Allomore nodded in his direction.

"He certainly does," he snapped.

"You did well to lie low when the Pretender's son was so close," Kilclath told him, returning to the original subject. "The news from south of the border is encouraging. If a retreat is imminent then all the more reason for us to be prepared."

"And will I remain neutral?"

"I assume that is your inclination."

"You know I have never been a fighting man."

Hughie's hackles rose, but Kilclath simply shifted an eyebrow. "That goes without saying. As usual, you will leave the fighting to others," he murmured.

* * *

The Prince's army had reached Derby. As the year had faded the men from Glenshellich had threaded their way down strange roads, through unfamiliar towns, yet always with England's capital in their sights. The lure of home may have grown stronger to some as their distance from it widened, but MacSomhairle's clansmen had stolen only a fleeting backward glance before they crossed the Esk and turned their eyes southward.

Carlisle, Kendal, Lancaster, Preston all heard the proclamation of the new and rightful king, but while many cheered more remained silent. The promised support had proved slow in presenting itself and the Prince's advisors were soon exchanging words of alarm. Manchester, and their numbers swelled again, but not by enough. There was an uncanny hesitation in the sleeping countryside as the Jacobites marched through it, unopposed, but unsupported. Then had come Derby and a decision.

"Cumberland is on his way to London," Ardshiel told Donald. "Where an army is said already to have formed. Wade is travelling south at great speed and we would be hopelessly outnumbered, fighting a superior force in a strange country. I fear there is little alternative but retreat."

Donald was unable to hide his despair. "We must gain further support," he insisted. "The Welsh have not had time to gather. Everyone thus far has cheered us on our way."

"Token support is not enough. We need men and arms, not empty promises. Campaigns are not won with toasts and pledges."

"The French, then," Donald implored. "They must be encouraged by our great success this far. The men are still eager for action. They would not see a retreat as a tactic. They would see it as a defeat. Arms and soldiers may win wars, but if the heart is lacking there can be no victory. We must push onwards."

But Ardshiel was unmoved by his entreaties. "You may prefer to wait until morning to tell your men of the decision," he said wearily. "But it has been made and there will be no reversing it. If it is any comfort the Prince feels as you do. The Council has over-ruled him." He sighed again. "We will begin our march north at dawn tomorrow morning."

So Donald spent the night sulking, along with his prince. Hugh tried to ease their spirits with brandy but the cure was no longer effective. Later Donald lay sleepless in their billet, listening to Hugh's gentle snores, and trying not to give way to bitterness. He was a soldier now, first and foremost. That had been his comfort. It must be his consolation.

The next morning he issued his command and his eyes did not flinch from the stunned faces of his men. But he knew they understood how reluctantly he spoke the order. Like him they could only despair and silently obey.

The sun now rose on the opposite side of an army marching more to the beat of jeers than applause. Manchester mocked as Wade pursued them. Beset with problems with ammunition and supplies they reached Penrith where their spirits were somewhat restored by a brief skirmish with dragoons at Cliffton. It proved a useful confrontation, which halted Cumberland's forces and gave the Prince time to reach Carlisle. They crossed back into Scotland on the day he celebrated his birthday, fording the swollen Esk with spirits still buoyant. For, as Hugh had been quick to point out, they had taken a tiny force into a great country and shown the Elector the appalling weakness of his defences. They had marched into the heart of his realm and met scant resistance. They had come home simply to re-gather their strength.

"We will conquer yet," cried Hugh, and Donald gazed with pride on his men, still brave, still eager, ready to face weeks more of harsh winter on the road. Euan stood proud as ever at his right hand, armed with his tales of their glen and its legends. Kenneth held his pipes high and played a new tune for their homecoming though the swirling waters reached his waist.

"You are right, my friend!" cried Donald, as he flung his arm around Hugh's shoulder. "You are right. We will conquer yet!"

* * *

Every fireplace in the House of the Eagle was stacked with fiercely glowing peat yet somehow the chill remained, as if the building no longer had a heart to warm. Jean Petrie crept silently along the upper corridor towards the head of the stairs, trailing her hand lightly across the polished banister and gazing, one by one, at the portraits hanging on the panelled walls: generations of Campbells of Kilclath, solemn men with shrewd eyes and far sighted stares, dressed according to their eras in plaid and doublet, tunic and hose. Halfway down the gallery a sudden draught rustled her hair and the sound of a footfall made her turn. She found herself staring into the flesh and blood features of Kilclath's young clerk. She had exchanged few words with him, but she had not mistaken the shy admiration in his eyes when he looked at her. He nodded awkwardly and for a moment it seemed to her that he might be the closest thing in this mausoleum to a kindred spirit. She flashed him an artful smile.

He was equally taken aback. "Jean," he gasped. "I mean, Miss Petrie..."

She let out a peal of laughter. "Miss Petrie!" she echoed. "You are very polite, to be sure, Mr Bothwell," she added with emphasis, then lowered her voice. "So what do you think?"

"Think...?" he stuttered.

Jean let her wide eyes travel the length and depth of the vast marble stairway.

"Is it what you expected?"

James had not been sure what to expect. Grandeur, certainly, but not on this scale. Yet Kilclath still preferred his cramped Edinburgh quarters, and James could almost understand why. He was about to open his mouth to say so when she pressed her finger to her lips and took his hand. Embarrassed, he let her lead him down the stairs, to the lower hallway and the entrance to the servants' quarters.

"It reminds me," began James, thinking of a play he had once seen about the old Scottish king, Macbeth, and the pageant of kings stretching forward through time. They were stepping through the dynasty of Kilclath, which grew more powerful with each successive chieftain. Her lover, his patron, must be the most powerful of them all. It seemed strange that he had commissioned no portrait of his own.

He was about to finish his sentence when Hughie emerged from the servants' door and strode past them. Jean stepped back in alarm. James too recognised the change in the ghillie. In the city he was shadowy, furtive, a fish out of water, but here he flaunted a different status. He did not seem to feel the need to offer them the courtesy of a greeting.

Kilclath looked up from his desk inside the drawing room. "Ahh!" he exclaimed. "Come in. Come in, Jean."

James cleared his throat uncomfortably, but Kilclath seemed equally pleased to see him. "Hughie has gone to saddle himself a horse and spread the word among the tacksmen." He fixed James with an intense gaze. "So the time has come for you to consider your own position. You must do so very carefully." James flashed a look in Jean's direction, but Kilclath did not appear to be about to dismiss her. "You are young, James, and you do not lack conscience. You must ask yourself if enlisting with the Campbells - against the cause for which your father sacrificed everything – would be appropriate."

James felt his cheeks flush, but answered defiantly. "Will my father's ghost return to haunt me for choosing the path of common sense - a path that could lead to justice for his family at long last?"

"That is a question only you can answer," Kilclath replied slowly, and his eyes strayed to the portrait that hung above the fireplace. "We are all vulnerable to the scrutiny of our father's ghosts."

Jean studied the portrait. So this was the Old Fox. This was MacIolair. It was a pleasant face, almost kindly as its eyes gazed with a quiet pride through the window to the sharp peaks of the twin mountains. But just as she was about to turn away a blink of sunlight caught the canvas and the image changed. The eyes were no longer gentle, the expression no longer placid. The sunlight had made the Old Fox vindictive, challenging, ruthless. Jean had scarcely time to wonder who could have painted so complex an impression when she turned to see Mhairi standing in the doorway, still as stone, her eyes fixed on that same face. Jean held her breath and looked from one master to the other, then back at their servant and lastly at James who was watching her with puzzled eyes. But Mhairi and the Master were looking in one direction only. The gathering clouds had once again dimmed the room and the Old Fox was calm once more, benign and reassuring. Was that man they saw, she wondered, or the one she had glimpsed beneath the façade? In that moment she knew she must make it her mission to find out.

* * *

James' business was of an even more troubling nature, and his sister's proximity so tormented him that he was finally compelled to send her a note. He suspected she would have changed her mind about nothing, but he needed her to know he would be there to protect her when this affair was over, that his choice might shield her from whatever might be the consequences of hers.

They met on either side of the Bloody Burn, where the lands of Kilclath and Glenshellich locked horns under a struggling sun. Streaks of pink cloud drifted over the harsh peaks that reared huge and white against the pale sky as Christie waited. She heard the metallic ringing of his horse's hooves across the iron hard earth long before she saw him ride towards her over the field of stones. Her face was numbed by the wind that swept from inside the valley and she huddled against her garron's flank, taking some comfort in its warmth as she watched the slight figure gallop to the burn's edge, dismount and begin to walk towards her. Weeks of frost had imprisoned the pebbles in ice, yet although the burn that separated them was narrowed it gaped to Christie like a chasm.

"Will you not come across?" she asked him.

He shook his head. "I would be doubly unwelcome now in MacSomhairle's lands. In a few days I ride with Kilclath to meet with General Mamore, to join with the Campbells in defence of the realm."

She gazed miserably across the sparkling water. "What have we become, James?" she whispered.

He met her gaze squarely. "I am about to become a soldier in the army of King George, and to seize the opportunity to redeem our family's reputation - for your sake as much as my own."

"Your father would call that treachery."

"Treachery!" He hurled the word back at her. "In God's name, Christie, when will you come to your senses?"

"Take no part in this affair, James, I beg of you."

"Our father can no longer dictate our lives." But the sight of her forlorn figure made him relent. "Please, Christie," he implored. "We quarrelled on our last meeting. I hoped today we could make amends."

"The last thing I want is for us to quarrel." Her voice faltered. The sight of him, so proud and defiant, so young and in need of her was almost impossible to bear. "What does Kilclath advise?"

"We have discussed the implications. The decision is mine alone."

"Are you sure he acts in your best interests?"

"Of course."

"And bears no grudges?"

"Why should he?"

Christie had no answer. Just how much did either of them know about the Master of the Stones? She felt her face grow hot, as it did each time she remembered the passion of her hours with him on the Pentland Hills. With or without grudges Kilclath achieved control in subtle ways and she did not believe he would relinquish it lightly. Perhaps she and James were no more than pawns in his complex game. Their lives so far had been controlled by other people's pasts: now they had become embroiled in a deadlier present where they could not even be sure of each other. She had no idea who was to blame for it, or how to find a way back.

"Perhaps none of us can escape," she whispered.

"We must each make our own future." His voice took on an urgent tone. "The Prince's army have not found support in England. The Argyll men are in training. A different reception has been prepared for their return."

Christie remained silent, too confused to argue. James took a step towards her, but remained on the other side of the water. "I will be there for you, Christie, when all this is over," he said. "You will need my help and I promise I will never fail you. Until then, it seems we must bid each other goodbye."

She did not answer. She could not bring herself to say goodbye to her brother. She could only watch in cold despair as he remounted his horse and spurred it eastward. A fresh breeze swept the mist from the mountain and whipped his plaid to a tail behind him. Numb with more than cold Christie watched him shrink, with each stride becoming more and more lost to her as he faded into the depth of Kilclath. She continued to stare, long after he had disappeared, shivering at last at the emptiness the cold wind carried. James had confirmed their fears of the mustering of Campbells, the government's reorganising of its forces. They already knew that the king's son himself had been recalled to England to protect his father's realm. But another king's son was still marching, lifted by the tunes of the mountains and the memory of a glorious past. With him were Donald, and Andrew, Euan MacMichael and Kenneth MacCombie. A tear trickled down her face and she rubbed her cheek against the garron's ear.

Never in her life had she felt so alone.

* * *

Jean watched the Master's clerk gallop back into the courtyard as she made her way towards the kitchen quarters. The sun was almost at its height and she had not seen Mhairi since the night before. In a perverse way she was missing her company. They could hardly be described as close, yet a kind of companionship had grown between them, strong enough for Jean to be certain that Mhairi was less comfortable even than herself in this Valley of Stones.

Deliberately staying out of sight of the other servants she crept along the narrow corridor, hearing the quick Gaelic tongues from the kitchen above the clanging and shuffling, yet recognising none as Mhairi's. She slipped past the entrance and all the way to where a studded oak door swung slightly ajar. As she drew closer she caught the sounds of splashing mixed with a peculiar mumbled crooning, and through the gap in the door she saw a woman standing naked beside a wooden barrel tipping water from a jug over her tangled brown hair. What she was crooning sounded like a lullaby and she seemed lost in a world all her own. Then she turned, and Jean saw that it was Mhairi. The winter sun shafted through the weathered shutters highlighting every curve of her body as she kept up her almost mystical ablution. Her figure was perfectly formed, remarkably so for one of her age, but through the tears that had sprung to her eyes Jean could distinguish every weal and scar that ravaged the flesh on her back. For minutes she could only lean against the wall for support as the sad fragments of Mhairi's lullaby wrapped themselves around her heart.

At last she felt strong enough to tiptoe back down the corridor. Sickness churned in her stomach. In all her years in the violent Chapel Land she had seen nothing to rival the torture carved on the body of Kilclath's servant woman. She did not wait to knock on the door of the Master's study but burst in to confront him. He had not moved from his desk but as he looked up his surprise turned to alarm when he saw the outrage on her face.

"Mhairi's back," she demanded. "Tell me."

He knew exactly what she had seen. His shoulders slumped and he ran his hands over his face and through his hair. For a split second he glanced up at his father's portrait on the wall.

"I cannot speak of it, Jean."

"Then Mhairi will."

But that was the last thing he wanted. "She displeased my father," he muttered.

"Displeased!" Jean echoed. "What depth of displeasure leads to a torture like that?"

Again his voice faltered. "I cannot say."

"You have to say," she insisted.

"Jean, Jean!" He had never pleaded with her before, but even his plea was no match for her ferocious compassion.

"Was Mhairi one of his whores?"

For a moment she wondered if she might have gone too far. A terrible expression crossed his face, changing it as the sun had changed the painted likeness of his father. But the moment passed. "She was traded from Glenshellich in the lawless days before the last Rising," he answered bleakly, turning away from the look of horror on her face.

"Traded!"

"Sometimes women were bartered along with the cattle. Especially troublesome women like Mhairi."

Jean was struggling to understand. How could Mhairi with her gloomy silences, her distant stares, her childlike giggle, ever be described as troublesome?

"When she first came here," Kilclath went on, "I was little more than an infant. But for me she always had a smile and a kind word. I remember her best – " He stopped suddenly. Jean scarcely dared breathe, but her eyes never left him as he drew breath and continued, "for soothing my grief when I lost my mother." He fell into another brief silence. "But my father also turned to her. And it was many years before she could escape."

"Escape?"

"I learned later she made first for Glenshellich. But John Stewart was in exile. His glen was impoverished and his people disinclined to charity. She found her way to Inverness, and that," he paused again and gave a strange smile, "that is where her life first touched those who would touch yours. She found a brothel there, where she worked alongside Hannah Bain and thrived as well as a whore can thrive any-where." Jean's eyes grew wide as he reached out and gently took her hand. "When I was deemed old enough to learn the world's ways it was there my father sent me. I recognised Mhairi straight away. She brought me whisky and we reminded ourselves of our old times together. When we had both drunk too much she showed me her scars." He paused, then moved on quickly. "Hannah had already taken the road south that led to the Chapel Land and your mother. With my conscience money Mhairi could lie low for a while in Inverness. But when my father died she came with me to Edinburgh, and there she has remained ever since."

"Conscience money," Jean echoed.

"As I have said, she showed me her scars."

"It happened here," Jean whispered.

His eyes narrowed. "She has nothing to fear now in the House of the Eagle."

"Except her memories." For a moment Jean looked puzzled. "She could have stayed in Edinburgh."

He smiled. "Perhaps she felt the need to watch over you."

Jean let the suggestion settle in her head. She looked up again at the Old Fox. "Your father . . ." she began.

But he held his other hand to his lips. "Let us speak of him no more, Jean. He can be no threat now - to Mhairi or anyone."

"Yet he still fills this house." When he did not answer she added in scarcely more than a whisper. "And that's why you stay away."

He smiled sadly. "It seems you know me too well, Jean. You read my heart." Then his manner changed. "Yet our business here is almost done. Neither you nor Mhairi need ever return."

Jean looked again at the portrait and felt a cold anger rise in her. You'll not get the better of me, she told the image. This whore's daughter from the Chapel Land is more than a match for your devilry. Jean could speak his language, in whatever tongue, and her voice was living while his was dead. She gazed levelly into his son's eyes.

"I'll come back any time," she told him. "Any time at all."

* * *

Andra' MacAslan steered his garrons through the bitter April wind. He had been disappointed to find the Valley of Stones so empty. The Campbells were in arms of course and the Master would not have been slow in leading out his forces, especially on so advantageous a campaign. But Andra' was as familiar a figure in Kilclath as he was in any of the western glens. He had been particularly welcome this time, for he carried more than silks and velvet, pots and pans. He carried news.

He drew his cloak around himself. The winter might have blown itself out but spring was proving as unsettled as ever. Glenshellich would bring him scant business, he reflected grimly, for those who remained would have little coin and less notion for his merchandise.

"Come on, my boys, " he urged his garrons. "No idling like your cousins up on yonder slopes. There's longer legging than this ahead. A single nights rest at the clachan's the best you'll have to look forward to."

The beasts plodded steadily down the rutted track in cheerful ignorance, splashing through the puddles that sparkled in a sudden burst of sunlight. Andra' hummed a low tune in accompaniment to the slow rattle of his wares. Was it just his imagination, or was the land more silent than usual? He raised his eyes to the giant's mountain and felt a chill whisper through his bones as he passed under its shadow. The clouds were gathering away to the west and already cloaked the higher peaks. The sky held a wheen of rain after all, he decided, nudging his beasts to quicken their pace. He reached the house of Glenshellich as the first big drops began to fall.

The girl with the golden hair opened the door. He had met her just the once, but remembered well her smile and her shining eyes, though he noticed they held a different expression today. He could understand the reason for it, so did not waste her time with pleasantries.

"Trade will be poor here at present, Andra," she sighed.

He inclined his head sympathetically. "A sair time," he began, and craned his neck towards the movement he sensed in the hall. But Eilidh spared him barely a glance as she stepped aside to let her mistress past. Andra' removed his bonnet and bowed low.

"What news do you bring from the road?" Helen asked eagerly. "Is there anything at all of good cheer?"

He drew his brows together. "Good cheer's in short supply for the Prince's friends, my lady. But there's bad news in plenty. How much have you heard yoursel's?"

He had a fair idea when he looked at her drawn face. Despite her swelling stomach dark purple shadows ringed her eyes.

"We hear only that they are in Inverness while the English army approaches from the east. But there has been no other word for nigh on two weeks. We hoped they might have found time to return, even for a day, but it seems Donald will not leave the Prince, and the men will not leave Donald."

Andra' nodded. "Though there's plenty persuaded differently. The army's a' ower the place. I hear of skirmishes over on the Black Isle, but Inverness itsel' is quiet enough, they say. Your side blew up the fort and seem well in command."

"But we cannot believe things go well," Christie observed.

"No," Andra' agreed. "Maybe no'. Mind, the good folk o' Aberdeen are none too pleased with the so-called duke and his army making free with their homes and possessions – the breathing ones an a'," he added with a wink at Eilidh. "Well who kens what'll come of it," he sighed. "Though I'll likely see for mysel' soon enough, for I'm Inverness bound." And should have gone there straight, he thought, instead of dallying in these deserted lands where none had the heart for buying and selling. The girl forced a smile. Maybe she had read his mind.

"Come away Andra'. No doubt you'll have something to interest us. And Eilidh will surely manage to find a bite for you."

Eilidh snorted, but led the way while Helen stood gazing at Christie. They were sharing exactly the same thought. Christie's resolve might have been formed in an instant, but she knew there was nothing on earth that could change it. She grabbed her cloak and hurried down the track to the clachan, and it seemed no coincidence that the first person she encountered was Meg MacCombie.

"Andra' MacAslan is at the house," she gasped. "And bound for Inverness."

Meg stared back at her. "Inverness, Meg," Christie repeated. Meg's eyes widened. It was a strange and wayward idea, but one of the very kind to appeal to her. She looked into Christie's fierce eyes and the newly set lines around her mouth and thought how these months had changed them all.

"Has time not been so hard to bear because of our ignorance?" Christie breathed. "You have felt it, at least as much as anyone."

Meg looked up at the mountain. The cloud was breaking again, drifting to expose the sharp peak against the brightening sky. She could almost make out the entrance to the giant's cave

"Well?" urged Christie.

"I will come with you of course," Meg said simply. "We are of the same mind. Domhnull is desperate for news of his father." When Christie looked away she added pointedly, "and also of his chieftain."

It was not so easy to persuade Andra' to have them accompany him. Their concern was for the rebels and his was to steer the calmest course through dangerous waters. But the women were determined and finally had their way.

"Were I not with child nothing could keep me from coming with you," Helen assured them, but Christie put her arm around her shoulders.

"Donald needs you here and safe," she told her. "And Fraser and Eilidh with you." As she spoke she shot a warning at her old friend. She knew he would have given anything to take the road with them, and she knew why. "Not that we will be in any danger," she added quickly. "And your fighting days are long past."

Fraser scowled. It was beginning to look more and more as if history were about to repeat itself and, if so, Inverness at present would be no place for women, especially women under the dubious protection of Andra' MacAslan. He made his own way to the clachan to consult with Catriona, but was surprised to find her resigned to the plan.

"The more voices in Inverness speaking reason, the better all of our chances," she told him. "It is not impossible that the Prince might grant Christie an audience. Remember also that she has friends on both sides." Catriona tried to smile, but Fraser could see that despite her words she was deeply troubled. "I think so often of her father," she breathed. "More and more as the years go on. I cannot believe his life was sacrificed for nothing."

"We are the only ones left," he said sadly.

"And we must stay strong," she told him. "For I fear our strength will be needed as never before."

That evening, as dusk began descend, Fraser took a hearty supper of venison with Eilidh and Andra' in the cosy kitchen of Glenshellich House. Helen sat in the firelight of her room, her feather quill scraping across the parchment as she poured out her thoughts, first to Donald and then to his brother. Only Christie heard Domhnull MacCombie's urgent hammering on the door. When she opened it he pulled her outside.

"My grandmother must speak with you," he gasped. "She must speak with you tonight."

Christie hung back. "I am busy, Domhnull," she told him. "It will soon be dark. I cannot come."

"You must come," he insisted. "She must tell you the *Faisneachd* before you go to Inverness."

Christie stared at him. He might have been inviting her simply to sup at his fireside, instead of to be told his glen's greatest mystery.

"The *Faisneachd*!" she breathed.

"That is what she said," Domhnull declared with the same calm understatement. Eilidh drifted past the doorway on her way to her mistress.

"I am going with Domhnull to the clachan," Christie told her.

Eilidh stared after them, and then gently closed the door.

Christie had never before set foot inside Beathag's hut. As they stumbled up the hillside the old woman appeared from inside. With a stream of invective and waving of her arms she dismissed Domhnull, who turned obediently and scampered back towards the clachan. Christie had not expected to be alone with Beathag and her sense of anticipation gave way to alarm as she was led into a reeking gloom colder even than the air outside. Beathag had no English, and spoke low in her own tongue as she pushed Christie towards a stool at the fireside.

"It is late you are in coming."

Christie's eyes were already smarting. Somewhere through the silence she could hear a steady drumming she knew was her own heart. There was no escape from the scrutiny of Beathag's sunken black stare. The old witch crouched low beside her and at her feet Luath gnawed casually at his charred bone.

"You were certain, then, I would come?" Christie breathed.

"Who else would tell you that which you need to know? Not the old men, for their councils are not for such as you. Not Catriona MacMichael, though she knows the *Faisneachd* well." She paused and her eyes glinted wickedly. "And of whom it speaks."

Christie leaned closer and Beathag stretched out her twisted hand to offer her an old clay pipe. Coughing, Christie shook her head, forcing herself to resist the almost overpowering urge to turn and run, to feel the bracken spring under her feet and breathe clean air. But she knew this chance would not come again. She must share Beathag's moment of bright-eyed triumph, and hold her breath as the old witch prepared to unlock her story of past and future.

"The river will run red but will not quench the flames," Beathag muttered. "Their smoke will shroud Beinn Feodag for a hundred years." Then her eyes narrowed. "With this war it will come. And we will see it, you and I."

Christie was no longer breathing. She did not dare to. She seemed to be drifting with the reeking trails that stroked their way up to the tiny hole in the thatch, drifting around the words of the old woman, words that were not her words but only issuing through her. Beathag cackled with satisfaction. At last she had become part of the secret, part of the destiny. She had no need to mutter the *Faisneachd* like the old men. She could recite it proudly to the one of whom it spoke. Retreating into the dark corners of her mind she could become one with those old seers. Her voice began as a hoarse whisper, but soon rose to a wailing chant.

"The first son of Samuel cast his seed in the moonlight. The second son of a second son will reap their bitter harvest. Seek him when the sun has fired the lake and the bolt has pierced the rain. Seek him in the time of the stranger saved from the sea, the woman with the mark of the knife. Cherish the days of his youth, for when the boy is a man will the time fall, when the last son of Samuel leads his clan to the death of their hearts." Beathag paused and squinted through the smoke, making sure that Christie was drawn with her inside the spell. There could be no doubting it. Satisfied, Beathag nodded and continued. "So told Lachlan Mor, the taibhsear, in the time of An Ciobar, Lachlan Mor who prophesied the murder of the queen from France and the end of the kingdom, who told of the false monarch from across the sea and the treachery he would make in men's hearts."

She paused again and drew a grating breath. Christie's head reeled. "Lachlan Mor..?" she breathed.

"Lachlan Mor MacCombie, many many times great grandfather of Angus Ban." Beathag chuckled, reached out and grabbed Christie's arm. "Who told us to look to the one with the sun in her eyes, the moon in her hair, the divided heart, for she will scatter the seed of Samuel and a new taibhsear will see new visions in a new land. Look not to the second son before the night of no shadows, look not to him until his deeds have made his soul weep, until he has plunged a deadly knife into his brother for ripping his heart more savagely than a hundred dirks." She stopped suddenly. Christie felt as if a cold hand had reached inside her and was twisting at her own heart. But Beathag had not finished. Her eyes glinted in the tiny flame that flickered from the hearth. "His brother will dig a grave he will breathe in, and worms will eat his living flesh. Because of him the glens will empty. No smoke will rise from the clachans and the pibroch will sound only laments. But the songs of the women and the children will be his songs, even though the sons of Samuel will be no more."

Beathag's voice faded into silence. The telling of her tale had transported her at last to the world she had aspired to for so long. She puffed out her skinny chest in a gesture that was at once proud and pathetic, her head tilted, waiting for Christie's response. For a long time Christie could only stare into the grey embers, and for all that time the only sound to break the silence was the gentle gnawing of Luath at his bone.

"It is …. quite terrible," she said at last.

"To some it is terrible," agreed Beathag. She had shrivelled back to herself again. "To Euan MacMichael it is terrible, and to his mother. To you perhaps, also."

"It does not tell of MacSomhairle's death," Christie breathed at last.

"A man can die many times. The *Faisneachd* tells of a different death."

"You do know, Beathag, that we go to Inverness in the morning, Meg and I?"

The old woman inclined her head, and then a panic seemed to seize her. "She will come to me before she goes!"

"Of course," Christie assured her. "We will not leave without saying goodbye." She bent down and lightly touched Beathag's head. The old woman was weary, tiny and drained by the telling of her tale, lost once more in the trails of smoke that wrapped and blackened her. Christie crouched through the door of the hut and stumbled out into a fresh air, now as alien as the stench inside had been earlier. She clutched at one of the giant's stones for support and her breath joined with the mist that sprinkled its moisture over the bracken. "*The glens will empty and no songs will rise from the clachans.*" As she gazed down at the deserted village, where no children played and no women gossiped in the waning light, she could almost believe that *Faisneachd* might already be coming to pass.

* * *

Catriona MacMichael regarded Andra' with a worried frown and wondered yet again if she should have done more to try to dissuade Christie and Meg from their venture.

"Are you sure the main road will be safe?" she asked him for the third time.

"Do you have no' a grain of faith in me, woman?" he grumbled, doing his best to make light of his own reservations. "A man who's travelled this route nigh on thirty years with scarce an incident."

"You are hardly the most tempting prospect even in times of peace. And to my knowledge you have never before ridden towards a war. I can only trust you'll put their safety before your own" she added grimly.

Andra looked abashed. "I would lay down my life for the ladies," he assured her.

Helen heaved a tearful sigh as he fastened down his packs. Catriona bent close to Christie's ear. "God go with you," she breathed. "Do not bring back tidings we dread."

Fraser shook his head sadly as he watched their figures sway into the distance down the track to the clachan. Why was he so ill at ease, so restless at being left behind? Out on the lochan Angus Ban's boat drifted towards the deeper waters. Fraser resigned himself. Some things never changed, he thought. Maybe they were the things that mattered most of all.

In the clachan Domhnull was pacing excitedly beside his mother.

"Andra' tells me there are boys in the army. Boys of my age."

Christie threw the peddlar a ferocious look.

"Well," he stammered. "Maybe just a bittie older."

"Domhnull knows he is needed here." Christie ruffled his thick brown hair. "It is the most important job we have left you with," she told him softly, "to be the man and help Fraser guard the house."

Domhnull kicked the ground but was pacified. Christie blinked away a tear as Meg took him in her arms and held him close. Then she looked for a long time into his face. "And your great-grandmother, Domhnull. You will mind her too, will you not?"

He nodded as slowly the little group began to make their way through the clachan, raising their hands solemnly to the women and children who appeared in the cottage doorways. The early mist was clearing and the day gave promise of being fine. They rode for the most part in silence, each wrapped in their own thoughts, Meg and

Christie keeping their distance behind the peddlar whose eyes darted constantly from side to side of the uneven track. Andra' was determined to make at least some business along the route, so they slept a night in a Cameron croft on the shores of Loch Arkaig where they learned that Lochiel had gathered his men and marched to Inverness. The same information met them at Fort Augustus, as they pressed on with growing haste.

"They are all there," Meg whispered and reached out to grip Christie's arm. Her eyes grew tight. "Domhnull MacSomhairle may be ready to sacrifice his life. But the black cloud did not hang above his head."

Christie did not understand. Black cloud or not she had her own terrible sense of foreboding as she thought back to her last encounter with Donald. Wherever he was, she was almost certain, he must by now have lost all hope.

* * *

Donald was standing beside his brother a few paces ahead of their men. The army was drawn up outside the graceful walls of Culloden House, the stately home the Prince had made his headquarters. Like all the Jacobite army Donald was tired, hungry and disheartened. Weeks of wasted effort with barely enough food to keep body and soul together had taken their toll. He was finding it difficult to meet his brother's eyes, but Andrew was reluctant to give way to despair.

"We have not lost a battle yet," he declared, hoping his voice did not sound as feeble as his words. "And the men have not lost their spirit."

"I wish I could believe it," Donald answered bleakly and gazed around their ranks. It was strange how clearly he could see them now, almost as if he had already ceased to be one of them. But if he had prepared himself for his own fate it was another matter altogether to take responsibility for theirs. They stood stoically before him in the sharp wind, their eyes dull, their stomachs empty, waiting for the orders he was ever more reluctant to give. For days now he had witnessed the squabbling of his leaders. For weeks he had despaired at the fragmentation of their army. Lord George Murray galloped past to join his Athollmen, and Donald saw his own hopelessness mirrored in the commander's face. The Prince had not taken Murray's advice on the choice of battleground, perhaps because his natural caution had seemed for so long more like the acceptance of defeat. In Donald's darkest moments it seemed to him that their leader had already lost interest in the campaign, even that he had almost ceased to care about the condition and fate of his men. He laid an arm across Andrew's shoulder as Hugh Fettes stumbled towards them.

"Cumberland has camped his army in Nairn," Hugh announced. "We are to march on them tonight."

Andrew stared at him in horror. "But the men have not eaten since yesterday, and are not likely to today."

Hugh made a face. "I believe," he replied grimly, "there are those among our leaders who maintain they will fight all the more furiously on empty stomachs."

Donald strode after the disappearing Lord George. "What is this latest scheme?" he demanded. "Has it your approval?"

The commander turned darkly to face him. "It is the best opportunity I can see. Look around you at the lie of this land and tell me how much hope rests here."

Donald's eyes scanned the barren moor that stretched before them. There was no cover, no protection, no secret places from which to spring. "It seems we must accept any order, then, and any fate," he said at last. "What a sorry end to all our hopes."

Lord George looked down sadly from his horse. "You will try once more for us, Donald," he urged softly. "Your men have equipped themselves with great honour so far. However dark it may appear, remember that God is on our side."

Donald was no longer sure of it, but he stepped aside to let Lord George press his horse slowly past. Then he returned to stand coldly beside Ardshiel as they watched the Prince, buoyed by his latest gamble, ride amongst them as eagerly as ever.

* * *

Jean Petrie slipped through the back door of The Ensign and into the shadows of Bella's close. The city's wynds were alive with stories, rumours and counter-rumours. The Duke of Cumberland was sweeping westwards from Aberdeen with a force no army could match, cheered all the way by his loyal subjects. The Duke of Cumberland had made himself enemies in every town and village for the looting and the coarseness of his troops. On the other side, the Prince had clansmen everywhere north of the Great Glen, the Prince was already in France, the Prince had lost half his army. Wherever the truth might have rested Jean had more pressing concerns of a personal nature and had come to seek Bella's advice.

"I ken a woman who'd do it tomorrow," Bella said. "No questions asked." Then she fixed a stern eye on her protégée. "I thought I had you better taught."

"If we're talking butchery you can forget it."

Bella raised the etched line of her eyebrows. "We're talking potions as a matter of fact. Potions that have never failed yet, to the best of my knowledge."

"And if I choose not to use them?"

Bella gaped at her as if she had taken complete leave of her senses.

"What would he do, Bella? That's what I came to ask, not how best to get rid of it."

Bella still stared, but a different expression had crept over her face, sly, secretive, almost fearful. "What would he do?" she repeated softly. "Dear knows, Jean, dear knows. But I ken what those who watch him," she screwed up her face and tapped her forehead, "would do, if you follow me, hen." Jean stared back at her with wide eyes, eyes that Bella had never been able to resist. "Dinna' make me tell their secrets, Jean. I thought to keep you safe from them."

"More secrets?"

"Secrets no' his, hen, nor of his making. Other people's secrets are his burden, other people's sins. Geordie Campbell's cursed, Jean, cursed until he gives Kilclath an heir. And for my sins you're preventing it. It was the last thing ever I wanted when I sent you to him."

"How would a child of mine prevent him having an heir?"

Bella drew back, as if fearing a blow. "You're no' the first to have said that," she whispered, before her voice took on a whining plea. "So come on, Jean, hen, will I no' just send for Agnes right now?"

Jean's mind raced. Bella might have taken her under her dubious wing, but compassion was not her strongest suit. As far as Bella was concerned those on either cusp of birth and death owed their existence to the convenience of the living. She had personally despatched more than a few in her time, from her own womb included if rumour spoke true.

"I tell you what, Bella," Jean said. "It's early days. I've missed before and nothing's come of it. Maybe we should just wait and see."

Bella squinted suspiciously at her. "Wait and see's no always the best plan for yoursel'" she warned. "Wait and see's too often left me short staffed."

"But that's hardly a problem in my case – unless you're thinking to offer me a position."

Bella shook her head. "It's an upstart you've gotten, Jean Petrie, after all. I might have kent it. You've been too long under his roof, too close to his business. But Kilclath business has aye been bad business, so take my advice and get out of it now." She leaned closer and gave Jean the full impact of her gin soaked breath. "A whore's already given Kilclath an heir. If it happens again they say it'll be the last."

Jean felt her heart pounding. But she met Bella's eyes defiantly.

"Why are you telling me this, Bella?" she asked. "Remember how you kept me for him, pure and untouched?" Bella looked as if she might be nursing serious regrets, but this Jean was not the same one who had left the Chapel Land eight years before. What's more she had become much more than simply what the Master had made her. "I am not a whore," she repeated slowly. "And I promise you now, there's no curse in this world that will come to him through me."

* * *

The chill night air woke Donald before Euan's voice. The first thing he was conscious of was the gnawing in his belly, the second was the need to put hunger out of his mind. He noticed that the numbers on the field had thinned since he was last awake, and little wonder, he thought, though they risked their lives for their desertion.

"We must make ready," Euan urged.

Fires crackled on the black moor behind them as they began their dismal and silent trudge eastwards. There was scant encouragement to be had from their Lieutenant General as their aching legs stumbled in relentless monotony over the rough heather and clutching quagmires. Men fell exhausted, their muttered complaints unheard above the desperate whinnies of the horses. Iain MacCombie staggered at the flank and made no attempt to raise himself. Donald made no attempt to rouse him and the clan floundered on through the driving rain.

At last a general halt was called and voices rose in dissent.

"This is no way," muttered Euan darkly at Donald's side.

"There is no way," gasped Donald as his ears strained to hear their leaders' words. Instead came the bitter voice of Kenneth MacCombie.

"If we must die we should not do so in darkness where a man cannot be cheered by the deeds of his brother. Give us the light to see our fate and know it."

For himself, Donald no longer cared how or where he died. He only prayed the end would come soon, while he could still stand upright, before he screamed his despair to his clan.

"We have walked three times this distance on the giant's mountain, and thought nothing of it," gasped Euan.

"It is the spirit, not the body, that is defeated," Donald muttered and lifted his eyes as he sensed the day growing from the east. The camp at Balblair would soon be alert, soldiers would be stumbling from their tents, hastily buttoning their red jackets in the dawning light. The Prince's horse reared among them.

"March back, my lads!" he cried. "We shall meet them later. March back and our chance will come!"

Grey light filtered through the shifting clouds as his army wheeled about to return the way they had come. Not a word now passed among the men from Glenshellich, no tales now from Euan MacMichael who had raised their spirits so often through the long winter treks. They seemed less like men than cattle, driven back to the windswept confines of Culloden, past Iain MacCombie and the others like him who lay as the strewn debris of their passage.

Back on the moor they flung themselves to the ground, careless of the damp that seeped from the heather, wearied almost beyond sleep. Donald looked down on them and believed his heart would break. Twenty-six men he had once called his own, had been proud to drill and lead, men who had left their glen in brave and giant strength, but now lay grey and wasted on this featureless waste. Donald's pride in them had shrivelled to a desperate shame of himself. Even these, he thought, even these have been brought to their doom by my tainted love.

Gently he shook Andrew by the shoulder. His brother blinked, drifting in and out of oblivion.

"Andrew!" he hissed urgently. At last there was a trace of a response. "Andrew," he pressed, "There is one more thing I need from you."

Andrew groaned and turned over onto his side, but Donald shook him again.

"Andrew!" he insisted. "Look at our men. They must have food. I need you to find the strength to go into the town."

Andrew was awake now. "Why me?" he complained.

"Because you still have distance in your legs."

Andrew looked at him with mounting suspicion. "Is that the order of my chieftain?" he asked finally.

"It is," Donald declared. "Bring us bread. I will not have the men from Glenshellich go into battle with empty stomachs."

Slowly Andrew pulled himself to his feet, and every muscle in his body cried out against it.

"Take Hugh with you," Donald added carelessly.

Andrew looked deep into his brother's eyes. He thought he understood Donald's reasoning. "You know there will be little food to be had." He ground his knuckles into his eyes, then let them roam the darkness that lay across the sleeping moor, the untidy lines and huddles of sleeping men. So there was to be no sleep even now for him, or for Hugh Fettes either. He gripped Donald's hand tighter than he had ever done, and lurched into the murky dawn.

Donald moved next towards his piper. Kenneth lay motionless, his pipes clasped to his breast. Donald gazed for a long time at the peaceful dignity of his slumber. He thought of the lapping of the water around Angus Ban's boat, the rustle of shellfish as they poured from net to shingle, the laughter of the woman who waited. He laid his hand gently on Kenneth's head, and the piper opened his eyes.

"Tell me, Kenneth," Donald whispered softly, "if you can in your weariness, who it was brought you to this place."

Kenneth raised his head and studied the face of his chieftain. "It was the Prince led you to this spot, MacSomhairle, and you who led me. As you followed him, so I followed you. It is the way."

"Then it will be the way no longer," Donald whispered. "The way is wrong that has led you from your family. You should be sleeping safe under your own mountain this night. And it should not be the pipes you hold in your arms."

Kenneth stared at him in dumb amazement.

"It will be the way no longer," Donald repeated, louder this time, loud enough to wake Euan who turned onto his elbow and looked from piper to chieftain with growing dismay as Donald moved more quickly among his men, stirring them from their stupors. "The way is wrong that has brought us here to die. Others have come to their senses. The men from Glenshellich should do the same."

283

"Their senses!" breathed Euan.

Donald ignored him. "It is in no clansman's heart to run from his enemy, but our old loyalties will destroy us." He continued to move urgently from man to man and barely felt Euan's restraining hand on his arm. "Today we will face a force we cannot beat...." For a moment his voice faded but returned more strongly. "Get up, Angus, Lachlan, there will be no shame, no disgrace. It is my order and you will obey it. It is the last order ever I will give you."

In a silence dense with shock their stunned faces stared back at him. Finally Euan broke it.

"So it is a coward you have become now, Domhnull MacSomhairle," he spat, and the accusation fell like a hammer-blow on each man who heard it. "And now you seek to betray all of us as well as yourself." He swept his arm around the stunned and weary clansmen, grey shapes wrapped against the darkness of the morning. "When have men from Glenshellich ever turned their backs on the enemy? These are men who will do a man's work when the time comes, whether or not they have strength left to grasp their broadsword. We have come this far and we will not surrender." His voice broke at last, less with fury than with his bitter disappointment in the man he had loved and revered above all others. "When you lie safe in your traitor's bed I wonder if you will spare a thought for those who would not run."

Donald stared back at his oldest friend, his brother, sick to see the hatred in his eyes. It was a long time before he could find a response, but when he did his voice was strangely calm.

"I thought you would have known better than anyone, Eochain, that I will not lie safe in my bed ever again. I followed the Prince because I believed with all my heart in the justness of his cause. But you followed him because of me. If I had remained in Glenshellich you would have remained there also. I am still pledged to the Prince's cause. If I have betrayed anything," he turned to Euan, "it is the ancient duty to bind each of you to my fate. I betray that cause with no shame, for I find I am unable to deal out death to those I love."

Another silence fell, but a different silence, and this time it was Kenneth who broke it.

"We stand or fall with our chieftain. It is the way, MacSomhairle: the only way we know, the only way we wish to know."

Donald's vision blurred with his tears as he stared around them in the creeping grey light. One by one they pulled their plaids tight, sinking back into the oblivion of sleep, until only Euan remained standing beside his chieftain. The tears ran unashamedly down Donald's rough cheeks and the thin drizzle washed Euan's twisted features. He pulled out his dirk and held it, handle first, towards his chieftain.

"It is now then, the moment," he said softly. "And not so terrible as I have feared."

Donald's voice was still gentle. "What do you speak of, Euan?"

"You will kill me now, MacSomhairle, as has been foretold, in anger at my words and the pain they have caused in your heart. I only ask that you will not remember me as I was when I spoke them."

Donald took the dirk from his brother's hand and let it fall to the ground. "Tell me of the *Faisneachd*, Eochain," he said softly. "For my hearing it can be of no consequence now."

Euan picked up the weapon and thrust it frantically back into Donald's hand. But once again Donald let it fall and laid his hand lightly on Euan's wrist. His own anguish had left him and been replaced by a strange calm.

"I am to die, Eochain, tomorrow. That must be written also. Do not deny me the story of my fate, especially when it is the last shadow to darken the love we have always shared."

Euan gazed down at the dirk lying on the heather. Then he drew a breath and, silently begging his old chieftain's forgiveness, began to recite the very same words Christie had heard in Beathag's hovel on the slopes of Beinn Feodag. And as Donald listened he heard also the voice of his father. "It not for you to concern yourself with, Donald. The *Faisneachd* is the work of the devil. I have not raised you to believe in such superstition." Yet on Drumossie Moor in the darkening morning the words of Euan MacMichael rang louder, as he repeated the prophecy of Lachlan Mor, the story he had so long kept buried in his heart.

Donald gazed at him for a long time after he fell silent. At last he said, "I have loved you above all men, Eochain. There is no way, no madness, no *Faisneachd*, that could make me take your life. Always I have been your brother. Today I need you tell me that you are mine."

It had drained Euan, the telling of the tale. The world had become so disarrayed that nothing was familiar; nothing was safe. But in the midst of this hell there was one thing he knew beyond all doubt. He looked deep into the distance behind Donald's eyes and whispered, "I am your brother, Domhnull MacSomhairle. I have always been your brother, and I will be always, for as long as I live."

They slept side by side, for barely an hour, yet Donald awoke refreshed to the sound of Kenneth's pibroch. Around him men were beginning to stumble to their battle positions. The Camerons followed the Prince and ranged themselves to the right of the Appin regiment. Charles's face was paler than usual as he sat astride his gelding, but his voice remained light and full of cheer.

"Come on my lads! The hour has arrived for King James your sovereign." When Donald's men made little response he pulled up beside them. "Donald, my good fellow," he cried. "Are your men in brave spirits?"

"Indeed they are," Donald lied. "And ready to do their best for you this day."

"It will not be long now," the Prince called over his shoulder as he made his way along the gathering ranks. "And what have I to fear with brave lads like you behind me? The day will be ours…" His voice tailed into the wind as more of Donald's men fell into position behind him. "Do not despair, my brave lads. The day will be ours…."

Arranged behind Ardshiel now the clan waited as the rain fell and the mist swirled above their heads. Donald sent up a fleeting prayer that Andrew and Hugh were still finding their quest as impossible as he had hoped. Euan stretched his stiff limbs and Kenneth shifted his pipes on his shoulder as the strange quiet spread over them. To more than just the fanciful it seemed the quiet through which poured the prayers of men for their souls. From far away the ragged strain of a psalm drifted above the poignant wail of a solitary pibroch. Beyond the field there was still much movement as people ran in search of their clan, past beggars quarrelling already, their clutching fingers impatient for richer spoils. There were women too, Donald noticed, standing in the unsafe distance, in little knots amongst tradesman and schoolboys, ghoulishly drawn to the spectacle that awaited. Above the featureless moor the standard of Appin rapped against the wind and echoed in the flags all down the line.

Euan stood at Donald's right hand two paces ahead of their men, their eyes straining in the direction from which the enemy was expected. Neither felt the need to speak, both sensing that the time for words was over.

Donald prayed for Helen. His fears for her safety were growing but, God willing, Andrew would find his way home to protect her. It had all passed beyond his control, the guilt, the tenderness, the heartache, and at last he let his thoughts rest with Christie. In his mind he set her apart, in a place that could not be marred by conscience, a place where the feelings they had shared could grow unblemished into all that had been denied them.

Then he heard the sound of drumming, regular, insistent, growing steadily closer. Turning his eyes towards its direction he saw the thin scarlet and white line emerge through the mist and heard the faint and feeble jeers from his own ranks as the line drew closer and into formation.

Lord George turned from Ardshiel, his expression drawn into tight lines of despair.

"What news, sir?" Donald asked.

"No news," replied the commander. "Even today I nursed some hope that the Prince would change his mind. Vain hope, I fear. But we cannot refuse his orders, however ill advised."

Donald narrowed his eyes across the flat ground separating the two armies.

"What use are our swords and dirks if we are to be mown down before we reach our enemy?"

"It will be a sad day for us, Donald, I fear – " His voice broke off abruptly. From somewhere in the centre of the line that stretched through Fraser and Chattan to the MacDonald hordes, came a boom and a cloud of smoke. Well to the fore of the government ranks the young officer who commanded Cumberland's front line was nonchalantly brushing down his jacket and a soldier two ranks behind him was ripped in two. At that moment Belford received his order to fire.

Beside Donald, Euan stiffened. The men drew up their plaids and fingered their sword hilts, keeping their eyes pinned on Murray to their right, waiting only for his order. No order came, only the shots of the enemy, rolling slowly, soothing in the sound of their coming, until they struck their mark. Donald saw them rip the ranks of Lochiel and watched the Cameron chief cry words of dismay and fury to their general.

"We must go." Euan urged, tight with restraint at Donald's shoulder, his eyes on the shots that bounced on in their devastating tide of destruction. He only needed Donald's word to charge, it seemed, as around them the noise grew, the cries of men and the clatter of swords on targes. Ahead Murray's commands were lost in the clamour as the eyes of the clansmen sought the enemy commander. All along their lines the highland artillery spun with the hopeless aim of pinning that stout figure, whom none could reach or even distinguish through the thickening smoke.

"No!" Donald tried to shout. "No! Their front line!" But his words were lost before they crossed his lips in the din and confusion. His men were jostling forward now, straining against the invisible leash that tethered them passive while their brothers were mown down. The round-shot still rolled slowly, unbelievably slowly, gently bounding and singing softly as it came. Surely, thought Donald this could do no harm? But even as he thought it he turned to his men.

"Scatter!" he yelled, but did not even hear his own warning. Behind him Angus MacCombie and Red Lachlan fell. For a moment his ears caught a thin complaint from Kenneth's pibroch as he stood firm beside his dead brother, his face spotted with his blood. In a blind fury Donald fought his way to Ardshiel.

"Go back to your ranks!" the chieftain yelled.

"Why are we not charging?"

"Lord George has sent to the Prince. Now get back!"

Donald returned, with no way of knowing that the order for the charge was mute in the hands of the young man who had died in the bearing of it. And so they endured more slaughter, despairing at the manner of their deaths. Minutes or hours passed. Time on Drumossie Moor had ceased for the men of Glenshellich, though far to the west in the shadows behind Beinn Feodag the day had already begun to descend with the hidden sun.

The cries grew stronger. "Loch Moy!" "Dumnaglass!" And suddenly the clansmen on their left were running, faces stained with mud and blood, wet plaids slapping numb thighs, hurling forward across the sodden ground. And finally Ardshiel was moved to follow them, his cry ringing high and clear through the air. "Creag-an-Sgairbh! – The Cormorant's Rock!"

The voices of the men from Glenshellich rose with it, a tiny part of the wild chorus that proclaimed their charge.

* * *

The road to Inverness was whipped with the same bitter squalls. Stray strands of hair were torn from beneath Christie's hood, slapping her eyes and stinging her cheeks.

"Look!" cried Meg, pointing, and Christie and Andra' followed her finger east to where smoke rose towards the murky sky.

"We are too late!" Christie breathed.

"We must make for town to learn the truth of this," muttered Andra, but his eyes strained towards Drumossie. "If need be we can find shelter. I fear it's an ill picked spot for a battle."

Meg and Christie dared not exchange a glance as they prepared to follow him.

* * *

In the confusion the right wing of the Prince's army met the Chattan men and they halted, bemused, as they took the grapeshot. To the right of them had been the dyke and behind it stood the Campbells. Ahead was a wall of red jackets and the popping of guns. With wild yells the Frasers threw down their pistols unfired and in a frenzy borne of nothing but despair prepared for their fate with only broadswords and targes, stumbling crazily over the dead and wounded that already littered their path.

"Creag-an-Sgairbh!" screamed Donald, and Euan's echo rose behind him. They could no longer see who had fallen but ran on, still urged from behind by the pibroch of Kenneth MacCombie. Then, suddenly, Donald fell, his features warped in pain. His men stopped on the instant and stood protectively around him while Euan dropped to his side and stared in horror at the shattered and bloody mess of bone and gristle that had once been the joint of his knee. Donald raised himself to his elbow and saw only bodies screaming and falling around him.

"Go on!" he urged. "Go on with Euan! He must lead you now!"

"No!" cried Euan. "It is nothing to me. I will not leave you."

It was Kenneth's yell that moved them as he sprang forward, the cry of Appin fierce on his lips. Then the Glenshellich men saw Ardshiel ahead.

"Go on!" Donald cried again, and this time they obeyed, even Euan, screaming his torment like a wild beast to the sky.

Donald watched them stumble beyond the screen of smoke into the flashing patchwork of scarlet and gave way to the tears of his own impotence. All around him were the dead and dying, washed in rain and blood. He turned his eyes to the wall and saw the plaids of the Campbells running to attack the Cameron men. At the sight of them a fury flooded his veins, the fierce spirit of An Ciobar who had crawled

290

from the stone valley of Kilclath with his tongue severed and his arms broken, the ruthless determination to look death full in the face and to spit in it. That same spirit would not lie in the marsh of Drumossie and wait for its end, but fight to salvage something from this wicked day.

Slowly he began to crawl forward, dragging his useless leg and ignoring the heaving of his stomach as his raw flesh grated over the rough earth. Men returning, wearied and sick, offered him their hands, but always he motioned them on, for there were those still charging and it was those his eyes followed and those whose goal he sought.

At that moment Kenneth MacCombie flung down his pipes and drew his broadsword. He had reached Barrel's frontline only to take a bent bayonet to his guts. Euan still hacked forward, though few were left to fight at his side. The musket fire passed him wide and none of the enemy dared confront the savagery of his attack. Then for a moment he stopped, arrested by the uncanny sight of a familiar face. For seconds the stricken eyes of James Hamilton held his in a grip of panic and terror. Some words seemed to show themselves on the boy's white lips and among them Euan imagined he recognised his own name. But the smoke thickened around him. When it cleared the boy had vanished and there were more pressing scores to be settled. Those whose fate it was to confront Euan MacMichael's wrath that day could not have known he was fighting for something more than his life. He was fighting for two men, with the vision of his helpless chieftain sprawled in the bracken urging him ever onwards.

But Donald had reached the soldiers. With an effort that almost sent him back to oblivion he pulled himself to his feet, for it would be unthinkable for MacSomhairle to meet his enemy on his knees. It was a Campbell who sprang towards a staggering Athollman and behind him came a soldier, his rifle poised to stab the clansman below his raised arm. Yet the Campbell's bayonet never found its mark for Donald Stewart's broadsword passed clean through him.

Euan saw it all through the blood that smeared his own eyes and began to force his way back to his chieftain's side. But there was fight-

ing and dying between them and the path was unclear. When next
Euan sighted him Donald had lost his sword and was reeling drunkenly, his arms flailing. Before Euan could reach him a soldier from the
thinning ranks was upon him and Euan watched in horror as the red
and white figure raised his rifle and brought down its blunted steel,
once, then twice, before, satisfied, he moved on.

* * *

Andrew saw the smoke rise above the moor at least two miles
distant and knew they were too late.

Hugh narrowed his eyes. "I say we make our escape. I say we
run."

Andrew flung himself down in despair. "I will run only to my
clan!" But his words sounded foolish even to himself.

"What use will we be to them now?" urged Hugh. "Let alone our
crumbs of stale bread."

Andrew's mind was in turmoil. He had no doubt what Donald's
reasons had been for sending them from the field. But his blood beat
against turning tail on his clan. He sank down onto the grassy track
and cursed all that had brought them to this place, their early victories,
the self-deception, the obstinacy of their leaders. Even more he cursed
himself for skulking yet again in Donald's shadow, a victim of his ill-
judged protection. Without it he would be dying with his clan, the
cry of Appin proud on his lips, instead of watching helplessly from this
unsought distance.

"Which way should we go?" he asked Hugh dully.

Hugh shrugged. "The sea is at our back. We would be sensible to
cross it. There will be fishing boats in Nairn harbour that could take
us at least some way clear."

Andrew thought he recognised relief and a kind of excitement on
Hugh's face. This particular adventure might have ended but a new
one, the dashing escape, already beckoned.

Hugh wrapped an arm around his shoulder. "Believe me, I understand your feelings, my friend," he urged. "But Donald would put your safety first. No-one would choose to desert their comrades, but what use would you be as a corpse?"

"I know it," whispered Andrew savagely. "I know it," and throwing his plaid across his shoulder he turned his back to the hills and his face towards the dark sea.

* * *

Soon there was an eerie quiet on the moor as the soldiers poked among the dead, gathering up discarded targes and muddied cockades. James Hamilton stood on the spot to which he had been rooted since the ceasing of fire, watching the sad little groups limp in retreat, around the litter of bodies that stared a sightless rebuke. He pictured them minutes before, numb fingers gripping broadswords, gashed legs pounding over the heather. Months before they would have tended their herds, fished the sea lochs, watched the firelight warm their old tales; perhaps sold bread in Edinburgh, mended chairs in Carlisle, swept streets in Inverness. Every body scattered here had its story. And every story shamed his own.

"Why do the troopers shoot the clansmen in the back?" he asked. "Why do they stab into the piles of dying?"

Kilclath's expression was solemn. "It is an ill way to end a profitable day's work," he agreed. "But we must rejoice at the conclusion whether its means justify it or not." He looked seriously at his young protégé and added, "I fear it could become an uglier business still." He surveyed the scene grimly. "I am removing myself to the town. You may join me if you wish."

James continued to stare helplessly about him. "I have no idea where I should be," he muttered. "I only know that I chose ill when I became an instrument of the slaughter of my countrymen."

Kilclath's expression was not without sympathy. "And had you chosen your father's path you would lie here too, another of the slaughtered. The standard these fools followed had its day a century ago. There is a chance of peace now at last in our land, and for that I thank God. Remove yourself from the carnage, James. Pity it if you must, weep for it if you will, but harbour no illusions and no regrets, for you are well rid of your inheritance this day."

But as James turned his face from the battlefield he knew he would never be rid of the sights of these last two hours. They would haunt his dreams forever. For the first time Kilclath's logic fell cold on his heart and he longed to hear again the wild emotion of Donald Stewart, the passion of his father's loyalty to their own King James. He had found himself among the victors, only to discover too late that their victory did not belong to him.

* * *

The stragglers were already stumbling into Inverness, where sentiments were undergoing a hasty reversal, alarmingly reinforced by the British Army and the tales that the first witnesses bore. A young officer stood in the roadway shouting orders into the panic, but the news was too fresh and alarming for them to be heeded. Perhaps unwisely it was this young officer who Andra' MacAslan approached.

"Maybe you could inform me, sir, what ails this town today?"

The young man regarded him with derision, but Andra' took no offence. "Would it by any chance concern the rebels who have so recently jeopardised the safety of our realm?" he continued.

The officer's expression grew more contemptuous still. "I am amazed at your ignorance, being so close at hand."

"We are newly arrived, sir, just minutes since." He lowered his voice and added confidentially, "I had hoped to be engaging in my appointed trade as seller of wares."

"In that case you could not have chosen a more unfortunate time," the officer sneered.

Christie was no longer able to contain herself. She thrust forward. "What is the news of the battle?"

The officer swung the focus of his irritation from the peddlar onto her. "You sound most concerned, madam. For which party might I enquire?"

"She has an interest in both," Andra cut in hurriedly. "And a most unguarded tongue. Would you please mind your impatience, Miss Hamilton, for the officer has more to concern himself with than the interrogation of a forward young lady." Christie threw him a look of fury, which he ignored. "Excuse me sir and thank you again for your attention".

All four turned suddenly, startled by a muffled cry drifting from the end of the adjoining close. A scream followed it. The very air was restless and soaked in danger. Andra' threw another apprehensive glance over his shoulder. Common profiteering was one thing, but placing yourself in such proximity to the front line was quite another. And there was the matter of the young ladies, rebels the pair and in no mind or condition to conceal either their involvement or distress. Luckily what happened next went some way to improve his state of mind, for Christie clutched his arm, gripping it so fiercely that he cried out, before she detached herself and took several halting steps forward.

Coming towards her was her brother, and as she saw him so his eyes fell on her. The fire that had burned in them on their last meeting had been replaced by an expression of glazed horror. Locks of unkempt hair hung over his forehead and his once white gaiters and cuffs were stained scarlet. They walked towards each other, James's breath heaving in great gasps, until he finally fell into her arms and buried his face in her neck. For a long time they stood wrapped together, while she gently stroked back his clotted hair. When she looked up her heart gave a leap. Standing at James's back was the grave figure of the Master of the Stones. Desperately pushing their last encounter from her mind she strove to maintain his detached gaze.

"He is but a boy," she breathed. "And not ready to kill."

The eyes of the Master of the Stones did not leave her. She knew too well what they saw. "He killed no-one," he stated briefly. "But he will kill the reputation of King George's Army if he continues this public exhibition." Meg moved a step closer to Christie in a gesture of support but Kilclath spared her the barest of glances. "Come to my room with him," he instructed. "And bring your raggle-taggle following."

Andra' prickled, but followed with some relief nevertheless, though Meg's acquiescence was more grudging and she laid on the Master a scowl every bit as dark as his own.

Kilclath led them down a drab close and up a narrow wooden stair that smelt of fish and polish, laced with urine. On the second level he turned onto the landing and kicked open a door into a stark room with splintered floorboards, a table, two chairs and an ancient dresser. He positioned himself on the other side of the table and regarded them solemnly.

"You must understand that the rebels are routed. The field resembled a bloodbath when we left it." Christie continued to stare in horror as he went on bluntly. "The road to town is littered with the bodies of those who tried to escape. The Duke of Cumberland's soldiers, as you have seen, are already in control here."

Meg could keep silent no longer. "The Appin men?" she stammered.

Kilclath kept his cold gaze on her. "I cannot enlighten you as to the exact fate of MacSomhairle and his clan, but you can be certain that, alive or dead, things will not be well with them."

"They are dead! They are all dead! There is carnage on the moor!" James cried and Meg's face grew tight. Seeing it he tried to pull himself together and stretched out his hand to her. She clutched it blindly. Kilclath studied the exchange dispassionately before returning his attention to Christie.

"The Duke is attending to matters there now."

She stared back at him. "With his medical officers?"

"It is his victory. To be celebrated as he thinks fit."

They held each other's eyes and this time Christie was not the first to look away. Cold anger had come to her rescue. "And you will celebrate with him?"

Her challenge seemed to trouble him, although his gaze remained cool.

"It is not," he replied, "what I would have hoped for. But treason has its price."

Meg's grip had tightened on James's hand and her face had turned ashen. Christie looked pleadingly at Kilclath. " Our friends are there. Her husband is MacSomhairle's piper. What can we do to help them?"

"It would certainly not be safe for," he hesitated and threw a doubtful glance at Meg, "ladies, to spend long out of doors here at present. I will arrange temporary lodging for you, and escort back to Glenshellich if necessary. Meanwhile I must report back for duty. I advise you to wait here until I can send someone with directions." He looked at James and frowned. "I will excuse you for the rest of the day in order to take care of your sister."

* * *

Euan MacMichael lay beside Kenneth MacCombie and his chieftain. He was unwounded but he lay as one dead. The chill of evening fell, while around them drifted a low, regular chorus of the dying. Then Kenneth lifted his head. "Go, Eochain," he whispered. "While there is still time."

"And leave him to their mercy?"

Euan stared dully into the ashen face of their chieftain. He fumbled inside his plaid for the brandy flask. He pressed it to Donald's lips and thought he heard him moan.

"Check his wounds," came the piper's voice again.

Euan was afraid to touch Donald's flesh. He remembered too clearly the soldier's stabbing bayonet. Yet his chieftain still lived. Euan closed his eyes tight and thought of his father. If he could fill his mind, heart and soul with him, then perhaps he could absorb something of his skill. His fingers found the wound, but they jerked back, red and sticky with congealing blood.

"There is shelter nearby," Kenneth breathed.

In the fading light Euan's eyes roamed the horizon, studded with the glow from the soldiers' fires and darkened by their shadows. He judged that alone he could easily cover the distance to the sheds and barns: with the burden of his chieftain he did not think it possible. But every so often a gap appeared in the line of guards. They were relaxing after their victory. The rebels were going nowhere and could be dealt with at leisure. Bursts of rough laughter merged grotesquely with dying cries. Euan eased his arms under his chieftain's shoulders and heard him moan again. He tested his weight.

"I will leave you MacSomhairle's flask, Kenneth," he whispered.

"Do not be a fool, Eochain MacMichael."

Euan briefly grasped the piper's hand. He must take the chance. He heaved his chieftain across his shoulders and Kenneth watched the reeling figure fade against the darkening sky. Then he sank back into the heather, closed his eyes with a half-formed prayer, and waited to die.

He had no idea how long he lay before he saw the English soldier, silhouetted against the glow of the fires, trailing two shadows that crouched and bent around the mounds of the dead. Darkness had settled completely now and the barn was no longer visible. He would never know if Euan had carried MacSomhairle to safety, for the soldier was on his knees beside him. He closed his eyes and thought of Meg and heard her say his name. When he opened them she was there, gazing down at him and he marvelled at the kindness of death. Then he realised that this soldier was not stabbing, nor shooting. He was clutching the muddied bundle of his own pipes. Meg pressed a flask to his lips and when their eyes met she began to whisper, secretly in their own tongue, of their home, the sunset over the lochan, the mist on the mountain. When she spoke of Domhnull her eyes were warm and soft. He saw no pain in them, no sadness. "Your son," she whispered, "will hear of your deeds this day. He will play them on your pipes for MacSomhairle." She smiled. "And one day he will play them for my mother in America." Kenneth tried to speak, but his voice had left him. "But you," Meg whispered, "have taken me to a place more wonderful by far." Those were the last living words that Kenneth heard. He did not know the moment his death came, save that his happiness ceased to be marred by the pain of his wounds. For a long time Meg cradled and rocked him and James and Christie crouched beside them. James looked down at Meg's black hair as it fell across her husband's face and wondered how anyone could bear such anguish. He did not dare think of his own unworthiness, the disgrace he had brought to the living and the dead. Then Meg raised her head and looked deep into his eyes. Tentatively he held out the pipes, but she shook her head. Somehow he understood that a different bargain was being struck. As if in confirmation she took his hand and laid it first on Kenneth's brow, then on the pipes. He had the strangely comforting sense that she was blessing him even as she bade him farewell.

"Domhnull," she whispered, "will play a pibroch for my mother in America. And you will be there to hear it."

Christie scarcely dared breathe. Something not of this world bound them, four souls in a strange limbo between past and future, life and death. But when Meg finally turned her eyes on her she knew why Beathag had so desperately needed to say goodbye. Suddenly Meg threw back her head and let loose a final cry that seemed to pierce the very night itself. It was a cry that gave voice to the dying, unearthly, tortured yet defiant, a cry that brought comfort to the vanquished but froze the very souls of their conquerors. Two soldiers came running towards her, and Meg rose to meet them. Christie watched in horror, too late to stop her, as she ran heedlessly towards their raised guns, cursing them in words they could not translate but could not fail to understand, while behind her the ragged heaps of the dead cast their monstrous shadows. James sped after her, but even as he ran he knew he would be too late. He heard the short report and saw the wisp of smoke rise gently through the firelight. He threw himself down beside Meg's body in the heather, and then looked up past the white gaiters and red coat to the coarse, hard face.

The soldier spat. "Damned savage!"

James rose, quite calmly, to his feet. "That was murder," he said softly. "Like all your deeds this day," and very slowly he raised his own musket to point directly between the soldier's incredulous eyes. He held it there until disbelief gave way to fear, and then, with a ruthless grin, let his hand fall to his side.

He heard the soldier's teeth rattle in his head. "Bloody fool," he stuttered.

"A fool who will remember your face," James answered softly, before a breathless officer reached them. He dismissed the soldier with a brusque nod of his head.

"What in God's name is going on?"

"I serve under Kilclath," James told him, in a tone every bit as aloof as his commander's. "And we do not condone butchery."

The officer eyed him angrily, but had no wish to tangle with the Master of the Stones. "Return to your post, then, at once," he ordered.

James stood his ground until the officer was out of sight. He had no intention of obeying. There was no post in the British Army he would return to ever again. He had been trusted with a commission far more important. He lifted Meg's body over his shoulder and carried her back to where Christie still crouched beside Kenneth.

"We are truly in hell," Christie breathed.

James laid Meg beside her husband and covered them both with Kenneth's bloody plaid. Then he crossed himself and cupped Christie's chin with his hand. "Maybe so. But these two are not. They have gone to a better place." Christie stared in amazement at the newfound strength in him. "Meanwhile," he went on, "we have another task. I think it would have our father's blessing. Let it be the last time I will need a traitor's uniform to protect me."

So for hours that night Christie Hamilton and her brother dressed the wounds of the dying clansmen and spoke soft words to them in their own tongue. They were not alone for others had been drawn there, women scoffed at and insulted by the soldiers but impervious to their taunts. And Christie looked into every face as she searched for Donald, for Andrew, for Euan, even for Hugh, but she looked in vain among the dead of Glenshellich. In the first cold light of dawn they returned to where Meg and Kenneth lay, at peace in each other's arms. James picked up the pipes and pulled the oak leaf from Kenneth's bonnet.

"Come then, Christie," he said softly. "It is time to try to find a way home."

* * *

Andra' MacAslan's eyes sprang open. A fearful scuffling was going on outside the brothel on the banks of the Ness where he had been forced to take his rest, not the usual scuffling that could be heard on most nights in the alleyway but something more frantic, something more desperate altogether. He struggled to his feet and moved to the window, but the brawl had moved to the lobby inside. He heard the creak of quick footsteps on the stair and tiptoed to lean his ear against the door. From the other side came rasps of breath drawn in desperation.

"For the love of Jesus and all the saints, let me in," a voice hissed. Then, "It is you, Andra'?"

Andra' drew back warily. "And who might you be?" he enquired, already beginning to nurse his suspicions. He swore inwardly. He had surely put himself in enough danger for one day.

Another curse followed. "Just let me in! For I know it is you, Andra'!" The voice grew more desperate still. "And if you do not open this door I am a dead man."

And that might be no bad thing, thought Andra'. It would certainly be a heaven sent release to one who had always occupied a special place in his heart. Angus Mac Ich Allach, once a young and handsome enough fellow, had succumbed over the years to his own fecklessness and fondness for whisky. With it he had lost the love, though perhaps love was too strong a word, of a good woman, Andra's own niece, whose dwelling he was contemplating making his next port of call as soon as he could escape the clutches of the women from Glenshellich. Morag had been a foolish lassie, learning sense too late. Now she was left with two bairns and a croft to keep while her fine suitor trawled the stews of Inverness. Like many another Morag had fallen young with Angus' child, and like many another had come to rue the day. Now her bonnie face was hardened by years of toiling to raise hungry bairns by the sweat of her own brow. Andra' swore again. Blood was thicker than water. He lifted the latch and Angus' fell inside, stinking of whisky and the sewer. Before he closed the door at his back Andra' heard another movement, a footstep furtive as a softly drawn dirk.

Angus fell cowering to the corner. What a specimen, Andra' thought grimly, what a disgrace to the lassie who in ten years with him had lost every ounce of the joy that had once shone from her. Angus Mac Ich Allach was a sorry picture indeed as he snivelled among the cobwebs. Angrily Andra' motioned him to silence and listened again. This time the footfall was louder. Angus clutched at Andra's jacket as if it was his last hope in an unforgiving world. Andra' took a step backwards in disgust.

The door groaned with the weight of muscle behind it and the thin wood bulged and splintered. Angus fell back again and buried his face in his plaid as the lock burst to reveal two clansmen, gathering measured breaths, their eyes hard with intent. Andra' backed into the shadows, but it was him that the older clansman addressed.

"If you would please to excuse us," he said softly. "We have last business from our chief." He pulled out his dirk.

"No!" screamed Angus, throwing himself once more at Andra's feet.

The second man took a step towards Andra'. "A friend of yours?" he enquired.

"Most certainly not," Andra assured him, trying his best to disentangle Angus' fingers from his jacket. "A distant relative – by marriage," he added, in case there might still be any doubt.

"Then we are come to do his wife a service," the man snarled. "His widow, I should more likely say, for this dog fled from the field at the first sound of the English guns. He has brought disgrace to his tacksman whose justice we now serve."

Angus convulsed, but to Andra's amazement found spirit enough to answer back. "Who forced me from my home and my plough and my bairns who will now be left to starve!"

The older clansman turned again to Andra' "It is good that his last words are of his bairns. You will tell that, I trust, to his widow, for we will be many miles away by tomorrow's nightfall."

"Though not as far as Angus Mac Ich Allach," added the younger one and drew out his dirk. A single thrust plunged its point through Angus' breastbone with such force that it appeared immediately between his shoulder blades. Andra', who had never before seen a killing so close at hand, was surprised to find himself more fascinated than afraid. The older clansman eased his brogue under Angus' ribs and rolled him over while the younger gripped his arms and hoisted him across his shoulder.

They left the door creaking gently in the draught that blew from the street, and before long Andra' heard a discreet splash, too soft to be noticed on this night of greater evils, which, perhaps fittingly, was the last sound on earth that Angus Mac Ich Allach would ever make.

* * *

"You are an Appin man," came a voice from the corner of the barn, "and have no wounds?" The voice held a note of wonder, for few from the army's left wing has emerged unscathed.

"I am indeed unharmed," Euan agreed. "But my chieftain is...." He choked on the sob that rose in his throat. The struggle through the heather to reach the brief safety of the barn had perhaps been a mistake after all. Euan was afraid even to look at Donald. "He is, as you see."

The voice became a man, ragged and wiry with lank hair clotted with blood. His eyes gleamed with a strange light and he pulled himself across the earth with one bloodstained arm, keeping the other clamped to his side.

"Show me!"

Euan made room for him and watched as he ran his good hand over MacSomhairle's shoulder and gently peeled the blood soaked shirt from his body. The wounds gaped wider and angrier even than Euan had dared to imagine.

"Best make good your own escape," the man whispered.

Euan shook his head helplessly. "I cannot leave him."

"Then I fear two more lives will be lost from the green shores. The soldiers will come before too long. He must not stay, yet he cannot be moved." He looked down at Donald again and he shook his head. "His leg also?"

Euan felt the despair rise in his throat. So the struggle to the barn had been in vain. The man ran his hand gently over Donald's thigh just above his shattered kneecap.

"I have water, only a little…" he murmured.

"I have my shirt." Even as he spoke Euan stripped the shirt from his body and began to tear at it, for he sensed something about this strange man that gave him cause for hope.

"It is not clean," the stranger said. "But that is a risk we must take."

Together they wiped the blood from the three bayonet wounds on Donald's chest.

"You are a healer," Euan breathed.

"Not me. My father was a healer."

"As was mine," gasped Euan and dared once more to wonder if perhaps between them they might have inherited enough to save Mac-Somhairle. The clansman continued to wipe the wounds, carefully, tenderly, muttering and whispering until at last he looked up.

"Bind his chest."

Euan tied the strips of his shirt as tightly as he could.

"Do you have money?" the clansman asked.

Euan raked in his pouch. He found a few coins and took more from Donald's. He handed them to the man. "This is all."

The man let the coins trickle through his fingers. "I will offer them to the guards for my escape. If they accept I can die alone, away from this carnage. It is chance for us both. While I speak with them you must make an escape."

"Are you sure?"

For the first time the stranger lifted his other hand from his side. A mess of guts was ready to spill from the scarlet hole.

Euan cursed softly. "Then God go with you." He briefly clasped the man's arm. "There will a song of you if we find our way home."

Stealthily, with his chieftain's lifeless body bound across his shoulders, Euan followed the unknown clansman through the shadows towards the guard. All around them hung the stench of smoke and death, though few sounds now disturbed the moor's quiet. Euan heard the slow tramping of his feet above the pounding of his heart, while all the time his eyes strained to keep sight of the frail silhouette lurching ahead along the line of the soldiers' fires.

"Stop!" a voice called and Euan caught the mumbling pleas of the clansman as they mixed with the strange English accents. Their scornful bargaining faded as he stumbled further into the blackness. The wind bit through his plaid and froze his naked chest. He heard no more shots and staggered on under the dead weight of his chieftain. To the north the lights of Inverness struggled towards the hidden stars and some blinked on the black water of the firth, but darkness engulfed Euan MacMichael, its blanket at once his protection and his danger. Only instinct told him the way west, the way he must travel through the hills of Mackintosh and MacDonald, then south to where the cattle of the Camerons grazed, south again and west to the shores of green where Loch Linnhe lapped gently in the quiet evenings, and finally west and north to Glenshellich. But before the next dawn, he must find shelter in the hills around the waters of the Great Loch. He must make time for MacSomhairle to rest and find some strength. Euan MacMichael struggled on, damp and chilled to the bone, his eyes on the ground, his legs aching beyond weariness. For hours, if hours there still were, his numb mind fought sleep, his raw feet trampled through heather and marsh, until at last the blackness turned to chill grey and the pewter waters of Loch Ness stretched before him. Now that he had light his eyes scanned the hillside for hidden places. He began to climb among unfamiliar rocks that spun before his eyes and took on wild and threatening shapes. At last, exhausted even beyond caring of their fate, he slumped against one of them. It took another eternity to lay MacSomhairle's body beneath the craggy overhang, to wrap it carefully once more in its plaid, and to listen and feel for a sign of life. It was faint, but still there, a tiny breath through grey lips, a trace of warmth in the pit of his arm. Euan tried to find strength for a final prayer but the world around him was fading. He pulled his own plaid tight and collapsed into unconsciousness.

* * *

By afternoon of the next day James Hamilton had still not reported for duty. More alarmingly, from Kilclath's point of view, his sister and her companion had clearly made no use of the lodgings he had organised for them. Hughie McIvor was finally despatched to discover the whereabouts of the peddlar in whose improbable company they had last been seen.

Hughie slunk through the town's narrow wynds, their familiar drabness transformed by red and white uniforms, impatient officers appeasing anxious townsfolk, swaggering soldiers squabbling over their spoils, jeering as each new batch of ragged and pathetic prisoners was marshalled to the overcrowding gaols. In the distance he could hear the carpenters steadily hammering nails into the gibbets that would be the next destination for most of them. Hughie had a lifetime's acquaintance with the town's less reputable quarters, the streets beyond the Crown where the gabled sandstone buildings gave way to squalid turf huts with their upturned baskets for chimneys. Where the two districts merged lurked the secret places, haunts of shame for the God fearing and damned alike to indulge their guilty pleasures. Hughie had frequented these brothels before ever he sprouted a beard, as had his own father before him. But he remembered best the countless vigils, ankle deep in gutter filth, dirk in hand, while he waited for the Old Fox to finish his business. Padding past the splintered shutters he closed his ears to the ghostly chorus of pleas and whimpers and more chilling silences his master had so often left behind him. He read again the message on the plaque on the wall. *The voice of the Lord shaketh the wilderness. The voice of the Lord divideth the flames of fire.*

He stopped and listened. "I am looking for Andra' MacAslan," he announced in Gaelic to a barefoot crone who eyed him from inside a close.

"Who needs him?" she snapped.

"An officer of the Duke."

She nodded her head in the direction of the ramshackle, three housed building leaning over the gently lapping River Ness. He gave her a coin and a wink and made his way inside.

Andra' gave every appearance of having been wakened from a long overdue slumber, though the look he threw the Master's ghillie was remarkably shrewd. He had not made his forays through Kilclath blindfold. He struggled into his jacket and hurried after Hughie as he led him back to the Master's quarter.

"Travelling companions, your lordship," he explained. "And no more than that I can assure you. We fell in on the road and soon fell out again in the town."

The cool gaze Kilclath fixed him with suggested that anything Andra' might have to say could hold little interest.

"It would be unwise to be anything but honest with us, under present circumstance."

"Indeed, unwise, to be sure," gushed Andra', desperate to avoid a repeat of anything like his previous night's adventure. He gave a discreet cough. "But the truth of the matter is I did not think it necessary, or indeed appropriate, to inform the ladies of my whereabouts."

"So you have not seen them since...?" Kilclath waited for Andra' to elaborate.

"Since the young gentleman was about to show them to their rooms, your honour."

"And you have not seen the young gentleman either?"

Andra' shook his head glumly. Dishonesty might be unwise, but honesty in this case more so. Andra' had no intention of mentioning the fact that he had spent the morning procuring two underfed and badly used ponies for the young lady and gentleman in question, or that he had last seen them taking the road west. It was also too soon to deliver the letter he had been entrusted with passing on to this chieftain and now king's officer. Someone with no connection to himself could dispatch it in a day or two, when the Hamiltons and their bitter tidings had made their way back to Glenshellich. After that, well Andra's memory could be as unreliable as anyone's.

He breathed a hearty sigh of relief as the cold street air hit his face. His garrons should be well rested by tomorrow and fit to carry him and his own bitter tidings to what he sincerely hoped would be a safer place.

* * *

The very sky seemed to weep as Christie Hamilton and her brother took the way west, along the same road she and Meg and Andra' had travelled only two days before. The brooding hills were streaked with shadows and reflected in the wind blown waters of the loch. Needles of rain stung their faces and made puddles of the potholes. James rattled his sluggish pony's reins but the beast would go no faster. It had been a miracle Andra' had found mounts for them at all, since every garron and packhorse had been speedily requisitioned, first by one army then the other. The track was almost deserted. The soldiers had more pressing business still in Inverness and on the moor. Christie did not let herself think of the scene they had left behind them that morning, the sight of the calm dead faces of Meg and Kenneth, the tortured cries and moans of those who foolishly believed that mercy might still exist. She did not let herself think of the wickedly mutilated bodies by the roadside, the knots of prisoners gasping for food and water, cringing under the slashing blades of the troopers. They had found fifteen Glenshellich men dead on the field and two dying, a grisly list to take home to their widows, their mothers, their orphaned children. For those they had not found, for Euan, for Donald, for Andrew, for Hugh, for Iain MacCombie, for Charles Edward himself, they could only cling to a forlorn hope.

"Will Kilclath understand?" she asked her brother. "Or will he see this as another betrayal?"

"He will receive my letter soon," James said. "And I hope he will understand, though it is hard to believe his friendship will survive my desertion."

Christie was inclined to agree. She only hoped that between them they had not turned him into an enemy. But it was easier not to think of him at all. Instead she said, "You and I were born tied to the cause of the Stuarts. Perhaps there was never a choice."

"I will serve no cause ever again," James declared, "save that of common humanity and justice. I have witnessed more than enough of the ways of kings."

They saw no red coat other than his own as they followed the road past Fort Augustus. Once they passed a knot of squabbling beggars who fled with their ill gotten spoils into the hills at the sight of James. Once they met a group of herdsmen, mainly young boys with dogs snapping impatiently, who scampered past without a greeting. From time to time they imagined they saw movement on the higher slopes and at those times Christie wondered if her brother would be safer in different clothes. But the further west they journeyed the more silent the land became. At last darkness and the eerie mist made them rest for another night in Cameron country. The horses were glad of their chance to graze in the open and seemed stronger and more willing when they set out again in the hazy dawn, though James and Christie felt their hearts grow heavier the closer they came to Glenshellich.

The drizzle continued softly as they passed the Watcher's Stone. Ahead of them the lights from the clachan glowed dimly through the dusk, and Christie finally understood the cold reality of the empty glen. Their homecoming went unnoticed by all save the softly lowing cattle and Beathag whose dim eyes peered through the crack in her doorway. She saw nothing, but had no need of the first sight when her second had already told her what tidings these riders brought. Luath looked up from his bone and gave a mournful little whimper as James and Christie bent their heads into the shadow of the track that led to the house. Weariness dragged down Christie's heart. Now they were home she could not bear the thought of telling what she had witnessed. She had a vague impression of Fraser's solemn face in the lamplight, and of Catriona drifting behind him. Somewhere too, she knew, were Helen and Eilidh of the scarlet face but their images faded and she fell back into the welcome darkness inside her brother's arms.

* * *

Hugh Fettes stumbled as the musket prodded him forward. He choked, spraying the contents of his mouth across the back of the red coat ahead. His reward was a sharp blow to the temple.

"Damn you, you bastard," he muttered to the sergeant responsible.

"Not me that's damned, mate," was the cheerful reply.

Andrew turned his head away and tried not to imagine the scene at the croft they had left behind. His nostrils still held the acrid stench of the smoke from the barn; the cries of the woman who had sheltered them still rang in his ears. They had bound his hands and marched him away before he could go to her aid. He prayed the soldiers had been content to let the burning of her barn suffice as punishment, but the sights they passed on the road into Inverness soon told him that this was not a time for prayers to be heard.

Only when they staggered into the town did they realised the true enormity of their defeat. The citizens who had joked with them days before now jeered and spat and jumped to obey every order and whim of their new masters. Keeping their heads high, Hugh and Andrew were marched through the babbling crowds to the Tolbooth where they were hurled into an airless cell, its damp stone walls already bulging with bedraggled and wounded men, its floor already awash with effluent and blood.

Andrew leaned against the crumbling stone and closed his eyes. The cell was not noisy, for the inmates had neither inclination nor energy for conversation, but their groaning made sleep impossible. At last he turned to Hugh who was hunched over his knees, gazing around him in despair.

"We are gentlemen," Hugh breathed.

Andrew had no idea to whom the remark was addressed, but heard a soft voice echo, "Gentlemen!" An unpleasant chuckle followed. In the corner, through the dim light, he could make out shaking hands with palms held upwards, and the whites of someone's eyes. The metal door grated open then clanged with merciless finality as two more wretches were flung inside

"Hell must have its share of gentlemen," Hugh whispered. Andrew shuddered and tried to make his way towards an old man who writhed and groaned on the filthy floor. He dug deep into his pocket and pulled out a crust of bread.

"Feed the healthy first," a voice hissed from the shadows. "Why waste bread on the dying?"

Andrew slumped back and let his head fall into his hands. Why indeed? And what use were his paltry scraps to any of them anyway? He tore a strip from his shirt and began to wipe the ugly wound on the old man's shoulder. Without proper cleansing and treatment the festering would become dangerous. There was a smell of death in the air. Perhaps some of these stretched out along the walls of the cell had already passed through its gates. Andrew looked around him and was met with blank and hopeless stares.

"What happened on the moor?" he breathed.

Some of those with enough strength took up their stories, but to relive that last battle was too humiliating. Soon the prisoners consoled themselves with prouder memories: Falkirk, Prestonpans, older conflicts buried in the ancient lore of their clans. But as the minutes stretched to hours the voices dwindled. Wounds festered and the sickness turned to fever as the foetid air choked them. Hugh vomited and grew faint, mumbling nonsense. Then came silence as the cold hours followed one upon the other, until it was no longer possible to distinguish night from day and still they were brought no food or water.

"Why are we here?" Hugh moaned in a rare lucid moment.

"We are all rebels, and treason knows no rank," Andrew told him grimly. "We are doomed as surely as those who perished on the moor." Donald's futile scheme for their safety had been just another misfortune and Andrew had no sense of any of their fates. His gift was silent. There was nothing more to do but wait for whatever the victors had in store.

* * *

Edinburgh buzzed with excitement. The Prince had once again been victorious and soon the country would be back safely in his army's hands. Gavin MacVey listened to Alison's outpourings of jubilation with a half raised eyebrow, and the next day's more reliable information proved his scepticism well founded. Before too long the guns from the Castle were firing a different salute, a salute echoed by the warships off Leith as the Whigs of the city breathed hearty sighs of relief. Alison took to her bedchamber in mourning and refused food for two nights and two days. When she did rejoin the world of the living she would receive no presence but Kirsty's for days more. Never again would candles glow from her window or taunts gush from her lips. Never again would she raise a glass or drop a curtsey to the one true king. Yet neither would she ever condemn the recklessness that had brought her Prince briefly home to glory, or apportion him the slightest blame, for deep in the ruins of Alison's shattered heart the petals of the white rose would never wither.

EUAN

Andra' MacAslan was not singing as he guided his garrons down the track by the loch's edge. The past few days were not ones he would care to repeat, and who was to say what further dangers might lurk in the weeks and months ahead? He could not keep his eyes from straying fearfully to the hillside. Better by far to have taken the road east as he had first intended, through townships where canny merchants looked to their own business and kept their fingers out of the pies of kings. But not for the first time in his recent past his good sense had betrayed him: in fact had apparently deserted him altogether. His wares clattered and rang behind him, broadcasting his presence to every desperate cut-throat for miles around. And Morag would hear the news soon enough without this tomfool detour into rebel territory. He shuddered as he recalled the dark eyes of the Master of the Stones, drilling into his, and for all he knew seeing right through the lies that had stammered from his lips. Andra' shook his head at his own folly. First he had landed himself up to his neck for the sake of a bonnie face and a pleading eye, and now there was the matter of his niece.

He judged his position. Ten miles or so to go and the clatter of his passage echoed more noisily as the gorge closed in around him. Andra' cursed the rebels with all his heart, savages that they were with their heathen ways, deserving of all they'd got for making the country's highways unfit for honest men, well near enough honest men. With luck the girl would be home by now, and her brother who had too late learned the ways of war. Andra' had been familiar with those ways all his life, but from a safer distance. His unease grew as he passed under a rock's shadow. He had the sense of eyes in the heather. It was grim country indeed, these highlands he had come to know so well yet never grown used to. On days like this when the clouds hung low and the mist obscured the mountains it was a land that chilled his heart with its damp and its silence.

He swore again as he thought of Angus. Morag would be disgraced by his cowardice and her son shamed, but at least she would be free of him. Maybe Andra' would take the boy himself. There would be no future on the slopes of Loch Ness with the wrath of the MacKenzies simmering, for while just one of them lived the story of Angus' treachery would never be forgotten. But shame or no shame, Morag was deserving of the truth, and it seemed to Andra' that he was the one best placed to tell it.

If he was given the chance. In less than a second after turning his attention back to the road a cold steel was at his throat. Instantly he dropped his reins, threw up his hands and froze on the seat of his cart, a statue in stone save for his terrified eyes, which swivelled in their sockets, needing yet dreading to catch a glimpse of his attacker.

"I have you," a voice hissed in English, "so do not even think to struggle." The knife slipped from Andra's throat, but his arms remained pinned as his assailant dragged him from his perch. He finally summoned the courage to turn his head but what he saw was hardly reassuring. Towering above him was a huge clansman, ragged and terrifying, an expanse of naked chest gleaming from beneath a soiled and steaming plaid. Andra' tried to control his trembling and introduce his wits.

"Well, well," he bluffed. "A fine object for an innocent traveller to be stumbling upon. Is it to be murder then, or just the plain daylight robbery?"

The man gave a native curse and let his arm fall to his side. He took a step backwards and sheathed his dirk, though Andra' noted with some alarm that it was stained all the way along the blade. "It is yourself Andra," he exclaimed. "Do you not know me?"

Now that Andra' came to think of it there was something familiar about the fellow. He looked again, ready to answer in the negative until he noticed the bedraggled sprig of oak in the man's bonnet.

"It is me Andra', Euan MacMichael, son of Euan the healer and Catriona from Glenshellich."

Andra' gaped back at him. This was a co-incidence too far.

"It is God's will that you are passing," Euan told him. "For Mac-Somhairle is on the hillside and near to death if I cannot find him shelter and rest. Yet for both our sakes I can carry him no further."

Andra' exchanged a few words of his own with his maker, but had already resigned himself to Euan's next demand. "I'm bound for my niece's croft then, just south of Foyers," he sighed. "I daresay we could take him there in the cart."

No sooner had the words crossed his lips than Euan sprang back into the hillside and bounded out of sight. Andra's troubled eyes gazed after him. Bad enough to be the bearer of bad tiding, but to bring two rebels along with it was evil luck indeed. Yet if MacSomhairle was wounded in the heather then his man would think nothing of cutting an old peddlar's throat for his horses, old acquaintance of his mother's or no. He sat back and looked about him. The mist was clearing and a patch of blue had appeared in the sky. Before long he saw Euan returning, his chieftain slung across his shoulders. Andra' grew uneasier still, yet felt obliged to offer some help. He tethered the cart and glancing both ways down the track began to climb towards them. He could see immediately that the situation was desperate.

"How long's he been like this?" he whispered.

"The wounds are from the battle," Euan told him. "I have dressed them with some sphagnum moss and bound him with my shirt, but he must be properly rested and treated."

"Is he conscious?"

"He has sometimes been. It is better when he is not." Euan took a deep breath. He felt close to tears. He could not remember when he had been so glad to see another human being. Although Andra's reaction was entirely the opposite he began to rearrange his wares to make enough space on the cart for the chieftain to be carried as comfortably as was possible.

"I'll be truthful, it's no' looking good," Andra' muttered.

"It looks better than it has done for the past two days," Euan answered, tightening Andra's leather strapping and wedging Donald between a pile of worsted cloth and the side of the cart. He wrapped his own bonnet around a stone for a pillow and placed it gently beneath his head. For a brief moment Donald opened his eyes. He saw the blue sky and Euan's face gazing down at him. He heard a horse's gentle whinny and felt the jarring of the cart as it began its unsteady motion forward. But it was all too much. His empty stomach heaved and his leg throbbed unbearably.

"We are on our way to safety now," Euan told him, but the safety that Donald craved was beckoning him again. He felt himself slipping towards it as he loosened his grip on his brother's hand.

* * *

Andrew was dreaming he was slung across the back of a horse that plodded and swayed, its rhythm lulling him into a treacherous security. He was being carried past the Watcher's Stone, and he opened his eyes in sudden panic. He was being carried the wrong way, not into Glenshellich but out of it, and above his head an eagle swooped and soared. He was brought back to reality by the clanging of metal and a harsh voice, cursing in a strange accent.

"Jesus, the stink!" The guard coughed violently, then Andrew heard the rattle of keys and the sound of something being dragged. A rough hand grabbed his arm.

"Get up, dog!"

Andrew felt the sting of the man's spittle on his face as he was pulled to his feet.

"Do as you're told right away, you rebel scum," he was told.

He stared defiantly into the guard's unshaven face. "Do not you presume to address a single man here as scum," he snarled. "We are prisoners of war and must be treated as such."

This time the guard's fist struck him full in the mouth and sent him spinning across the floor. He heard groans as the others in the cell stirred, but the guard ignored them. "Now get up and show some respect for the captain!"

The Master of the Stones was required to stoop to gain entrance before he took two paces inside. He held a handkerchief in his hand, but unlike the guard did not raise it to his face. If the scene before his eyes appalled him he gave no sign of it.

"Mr Andrew Stewart of Glenshellich, I believe," he said slowly, and let his eyes move from Andrew's bloody face to the figure still sleeping beside him. "And Mr Fettes of Ballingry, by my life. Treason exacts a sharp price, does it not?" He turned towards the guard. "When did these men last receive food and drink?"

"I cannot say, sir."

"How long have they been lodged here?"

"Two days, some, others since the battle."

"And what have your orders been during that time?"

"None concerning food, sir."

Kilclath allowed the tension to linger for some seconds. "Then I must compensate for General Hawley's oversight," he stated unambiguously, "and give you different orders. Meal and water will be provided immediately, as will bandages and medicines. I will personally find a surgeon to perform any operations that can still be usefully carried out."

"There are three dead men here, Kilclath," Andrew broke in, almost overcome with relief. "We have stripped them and lain them in that corner."

"Remove them immediately," Kilclath barked to the guard. He came further inside the cell and was finally compelled to cover his face. "I will make a list of the names of these prisoners."

Andrew watched his face darken as he noted each name and dared to step forward. "Do you have the names of those wounded – or killed – on the field?" he asked.

Kilclath's expression immediately hardened. "Why would I exchange information of that nature with a captured rebel?"

"From common humanity." Andrew did not flinch from Kilcath's cold gaze. "And from honour."

"Honour," echoed Kilclath. "I fear, Mr Stewart, that your interpretation of that word and mine may differ somewhat." He shook his quill, passed it to the guard, and without looking up added, "Though I have not, as yet, found mention of your brother in any report."

* * *

Morag Mackenzie was surprised to find herself singing as she drew her pail through the burn. It had been a long time since she had the heart for songs, but somehow today was different. Morag wondered if she should be ashamed, since terrible news had filtered down the glen, clachan by clachan, croft by croft, news of a bloody slaughter and the end of all hope for the Prince and his men. Morag had tried hard not to be glad, but could only believe it served them right. She remembered the MacKenzies coming for Angus, drawn dirks at the ready, threatening to fire the thatch above her children's heads. If they lay dead for their pains then she for one would not mourn them. One chief was as bad as another and one king would no doubt be the same. She let the water flow into the pail and lifted it onto the bank, as she did so catching a sound in the distance, a familiar sound she had not heard for many a month. She stood up and ran her hands down her skirt, feeling the year's first real warmth in the spring sunshine. Her Uncle Andra's cart toppled into view, led by his faithful garrons, leaning almost sideways on the incline under the uneven weight of its wares.

318

A man walked beside him. They were too far off for her to be sure, but her immediate thought was that it was Angus safely returned. She watched them draw closer, ashamed that her first reaction had been disappointment, and her second relief when she recognised that the man beside her uncle was a stranger.

The peddlar was wearing a more serious face than usual. He patted her fondly on the shoulder and drew her aside, while the stranger, an alarming and unkempt clansman, leaned anxiously over the cart.

"I'm sorry to be bringing this to your door, Morag, my quinie," Andra' began, and lowered his voice to a whisper. "Rebels. One walking and one close to death in the wagon – the chieftain of Glenshellich no less."

Morag lifted the corner of the sacking that covered the cart and drew back with a gasp. Close to death was an understatement, for she had never in her life seen a man closer. The chieftain of Glenshellich's face was a pale shade of grey, his cheeks were drawn like parchment and hardly a breath escaped his cracked lips. The clansman was hovering at her shoulder and she looked up into his face, immediately understanding the need to hide her dismay. Then she ran her hand over the chieftain's chest and lowered her head to listen for his heartbeat.

"The two of you had better take him inside," she said quickly. "Lay him onto my own bed and bank up the fire. Iain!" she shouted, and a ragged barefoot boy appeared suddenly from behind the cottage. "Go you and collect some sphagnum moss and foxglove." She thrust the pail of water into his hands. "But first set this upon the fire." She glanced down again at the chieftain. "Quickly!"

Euan and Andra', one at each end, gently carried Donald inside. It seemed to Euan that his weight grew heavier each time he lifted him, which was odd considering he had not eaten for at least three days. Euan's own hunger had been kept at bay with a few handfuls of meal stolen from an abandoned croft.

There were sheets on the bed where they laid Donald, and while the water warmed Morag carefully peeled away his clothes. A small girl crept from the shadows beside the fire and carried them away. Morag looked down at the exposed wounds on Donald's chest and laid her hand on his brow.

"He must be a strong man to have survived these," she breathed.

"He is a strong man," whispered Euan.

"And you a stronger one, to have brought him this far."

Andra' crept closer, looked down, then retreated to the fireside. They would be kept busy with the nursing so he could postpone the telling of both his sorry tales. He felt the temperature of the water and poured it into a jug. Little Janet carried it over to her mother who began to wipe the dirt from Donald's wounds. Euan remained silent at her shoulder and before too long Iain brought in the moss, which he had already rinsed in the burn and now spread in front of the fire to dry. Euan soon recognised the familiar and comforting scents of infusing herbs.

Donald stirred from time to time and moaned softly. Once he cried out, but mostly he remained unconscious. When his chest was bathed and covered and the healing infusion placed beside his head Morag turned to Euan.

"It could be you'll need a sharp dirk - and a stronger stomach," she added. "It is not these wounds that threaten him. These will heal. Look!" she let her finger trace the edge of the weal that stretched above his ribcage. "It has already begun to knit itself." Then her face grew grave. "This is the danger."

Euan forced his eyes where he had not dared to let them rest since the battle, for in his heart he had known where the real threat lay. He had smelt it. It was a smell he had long ago learned to fear.

"We might be best to . . "

But he did not let her finish. "No!" he cried.

She was studying Donald's knee. Euan watched her face, scarcely daring to breathe, and with all his heart tried desperately to summon the spirit of his father. But the healer did not come. Euan had no choice but to put his faith in this stranger. He watched her calloused fingers with their cracked nails tenderly probe the mess of flesh and puss, bone and gristle, all that remained of Donald's knee. They were strong hands, well used to toil. Euan watched the concentration on her face, the soft shadows in the pockets of her eyes, the full lips parting as if whispering a familiar incantation.

"Uncle Andra'," she said at last, never once taking her eyes from Donald's face. The peddlar rose from his gloomy vigil at the fireside to join them. "Do you have brandy?"

Of course he did. "A wee pickle maybe," he told her.

"Iain." The boy looked up immediately. "Find me maggots." She looked up at Euan. "We will try that way first."

"First?" breathed Andra'.

Morag nodded towards Euan. "He knows what I mean."

"My father once cut off a man's leg," Euan breathed, and his face twisted as he imagined how he would take his dirk to Donald's flesh and bone, a butcher at a carcass. His stomach heaved. "The man died."

"Yet I know a blacksmith in Fort Augustus who has lived for thirty years with less leg than you would leave your chief," she told him. "It was a surgeon in the last war, I believe."

"A surgeon," groaned Euan.

She laid her hand on his arm. "We will try every other way before that one."

Iain Mackenzie had been with his dog when it killed the rat in the steading. Now there was another beside it and both carcasses crawled and moved. He took his own knife and scraped the maggots away, carefully scooping and tipping them into the pot he had brought from the stove. Then he hurried back inside.

Euan had raised Donald's head and Morag tipped Andra's flask to his lips. He spluttered and spat it back at them, but they persisted and after a while Morag nodded. "That will do. I will try now." She held out her hand. Euan reached inside his sock and pulled out his skean dhu. She took it and sent the boy to sharpen it. When he returned she tested the blade and drew a long breath.

Euan blanched beside her and Andra' returned to his ingle.

"Iain," Morag told her son. "You must help me. I am sorry." Then she lowered her head and whispered the last three words again in Donald's ear.

Euan did not dare watch. He felt the boy grow tense and heard him retch as Morag set about her grisly task. To begin with Donald was oblivious as she pared his rotting flesh, but before long the pain reached inside his consciousness and he screamed out. Euan gasped and sobbed and was about to turn away when Morag snatched his hand.

"You must hold him!" she hissed. "You must."

Beside her the boy gathered the scraps of Donald's flesh and fragments of bone into the bowl and vomited onto the floor. Sickness churned in Euan's stomach but he gripped his chieftain's shoulders and kept his eyes on the quick deft hands of the woman. At last she seemed satisfied. Donald collapsed with a tiny moan as she poured on the maggots and wrapped a cloth loosely around them. Euan forced more brandy between Donald's lips and felt the woman's hand lightly on his wrist.

"Sleep is his best chance now," she said softly, and Euan was somehow comforted by the words his father had used so often. Morag's eyes were tired as she gazed down at Donald's face, calm now in the creeping lamplight. She reached out her hand for the flask. Euan passed it to her and she took a long draught.

"You are a healer," he whispered.

"I was for a moment," she answered. "And found I knew things I have not been taught." Euan found himself trembling and his shoulders heaved with sobs. Morag took his hand and led him to the fireside. The children glanced uncertainly towards the daylight streaking through the doorway.

"Go on then," she told them. "But not too far. And if you see anyone at all you must come inside right away."

Euan was gazing numbly into the smoking embers.

"I have broth and meal," Morag told him. "Once you have eaten you can rest. All we can do now is pray."

When Euan had finally fallen into his own sleep Morag sat down opposite the peddlar at the fireside. "As ever, Uncle Andra'," she sighed, "You are not the easiest of guests."

"This wasna the trouble I'd thought to be coming with," he told her. "But I may's well get the whole lot off my chest." He drew a determined breath. "Angus is dead."

She stared at him and he could not tell from her expression what emotions were battling inside her. She glanced instinctively towards the doorway and Andra' heard the sounds of the children's voices as they played.

"He is dead," she repeated at last. "In the battle?"

He shook his head. "Would that it had been." And quietly he told her the truth, for he owed her that at least.

"Then Iain must know too," she said at last. "The truth."

"It might be for the best," Andra' agreed. "For I doubt the Mac-Kenzies will keep it secret. They wished as much for his disgrace as his death."

"Yet Angus' son is also a Mackenzie, and might be a truer one."

"You canna' protect him from his father's shame."

She kept her eyes fixed on the glowing peats. "Where will we go?" she said at last.

Andra' had wondered the same thing. Their life here, poor as it was, would be worth even less with no man, even a man such as Angus Mac Ich Allach. A tear sprang from Morag's eye and Andra' reached out and patted her hand

"It's good you shed tears for him," he said. "But he's no loss to you, hen. We'll find a place for you in the town. A lassie like you can turn her hand to anything." He lowered his voice. "And these two might pay you well."

"Not if the chieftain dies."

Andra' crept over to where the Glenshellich men lay, MacSom-hairle pale and scarcely breathing on Morag's bed and his henchman in a solid slumber on the floor beside him. He sighed. "I've a tale to tell him in the morning as sorry as the one I've told you. On the same subject. Death."

"And I should grieve," she sighed. "I should grieve for my husband, though it's hard to find anything in Angus I'll be sorry to lose. He's taken my heart, Uncle Andra' and drained it dry of everything but love for my bairns. He would have taken Iain and turned him into another such as himself."

It was true, thought Andra'. The MacKenzies had at least spared Angus' son that sorry destiny. He put his arm around Morag's shoulders, drew her close and kissed her cheek. There was no need to waste their prayers on her husband's body sinking or drifting or bobbing out to sea. If God had any mercy left he would surely find a more deserving place to send it.

* * *

The fact that Kilclath was making a second visit to the cell gave Andrew fresh heart. "I have some medical training if supplies could be arranged," he ventured.

Kilclath's eyes narrowed. "I will do what I can," he said briefly, and moved on.

His provision turned out to be meagre, less than half a pound of meal, but enough to keep them from starvation.

"Did we treat them like this?" Hugh cried out. "Those prisoners from Carlisle, from Falkirk? Bastards!" he screamed. "Swill out this pigsty before we all die of the plague!" Andrew placed a restraining hand on his arm, but the tread of the guard in the passage grew quicker and closer. The door swung wide and two soldiers appeared. They grabbed Hugh and clapped fetters onto his wrists. Andrew took two steps back and watched in silence. To intervene would not only have been futile but would have brought the same punishment on himself, and he needed his strength for those who could no longer help themselves. There would be more of them dead before long. Andrew winced to see how the metal cut into Hugh's flesh as he thrashed and cursed in frustration. Another night passed. Somewhere in the course of it two boys were thrown into the cell. When Andrew woke he saw them cowering together in the corner.

"Why have you been taken?" he asked them.

"We were searching for our fathers on the field," the smaller boy snivelled. "We were sent to find them, dead or alive, but the guards took us and brought us here. They gave us no chance to explain."

Andrew stared at them in horror. They could have been no more than fourteen years old. Surely the fact that they wore the plaid and the philibeg was not enough to seal their fate? He crawled over to where Hugh slumped against the wall, and saw that his wrists had swollen to almost twice their size, making his shackles invisible.

"Stay strong, Hugh," Andrew warned him softly. "For we must live to tell of this."

The sickness grew worse. It crept through the alleyways and wynds of the town and hung over the uneasy inhabitants. The stench of it poisoned the very air until there was no loft or cellar it did not infect. Few officers were bold enough to complain to the Duke, but the Master of the Stones was one who did. He grew increasingly frustrated at the British Army's handling of its victory and his irritation was increased by his personal concerns since receiving James Hamilton's note. It had affected him more than he cared to acknowledge. Allomore's son would be forever in his debt, but could no longer bring himself to serve the cause of the House of Hanover. He trusted the Master would appreciate his position and forgive it, but would understand if he wished to sever their connection. Kilclath did not. He had given his support to James Hamilton for a reason and its purpose remained unserved. But his pride and reputation had been damaged by the boy's rejection, and thoughts of his sister were uncomfortably intruding on his peace of mind. He wished Jean were with him, in fact was seriously considering suggesting that she travelled north, either to Inverness or to the Valley of Stones itself. The barbarity of the prisons appalled him. Kilclath believed in due and just punishment but not when it threatened the dignity of his race. The abrupt dismissal he received from the king's son did nothing to restore his pride. Since his complaints were so unceremoniously ignored he resolved to set about freeing himself from his commission with all possible haste. He sought permission to petition General Mamore for his release and was at least relieved of his immediate duties. He left for Fort Augustus with a bitter taste in his mouth, on a route that others, with more sinister concerns, would soon be taking also.

Meanwhile Andrew watched more of his countrymen die in their squalid cell, writhing in filth and meeting no compassion. He bathed Hugh's wrists where the strained flesh broke and festered, and tried to contain his fury at the cruelty of their captors. For he saw that the thread of sanity was stretching to breaking point in them all as the days passed in their unrelieved gloom and the nights came cold and unrecognised. Each morning the prisoners held out their filthy shirts to receive their pitiful rations of meal and each day they grew sicker and more desperate and died. Sometimes they whispered together softly in their own tongue of the sweetness of the air to the west, and remembered the cries of the gulls in the still evenings. Sometimes as he listened to their stories Andrew Stewart, who bore a king's name, felt his spirit stir, and vowed that their suffering would be avenged. His prayers grew more desperate as hunger gnawed in his stomach and bitterness tore at his soul.

When the guards discovered two more dead bodies to remove Andrew grabbed the arm of one of them. "How much longer are we to be kept here?"

"That aint your concern, mate," the guard replied, carelessly. "Mine neither. Till you die, like enough. There don't seem no other way out."

"I wish to talk with the captain who arranged our medicines."

"Captain Campbell? He ain't here no more. Gone west, they say."

Andrew's heart sank. "Then for the love of God let me speak to someone in authority. I have medical training. I could help these men.

Half of them had no need to die of their wounds." He paused and added. "This is not what a member of a civilised nation expects."

"Civilised!" snorted the guard and looked about him and spat. Then he lowered his voice. "Going to tell me what that word means, Mr Doctor? 'Cause for sure I don't know. I ain't seen much civilisation since I left home, aged ten. Took Geordie's shilling for this life of luxury. If I'm lucky I'll avoid the whip. If not there's always the noose. A thrust in the guts is the same wherever it comes from, mate. One prison's much the same as another. Civilization! Civilisation ain't in it for the likes of me, or for you now, either." Having warmed to his subject the soldier leaned closer. "War ain't a parlour game, Mr Doctor. It ain't polite. It don't even stick by the rules. Maybe that's where you and your kind made your mistake, with your fine prince and your talk of glory. Here's where it's brought you, and serves you right, is all I can say." But his expression softened. "I'll have a word with Captain Dunlop about your medicine, not that it's likely to do much good. He ain't got a lot of sympathy for any of you, the captain." His eyes fell on Hugh. "Right mess, eh!" he observed, and took a key from the leather ring at his belt. "I think we can have these off. Don't reckon there's much harm he can do now."

Andrew fell back beside Hugh, who had not even noticed the guard's act of charity, but continued to groan through another fitful sleep. His freed wrists and hands, deformed by their swelling began to twitch grotesquely. Andrew trickled some precious water from his flask over them.

The guard was as good as his word. He returned with a summons for Andrew to see the Captain. With his own hands shackled now Andrew followed him through the stinking passage, past other bulging cells humming with the same chorus of misery, into a bare room where an officer sat behind a heavy oak table. The first thing Andrew noticed was the cold gleam in his eyes.

"Mr Stewart," he sneered. "Of Glenshellich. Not the most fortunate of names to be burdened with just now."

"It is name I bear with pride."

Another icy flash from the officer's eyes silenced him. "And how much pride do you think you and your fellow savages will have left when our work here's done?"

Andrew saw no trace of mercy in his face. He was Scot, but from far south of the Highland line. Andrew's regret at the absence of Kilclath grew stronger. He swallowed and began his request. "I have asked for medical supplies to be sent to the cells. Common humanity demands it."

"Common humanity!" Captain Dunlop repeated. "Your side is known for that, I hear. They tell me a man had his throat cut last week for a loaf of bread."

Andrew ignored the jibe. "The conditions the prisoners are expected to suffer are beyond endurance. And no credit whatever to the British Army."

"Worse than your smoking huts in the glens?" the Captain sneered. "Where the cattle sleep alongside the bairns?" He was a cruel man this Captain Dunlop, Andrew decided miserably, a man without compassion.

"Ignorance of our people and their way of life is understandable," he retorted, "so long as they can be treated like human beings."

"Ignorance, is it now?" the captain fired back. "Human beings? Let me tell you this, Mr Stewart. There are men in this army who might feel like disagreeing, men with good cause no' to consider them human at all. There wasna' a great deal of humanity in what came charging at them on Drumossie, or Prestonpans, or Falkirk. So maybe its time we started to introduce it."

"Some would say," Andrew countered coolly, "That understanding is the key to tolerance."

Captain Dunlop stared at him with still more contempt. "Well," he sneered, "I'll no' say yeah or nay to that one. But your fine sentiments dinna' go down well here, so perhaps you'll confine yourself to answering my particular questions from now on. For a start, I'd be interested to hear what part you played in the battle."

"I had no part in it. I was not on the field."

"But your clan was. Under the leadership of your brother, who likes to call himself MacSomhairle."

"I have no idea."

"I think you have a damned good idea. I need a list of the Appin chieftains who presented themselves on Drumossie, and you look like the very man to oblige."

"I can give you no such list."

"I suggest you think again."

"Is this a trial, Captain?"

"Your trial'll come soon enough. Meanwhile here's some names to refresh your memory. Ardshiel, Achnacone, Ballachulish, Glenshellich..." As he reeled them off, one by one, the list, even in his harsh accent, was music to Andrew's ears.

"As I have said, Captain, I am afraid I can be of no help,"

Captain Dunlop leaned back in his chair and heaved an apparently regretful sigh. "Och well," he conceded with a shrug. "It's no great matter. They'll all be rounded up sooner or later." He paused and stared hard into Andrew's face. "So to your own crime, then," he went on. "Andrew Stewart of Glenshellich, you served in the Appin regiment as Lieutenant and sometime medical officer. You campaigned from Edinburgh into England and back to Inverness, which put you in arms against King George for near enough seven months. High treason, Mr Stewart, for which the penalty is death."

"But as you have already said, this is not a trial. I need say nothing at present and I shall not."

Captain Dunlop shrugged. "You'll say it all eventually, with a wee bit persuasion. Like all the rest."

"And my request for medicines?"

Captain Dunlop repaid his cold stare with interest. "Not granted."

* * *

329

It was afternoon of the next day before Euan MacMichael stirred. The dark room spun about him as his eyes fell into focus. He heaved himself upright and saw that Donald was lying calm and still on the bed beside him. Too still. Euan listened, almost afraid to breathe himself, until at last the sound came, faint and uneven, but there.

"He is stronger, I am sure of it." He had not heard the woman come up behind him. She held out a steaming bowl. Euan turned his eyes to the corner where the peddlar was hunched, still staring into the fire exactly as he had been when Euan last looked his way. "Take it," the woman urged. Euan looked again at his sleeping chieftain. "He has had a little water," she reassured him. "It is you who must eat. You have used more strength than you have left." Euan did not doubt that she was right. He took the bowl from her hands. To begin with he sipped the broth slowly, but soon found himself swallowing mouthfuls. She brought him bannocks, which he devoured with the same desperation until his stomach ached with the strange sensation of being full.

"Forgive me!" he gasped.

Her eyes grew tender as they gazed first at him then at the sleeping chieftain. Euan too studied Donald's face. Was it only his hope that made it appear less drawn and grey? He saw that Donald's knee had a new dressing and wondered how much of her own sleep the woman had sacrificed.

"We are forever in your debt."

"The fever could return." She passed her finger lightly over Donald's dank hair. "We must keep praying."

"It seems I have been praying forever."

She looked up at him with calm and steady eyes. "We are all in God's hands."

In his seat beside the fire Andra' gave a shudder. All this talk of God was making him uncomfortable. Their maker had been absent so often this last while he was beginning to wonder if he had changed sides too. He glanced over to the chieftain's bedside where Morag was spreading the plaid over Euan MacMichael. She did not appear to resent this trouble he had brought to her door: in fact it seemed quite the reverse. She stood up and walked slowly towards him.

"We are all in God's hands, Uncle Andra'" she repeated. "So perhaps it's time he heard some prayers from you."

* * *

Major General Sir John Campbell of Mamore was doing nothing to improve his kinsman's temper.

"So the conduct of affairs in Inverness is not to your liking," he murmured.

Kilclath drew up a chair and flung himself into it. He was still weary from his journey down the Great Glen. "My association with such an army is not to my liking."

"But fear will lead to unaccountable things, George," Mamore observed slowly. "As will ignorance." He drew a long sigh. "Though I have heard stories myself to cause some alarm." He took another deep breath and looked seriously across the table. "However, we have our duty."

"The rebels are surely dispersed beyond all hope of reforming as a serious fighting force. What more can the government require?"

Again, the uncomfortable pause. "It seems that this time defeat alone will not suffice. Our commander in chief intends to ensure that such insurgence will not occur again." He narrowed his eyes. "Since the measures taken thirty years ago have proved themselves so inadequate his companies will be advancing through the glens."

"But not my company, I trust. I am come to request relief from my commission."

Mamore sighed. "I am afraid it will not be that simple." His eyes narrowed further. "It is perhaps an opportunity we should welcome, for the settling of old scores, yet...."

"There are more appropriate ways." Kilclath finished for him.

"As you say. Unfortunately there are still those in this land who have not learned their lesson, and our orders are to teach them more effectively. We cannot afford to allow compassion to override common sense at this particular time, which is why I will not be releasing you, at least for the foreseeable future." He ignored his kinsman's obvious dismay and added slyly, "I notice that MacSomhairle's name is not among those of the dead or those taken prisoner."

"Although I encountered his brother in the Tolbooth of Inverness."

"Did you indeed?" The general sighed. "Then I suppose I am sorry for it. There can only be one destination for those who fester there."

* * *

Euan MacMichael's head slumped against the stone ingle. Andra' stared at his clenched knuckles gleaming in the fire's faint glow and wondered how much it was possible for a man bear, even a man as robust as this son of Glenshellich's healer. Dusk had fallen and a chill from the hillside blew through the rafters. Andra' pulled his jacket closer. Morag's roof had been in sore need of attention for his last few visits, but this time it was the least of her concerns. For three days and two nights the maggots from the rats' carcasses had worked to clean MacSomhairle's flesh. Now his wound was packed and bound, and he slept soundly. The wound that Andra' himself had just delivered to Euan MacMichael was of a different kind. While the children played a solemn game with pebbles in the corner Andra' and Morag watched him with grave faces.

"It's sair I am to be the bearer of such news," Andra' muttered.

Euan did not raise his head but a huge sob rose from the depths of him. Morag reached out and touched his shoulder.

"There is no shame in tears," she told him. "You are surely among friends here."

Slowly he lifted his head to meet her eyes. He could find no words, but was glad that her hand was still on his shoulder.

"A grievous time," Andra' sighed.

"More grievous for these men, Uncle Andra'," Morag said. "They have lost those they loved. I am sorry for Angus's death for his sake, but not for mine, nor," she threw another quick glance towards the corner where her children remained intent on their game, "for theirs."

"Though it could be you're out of one trap into a worse one," her uncle observed grimly.

Morag stood up and moved across to the bed where Donald still slept soundly. Little Janet looked up from her game and scrambled up to join her. They stood together looking down at Donald's peaceful face. "The dying is over," Morag whispered. She closed her eyes and felt the power flood through her, the same strength and confidence, the same strange sense of belonging she had felt when she first tended him. Euan was studying her closely. But perhaps it was too soon for him to trust her. He needed time now for his own healing to begin.

"I am sorry to have brought this trouble upon you," Euan whispered.

"You did not," she said, and added with a smile. "As usual it's Uncle Andra' we have to thank for that."

* * *

On a cold spring morning Andrew, Hugh and those of their cellmates who could still stand were marched through the closed streets of Inverness towards the waters of the firth. After their weeks of confinement the fresh air was a shock to their lungs and they coughed and reeled like drunkards. The citizens of the town watched them pass in their chains, some with hooded glances of shame, others with a gruesome fascination, but the prisoners' eyes were dazzled by the day's brightness. They did not see the transport ships that rocked on the calm water, starkly picturesque from a distance, but already bulging with their miserable cargo.

"Drink deep of this air, Hugh," Andrew whispered, leaning in his chains towards the sad shell of the young Master of Ballingry. Hugh seemed so beyond caring that Andrew wondered if he even heard him.

His eyes were fixed blankly ahead as the prisoners were crammed onto a small rowing boat, which soon began to pull towards the merchantman, "Jane of Leith". Andrew did not look at Hugh's haggard face, but instead watched the town sway with the boat's motion as it shrank to a memory.

"The invaders take us in chains from our own land," a voice piped behind him. "But in the air I feel only the pull of Kintail, the mountains dark in the wind from the west."

"They are looting in the hills and burning," another voice hissed, a tacksman, not a bard. "That is what I heard in the street. They are laying a trail of death down the Great Glen. Out country is breathing its last."

"No!" cried Andrew fiercely as the fresh wind lifted his dank hair. "There will always be those who survive to restore our lands." And he thought of Christie, of Helen, of Meg, of all the desperate, brave women who waited. But who would there be to take them the news they dreaded, or even to know it? Miserably he climbed the rope to his new prison.

They were hustled along the slimy deck and, one by one, dropped down the lifted grating of the small square that opened onto the hold. But long before that they caught the stench, worse by far than the one that had filled the air in the Tolbooth. Hugh grabbed Andrew's arm, his face a staring mask of horror.

"No!" he screamed, as he struggled against the unyielding arm of the guard. "We are gentlemen! You cannot treat us in this way!"

"We'll see who's gentlemen," sneered the guard and jabbed his musket between Hugh's shoulders. "And you'll find out how we treat rebel scum who speak out of turn. Now keep your mouth shut unless you want me to shut it for good." And he pushed Hugh forward into the blackness that was the belly of the "Jane of Leith."

Andrew was flung beside a boy stretched half naked across the ballast. A vicious wound ran from his thigh to this knee and his yellow eyes rolled towards the square of daylight.

"Water," he gasped, but as if he knew his plea was futile he let fall an arm that was little more than skin wrapped around bone.

"I have none," Andrew answered. He lifted his head towards the deck and repeated the boy's request. He heard rough laughter above them as a metal cup swung from a tattered rope above the grating. Andrew snatched it and tipped it against the boy's lips, but immediately the boy spat and swore.

"Pish!" he cried. Andrew threw the cup down in horror. The boy screamed another bitter curse through the grating, but the only response was more laughter. Hugh was lying only yards away, but more bodies separated them.

"We are truly in hell." Hugh's voice was a hoarse whisper. "We are dead already. You are no longer Andrew Stewart of Glenshellich. I am no longer Hugh Fettes of Ballingry. We are worse than cattle. What does it signify now that we have dined at a prince's table?"

That night as their stomachs heaved with the alien sea-swell, Andrew's dreams returned: nightmare visions of limbless and tortured men, all with rolling eyes, hundreds upon hundreds, thousands upon thousands, moaning and heaving as they were trampled by laughing devils in red coats. He saw Kenneth MacCombie, his head rent from crown to chin. He saw Euan MacMichael starved to a skeleton. He saw Donald, a livid stump where his arm had hung, and he cried out in terror until the bard's hand on his brow woke him and the nightmare vision became the reality of the hold of the "Jane of Leith". Men were still dying around him, but they were strangers. Donald and Euan and Kenneth were somewhere else.

* * *

Christie too was plagued by nightmares. The scenes on the moor returned to haunt her nights' darkest hours: the cries and moans of the dying clansmen, the jeers of the soldiers, the dead faces of the piper and his wife. Each night she forced herself awake, her brow soaking and her throat dry, and each night Catriona MacMichael dozed in the rocking chair beside her, ready to soothe her back to sleep. As she rocked Catriona thought many things, for she knew that the time had at last come for her own debt to be repaid. It was the reason her life had been spared and now she must rise above her own pain to help ease the pain of others. Sitting at Christie's bedside whispering her soothing words Catriona was more and more certain that this was only the beginning. True happiness, however brief, was a treacherous gift that would sooner or later demand a cruel price. She and this girl were alike in so many ways. Now it seemed that even their destinies were walking hand in hand.

Six days after the battle Iain MacCombie had returned to the glen. He had slept on the road to Nairn for a night and a day, oblivious of the distant battle blasts, and had woken only with the thundering hooves of a battalion out to take revenge on any who might try to make an escape. He had returned the field and found it ringed by the fires of the Sassenach soldiers. Through their flickering shadows and his own bitter tears of shame he had seen the bodies of his brothers. His first instinct had been to draw his dirk and run screaming to his death, hoping at least to take a red coated devil with him; but an old man of Clanranald had counselled a wiser course and pointed him again towards Nairn where the two had taken shelter for the night in a fisherman's bothy. The next day he had retraced his steps westward, passing by the confines of Culloden House where the devils were going about their bloody business of searching the nearby outhouses for skulking rebels and setting alight any barns that might have given them shelter. He heard on the road that eighteen men alone had died from the firing of one barn. Iain had returned to Glenshellich to admit his disgrace at sleeping while his brothers gave their lives. He had come home to await his punishment.

James and Domhnull had been on the lochan, fishing from Angus Ban's boat, when Iain skulked past the Watcher's Stone.

"So at least you have one grandson," James said at the same time laying a comforting arm across Domhnull's shoulders.

If Angus was grateful he gave no sign of it. "This war has made many orphans," he muttered. "There will be more still to come." His sightless eyes turned towards the mountain, dark under the gathering clouds. "You must show Domhnull the giant's cave," he told James. "Your sister knows the way."

"I know the way," Domhnull declared.

The old man was suddenly alert. His bony fingers gripped the boy's wrist. "Which way?" he hissed.

Domhnull did not flinch from the old man's blind challenge. "Until I have grown some more there is only one way," he answered calmly.

Angus drew back. James looked from one to the other as the old man let out a little breath. "You crossed An Ciobar's Ridge?" he gasped.

Domhnull nodded, and then remembered that the old man would not see.

"I did," he said.

James was still mystified. "An Ciobar's Ridge?"

"At the other side of the mountain," Angus wheezed, "high up, near the summit, there is a ridge where a man cannot walk upright, only crawl, for the drop on either side is too sheer and too deep. They say An Ciobar once led seven hostages from Kilclath across it to their deaths. They say their bones still gleam white among the scree, along with the bones of the foolish of this glen who thought they could take the same road."

James turned his head slowly and studied Domhnull MacCombie. "Are you saying you have taken that road, Domhnull?"

Domhnull remained silent.

Angus let out a different breath. "Fortune might smile on you once," he warned. "But may you grow fast, my boy, so that other paths will open to you. It would not be wise to tempt the giant too often."

* * *

"In the far off days before your father's grandfather, or even his father's grandfather before him, my mountain was the home of giants."

"Giants!" gasped young Iain MacKenzie.

"A whole family of them. And being giants they were squabblesome and bad tempered, so that when their mother and father died all that the three brothers could find to do was quarrel."

"What did they quarrel about?" interrupted the boy.

"It's a well known fact that giants can quarrel about anything at all . . ."

"Much like chieftains, then," broke in Iain's mother.

Euan looked up from stool he was mending and gave a low chuckle.

"Much like chieftains indeed," agreed Donald with a smile, before returning to his story. "But these three giants quarrelled mostly about which of them should fall heir to the cave where they lived. None of them could agree because none of them wanted to leave the mountain: not Finn, not Torphaig, and especially not Feodag, the eldest and the most fearsome."

The boy continued to gaze into the chieftain's face. He remembered the three days and three nights his mother and the soldier had scarcely left his bedside. He remembered how he and his sister had gathered fresh herbs and moss each day until now, all these weeks later, the chieftain was sitting up and supping rabbit broth and telling his stories about giants.

"At last Feodag devised a plan," the chieftain went on. "He sent his brother Finn on an errand to Kintail to search out and bring home the stag with the silver antlers that lived by the sound of Sleat, and he sent his brother Torphaig way beyond the Mountains of the Eagles to lift all the cattle he could find on the way. Unknown to them, he charged his two tame crows to follow and watch to see that his brothers obeyed his instructions. While they were gone Feodag himself collected stones from all the mountaintops around Glenshellich, stones that would seem to you and me ten times bigger than the biggest of boulders, and just before the sun set over the lochan on the seventh day one of his crows returned. Exactly as Feodag had suspected, his brothers had betrayed him. They had penned all the cattle in Kilclath and had killed the stag to turn its silver antlers into pins for their plaids.

Feodag waited for them to return, but he did not wait to hear their lies. When they were halfway up the mountain he picked up his stones and hurled them, one by one, from the mouth of the cave. Down they fell, like a shower of deadly hail, gathering speed until they became lethal as balls blasted from a cannon. Each time the brothers strove for the cave it was the same thing, until Torphaig's legs were broken in twenty places and Finn's eyes had been pelted completely blind. When at last they gave up their struggle Feodag's crows pointed Torphaig the way northwards and Finn carried him right to the wild waters of the furthest Minch where an undiscovered cave was hidden in the high cliffs. There they began a new life and Feodag was left in peace to set about founding his own family."

"Who with?"

But Donald was tired. He rested his head back against the blanket and closed his eyes. "That will have to be a story for another time," he said softly.

* * *

Domhnull MacCombie inched his way across the ridge. The grey clouds hung above his head and spat a careless drizzle. Every so often his foot dislodged a stone, which slipped and bounced down the seemingly endless drop on either side. Christie raised her hand to her mouth, scarcely daring to breathe as Domhnull crawled closer.

"He will not fall," James assured her in a whisper, and tightened his grip on her arm. They were standing on the ledge that ran twenty yards around the mountainside from Feodag's cave. James had found his own leap of faith surprisingly easy, considering he had never in his life before climbed a mountain. But the path that he and Christie had followed to the giant's cave, the only path she knew, was a stroll compared with the precipitous route a boy of Domhnull's height was forced to take. Although Meg's son was confident, his features set in concentration, his limbs moving with a cat's slow grace, James found himself fervently echoing old Angus's hope that he would indeed grow quickly.

He kept his grip firm on Christie's arm, sensing that her instinct would be to reach out and pull Domhnull to the comparative safety of the ledge. Domhnull seemed to sense the same, for he paused before he reached them and looked briefly behind him. Droplets of rain misted the air and James was struck with the sudden memory of Meg's feather light laughter.

"I would not dare take your way, even if my life depended on it," he told Domhnull when at last he stood safely beside them. Christie said nothing but clutched the boy so tightly that he became one with the pounding of her heart.

For weeks the glen below them had held its breath. It seemed that Helen waited only for the time to pass until her confinement and her husband's return. She had ignored her father's repeated pleas to return to the Glen of the Black Cattle, for she shared Iain MacCombie's conviction that Donald was alive and would find his way home. Even so, she had become a pale shadow of the girl she had once been. Her face had lost its colour and her eyes their glow. She hid more and more within her own room, with only the devoted Eilidh for company, increasingly prey to strange notions and fantasies. Catriona caught her one morning outside the stables, squinting up at the mountain and dodging behind the stall. Helen would not say what she felt the need to conceal herself from.

"It's Beathag, I doubt," Fraser muttered. "And little wonder, for it's like she's casting her evil eye on us all."

"Not us, Fraser."

"Aye us. She's lost what little mind and sense she ever had. Grief's driven out her senses this time and no mistake."

"Each generation," Catriona murmured. "Each generation passes from her and yet she is still here. Perhaps that is her curse, her burden."

"Then it's to be hoped she'll no' outlive the boy."

Catriona's face grew thoughtful. The strain of waiting was becoming intolerable for them all. Each day they gazed towards the Watcher's Stone, each day hoping and praying with hearts that did not dare to hope, hearts close to breaking. Catriona did not think she was the only one who saw the ghosts, so many now, so many more than the living. She and Fraser were stranded in this dismal present while the future closed darkly around them. And for Catriona the future held the worst fear of all.

Each day Beathag ranged the mountainside, wailing her chilling grief, her frailty somehow more terrifying than her old black magic. And to Helen it seemed that the old woman was adding her own curses to a glen already cursed. In her worst moments she could almost believe Beathag was laying an evil eye on her unborn child, reminding her that this land was not hers, that when MacSomhairle was not with her she would remain a stranger.

Of the wider world at first they had received no news at all. Then came rumours from the north and east, creeping closer, rumours of plundering, of cattle driven to the forts, of clachans burned to the ground. Murdo Ban returned from Cairnill with repeated pleas, but Helen was adamant. What if Donald should return and find her gone? Besides her confinement drew closer. It would not be safe to travel even on less hazardous roads. There was nothing for any of them to do but wait and pray.

* * *

The "Jane of Leith" sailed at the end of May, carrying its doomed cargo to a deadly destination. The merchantman's tattered sails drove it through the sea days and nights, whether a thin sun glinted on the waves or cold moonlight streaked the black sea with silver. Riding high seas, battling fierce gales, the ship swayed southwards while the prisoners groaned and spewed across the soiled hold and watched the lice crawl from one naked chest to another. On calmer days the stronger among them murmured to each other of old lives gone forever, though not once did Hugh Fettes boast of the distant glories of a foreign court. Not once did he recall nights squandered in gaming rooms and secret bedchambers. His wasting body no longer yearned for France's finest claret and brandy but craved only the pure cold water that danced through Ballingry's burns and his dreams.

The prisoners in the hold of the "Jane of Leith" had grown accustomed to the stench in their nostrils, the hunger that gnawed their stomachs day and night. All that flourished was disease, striking with a savagery as indiscriminate as their captors' whims. Andrew saw one man tied with rope, plunged into the cold sea and come to the surface dead on the starboard side.

Days turned to weeks until a different motion and strange accents on deck told them they were in new waters. Andrew looked through the hatch that had been his frame on the world and saw a cluster of gaiters. Stretching his swollen legs he tried to rouse Hugh whose only response was a feeble groan. An old man, once a blacksmith from Tiree, shuffled closer in his chains.

"You are the fittest here, Glenshellich." It was a sad indictment that Andrew could not deny. "So stay strong," the blacksmith continued. "To tell our story."

"I fear we will all be condemned before we have that chance," Andrew muttered bitterly.

The old man's eyes glinted with sudden ferocity. When the words tumbled from him they held all the passion of his numbered days. "I was forced from my home when Tearlach came," he hissed. "They promised if I did not join him my house would burn, my cattle would be taken. I did not follow him willingly, but I tell you this," his voice faltered only briefly. "I tell you this: had I seen such an end I would have run to his side, my sword gleaming. I would die a hundred deaths, suffer a hundred journeys in this ship of hell to tell the world of the wickedness of this German king. I will die in the cause of King James though I never lived in it, though I cared nothing for it in my whole life."

Andrew's reached for the old man's arm but his chains slithered and grew taut. He could not touch him: he could only grip his eyes as he heard the thundering of feet and barrels across the planks of the deck and the snatched orders that followed. They had grown so used to the sea's moods that the strange calm of these waters made them uneasy.

For what seemed like hours more not a soul came near the prisoners. They lay, beyond weariness, in the gently creaking hold, until at last an officer thrust his head through the hatch. He swore, recoiled and barked an order for them to gather on deck. Few were strong enough to climb the ladder unaided. The day's brightness was torture to their eyes and they retched and spewed with the shock of the fresh air. The guards stepped as far back as the rails would allow and watched in disgust while the officer addressed them.

"You will henceforth be transferred to our sister ship, the "Pamela". He paused as if waiting for a reaction, but there was none from the prisoners whatever. "Save two of your rebel number." His face registered deeper distaste. "Step forward Andrew Stewart of Glenshellich, acting medical officer with the Pretender's army, and step forward Mr Hugh Fettes of Ballingry." Andrew managed to stagger two paces, but Hugh had to be dragged upright, his head slumping loosely onto his chest. When Andrew made a move to support him he felt the crack of a pistol butt on his arm. "You are to be housed with Mr John Howard in the borough of Southwark," the officer went on. "Where you will await your trial for treason."

The other prisoners were prodded towards the small boats clustering at the "Jane of Leith's" starboard side. As he shambled past the old blacksmith fixed Andrew with a last penetrating gaze. "Remember," he hissed. "My sword gleaming for the Prince."

"I will remember," Andrew barely whispered in reply as he lowered his eyes to the splintered deck. There would be little chance for any of them to tell their tale, and none at all for himself or for Hugh. For their offence there could be only one verdict, and only one sentence.

* * *

Jean Petrie had never before received a letter from the Master. She studied the seal for a long time, half in excitement, half in apprehension. Mhairi looked impassively at Hughie who twitched in the kitchen's shadows. He greatly resented being parted from his master, especially on such an unworthy errand. Mhairi muttered what might have been a rebuke, but Hughie's only response was a darker glower. He was impatient to receive the reply and be gone.

Jean turned away, but although her swelling belly was still concealed beneath the hoops of her skirt she sensed that Hughie had guessed her secret.

"I write in haste," she read, and judging by his careless hand the Master was telling the truth. "But you have been greatly in my thoughts during these dark days, as well as in my dreams at night." Jean felt herself flush. "I have not written before because I hoped, in fact fully intended, to be relieved of my military duties long before today. Now, however, it appears that I am to lead a series of sorties into the rebel lands. I miss you, Jean." A little gasp escaped her lips. His uncharacteristically spontaneous tone continued. "All here is discord. Our government's notion of punishment is out of all proportion to the offences, although it is perhaps opportune that I have been made an instrument of its retribution. Please send me your thoughts, which are bound to cheer me in this miserable sojourn. Hughie will act as your messenger as he has done for me, though I know he will be anxious to return with all haste. He at least seems to be enjoying his duties...."

Jean held the parchment to her lips then hugged it to her chest. Mhairi and Hughie exchanged another covert look. Jean was still not sure exactly how much Mhairi suspected, but Hughie's agitation left her in no doubt that she would have to decide quickly whether or not to give the Master her news. Despite Bella's disapproval she had held to her determination to keep their child and she knew that nothing now would make her change her mind. She fetched parchment and a quill and sat down at the table. There would be time enough to discuss that part of the future, she decided, when she and the Master were reunited.

* * *

"There we are gentlemen," announced Andrew's new gaoler. "Not the best furnished of apartments, but I daresay preferable to your previous lodgings."

The attic was cramped and airless by any standards, but it seemed to Andrew as sweet-smelling a room as he had ever set foot in. On a rickety table in the corner were four books, and a small window in the roof let in sufficient daylight to read them. Five mattresses lay on the floor; three holding bodies apparently asleep, although one occupant raised his head to glance dispassionately at the new arrivals.

Andrew looked again at Mr Messenger Howard. He was barely an inch above five feet, but his bustling self-importance compensated for any presence his height denied him. His eyes shifted in the weak light. "I hope my hospitality will be to your taste, gentlemen." And it seemed he could not resist adding, "though I suspect you will find a more permanent resting place before too long."

"On the scaffold God will show us mercy," intoned the man on the mattress and Andrew noticed the bible open on the floor beside him. The messenger threw him an unsympathetic look.

"For your sake we'll hope so, Mr McBride." He rubbed his hands in mock cheerfulness. "Well gentlemen, I'll leave you to make your own introductions. No doubt you'll have plenty to discuss. My man will be outside the door should you require anything further."

Hugh had been practically carried to the attic. It was as if this last move had set the final seal on his spirit. For weeks he had lain in filth but still nursed faint hopes for some kind of future. Now he seemed ready to await death, albeit on a half-clean mattress. Andrew stretched out beside him as the forms of their three companions blurred before his eyes.

When next he stirred it seemed still to be morning. He felt surprisingly refreshed and also hungry. Bread and cheese lay on a tray beside him and he attacked it greedily, unembarrassed by the scrutiny of three pairs of eyes. Beside him Hugh slept on.

"I am sorry, gentlemen," Andrew said when he had eaten his fill, "but a starving man forgets his manners."

345

"You were brought here on the transports?" asked the youngest of his new companions, a boy with lank blonde hair falling loosely over a friendly face. He spoke with an English north-country accent. Andrew nodded and the boy looked towards the sleeping Hugh.

"Can't have been much of a trip."

Andrew did not reply. Although he was out of the hold of the "Jane of Leith" the horror of it was fresh in his mind. He tried not to think of those who had shared it with him lying, as he was sure they must be, in one as bad or even worse. Instead he turned his attention to his new companion and discovered him to be one Joseph Burns, taken prisoner at Carlisle for no greater crime than selling stolen horses to the rebels. His trial had been postponed once but could take place at any time, as could that of the others.

"This here's Martin." Joseph indicated a raffish fellow of about Andrew's own age. "Martin O'Day from Donegal, assigned to the Manchester Regiment before the rest of you marched back north. And our pious friend in the corner is John McBride from Newcastle." Both men seemed quite content to have Joseph relate their histories. In fact it appeared they were too weary by far to be interested even in themselves.

"We've been here since March," Joseph went on. "And starting to hope they'd forgotten us, but no such luck. The trials are all ending one way. Yet I'll not deny the Prince for all that."

Andrew shook his head sadly. "Nor more will I," he agreed.

Joseph's eyes grew eager. "So were you there at the last battle?"

As Andrew told him his story the boy gazed at him in awe. "They were some fellows, those highlanders," he exclaimed. "They could put the wind up anyone, I reckon."

Andrew managed a small smile though his eyes were moist.

"It stirred us all to see them," Joseph went on. "They put fire in us, Mr Stewart. Whatever happens it was the best adventure. Whatever happens I'm proud to have been part of it."

Whatever happens, thought Andrew, knowing that he was still very far from being ready to sacrifice his life. Joseph's hushed voice broke again into his thoughts. "They say the Bonnie Prince has not been caught."

Andrew felt a stab of shame to realise that this was the first time in weeks he had given so much as a thought to the fate of their leader. Strange how quickly in the foul cells of Inverness and the stinking hold of the "Jane of Leith" he had been forgotten.

* * *

The trench in Morag MacKenzie's barn was still not wide or deep enough to hold two men. As Euan dug he wished it did not so closely resemble a grave. But he could console himself with the thought that fortune had smiled on them so far. Each time the troops had marched on the road down the lochside they had passed the croft by. Every day young Iain MacKenzie concealed himself in the heather on the slopes above, keeping watch and gathering news. All of it was bad. The red and white platoons were marching relentlessly, setting fire to crofts and stealing cattle. Rumour had it that for miles around Fort Augustus the hills were black with plundered herds. But still no soldiers had found the track to Morag MacKenzie's croft.

Donald lay on the bed and watched Morag slice the deer's flesh with Euan's dirk. He was fascinated by the motion of her arms, the energy with which she went about every task, her reassuring combination of grace and strength. For weeks her resourcefulness had amazed him. She looked round and gave a quick smile.

"You knew I was watching you."

"I have eyes in the back of my head," she joked.

"We must leave your family in peace soon," he said sadly.

She turned away from the deer's carcass and came to perch on the edge of the bed. "It is strange," she said softly, "how I have come to feel that you are our family now." He reached out and took her hand as she added. "They say that saving a life brings great responsibility."

"You have been listening to too many of my stories."

Her eyes shone back at him. In his old life he would not have spared her a second glance, yet in this world she was beautiful, and he knew she was becoming even more so to Euan. Something about her mixture of strength and compassion reminded Donald of Catriona.

"What will you do?" he asked softly.

She sighed. "I daresay I'll take Uncle Andra's advice and go to Inverness. Not that I've much love for towns, but it will be safer, for the children too. Then –" her voice faltered, "who knows?"

"Who knows what will become of any of us?" Donald whispered.

She pulled her eyes away from him. "It'll be long enough anyway before you can even think to travel."

"The weather is warmer." He took her hand again. "When Euan has finished digging the pit we must pretend that I am hiding from you too."

"If that's what you want," she told him. "But you'll be lying in no pit until your legs can carry you there."

He grinned. "You strike a hard bargain, Mistress MacKenzie." With a huge effort he pulled himself up in the bed. The very effort of it sent the room into orbit. He was weaker than he had dared to imagine. Very slowly he twisted himself around, wincing as the pain of the unfamiliar movement seared through his chest. He swung his good leg carefully over the side of the bed and held out his hand to Morag. She pulled his arm over her shoulder and they exchanged a determined look. Then she stood up and braced herself to take his full weight.

He had barely hopped a pace from the bed before he collapsed with a yell that brought Euan running from the barn. Quickly the big man lifted him and with Morag's help arranged him back on the bed. Donald felt tears of disappointment spring from his eyes.

"Perhaps we shouldn't..." Morag began.

"No, no," Euan interrupted. "It was good that he tried. He must find a way to walk again." Euan knew perfectly well that he could not carry his chieftain back to Glenshellich. He knew that each day they remained at the croft put Morag and her family in more danger. That night, as Donald dozed and the children slept soundly in their box beds, he held her eyes across the shadows from the fire.

"Nowhere will be safe," she whispered. "Especially not your glen. That's the first place they'll look for him."

"Yet we cannot leave it unprotected."

"It might be best protected without the two of you in it."

Euan drew a heavy breath. If what they were hearing was true, then nowhere and no one in their lands could count themselves safe from this government's revenge.

"The soldiers have passed us by so far," she insisted. "You have a place to hide him now."

"But we put you in deadly danger."

She held his eyes for a long time before she answered. "I have never in my life met such men as you," she said at last. "Men who tell stories to children, men who mend roofs as well as they fight wars, men with gentle hearts who cry real tears."

"Domhnull MacSomhairle has never been afraid to cry," Euan whispered. "And as for myself, this last while, I have not been able to help it."

"Broken hearts can heal."

"Sometimes I wonder if the heart of our country itself is broken."

"The strong will always survive."

"You are strong," he told her.

"But I was not always."

Euan fell silent for a while. This was a new idea to him, that strength could be forged with suffering as much as with victory. He studied her face, licked into light and shadows by the fire's glow. It was a face a man would never grow tired of. To break the silence she whispered, "When will you tell him about his piper and his wife?"

"When he has passed the Watcher's Stone that guards our glen," Euan answered. "For he could not carry such grief as that on the road we must take." He paused and his eyes drilled deep into hers. "Mac-Somhairle believed that he would be the one to die. I am sure he prayed for it."

"And you prevented his prayer from being answered."

Euan thought for a while. "I have a picture in my mind," he said at last, "of the sun rising above the giant's mountain and children running through the clachan. I see the water of the lochan shining and I hear the gulls call as they dive to catch their fish. On the lower slope are all the grazing cattle. My cattle," he added with a trace of embarrassment. "It is the only future I have ever imagined." He drew a long sigh. "But now it seems my life must take me far from Glenshellich."

"And you can make no picture of it anywhere else?" she asked him gently. He shook his head and her expression grew more serious. "Then tell me, Euan, is MacSomhairle in your picture of the cattle and your glen?"

Euan raised his head and gazed into her eyes. Of course MacSomhairle was there. He could make no picture of a future that did not contain him. MacSomhairle was there, with the children and the dogs running at his heels, but she was there too, stepping out of his mother's cottage with Iain and Janet as if she had lived there all her life. Without this war he would never have known her, yet because of this war he could never make his new dream come true.

"You are all in my picture," he said softly, and she touched his face before she stood up and made her way to the corner to lie down beside her children. Euan sat for a long time alone by the fireside and thought of everything that had brought them to this place. He thought of his mother and father and the lost years of their exile. He thought of the old MacSomhairle and the Prince, and the daughters of Allomore and Cairnill. Then he looked across the room and watched Morag stir in the soft dusk. He gazed at her sleeping face for a long time and wondered what it would be like to hold her in his arms and feel the warm curves of her body against his. At last he crept across to the bed where Donald lay in his calm sleep and stretched himself across the floor at his feet.

* * *

Two lackeys carried Hugh Fettes' body from Messenger Howard's attic, bumping it from wall to wall down the narrow staircase. Andrew prayed for his friend's soul and gave thanks that Hugh had at least been spared the horrors that still lay ahead for him. That night he started from his sleep, a sweat cold on his forehead, his limbs twitching as if they already jerked on the gallows. This was not another of the nightmares that had haunted him since his capture: this was his curse, the vision so vivid that the smoke and burning singed his waking nostrils. The house of Glenshellich, the whole clachan lay in flames, and it was not the prisoners in the hold of the "Jane of Leith" he could hear moaning, but Helen. Trembling he closed his eyes and the moans turned to a harsh, crazed curse, that dwindled to silence. Only Helen's calm face remained, shining white in the moonlight. He stared through the tiny skylight at his own moon, half light, half shadow, an undecided, unfinished moon. He could no longer separate truth from illusion, dreams from visions. But as he saw Meg's face framed in the skylight, and heard Kenneth's pipes play their haunting pibroch it seemed to him that they had come to show him a way home.

* * *

It was mid-May when the soldiers arrived at Morag McKenzie's croft. A troop of a dozen or so beat their way up the track, between the straggling hawthorn hedge and yellow gorse, past the tumbledown barn where the outlawed chieftain of Glenshellich lay concealed in the blackness of his trench. When Iain had stumbled home bearing his frantic warning there had been barely enough time for his mother and Euan to carry Donald to the barn and cover him with the stick woven palette and heather. They had no time at all to remind themselves of their own plan.

Donald could only listen to the tramping of feet growing ever closer. He heard the harsh orders barked in alien accents and bitter frustration sickened his soul.

The sergeant ordered his men to halt ten yards from the cottage door. After a few moments Morag MacKenzie and her two children crept from its murky interior.

"Into the open with you," the sergeant snapped.

Morag, Janet and Iain stared back at him with wide and terrified eyes.

"Don't speak no word of English most like," a scarred trooper muttered. He raised his eyes fearfully to the hills. The very land had a different language, hostile and sinister: its dismal sky weighed down on them and weighed them down day and night. The sergeant grabbed Iain roughly by the shoulder and threw him onto the ground. Morag flew to his side and the sergeant dealt a swift blow to her temple.

"Damned savages!" the soldier spat.

Morag gathered Iain into her arms as Euan came lurching from behind the barn.

"Mother!" Janet shouted in panic. Morag raised her head and looked pleadingly around the platoon. A silence had fallen over them at the sight of Euan. Several of them exchanged uneasy glances.

"Jesus!" breathed the sergeant as Euan lurched forward, his eyes rolling crazily.

"You must excuse him," Morag pleaded. She made a gesture with her hand at her head. "He is not in his right mind."

"Did the battle take his wits or is it the natural state of him?" The sergeant sneered. Some of his troopers laughed, while others looked at Morag with a different interest. Euan felt his heart race and his spirits freeze. Their plan was not going to work and there was nothing one man could do against all these soldiers. If he fought to the death he could take no more than three of them with him. Like his chieftain Euan MacMichael was more helpless than he had ever been in his life.

"He was not at the battle," Morag answered, still miraculously calm. If she was afraid she gave not a single sign of it. She pulled Iain to his feet and stood with her arms around each of her children. Her hand moved gently over Janet's head.

Euan did not need to pretend his fear, but their plan depended on how he showed it. He was a half-wit and his wife was to be pitied, for his children were wiser than their father. Taking his own cue Iain stepped forward and pulled at Morag's sleeve.

"He will have a fit!" he whispered in English. "Look at his eyes!"

Euan set his eyes once more to rolling in his head. Iain edged towards him and tried to take his arm, but Euan shook him off and fell back, quaking, twitching and cowering against the cottage wall.

Morag addressed the troopers again. "How do you think he could he fight in a battle? What use would a fool such as he be to the Prince?"

Entombed in his earthy darkness Donald held his breath. He could hear only sporadic and muffled voices: nothing at all of what they might be saying. When at last the barn door creaked open he almost hoped he would be discovered. But even if he was there could be no guarantee the others would be reprieved. For their sakes as much as for his own he could only force himself to lie tortured and silent. After a few moments he heard the door swing shut.

"What d'you think?" the scar-faced trooper muttered to the man next to him.

"Waste of time," came the reply. They had been sensible to give this den a wide berth before. "Angus Mac Ich Allach MacKenzie." He spat and turned to Morag again. "You would better be rid of him."

A second's alarm flashed in Morag's eye, for how could these soldiers know of Angus?

"Though he once did us quite a favour, I believe," declared the sergeant, stepping up to Euan in what he clearly thought was a threatening manner. Euan still quaked against the wall with his eyes half-crazed, but his heart was beating furiously. "So maybe we should do his wife one," the sergeant went on, and Euan smelt the foulness of his breath. His fists clenched behind him. "If you like, boys. After me of course."

Two of his men seized Morag's shoulders and held her in a brutal grip while and two more pulled off her bodice and skirt. A sharp blow from the sergeant's rifle butt silenced Euan's anguished yell. Iain struggled free from the soldier who had held him, but another caught him, laughed and spun him around, then let him go. To them it was nothing more than a careless game. The sergeant advanced towards Morag, unbuckling his belt, lust glinting from his eyes. Euan struggled to steady his head, but there was not a thing he could do. One by one, in a relentless procession, the soldiers took her as her children cowered behind him and hid their eyes. And with each ruthless thrust, murder filled Euan's heart and soul. He forced himself against the damp stone wall, bitter sobs tearing him apart, but all through her ordeal Morag MacKenzie made not a sound. She lay on the rough slope where the redcoats had pushed her and she lay as one dead, so still that when the last of them had spat his contempt and joined the reformed ranks, when the column had marched back up the track and Euan finally crawled across the heather to her side he believed for one heart stopping moment that they had killed her.

Donald heard the sergeant shout the final command, then for a long time heard nothing else. At last he began to push at the palette until he managed to dislodge it sideways. A little light squeezed through as he raised his arms and tried to grip the side of the trench. But he lacked the strength and sank back again in despair. There was nothing he could do but wait. At last the barn door creaked and a wider strip of daylight opened. Euan, still sobbing like a child, pulled away the palette. Donald reached out and grabbed his hand as Janet's face appeared behind him.

"The soldiers hurt my mother," was all she said.

Donald gazed up at her. "Then get me out," he ordered, for he knew with her words that his own pain must become as nothing. He must learn to live with it and endure it for as long as need be, for this uselessness must come to an end. He was a son of Samuel, not a cripple to be nursed and pitied. "The stick," he demanded. Janet passed it down to him and her brother and Euan MacMichael reached into the trench and pulled him up onto the earthen floor of the barn. Then Donald stood up. Wedging the crutch under his armpit and

354

leaning his other arm over Euan's shoulder he took a step, and this time he did not fall. Gritting his teeth he forced another step, then another, until he could look across to the bank where Morag lay as the soldiers had left her but covered now with Euan's plaid. She raised her head and their eyes met.

"Go to her," Donald breathed, and when Euan hesitated he repeated his command. "Go to her, Euan." He lowered himself onto the boulder that leaned against the side of the barn. "Take her and wash their filth away."

The MacKenzie's croft had been built at the head of a narrow glen beside a burn that had its source high in the hills above. The water followed a tortuous course through the hard and soft rocks, damming naturally from time to time and forming occasional pools in times of high rain. But behind a small outcrop, scarcely higher than the croft itself, was a pool that was never drained, a place where the children splashed and swam and where in happier days Morag and Angus had once laughed and made love. It was to this pool that Euan carried her still rigid body, and there he laid her in the cool water, gently stripping away the torn remnants of her clothes and stroking back her soft brown hair. Supporting her with one arm he shook off his own shirt and waded in beside her, sinking his shoulders beneath the surface and feeling the quick gentle current wrap itself around them.

Donald swallowed back the fierce ache in his throat and reached out to touch Janet's silky hair. "Have I ever told you about the time the son of Red Fergus the herdsman escaped from the water horse?" he asked. Iain dragged his eyes back from the outcrop behind the croft and Janet gazed up into Donald's face. "Since Euan is gone to make your mother better I think we have time for a story," he added gently.

"What did the soldiers do to her?" Janet asked him.

Donald threw an anxious glance at Iain. Janet might not understand, but her brother certainly did. He pulled her closer to him. "They hurt her in a way that wicked men sometimes do, men who believe that a woman is weaker and less worthy than them. But I promise your mother's spirit is stronger than any soldier's, Janet Mac-Kenzie."

"So she won't die?"

"Not for a very long time, I am sure," he said softly. "And you must try to put this day from your mind. The soldiers will not be back." Donald spoke with a confidence he did not feel. The time had surely come for Morag to take her children to a safer place. If Andra' had not yet found a way to set her up in town, then he and Euan must put their own minds to it.

"Who was dumb Fergus?"

Donald forced a smile and drew breath for his tale. Iain was still studying him, but in a different way. Nothing could change what had happened, but Donald was beginning to discover that time would bring healing if time could be granted. "He was a wily old tacksman from the eastern border of Glenshellich, much given to boasting and telling tall stories. But this story –" he lowered his voice. "This story is generally believed to be exactly and entirely the truth."

"Uncle Andra' once saw a water horse," Iain said. "In a sparkling loch far to the west."

"Then perhaps it was the same one."

"Tell us," pleaded Janet.

"One evening when Fergus was walking by the lochan he saw three horses. Two belonged to his neighbour, Black Allan Stewart of Branach, but the third was a magnificent beast, sleek and sturdy, with a flowing mane and tail. It followed him home along the shore and, fearing the worst but not wanting to lose this marvellous beast, he put a cow shackle around its neck and set it to gathering peats with his eldest son Murdo. Fergus soon began to boast about his new animal, how clever it was and how strong - as strong as any two of his neighbours' horses. But one spring day when Murdo was riding it home, without warning it became restless, tossing its head and shaking off its shackle. Without the shackle Murdo had no power over the beast at all, and could do nothing but let it gallop with him on its back, all the way to the shore of the lochan and into the water."

"And drowned?" breathed Janet.

Donald shook his head. "Whether he was drowned or not, Murdo was never seen anywhere in Glenshellich again."

"But the water horse was," Iain broke in, for he had learned to anticipate what might be coming in the chieftain's stories, and he did not think that this one had half run its course.

"Indeed, Iain, the water horse came back one starless night some three years later. Fergus heard it whinnying outside his door and recognised it at once. He put the same cow shackle on it and set it to work, but his younger son would not ride it, until Fergus grew angry and told his younger son he was no match for his brother. Fergus only wished that it had been him and not Murdo who had disappeared into the loch. Now that was a very terrible thing to say to a young man so much in awe of his father, so Fergus's younger son, whose name was Martin, knew that he must somehow find the courage to ride the horse. The first time he saddled it the horse was very docile and walked, then trotted gently up and down. The second time it cantered smoothly over the meadow and down the track that led to the lochan. By the third time Martin mounted it the horse believed it had tricked him into a sense of safety, so it shook its head free of the shackle, even though Martin had been expecting that very thing. The water horse galloped headlong down towards the lochan, past the herd of cattle and through the gateway at the head of the track. Martin had only one chance and he took it. He wedged his feet firmly against the pillars of the gatepost and the water horse shot from under him and down into the lochan before even it realised it had lost its rider."

"So Martin was safe?"

"Martin was safe," agreed Donald. "And as soon as Fergus saw how easily he might have lost both sons he started to appreciate Martin very much more."

"And the water horse?"

"Did not return again to the Glen of the Little Oak Trees," Donald concluded. "For they say that once a water horse has been outwitted it will find a new loch to inhabit, and new humans for its prey.

Now, Janet," he said, changing the subject with a slow smile. "I think you should go and find some clothes to take up to your mother." He turned to the boy. "And Iain, you will see how well you can bear my weight, for I am inclined to attempt another stroll."

* * *

The water of the pool was cool and clear and soothing, and at last Morag turned to look into Euan's face. It seemed to her that his pain was greater than her own, for at least her ordeal was over.

"You must forget this, Euan," she whispered, "and be thankful that we are all still alive."

"I am thankful," he told her. "For my life is more precious than it has ever been." She smiled and lightly touched his cheek, but he jerked his head away with another sob. "Yet how can I forgive myself for not stopping what they did to you?"

"How could I forgive you if you had tried to? For you would surely have died for your trouble. Anyway," she added as a cloud drifted above them and the burn's water turned to a silver streak across the pebbles. "You must believe that the soldiers did not touch me." He gazed at her in dismay. "They might have hurt my body," she went on softly. "But I was not inside my body." He could see in her eyes that she spoke no less than the truth. "I sent my spirit somewhere else, Euan," she repeated. "So you see, I do not need your remorse, and I do not need your pity."

"What I feel for you is not pity," Euan whispered. He reached for his plaid and stepped onto the bank, his body refreshed and strengthened as the water ran from his shoulders and the sun's warmth dried them. He held his plaid ready, and as he wrapped it around her he saw Janet making her way over the rise. "You have become my family," he said softly. "And no matter where in the world I must go, I promise there will be no distance great enough to keep me from returning to you."

* * *

In Glenshellich the old men, the boys and Iain MacCombie prepared to take the cattle to their summer grazing, but even though the hill pastures were budding green the women were strangely loath to leave the clachan. As Catriona MacMichael swept the year's dirt from the huts she thought she heard distant trails of lost laughter drift with the breeze. Then her ears caught a different sound, an unfamiliar, regular, thin beat, a drumming growing gradually closer. Domhnull MacCombie heard it too. He appeared from behind one of Feodag's stones and turned to Catriona with eyes full of dread.

Out on the lochan Angus Ban pulled in his net. It held a good haul for a clear summer's night: not as heavy as in the old days, but that was maybe just as well now that he had lost most of his own strength, now that he no longer had Kenneth to help him. The shoreline he rowed towards was an indistinct blend of soft colours, but his memory could distinguish the wild purple orchids, the pink milkwort and sea daisy hidden among the broom. And his ears were still keen, keen enough to catch the steady tattoo, quite unlike the mystic rhythm that now and then pulsed in his heart. He let the oars drift but his ears remained alert to the beat as it pounded closer.

Helen rose from the bed she had shared so briefly with her husband. She glimpsed her white face in the mirror, and the dark hollows that framed her eyes. Sometimes she believed a different person entirely looked back at her, no longer a sparkling girl but a woman almost as deranged as old Beathag, a woman dreading the day she must bring her child into a world she felt scarcely part of herself. Her only remedy would be Donald's safe return, a hope that grew fainter with every day that passed. All her life she had been treasured and protected and this adversity had taken a cruel toll. She gazed through the window towards the track that led to the empty clachan and saw only the clearing mist and the small shadows the sun's early rays etched around Feodag's scattered stones. She clutched the bedpost as a spasm stabbed her stomach. He must come back to her soon. Perhaps today would be the day. She struggled downstairs and Christie and Eilidh, from their different directions, both crossed the hallway anxiously to her side.

"What is it?" cried the servant woman.

"Come and sit down," Christie soothed, and led Helen to the wooden settle where she perched uncomfortably, struggling for breath. But although she tried to brush their concern aside, her spasms grew worse. Christie held her hands and looked fearfully at Eilidh.

"We must fetch Catriona."

Eilidh nodded, but could not tear herself away from her mistress. Perhaps it was best that she should be the one to stay, Christie decided. She would go herself to the clachan to find James and he could climb to the shieling for Catriona.

James was helping the women gather the cattle. They were only days away from moving the herd, and he would be going with them. Christie reached them at the same moment Iain MacCombie came tearing up the track.

"The red river has come!" he gasped. "It is flowing this way. Listen!"

They did, and James Hamilton could not mistake the beat that drummed in the distance. It was one he had not long ago marched to himself.

"Is there time drive the cattle?" Christie cried.

"We can herd them behind the burn and over An Ciobar's Pass," Iain told her. "I will do it."

Christie grabbed James' arm. "And then you must go to the cave."

He shook his head. "I cannot leave you all in the house without protection."

"Fraser and I will protect the house. You must take Domhnull to the cave. I will hear of nothing else," she insisted. "We have agreed it is the only way." Yet still James hesitated. "Domhnull is with Catriona at the shielings," Christie went on. "You must send her back down for Helen."

He looked down into her face and felt his heart twist. "But what of you?" he breathed.

She reached out and pulled him close. "Whatever happens," she whispered, "you and I have found each other. We will never be parted again, even by death."

A rough sob escaped him before he drew away. With a last desperate look behind him he followed Iain MacCombie to where the women of the clachan waited, impatiently swishing flies from the cattle's hides. Iain urged them forward and the shaggy black beasts began the climb towards the passage that twisted around the hidden slope of the Giant's Mountain. Christie turned her eyes towards the Watcher's Stone. The drumbeat grew louder and soon she could make out the scraping of hooves and the stamp of marching feet. Around her the empty glen waited as the red and white column approached.

At last the officer in charge of it drew to a halt.

"Miss Hamilton, once again, if my eyes do not deceive me."

The Master of the Stones sat dark and proud astride his gelding while his ghillie skulked at his knee, filthy and scowling as ever. Behind them ranged twenty or so foot soldiers standing patiently to attention.

Kilclath turned to address the man at their head. "So here we have it, Sergeant Gillespie. The Glen of the Little Oak Trees, whose master is another to have made the unwisest of choices." The sergeant's lip stretched into a brief, thin smile. "Am I to assume that you are the one in command here?" Kilclath inquired of Christie, the light mockery in his voice making her more uncomfortable still.

"Lady Glenshellich is close to her confinement," she said, but added softly so only he could hear. "This is a sick revenge."

The force of his penetrating eyes unsettled her entirely. "It is not my revenge," he answered in a lower voice. "But you may consider it fortunate that the government has chosen me as its instrument. I will see to it that MacSomhairle's glen does not suffer unduly for his treason."

Although she had no reason to doubt his words Christie's sense of disquiet grew. She and her brother had both, albeit unwillingly, betrayed him, and one glance at Hughie McIvor told her that betrayal had not been forgotten. Her heart raced and she struggled to control her breathing.

"The soldiers will be relieving you of some cattle as instructed," Kilclath went on and cast his eyes around the clachan and down to the shoreline. "Though you do seem remarkably lacking in livestock." Hughie scowled more deeply and let his contemptuous eyes rest on Christie. She shuddered. "I, of course, am seeking MacSomhairle," Kilclath went on. "An uncaptured rebel in arms."

"You will not find him here," Christie said softly.

Kilclath gave a sigh. "I did not expect to. But by making away with some of his possessions I will fulfil my immediate commission. Not perhaps to the total satisfaction of Captain Scott at Fort William, but I think in accord with the feelings of my kinsman General Mamore. So might I ask you do me the honour of escorting us to the house?"

His eyes were mocking yet held their old dark intensity. Trying to ignore their effect she fell into step beside him. Hughie walked at his other shoulder and the soldiers followed at a respectful distance, muttering suspiciously amongst themselves.

"The other matter of which we should speak is your brother," Kilclath went on. "A conflict of loyalties is unacceptable in a soldier. The government has little compassion for deserters."

"I hoped you might find it in you to understand what James did. And why."

"Then he must discuss that with me in person."

A short silence fell before she dared to ask, "Do you have any word of MacSomhairle?" She was disappointed to hear her voice tremble.

"Have you received none?" He spoke sharply, but his tone softened as he looked down at her. "My information is that he is not yet accounted for." He squinted up at the mountain. "His name has appeared in no official list," he went on, "whether that is good news or bad." He paused again. "I did, however, encounter his brother in the Tolbooth of Inverness."

"So Andrew is alive!" she gasped.

"Was alive. Presumably he will now be held in London, awaiting trial for treason."

Christie turned away from Hughie's savage grin. She knew as well as he did the sentence for a traitor. They proceeded in uneasy silence, the darkly solemn officer and the anxious girl stumbling to match his pace, while the soldiers drilled their eyes rigidly ahead. Gillespie's troopers had no doubt they had drawn the short straw with this officer. He was a high-lander. These were his neighbours, and this campaign had already shown how much more there was to unite than divide them.

On the slopes above them James urged the last of the black cattle into the pass to be penned by Iain MacCombie and his watchful dogs. He thought of his unspoken promise to the piper's wife and looked up at the dark mouth of Feodag's cave, then down at column snaking its way to the house. Once again he found himself torn in two. But Iain faced no such dilemma.

"We must stay hidden," he hissed. "There will be more need of us when the soldiers have gone."

Helen rose unsteadily to her feet as the Master of the Stones passed through the doorway of the house of Glenshellich for the second time. Eilidh stared into his face and knew that like her he was remembering the first. She edged protectively closer to her mistress.

Christie could see from the sudden gravity of Kilclath's expression that the sight of MacSomhairle's wife had come as a shock. He tried to disguise it by taking her hand and raising it to his lips.

"Kilclath!" she breathed.

"I regret I must renew our acquaintance under such unfortunate circumstances," he told her gently. "But I am afraid that your estates are in forfeit and your possessions the property of the crown."

Helen drew a little breath that turned to a gasp as she stumbled against Eilidh, who nervously traced the sign of the cross on her chest. Christie stepped in front of them.

"So will you burn their house around their ears?" she demanded. "As we hear is this army's custom."

"I have done this house disservice enough," he answered quietly, before he took two paces towards the study door and held it open.

"If you promise to remain in this room I guarantee you will not be disturbed."

"This is indeed a charming way of conducting a robbery," Christie retorted.

For an instant his eyes flashed and she wished the remark unsaid. But he made no reply, other than to bend a stiff bow to Helen before he turned and closed the door behind him.

Inside the stables the garrons whinnied and kicked, but above their agitation Hughie McIvor could hear the distinct strains of an old sea shanty. He crept closer and cocked his ears.

The singer clearly had no intention of changing his routine for a handful of redcoats. He cut short his song and whispered to MacSomhairle's mare, "That's the way, my beauty. And you too my boys," he added to the garrons. "Just let they red vermin try laying their filthy paws on any o' you..." But the vermin who slipped inside the stable behind him was not wearing a red coat. He was a clansman, lean and swarthy, with drawn back lips and gleaming eyes. In that moment Archie Fraser would have given a very great deal for the sight of a soldier.

Eilidh of the red face sat frozen at her mistress's side. Helen had so withdrawn into herself that she seemed completely untroubled by the tramping of boots in the rooms upstairs. Christie moved to the window and stared out anxiously. Catriona must surely have received her message by now. Kilclath's compassion at the sight of MacSomhairle's wife had convinced her they were in no personal danger, but even so she found it intolerable to be so enclosed and helpless. She turned back to Eilidh in desperation.

"You should stay here," breathed Eilidh, reading her mind.

"I need fresh air," Christie told her. She could hear the heavy feet tramping over floorboards directly above them and she could see soldiers crossing the yard as they removed Glenshellich's silver and crystal, pictures and drapes with ruthless efficiency. The carts at the door were already half full. Sergeant Gillespie cast a sour look around as Christie stepped out into the yard. He had every intention of reporting this unwarranted leniency to a higher authority than General Mamore. Gillespie was a lowlander himself and to his mind the Campbells were a liability one and all. Harsh measures were required to stamp out insurrection and harsh measures accorded well with his temperament. Lawlessness had been rife in these parts for too long and here was the perfect opportunity to end it once and for all, to purge the wilderness with the brand and the sword. He watched his soldiers haggle over their bounty without the satisfaction of a job well done.

Inside the stables Hughie McIvor drew his dirk and crept closer. This would be a silent death, a swift revenge for a kinsman's life, but first the old man must taste his fear. Hughie crooked his arm around Fraser's neck and tickled his chin with the knife's point. The old groom smelt the sour breath and acid sweat and heard his heart pounding above the mare's weak whinny of protest. Then he heard another sound, a scream as someone else hurled against him, startling Hughie off his balance. The ghillie swore and kicked and sheathed his dirk to free his hand to fight off this attacker, this wildcat woman. He tried to grip her pounding fists and fend off her kicking until a sharp command rang from the rafters and called him to stillness. Christie Hamilton's feet continued to bruise his shins while Fraser clutched his own throat and struggled for breath.

"Who is this man?" demanded Kilclath, stepping forward into the gloom.

Hughie made no answer. He turned away with a thwarted snarl.

"Who is he?" repeated the Master of the Stones.

"The one who fired the first shot," panted Fraser at last, "the day your bullet felled MacSomhairle."

Kilclath's brow was drawn dark. He looked for a long time at Fraser, then back at the ghillie. Last of all he turned his eyes on Christie as Hughie slunk away in the direction of the loaded carts. Fraser, still gasping, leaned back against the beam for support.

"You should go inside the house," Kilclath told him. "And join the others. Miss Hamilton is in no danger now." When Fraser had struggled half way across the courtyard he added softly, "Although she most certainly was – in the gravest danger." He was still studying her closely. She turned away from the effect of his scrutiny, though the sound of his voice had already set her trembling. He touched her shoulder. "I have already discovered your bedchamber," he told her. "When my men have done their duty I will be waiting there for you."

* * *

Domhnull MacCombie crouched at the mouth of the cave and stared into the abyss of his glen. All was still and silent. He could see the empty track to the house and if he strained his eyes he could make out the occasional figure, like a tiny bright ant, crossing the courtyard. He had not heard a single shot nor seen a single wisp of smoke, yet he knew that the man beside him was so tense that he scarcely dared to breathe.

"Could a person hide here for ever?" he whispered.

"No man can hide for ever." James's words came from the knowledge that hiding might be the only future for him now. He would never escape the shadow of the gallows noose that swung over all who deserted in time of war. The lands and title of Allomore were certainly lost to him forever and his heart was heavy with the understanding that the same must now be true for MacSomhairle and Glenshellich.

* * *

The study door was still shut. Christie slipped past it and up the staircase, drawn like a trembling moth to the Master's flame. He was standing beside her bed, dark, patient and inescapable.

"Wherever life leads us, whoever we may pledge ourselves to, we will feel this passion," he said softly. "Why should we pretend otherwise?"

Christie's breath was deep and uneven. "Then you do not believe I have betrayed you?"

"Betrothal was never the path we were destined to take."

He took a step towards her and she fell against him. He was right. What they shared was about danger, about breaking boundaries, abandoning everything but their own desire. His fingers were already loosening her bodice, impatiently and more roughly than before, with no attempt to disguise his own need. And as they tumbled together across the bed Christie had no other thought or feeling or memory beyond the overpowering immediacy of her passion.

Eilidh of the scarlet face looked across the study at Fraser sipping from his brandy glass at the empty fireside. The silence in the room was broken only by occasional strange sounds from above. She raised her eyes suspiciously towards the ceiling, and then turned them towards the window. The soldiers were growing restless. At last the study door slowly opened and Kilclath once again appeared on the threshold.

"We are ready to take our leave," he said.

Christie squeezed past him to kneel at Helen's side and Eilidh noticed the warm flush on her cheeks.

"I will ride with the soldiers to the Watcher's Stone," Christie told her, "and find Catriona, for she should have been here long before this." She paused and pressed on Helen's arm. "We are safe now. I promise."

Only Eilidh noticed the look that flickered between Allomore's daughter and the Master of the Stones. She watched them as they passed through the door and out into the yard, and once again, as if by some strange instinct, drew another small cross upon her chest.

Christie rode to the rear of Kilclath and his sergeant, beside the laden carts that trundled and veered along the track, brushed by the yellow broom. Her body was weak from their passion but this time she felt no shame, only a strange exhilaration. On the opposite side of the cart Hughie looked slyly up at the bare slopes of the giant's mountain. He could have sniffed out Glenshellich's herd in no time had it been required. The Master's eyes too strayed often to the craggy peak. The mist was beginning to fall and already covered the corrie's grey shadows. A sharp wind blew threads of it towards the clachan and Christie saw in the distance a blurred figure moving quickly ahead on the track.

Her heart gave a little lurch. Something was not right. The figure was stumbling, sometimes visible, sometimes hidden, and seemed to be in flight. At first Christie had thought it might be Beathag, but as they drew closer she saw to her dismay that it was Catriona MacMichael.

Kilclath drew his horse to a halt and Christie sensed a different kind of tension in Hughie McIvor as he edged closer. Catriona gave no indication that she was aware of their presence but continued her stumbling passage.

"Who is that?" Kilclath asked.

"I believe it is Catriona MacMichael, who teaches our children." Christie was still uneasy. She did not know why she added, "Foster mother to MacSomhairle."

"Indeed," commented Kilclath. "A person of undoubted importance." But there was something different in his tone too and a lowered glance passed between himself and his ghillie.

Ahead of them Catriona was still running and Christie began to feel genuine alarm. There could be little doubt that her flight through the gathering mist was growing desperate. Kilclath kicked his heels into his gelding's side and Hughie loped at its tail as they cantered ahead of the platoon.

"Wait, woman!" Kilclath shouted.

But Christie could see that Catriona had no intention of obeying his command. She gathered speed again and hurried past the door of her cottage. She ran on and on towards the Watcher's Stone, and although Kilclath drew rein Hughie's pace increased.

"Catriona!" Christie cried, for she was certain now that something must have happened to James. Catriona could only be acting in this strange way to provide a distraction. Kilclath kicked his horse back into action and overtook his ghillie.

"Why do you run from us?" he called, but still Catriona did not stop. Christie followed as he continued to pursue Catriona into the mist. When she reached them she was horrified to see that Catriona was cowering against the Watcher's Stone, clutching her plaid around her neck in apparent terror.

"I was afraid, sir," she stammered at last, her head held low. "I was afraid of the soldiers." Christie stared at her in horror. Even her voice was not her own.

Hughie's eyes were glinting. He left his master's side and began to advance on Catriona who turned her face into the damp rock.

"Look at me when I speak!" ordered the Master of the Stones. But something seemed amiss with his voice also. Christie moved closer to Catriona in a desperate bid to reassure her.

"What is wrong, Catriona?" she implored. "It is Kilclath. He means you no harm. The soldiers are leaving."

Still Catriona made no response other than to tremble more desperately still.

"Catriona!" Christie pleaded.

Sergeant Gillespie was not a patient man and his frustration was reaching breaking point. He jumped from his horse, pushed past the crouching Hughie and spun Catriona around with a force that sent her reeling backwards. Hughie took a step closer to his chieftain. "Speak to the officer, you highland bitch!" the sergeant spat. "Do you think he's got time to waste on the likes of you?"

Catriona made no attempt to save herself from her fall. Her hand still clutched her plaid to her throat as if her very life depended on it. But at last she raised her eyes to meet those of the Master of the Stones and Christie saw that every muscle of his face had frozen.

"I have asked you a question," he said softly, and Christie could not fathom the expression in his eyes. "Why did you run?" he repeated, but somehow this time it did not seem like the same question at all.

Catriona shrank even further into the rock. It was horrible, shameful, for Christie to witness her humiliation, yet she could not tear her eyes away. At last Kilclath drew his sword. Hughie's fingers moved on the handle of his dirk but he kept his eyes trained on his master. Slowly and deliberately the Master of the Stones raised his sword arm until he brought it whipping across Catriona's shoulders. The steel caught her plaid and dragged it from her body. For a hopeless moment she raised her arm to retrieve it, but let her hand fall weakly to her side.

A low growl issued from the throat of Hughie McIvor but his master made not a sound. He sat frozen in the saddle, staring down at the livid mark of the knife. Uncomprehending, but sick with compassion, Christie moved to kneel at Catriona's side, then looked up, only to see the anguish in the eyes of the healer's widow mirrored exactly in the eyes of the Master of the Stones.

* * *

A great crowd had gathered all the way from Edinburgh's Castle to its Cross to witness a grimy throng of chimney sweeps waving and dragging the tattered standards of the vanquished rebel army. Davie Dalgleish shook his head and solemnly doffed his bonnet, a gesture in marked contrast to the majority of his fellow spectators who jeered and giggled and mocked the comical antics. At the head of the raucous procession Edinburgh's chief hangman carried the Prince's colours, escorted by a detachment of Lee's foot and the city sheriffs. Gavin MacVey was not in their party, although he was a spectator. He caught Davie's eye but quickly looked away. It was not wise to recall old allegiances in the current climate, more prudent by far to cheer along with the rest as one by one the standards were ceremoniously burned. He did note with some small satisfaction, that the standard of Appin was not among them.

Further up the Lawnmarket Alison Bothwell kept well away from her window as only befitted a woman in mourning.

* * *

Sergeant Gillespie could find no explanation for this latest insanity in his commanding officer.

"What are the orders?" he yelled after the galloping figure as it disappeared into the mist. But his only answer was the sound of fading hoof-beats. Unusually Hughie McIvor had not followed his master. He loomed over Catriona MacMichael, his eyes drilling her with a loathing that had simmered for thirty years. He growled some savage Gaelic into her ear, but when he turned to the sergeant he spoke in perfectly formed English, so perfectly formed that the shock of it chilled Christie's soul.

"Did you not hear the officer, Sergeant Gillespie?"

Gillespie stared back, as much in amazement at Hughie's command of the language as in alarm at his master's flight.

"Then let me repeat the order," continued Hughie. "Take half your men back to burn the house. The rest can fire the village." He spat and gave Christie a sneer of triumph before he aimed a final vicious kick at Catriona's ribs. "Seek out this bitch's dwelling for your first brand," he hissed, before he turned and disappeared into the same mist that had swallowed his master.

From the mouth of the giant's cave James Hamilton could distinguish nothing. He had watched the red line proceed from the clachan to the house in what appeared to be an orderly fashion. He had watched the same line slowly return before the mist had fallen and he could see no more. But now he had no need of his eyes. He could smell the burning and even at his great height it caught his throat and sickened his heart. Then came the sounds, deadened in the dense air, cries of children and women's screams.A helpless sob tore his throat. Yet again he had made the wrong choice. He thrust his knuckles into his mouth but his sobs would not be silenced. The horror he had seen ravage Drumossie Moor had now reached Glenshellich.

Christie was screaming through the smoke at the sergeant and when he ignored her she grabbed his arm and kicked his ankles. He threw her aside with a curse and watched with satisfaction as his men went about their new duties. Whatever the reason for it he could be thankful that Kilclath had finally come to his senses. The cottage roofs were crackling and the flames reached high into the fog. Lumps of burning turf fell and kindled the heather as the women clutched their quaking children and wailed frantic prayers. Christie continued to wrench at his arm and he flung her to the ground. No damned fool girl would keep his lads from their sport now, even one who could speak so presumptuously to an officer. She would sing a different tune before the day was out.

"Stop it in the name of God!" she screamed again. Sergeant Gillespie raised the butt of his rifle and cracked it down on her head.

"And maybe that'll put paid to your damned raving!" he muttered and turned to give his men their marching orders.

Before long his fist hammered once more on the door of the House of Glenshellich, and this time he did not wait to be admitted.

"Take yourselves out into the yard!" he yelled, though he cared little whether those inside heard him or not. "We're here to finish the job."

Eilidh appeared at the top of the stairs, her red face pale with horror. Back inside her bedroom Helen moaned in pain and clutched at the covers. Fraser and Eilidh supported her down the staircase, and through the yard where already the soldiers were pulling the horses from the stables. Fraser watched them rear and kick and heard them snort and whinny as they were whipped past the stacks of sticks and straw piled against the doors and windows. He knew he would never see them again. Soon they would be serving new masters and all he had lived for here would be gone. The house of Glenshellich, the panels and portraits, the books and the drapes would be nothing but ashes on the earth and dust in the air.

Helen knew nothing of the carnage. She was barely conscious, though she squirmed and wept as Eilidh soothed her soaking brow and whispered words that brought no comfort. The soldiers bunched themselves apart, watching the flames flicker, leap and crackle as they gorged on the books in John Stewart's treasured library and on the bed where hours before Allomore's daughter and the Master of the Stones had tumbled in their stolen ecstasy. As quickly as their passion had ignited the soldiers' fire had engulfed the rafters, but before the roof submitted with a final roar another sound rose above it, a strangled, barely human cry. The soldiers turned as one to face the bent figure emerging through the red glare, running towards them grotesque and demented, more devil than woman. Beathag stumbled closer, discharging her glen's anguish more eloquently than their guns, more powerfully than swords or flames, and all who heard her knew the sound would echo through every day and night her curse left to them.

Sergeant Gillespie was the first to recover his composure, but his desperate order went unheeded as Beathag's twisted fingers tore at the soldiers' coats and faces. For a brief moment Helen stirred and understood at last that the curses were not for her. It was the sergeant himself who discharged his musket at the old woman's chest, taking aim as calmly as he would have done at a mad dog. She fell to the ground, just as her granddaughter had done, at the white-gaitered legs of a redcoat. Eilidh's hand stroked her mistress's brow and she whispered soothing words as her desperate eyes sought Fraser's. His face was twisted in grief and fury, a helpless old man whose world was smouldering to ashes. They stared together at the lifeless bundle of rags at the soldier's feet, knowing that Beathag's spirit, fierce as ever, had already flown to merge with the mist above the giant's mountain.

The flames still leapt as the soldiers assembled to march away. The rush and spluttering of them continued into the gathering dusk, as Eilidh stroked the cold, white face of her mistress, praying for a miracle, and Fraser slumped wretchedly beside them. At last Eilidh began to croon a soft song she had heard at her grandmother's fireside.

Carry me, carry me, higher than eagles, stronger than torrents, that rush from the west, carry me, carry me down through the valley, down through the green slopes to where I must rest.

MacSomhairle's wife had been so beautiful, serene as the lochan on a windless evening. Now she was grey and wasted, her eyes empty and her mind lost. As the smoke wrapped itself around them like a shroud Eilidh crossed herself and her heart grew cold.

And then, in an instant, the world changed. They were no longer alone. A familiar voice was speaking, calmly and with confidence.

"Fraser! Stir yourself!"

Catriona MacMichael was at Helen's side and James Hamilton laid his arm gently on Eilidh's shoulder. "There is nowhere we can take her," he whispered.

Eilidh knew it, even if her mistress had been in any condition to be moved.

"Fetch me water," Catriona instructed.

When James returned from the burn Catriona's eyes gripped his. "We must deliver MacSomhairle's child between us," she told him, and paused for barely a moment before adding, "MacIain Mhor."

In the grey half-light Helen drifted in and out of consciousness, unable to heed the soft entreaties from Catriona and Eilidh. Stifling a sob James tightened his grip on her shoulders and Fraser moved closer and took her hand. Her body twisted in agony, and James forced himself to pray through the timeless moments between her gasps. At last an infant's strangled cry rang through the air, and James felt warm tears on his cheeks. He watched Catriona wrap the child in her shawl and hand it to Helen, but Helen's eyes were distant and empty. Eilidh leaned close to her ear.

"You have a baby girl," she whispered. "A beautiful baby girl."

But Helen did not hear her. The embers of the House of Glenshellich glowed through the fleeting summer darkness and made shadows around Beathag's corpse. Catriona moved towards it, her eyes tight with sorrow.

"So time has proved you right, Beathag," she said at last. "Rest easy now with your ghosts and your prophets and I promise we will not let this new generation forget."

* * *

When Christie woke she was conscious only of blackness, though it was daylight, blackness and the stench of stale burning. She could see the grey sky above her head, and the charred remains of Catriona's rooftree. She turned her head and saw Domhnull asleep on the floor beside her. They were alone and all around them was silence. Then she remembered. She closed her eyes. It was simpler to fall back into the void.

When next she opened her eyes James was there, and instead of silence she could hear a feeble baby's cry. She sat up and saw Eilidh cradling a bundle in her arms, her eyes pleading as she gently tugged at Helen's plaid. The two women were dirty and bloodstained and glancing down at herself Christie saw she was the same. Her head throbbed as she tried to raise it from the pile of heather. She saw Helen shudder and push the bundle away. Eilidh threw an imploring look across the room and Domhnull lifted the baby from her arms and began to rock her gently. Then the piper's niece appeared and exchanged her own infant for Helen's. Shyly but proudly she prepared to hold her chieftain's child to her breast. James returned quietly to Christie's side and wiped her brow as she drifted back to sleep.

The next time she awoke it was to the sound of low voices. Her head no longer ached, but throbbed dully, producing a peculiar sense of unreality.

"She would at least be safe there." That was James.

"But the baby…?" Catriona's voice was uncertain.

"She has not looked at the baby," sighed Eilidh. "Not once."

"She's no' looked at anything or anyone. There's only one sight like to bring her to her senses now." Fraser's voice, at least, was strong.

"The child must stay with its mother." James sounded unusually decisive. "They will both be safer in the Glen of Black Cattle where there will surely be women enough to wet nurse. And of course Eilidh must go with her."

Eilidh heaved a great sigh. She had never in her life left Glenshellich. But wherever her mistress went she was bound to follow.

Christie opened her eyes and sat up. The small council had gathered close to where the door had once been, and Helen sat some distance apart, still lost in her own inaccessible world. Domhnull turned his anxious eyes from her to Christie, and nudged James who immediately crossed to her side.

* * *

Down at the lochside it seemed that nothing had changed. The pebbles glinted and the gulls dipped, their wings sweeping the quiet water. Iain MacCombie sat on the shingle watching old Angus make safe his boat.

"So can you say what is left for me?" he complained balefully. "I have betrayed my chieftain time after time after time."

Angus pretended to busy himself with the rope. He sensed a tide turning and at last dared begin to hope the worst might be over. This latest wickedness had taken a bitter toll, the life of his old sparring partner and, he had heard, the mind of his chieftain's wife. Angus knew that before the healing must come the retribution. Yet it was beginning to seem to him that what had been foretold was in fact no more or less than the passage of every man's life, the struggle, the grief, the heartache, and for the resilient, the survival.

"Your strength has always been your swiftness," Angus told him. "You will cover many miles to serve MacSomhairle, for many miles still lie between him and his destiny."

A flicker of light sprang into Iain's hooded eyes. "Then you believe MacSomhairle lives?"

The old man turned his face towards the mountain but made no answer.

* * *

"I have yet again played the coward's part," James whispered.

Christie gazed earnestly into his face. "Andrew has been taken to London," she whispered. "Remember Henry Matheson, the magistrate?"

"Alison's old beau?"

"I have been thinking…"

Catriona lifted her head to listen.

"Perhaps if you went to Alison," Christie urged, "and told her all that has happened, between you might find a way to save him."

"How can I desert you? Especially now."

"What is there left in Glenshellich for the soldiers to destroy?"

"There are still women. There are still children."

"We must move to the shielings," Catriona interrupted. "We can hunt and snare to survive. Angus will catch us fish. We will not starve until winter comes if we all pull together. But you will not be safe here," she told James. "Believe me."

"And what of Domhnull MacCombie?"

Catriona's voice was firm. "Come time, MacIain Mhor, he will have greater need of you." Then she turned to Christie. "You must go with your brother."

"No!" Christie cried.

"The Countess of Dalvey will protect you."

Christie felt hot tears spring to her eyes. It had never occurred to her that she should once more leave the glen. She thought back to the day of its destruction: the false sense of safety Kilclath had given them, the incomprehensible anguish of his betrayal. As if she read her mind Catriona took both her hands and grasped them tight.

"You must go with him," she repeated. "For I fear even more for you if you stay in Glenshellich."

* * *

A summer gloom hung over the Valley of Stones. The air was leaden under the grey sky as the Master rode rigid into the shadow of the twin peaks, his head high and his eyes dead. Hughie McIvor followed, with the satisfaction of a man who knew his time had come. For thirty years he had nursed his hatred, but not even in his wildest dreams could he have imagined how sweet would be his revenge. Now his promise to the old master was almost fulfilled. He remembered well the night he made it. Cold eyes had met across a bloodstained desk and sealed a silent pact. No matter how long it might take there would be retribution for the humiliating betrayal that had pierced the very heart of his chieftain's pride. And fate had added a personal stake. Hughie's kinsman's half blind eye had peered through countless fractured dreams, poison from the same wound, reminding him that the only remedy was the death of all those who had brought shame on the House of the Eagle. Strange to think that all the time he need have looked no further than Glenshellich.

Like the evening itself the house was sombre as they passed through the front door. No servants waited to welcome them and only memories followed the tall figure up the staircase, past the old portraits and down the cold corridor. His plaid covered him from head to toe as he strode from Hughie's sight, but what lay in the Master's heart was wrapped closer still, closer than ever before, so close as to have slipped beyond reach.

The ghillie waited a few moments at the foot of the stair, and then slunk inside the dim study. He looked up at the portrait above the desk and showed his broken teeth in a twisted grin.

For a second the Old Fox almost seemed to smile back.

* * *

"You must make your way in stealth," Christie told Iain. "For the land between here and the Glen of the Black Cattle will be alive with troops." She paused and added, "I know you lack neither the skill nor the courage."

Iain looked at her with suspicion, but saw she was in earnest. Then Christie turned to Eilidh, nervously clutching the baby. "You are their best protector, " she whispered, "for I know that Helen is more precious than life to you." Yet she was still uneasy, something still was not right. Finally she moved to Helen and took her into her arms. But Helen pulled away at once, rigid, as if her very lifeblood had been frozen and she had turned to unfeeling stone. From behind the charred walls of Catriona's cottage a white-faced Domhnull watched. Helen gazed back at him and her eyes took on a brief flicker of animation. She lifted the baby from Eilidh's arms, carried her to Domhnull and held her towards him.

"You cannot," James breathed. "You cannot! You are her mother."

Helen turned and fixed him with an even stranger look. She said not a word but let Eilidh guide her to where Iain waited. Eilidh looked helplessly behind her. Domhnull cuddled the child close and Christie saw tears in his eyes and a strange defiance as James moved to take her from him. But Helen had already turned away and was walking towards the Watcher's Stone, with Eilidh hurrying behind.

"The child will stay with us," said Catriona softly. "For the time being at least."

"Helen is her mother!" James repeated, but this time his words lacked their earlier conviction.

Helen and Eilidh were already close to the bend in the track. Iain remained, pacing indecisively, but when Catriona nodded in the direction of the retreating women he followed them without another backward glance.

Catriona laid her hand softly on James' arm. "Sometimes, MacIain Mhor," she told him, "Only a mother can choose when she must say goodbye."

* * *

The sun set orange over the Twin Mountains of the Eagles and its dying rays ignited each stark stone that scattered down the valley. No movement came from the shielings and the cattle slept as Iain MacCombie lifted his chieftain's wife across the foaming tributary that plunged to the Bloody Burn. Casting an anxious glance after it Eilidh of the red face hoisted her skirt and found her own foothold. Iain gave a brief nod to reassure her. He had passed this way unchallenged many times. He knew that around the rocky shoulder the valley narrowed, then widened again into marshland where hill ponies grazed and roamed at whim. He crept like a shadow towards their shadows, silent and fleet of foot, resolute and alert. MacSomhairle's wife's bewildered eyes followed him and Eilidh reached over and took her hand. With luck they would be clear of Kilclath by daybreak, riding Campbell garrons over safer routes, if such routes still existed. Whatever the dangers, Iain MacCombie was grateful for his chance to make amends.

* * *

Inside the blackened ruins of her cottage Catriona MacMichael crooned softly as she cradled her chieftain's baby and stroked her soft face. She had Helen's dark hair and her father's strong jaw. She was almost unbearably fragile, smooth and precious. Catriona shuddered at the contrast with her own scar. "It is this hand that has brought ruin to Glenshellich," she murmured. "And made her world collapse even as she struggled into it. I have held her father thus so many times. And each time I repeated the same prayer. It will not be easy for me to speak with God again."

Christie gazed at her with a terrible compassion. No matter what grief had touched her own life she knew it could be nothing in comparison with this. "So will you tell me?" she whispered.

Catriona nodded and at last raised her eyes. "How could the past remain a secret when there are so many who remember? I knew Glenshellich could not hide me forever. It is a long and sad story, Christie, yet perhaps you more than most have the right to hear it." As Christie moved to kneel beside her she reached out and clasped her hand. "Once I spoke to you of the man who took your father's title. I said I knew him but I did not tell you how well. David Hamilton is my brother."

As Christie stared at her in utter amazement Catriona went on. "All his life David was sly and cunning. While he pretended to admire your father for his loyalty to King James he sang a different tune in the Whig circles where he preferred to move. He was in a perfect position to gather information, and the intelligence he traded led to many downfalls and deaths. Perhaps it was inevitable that one day he would join forces with the Old Fox of Kilclath." Catriona paused again. She could not remember when she had last mentioned that name. "Kilclath," she repeated, "was driven by many demons, but by the time I was introduced to him he had one, over-riding, desire. His second wife had died in childbirth and her baby did not survive her. More than anything else Kilclath needed an heir. I was fifteen years old, strong and healthy, and David had devised his plan." Christie was holding her breath, still afraid to imagine what might be coming next. The baby gave a tiny whimper. Catriona eased her onto her shoulder and her eyes grew distant. "My brother took me to the House of the Eagle," she went on, "And, young and foolish as I was, I was impressed, impressed too, God help me, by its master. I knew nothing then of the world and its ways, and when it suited him Alexander Campbell could appear the most charming of men. Before that first visit was over Kilclath and my brother had discussed our betrothal." Catriona gave a sad smile. "Although I must have had some doubts," she went on. "For I sought your father's advice. I had always been a favourite of his and he was incensed when he heard of David's plan. Perhaps if he had told me the truth about all those good men ruined by my brother and Kilclath I would have made a different decision, but my brother's will and Kilclath's soft persuasion proved stronger. I married the Master of the Stones, and after a year I bore him a son. But long before that day I had come to realise my mistake."

Catriona had waited a long time to tell her story. Now she was reliving each dark and evil day and she felt the spirit drain from her again. "It is enough to say that within a month of our marriage I had come to both hate and fear my husband," she went on at last. "By the time our son was born I had no pride left and no hope, other than for my own death. A likeness of his first wife hung on the wall of the drawing room and I would sometimes sit beneath it. All the skill of the artist had not been able to hide the emptiness in her eyes, the same emptiness I saw reflected in my own each time I looked in a glass."

Catriona fell silent again and Christie sensed that the hardest part of her story was still to come. Outside the wagtails and swallows darted, their wings sending little black showers to dust the women's hair. "My life improved with the birth of our son," Catriona went on quietly. "I had given Kilclath what he needed and I began to see less of him. I was barely sixteen years old, but I had a child who depended on me: and it was my child who brought me back to life. I kept him by my side always, and as he grew we laughed and could be happy together." Catriona's eyes were moist and Christie felt the tears on her own cheeks. "But although his father treated me in public like a pampered child I had to choose my gowns carefully to hide my bruises."

It was all too easy for Christie to imagine: the stark valley where the sun never shone, the sharp twin peaks with their drifting cloud, the cold mansion with its cruel master where a child and his mother shared their brief, doomed happiness. A long and trembling breath escaped her.

"In time my husband's attention turned to Glenshellich," Catriona went on softly. "There was good grazing on the giant's mountain and Donald's uncle was always hard pressed for money. One day he and John Stewart came to the House of the Eagle to discuss terms. They left Euan in the courtyard guarding their horses and somehow we fell into conversation. When he looked into my eyes I knew he saw me as I was. But Donald's uncle was headstrong and could not be trusted any more than my husband. It was John Stewart who had always to put his affairs to rights. At that time there were great stirrings among the followers of King James and my husband saw a still more prosperous future for himself. He bided his time and waited for events to unfold. Then one night new friends came to the house, important friends from London who showed great interest in your father. They spoke of how their government was watching him, and foolishly I told them that your father was a wise and honourable man. I had no idea that I had committed an unforgivable sin, or how I was about to pay for it. Later that night, after my husband's guests had retired, I was summoned to his study. I was not afraid. My outburst had emboldened me and I gave him my opinion of himself and of his associates, my own brother among them. I told him that one day his son would learn of his wickedness and would come to despise him as I did."

She stopped again, her face full of pain. Once again she was in the study of the House of the Eagle, facing the Old Fox's cold fury. "I knew he was not alone," she whispered, and Christie was certain that Hughie McIvor had lurked there too. She could picture the menace glinting behind those yellow eyes. "That was when," Catriona continued slowly, "The Master drew his sword. I thought he was only toying with it, and still I defied him. I was leaning on the desk with my thumbs gripping its edge, and in a split second he raised his sword and with his full force brought it down. At first I had no idea what had happened. I felt no pain. Then when he raised the blade again I looked down...." Her voice finally faltered. "I looked down and saw...."

Christie gazed at her hand in horror. Before Catriona drew breath to continue she knew what she was going to say. "... Neither of us could have guessed that our son was hiding inside the shadows behind the open door. It was his scream that rang through the House of the Eagle, the scream of a four-year-old child caught in a nightmare beyond imagining. I went to him and took him in my arms, but his eyes were fixed on the carpet and what lay there, and all the time my blood was soaking his nightshirt. I took him to his bed and lay beside him until he slept, knowing I could no longer shield or protect him. So I kissed him goodbye, and while his father drained his brandy bottle I left the House of the Eagle and wandered out into the darkness of The Valley of Stones. All I sought was death. It might have broken my son's heart, but I told myself that with time all hearts could heal. He was the apple of his father's eye and the Old Fox would deny him nothing. I remember the singing of the burn as I waded into its water. I remember the relief of knowing that the end had come." She gave a strange, sad smile. "Except it was not the end at all. For I awoke and found myself in the House of Glenshellich."

* * *

Andra' MacAslan had been trying for a dozen miles to sneeze the stench of death from his nostrils. The world was going to the devil before his eyes. On the slopes above Loch Lochy he had been required to turn both priest and gravedigger to a family he had known all his travelling days. Inverness had been no safer the last time he left it. Dog ate dog and British officers flogged and hanged their own side as casually as they did the rebels. The captured and the injured decayed in airless stables, attics and outhouses, yet still the dispossessed flocked to the town in their droves until every last cranny bulged and festered. Disease would take its own toll before long. Andra' was not convinced that Morag and her bairns would be any safer in town than they were in their own croft, or that he would be himself for that matter.

Weeks had passed since the soldiers' raid and little news had filtered through to the fugitives from the outside world. Euan MacMichael no longer even sought it. His days were spent in shoring up the cottage, making safe the outbuildings, teaching Iain how best to husband the unfriendly soil. His nights were passed in Morag's bed, coaxing her body towards a gradual healing. He had taught himself to savour each precious hour as MacSomhairle began to move more easily, hopping now as far as the end of the track with his clumsy crooked gait. Euan knew their days in the croft were numbered. Soon they must begin to make their way home over the well-guarded slopes that lay between them and Glenshellich. And where that way would end Euan could not even dare to imagine.

* * *

The Duke of Cumberland spent just one night in Scotland's capital on his swift journey south, in a bed warmed for him months before by the Pretender's son. The commander of the king's forces had every confidence that the country north and west of the Great Glen was subdued, and was happy to leave the maintenance of the peace to others. His father's adoring subjects in London waited to hail him as their deliverer and he was impatient to savour each cheer and accolade.

"Stinking Billy, they're crying him, I hear," Bella Galbraith pronounced as she closed the door on her Canongate establishment for the final time. "Say what you like about Charlie, but his men kent how to enjoy themselves."

Jean would be glad to see them all go. Edinburgh was gloomy, the citizens cheering the winning side at last but cheering with only half their hearts. And the war was far from over. The Master was still trapped by it. Jean pined for him more and more with every day that passed. Bella gave another snort and cast a critical eye over the hoops that concealed the contours of Jean's belly.

"Have you telt him yet?"

"I'll tell him when he comes home."

"Home!" she snorted. "I doubt he'll get wind long before that, my lassie. There's Campbells by the hundred in the miles between you and him." She squinted meaningfully. "They tell me you've got quite the expert at the letter writing."

"Maybe. But some things need discussed face to face."

Jean began to saunter across the cobblestones down the darkening street. Bella watched the slow sway of her hips and the graceful set of her shoulders. Just like her mother, she thought, the day she had come knocking on her door, though unlike her mother Jean had a strength that had already taken her into orbits way beyond Bella's control. Yet as she set off after her it occurred to Bella they were all part of the same canvas, brushed in or scrubbed out by the devil's hand that designed the fate of all who fell within the power of the Old Fox of Kilclath.

"Jean!" she called, then bit her tongue. But it was too late: too late in more ways than one, she thought grimly, for even before Jean turned around Bella knew there were things she could no longer hide.

"I've a mind for a mouthful of the master's brandy."

Jean was not fooled. "So you've decided to tell me, Bella?"

"Tell you what?"

"Why you were so against me having his child."

They had reached the door of Kilclath's apartment and Bella closed it behind her. With a cool nod that indicated her new authority Jean dismissed the servant who lingered in the hall and Bella followed her into the Master's study. She waited while Jean poured two glasses of brandy and then sat down. Jean glanced at the Master's chair and although she chose the seat beside it her hesitation was not lost on Bella.

"Near enough mistress already, I see," she muttered slyly, though she supposed she could hardly resent a situation she had herself engineered. "So when are you expecting the proposal?"

Jean's indignation was genuine. "You should know I've never wanted anything from your arrangement but to be with him. Our child will have no claim on him but a little of his time, a little of his love."

Bella's snort this time was enough to make her choke on her brandy. Jean sprang to her aid but Bella brushed her aside. "A little," she spluttered at last. "A little. That's all it can ever be, hen." She wheezed herself back to coherence. "All that's mine will be yours one day," she went on. Jean opened her mouth in astonishment, but Bella motioned her to silence. "Dinna say a word. Who else of them's got the brains or the stomach for it? Besides, I promised your mother." To Jean's dismay a tear welled in Bella's eye. "We all had our soft spot for her if truth be told, hen, and no just poor Hannah Bain." She lowered her voice still further until it left her lips as less than a whisper. "And it's tormented me all these years, what she'd say if she knew where I'd sent you."

Jean's eyes widened with alarm. "What are you saying Bella?" she breathed.

"The House of Kilclath is cursed."

"Cursed?" Jean felt her blood run cold as Bella's eyes narrowed to slits.

"The last Master of the Stones will come out of the womb of a whore."

Anger came to Jean's rescue and straightaway banished her fear. "I am not a whore," she breathed, and for the very first time her words came with utter conviction.

"*You* are not." Bella emphasised the first word. "It was the Old Fox gave his name to one: too frantic for an heir to heed that old dead nonsense, as he cried it."

Jean was still gazing at her with wide eyes. "Are you saying the Master's mother was a whore?" she breathed at last.

Bella shook her head. "No' *his* mother," she said softly. "The mother of the one who *should* be master."

Jean felt her heart stop altogether. "Bella…?" she began, but Bella had only paused for a second.

"Geordie Campbell's a bastard, Jean. The Old Fox was already wedded when he went through that ceremony – already wedded to the whore who had taken his son and escaped with her life while she still could." Jean's eyes grew wider. Her heart fluttered and a strange elation flooded her veins. If that was all the reason for the Master's dark dreams then she could at last breathe easy. Bella's voice broke through again. "It's the cloud that's hung over Geordie Campbell's inheritance, the secret he's had to live with from the day his father breathed the truth in his ear, the reason he needs to give Kilclath its next Master and put the past behind him."

Jean stood up and refilled their glasses. Bella was consumed by another fit of coughing and Jean was alarmed to see dark red stains on the handkerchief she removed from her lips.

"Are you telling me this because ….." she whispered.

"Aye, hen, I could never pull a trick over on you. The more we ken the higher we climb, Jean, just so long as you mind there's some can ken too much for their own good. Like poor Hannah Bain."

"So what happened to this other son and his mother?"

Bella tapped the side of her nose and squeezed her eyelid into a slow wink.

"That's what none of them ken. The Old Fox would have it she'd died and the bairn with her – clutching at straws. Anyone fly enough to trick him at his own game would have an card or two up their sleeve." She paused. "Hannah used to say she took her boy and her wedding lines on a passage to America."

"And the Master?"

"Has just to bide his time and wait."

"Is that so bad, Bella?"

Bella gave her another sly and knowing wink. "Maybe you should tell me," she said. "Or maybe it all depends which is safest - kennin' too much, or kennin' too little."

* * *

Christie pulled the skean dhu from her stocking and drew her finger back from the cold blade. The jewelled hilt glinted in the sunlight, as if to remind her there were some things that flames or swords could not destroy. The message was hardly comforting. Tradition had brought them mountains of dead, burned clachans and empty glens. It seemed to Christie the time had come to cast it aside and seek a different path.

She watched the sturdy boy jump from his great-grandfather's boat and run to meet her across the shingle, as lightly as his mother had once run and as swiftly as both his fathers. He was the future, the son of MacSomhairle, bred from the best and the finest of his clan.

When he reached her she held the knife out to him.

"MacSomhairle's skean dhu!" he breathed.

"You must take care of it now, Domhnull. He wanted you to have it. One day, we must hope, he will tell you its story himself."

Domhnull studied the knife for a moment in silence, and then calmly slipped it inside his own stocking. "Is it true that you will be going away again?" he asked softly.

She put her arm around him and they sat together staring out over the blue water of the lochan. She noticed that he did not snuggle close as he once would have done but held himself rigid. "No-one can make promises in these uncertain times," she said at last. "But for now I do not think I will go with James to Edinburgh. I think it will be best for me to come with you and Catriona and the baby to the shielings."

* * *

388

On the evening before their trial Andrew prayed with his companions. They prayed for their families and for all those who had suffered in the name of King James. They prayed for the prisoners and for the Prince, and lastly for themselves. They did not ask for the courts to show mercy, only for the courage to meet their deaths bravely with heads held high.

Early in the morning they were escorted from the house and for the first time in many months Andrew found himself alone. He climbed onto the chair and from the chair onto the table beneath the roof top window. If he stretched his neck sideways he could catch a final sight of his roommates as they were marched through the narrow street. He felt the sun warm his face and almost envied them their last walk in the air of the world: three ordinary but brave men, small and dwarfed by the angle of his vision, flanked by their red-coated guards. It was a common enough sight in the streets of London that summer, but it was a picture that Andrew would keep in his heart. In the short time he had shared their company he had come to feel for them as brothers, and his cheeks were streaked with tears as he watched them disappear.

That night he was swamped by an almost unbearable loneliness. It was the isolation of uncertainty, a languishing between life and death with no idea of who might wait for him on either side. Once when he woke it seemed he was back in the hold of the "Jane of Leith", shackled and sick, with Hugh's bloated corpse rolling beside him. Another time he was crawling among the dead on a battlefield, each mutilated face a member of his clan. In the strangest vision of all his imagination exchanged one bare attic for another and he found himself looking down on the raddled bones of old Hannah Bain. As he stretched out his arm to pull the blanket over her face she jerked suddenly upright and gripped his shoulders. There was something she needed to tell him, a story she could not take with her to the grave. But when he woke it was to the thin toll of St Martin's Bell, the grey light of a London dawn and a future that shrank darker than ever.

* * *

Alison Bothwell dabbed a tear from the corner of her eye.

"So it is truly over," she sighed at last. "All over, all in ruins and only weeping left for us."

"No," urged James. "The trials in London have only just begun. And I was wondering if your old friend the magistrate…"

"Henry?" she exclaimed. "But .."

"Is there nothing he could do to help us?"

The idea might have not have occurred to Alison herself, but once planted bore immediate fruit. "I'll write him tonight," she declared.

"And I will deliver your letter in person," James told her. "For I intend to take the first available southbound coach."

Alison looked scathingly at his dishevelled clothes. "You'll ride no coach until the two of us have paid a visit to Mr Dalgleish," she told him, "and measured you up for a suit that'll no' arouse the suspicion of all and sundry. Are you forgetting there's a price on your own head?"

His eyes blazed back at her. "I have played the coward's part too often since I returned to my father's country, and brought nothing but shame on his memory. I promise you now I would sacrifice my life to save Andrew!"

Alison could see that he meant every word. It was a change of heart of which she entirely approved. Andrew had always been her favourite. She would be every bit as prepared to make a similar sacrifice herself.

"London!" she murmured to herself with a smile. "Maybe I'll not be writing that letter after all." She gave a chuckle. "I just wonder what Henry would have to say if I turned up on his doorstep."

* * *

"It's as true as I'm speaking to you now," gasped Davie. "My faither's got the suit sewn and Kirsty's set up in charge of the house." He stood back and waited for Jean's reaction. When none came he persisted. "It's no' the money, but I ken the Master would want to be told."

Jean stepped back quickly and ushered him inside.

"Since he was the one responsible by all accounts," Davie went on.

A movement in the doorway opposite told them they were not alone. Jean beckoned Mhairi closer.

"Responsible for what?" she asked.

"For burning Glenshellich, or some such God-forsaken place."

A low exclamation seemed to catch in Mhairi's throat. Jean ignored it. "So where's the Master now?" she demanded of Davie.

"How in the name would I ken that? All Kirsty told me was that your Mr Bothwell turned tail and ran at the battle and ended up at Glenshellich when the Master's soldiers raided it. Looking for him," he added with emphasis.

Another sound came from Mhairi, somewhere between anguish and dismay. Jean finally paid her some attention.

"What is it, Mhairi?"

Mhairi took two steps towards Davie and clutched at his arm.

"Glenshellich!" she breathed.

"Aye!" he snapped and quickly turned back to Jean. "So what's to be done about the reward?"

But Jean was not listening to him. She was staring at Mhairi's stricken face.

"What is it, Mhairi?" she repeated.

"Was he there?" Mhairi whispered to Davie.

"Have I no' already said?"

Mhairi turned her imploring eyes back to Jean. "Find him." The words were barely audible.

"The reward!" insisted Davie.

"In God's name shut your mouth about rewards!" Jean cried. "There'll be reward enough for you from the Master when he returns. Now you'd best take us to Mistress Bothwell's, for I'll not be thinking of betraying anyone until I've heard the other side of the story."

Kirsty's mouth gaped wider than the crack she opened in the door when she saw who stood on the threshold.

"Best let us in," Davie demanded.

Kirsty was not about to take instruction from the caddie, beholden to him as she might have been. Only one person was permitted to tell her what to do, but Alison showed no hesitation in ushering Jean and Mhairi inside.

"Away you and get a hold of Mr MacVey," she told Davie, "and we can all put our heads together over what's to be done." The she turned her scrutiny onto Jean. Never before had she seen her at such close quarters.

"My!" she exclaimed softly, and indicated a chair.

When James edged tentatively through the far door to join them Jean saw that he was leaner, paler, but somehow stronger by far than when she had last seen him.

"Will you forgive me, Jean?" he whispered.

Jean continued to stare at him. "Forgive who and for what?" she countered at last. "Mr Bothwell the clerk, or Mr Hamilton the fortune seeker?"

James' face relaxed into something like a smile. "Ensign Bothwell, the deserter, at present, I am afraid," he told her. "But I hope you will still think of me as a friend."

Jean's expression softened. "A friend of the Master's too?"

"Of course. Though I very much doubt he will still consider me as one."

"Then tell us your story."

James was only half way through it when Davie reappeared with Gavin. The old lawyer's expression was grave as he settled down to listen.

"So we know nothing of Donald," he said at last, "and this news of Andrew is grim indeed. There has been no mention of his name in any journal I have read so far, though that is not to say ...." His voice tailed off and he sat frowning for some moments. "But there is no doubt that Henry would be a good man to have on your side." He looked gravely into the faces of each one in turn and when his eyes reached Mhairi he frowned again. She stared back and then a sudden rush of Gaelic poured from her lips. Gavin grew momentarily pale. He turned back to James.

"You say Kilclath did not give the order direct. Do you know why that was?"

James met his gaze squarely. "I do," he said, "but I was given that information in the strictest confidence."

"I believe that this lady –" He nodded towards Mhairi, "needs to know."

James looked into the servant woman's eyes. There could be no mistaking the desperation of their appeal.

"It is not my secret," he said.

Another stream of Gaelic gushed from Mhairi's lips, but James could clearly distinguish one name amongst them: the name of Catriona MacMichael.

"It is too late for secrets," sighed Gavin.

Jean and Alison exchanged bemused stares. The atmosphere in the room had grown tense and troubled. Davie shuffled towards the door where Kirsty already stood, as if driven there by the force of Mhairi's outburst.

"It is too late for secrets," repeated Gavin, and this time his words were addressed to Jean. Mhairi mumbled some more and he nodded. "It seems you must go to Kilclath," he told Jean gravely. "For if ever the Master needed you he needs you now." He looked again at Mhairi whose frantic eyes spoke plainer than any words. "I will find a reliable guide and translator to go with you, for I suspect that anything will be safer at present than enlisting the aid of the Campbells."

* * *

Three days later they were on their way: Mistress Bothwell and her young companion on the London coach and Jean and Mhairi on the road bound for Kilclath.

"The Master chose well with you, Jean Petrie," the old lawyer said as he bid them goodbye. "And I've no doubt your mother would have fared better with better help."

"You knew my mother?" she asked in surprise.

He shook his head sadly. "Many's a time, lassie, many's a time. She was a bonnie woman, a good soul brought low, like so many in this evil world Bella knew that better than any, but I'll wager you'll find a way to rise above it, with or without Bella's help. Maybe with or without the Master's."

Mhairi had reverted to her customary silence and her familiarity with the English language had shrunk once more to the occasional word. Jean threw her a sideways look of irritation and dug her heels into the gelding's flank. She was glad to be leaving the city behind them: its summer reeks intensified by the bitter stench of death the wind sent southwards. Yet the same wind propelled James Hamilton and Jean thought of him and his intrepid companion, bumping and lurching as their carriage rattled through towns and villages, and a countryside that knew little and cared less for the way its government enforced the law on the savage side of the border. Jean hoped and prayed his adventure would have the result he sought. This year had changed the shape of all their destinies: hers and Mhairi's as much as anyone's. Gavin MacVey's young messenger rode silently at their side and the drover cantered ahead. He was a dark and morose fellow, but Gavin had assured her he was familiar with every trail south of the Great Glen. She hoped so, for he was leading them higher and higher along an increasingly narrow ledge that snaked above a foaming burn in spate.

Mhairi glanced down nervously and leaned into the cliff wall. Jean remembered the servant woman's fear in the house of the Eagle: she remembered the marks of the knife on her back. The drover reined his horse as the path narrowed to a foot's breadth. The sun was setting fast and for a brief moment it seemed that the water they looked down on no longer ran amber but a deep and vivid red.

* * *

Henry Matheson, comfortably settled in a handsome apartment off Sloane Square, received his guests with open armed delight. After listening gravely to their story he sat for a while considering.

"As far as I can tell the situation regarding the prisoners is fraught with confusion," he told them. "The transports arrived in June and are still anchored off the fort at Tilbury." He shook his head grimly and readjusted his wig. "They have provided a gruesome spectacle for the idly curious, as have the passages of the fort itself. But London does not have space for so huge a haul. We've had trials already and very unpleasant affairs they have been. These ghoulish public executions bring out the very worst in our citizens." Alison swallowed bravely as he went on. "But I daresay sympathy can scarcely be expected to lie with rebels who caused them such fear and panic."

"Perhaps your citizens would change their view had they witnessed what I have witnessed these past months: men and women shot down in cold blood, bodies mutilated, homes destroyed in flames." James declared.

"They will have little opportunity of discovering any of that, I fear." Henry sighed again. "The lords Balmerino and Kilmarnock were executed last week. They died bravely, but perhaps it is time to accept that the world has moved on." He stood up and called for a servant. "Now, you must make yourselves comfortable before we dine. Tomorrow I will set about my enquiries."

* * *

"The mighty giant Feodag had two sons and he brought them up to be strong and brave, to be fierce warriors but also to be skilled farmers and herdsmen. Eventually the time came for them to go out into the world and seek themselves wives. Aron was the eldest, proud and handsome. He had two requirements for his bride: great beauty and the power to sing as enchantingly as the selkies. He searched the country far and wide, north, south, east and west, and even crossed the sea to seek out such a one, but found none to capture his heart as he knew it could be captured. At last he decided he must make do with the best of them, a giantess with raven hair and sparkling eyes, and a voice so sweet it could lure the mermen from the very depth of the sea..."

* * *

Euan swam to the edge of the pool and clambered onto the shining rocks. He cupped Morag's face in his hand and tilted it towards him, gazing into her clear eyes while the fingers of his other hand stroked her soft cheeks and traced the smile she forced to her lips.

"Whatever happens, this has been our time," she whispered. "No-one can take it from us."

Euan was afraid to agree, for somehow her words made it sound as if their time was over, when he needed more than anything to make himself believe it had only just begun.

* * *

"But Fergus, the second son of Feodag," Donald went on, "did not have to look far at all for his bride. He found her tending the black cattle on the Mountain of the Eagle, and as soon as he saw her he knew his search was over. Her name was Aithin, and Fergus returned with her to Feodag's Mountain where they lived happily for many months; happily, that is, until Aron returned with his raven haired bride."

"Why should that stop them being happy?" interrupted Janet.

"Be quiet and listen," Iain told her.

Donald looked at them both seriously. "What do you think might be the reason?"

Over by the dung heap Andra' gave a snort, but bent his ear closer nevertheless. He would have to conjure up some stories of his own for them in the days and weeks to come.

"Because they chose the wrong brides?" suggested Janet.

Donald considered the suggestion seriously. "In a way," he agreed, "that is true. You see, when Aron saw Aithin he knew at once that she

396

was the one he had been looking for. Yet although she was pleasing to his eye, her beauty did not take his breath away; neither did she sing like the spirits of the sea. Even so, Aron knew that his brother's wife was all that he could ever want in a woman – all that he could ever want and all he could never have, for it was clear to him that Aithin would only ever love him as a brother, that her heart was completely bound to Fergus."

"So what did he do?" Iain demanded.

"He tried for many years to hide his love. And it is true that no one could have guessed how deeply he felt for Aithin. But all the time the pain was eating away at his heart," he told them softly, and Andra' thought he saw the corner of his eye moisten. "It was Aron's great misfortune to learn too late that love cannot be hunted down and captured. It comes of its own accord and seeks us out no matter what we do."

"Like Euan and our mother?" asked Janet.

"Very like Euan and your mother." The chieftain smiled but his eyes grew distant and Andra' was not convinced that Euan and Morag were foremost in his mind. He heaved his own deep sigh. The men from Glenshellich would be gone soon, skulking through the dangerous lands that once been their home, hiding as they might have to hide for the rest of their lives. The Prince had exacted a high price indeed, thought Andra', not for the first time. It was a price far greater than any sum the King in London might have set on his own reckless head: a price not counted in guineas but in broken hearts.

* * *

"Your nephew is lodged with a King's Messenger in Southwark," Henry announced, making no attempt to hide his glee. "Thank the lord that his rank sent him there rather than to one of the gaols. The date for his trial has not yet been set, which is also encouraging." He paused and fixed James with a solemn stare. "Nevertheless, I would urge you to set your plan in motion as soon as possible. Fates of rebels have been known to change with a careless signature." He gave a deep sigh. "The new dispossessed will be many, Allomore's son. They will follow the same path as your father." Alison patted her old friend's arm affectionately as he went on. "If, and it is an enormous if, if you can secure an escape from this Messenger Howard's house your only course will be to take ship out of the country. You both face sentences of death and the king's justice is not equivocal."

"Justice!" snorted Alison.

"Well, well, well, no matter," Henry went on. "What we next must do is make a close study of the house of this Messenger Howard." A sudden gleam shot from his eye. It was a long time since he had tasted anything like adventure. "Then we must make enquiries about sailings," he went on. "Though that would seem the least of our problems." His eyes almost twinkled at Alison. "And we must also consider who there will be – when the time comes - to accompany you on your journey home."

* * *

The door of Andrew's attic was unceremoniously flung open.

"Mr Stewart," announced the messenger, puffing out his chest and drawing himself up to his full fifty-nine inches. "You are to be afforded the privilege of repairing downstairs this evening."

The news had little effect. Andrew only asked wearily, "To what do I owe such an honour?"

"A gentleman, a gentleman of not inconsiderable influence, I might add, wishes to make himself known to you."

Andrew threw the messenger a look of distaste. "I scarcely believe a person of influence would show much interest in me."

"His name is Henry Matheson," the messenger continued. "Magistrate Henry Matheson, and an expatriate from your own country, I believe." He paused and cleared his throat. "I trust you will report favourably on the accommodation you have been provided with."

"Mr Howard," replied Andrew. "In comparison with my previous surroundings your accommodation is of the highest merit. Rest assured that I will not be slow to inform your influential magistrate of it. In respect of what a gentlemen should be entitled to expect I must allow him to draw his own conclusions."

When Messenger Howard closed the door behind him Andrew sank wearily back onto his mattress. Henry Matheson. He repeated the name several times to himself. He wondered vaguely what this new development might signify, but his thoughts soon took gloomier paths. Loneliness had darkened his spirits. Memories besieged him and brought increasing despair. The comfortless room pared to a single mattress, the flimsy chair, the splintered table, the bible, and the tiny roof window with its dismal outlook had all grown more oppressive as the summer faded. Soon would come autumn, muted in the city streets but spreading its poignant shades over an unfamiliar countryside. The season sank in Andrew's heart, for he feared that too many of those he loved would never see its golds and oranges. Sometimes he almost wished for his trial to come and bring an end to the interminable waiting. Sometimes he believed he would not be sorry to see an end of it all.

But as he followed his gaoler down the narrow staircase the next evening it was impossible not feel a stirring of anticipation. Messenger Howard led him into his sparse and shabby public room where a stout elderly gentleman with fiery features was struggling from his chair. His intense intake of breath at the sight of him reminded Andrew he must indeed present a sorry picture after his long captivity. It was only when Henry spoke that Andrew remembered where he seen him before.

"Mr Stewart," he began in bluff tones. "Perhaps you will recall meeting me in Edinburgh, why, it must be close on two years ago? I am here with particular news from your aunt." Andrew found his heart beating powerfully as he grasped the magistrate's hand. Henry paused to give his information the opportunity to register and to give himself a moment to recover from his dismay at Andrew's wasted appearance. "These have indeed been sorry months," he went on at last, "but I am here to remind you that you have not been forgotten, that you have friends in London even as we speak." He maintained his grip on Andrew's hand and kept his shrewd eyes fixed on Andrew's face. A harder light came into them as he added, "Friends in London I am certain you will be hearing from soon."

For the first time in many weeks Andrew felt a small spark of hope. "Might I ask which friends in particular? And if they have any news from home?"

Henry briefly looked away. Messenger Howard was alert, and although he maintained a discreet silence he could not disguise his curiosity.

"The news is good nowhere for those of the rebel persuasion," Henry answered carefully. "There has been much looting and burning in the glens, but it is to be hoped that the desire for vengeance is beginning to fade. The Prince has apparently slipped the net and many chiefs besides, but I am afraid I can bring no news of your brother." He held Andrew's eyes and Andrew knew his next words were for Mr Howard's benefit. "I hope you have the means to write a letter, for I know that your aunt is most anxious to receive word."

The messenger shuffled in his seat. "It can be arranged.".

"Good," said Henry briskly, pushing himself to his feet with even greater difficulty than before. "Write your letter and I will despatch my servant James for it tomorrow afternoon." He gave what appeared to be an impatient sigh. "It is time he did something for his keep. I took him on as a favour to his sister Christian – " Henry ignored Andrew's involuntary gasp – "Not that my domestic arrangements will be of any great interest to you." Messenger Howard shot him another look of suspicion but Henry returned it with a benign smile. "Be sure to tell your aunt how well you are treated here with Mr Howard, for I guarantee that she will be interested in every minute detail."

"I hope that any favours I may be granting Mr Stewart are within the confines of the law," the messenger muttered.

Henry patted his shoulder reassuringly. "Of course. Of course. Have no fear that any dealings between ourselves will be anything other than completely above board. Mr Stewart has no doubt had time to learn the error of his ways and will be seeking a pardon if at all possible. Meanwhile," he patted the messenger again, "I will give my boy a bottle of my best claret as a token of my appreciation – a token for yourself you understand, Mr Howard."

Andrew's sleep that night was sounder than it had been for many a month, and entirely untroubled by dreams.

* * *

Euan and his chieftain clung to the hillsides, bending their heads to the heather as they inched their painful way down the Great Glen. They spoke little, for their hearts were filled with the sadness of their leave-taking and the anxiety that increased each time they looked down on the charred ruins of crofts and deserted clachans. Sometimes they passed groups of stumbling women and children skirting the same hillsides. They all had the same tale to tell, of plunder, rape and burning. Like themselves they were reduced to sleeping concealed amongst the higher boulders, and picking what bare survival they could from this new wilderness.

Donald could cover no more than a few miles each day. Although his wounds had healed they had taken a heavy toll. Only the rage that flooded him kept his spirit strong, and the knowledge that he and Euan were closer than they had ever been, for they had never seen so clearly into each other's hearts.

* * *

James Hamilton arrived at the messenger's house early in the morning. Mr Howard was taking no chances with the security of his prisoner and had stationed a servant with a pistol outside the attic door. He personally accompanied James into the room and stood vigil beside him. Henry might have prepared James for his inevitable shock at Andrew's appearance, but nothing could have prepared him for the impact the sight of the broken figure had on his emotions. He turned away, reminding himself that he had not embarked on this mission to stumble at the first hurdle. He gave the kind of short bow he believed befitted a magistrate's manservant and stepped forward.

"A letter from your aunt," he said stiffly.

It was all that Andrew could do not to fall sobbing onto James' shoulder, but he too was painfully aware of the messenger's shrewd scrutiny. Without looking into James' face he reached out his hand. It was Mr Howard who took the scroll.

"All that your aunt knows of your family is in her letter," lied James. He turned to the messenger. "Mr Matheson says I am to return tomorrow for any correspondence from the prisoner."

Mr Howard was reading slowly. A frown of concentration was on his face and James shot Andrew a quick glance. If anything was to be read between the lines the messenger was not the person to do it. He nodded briefly and passed the letter to Andrew.

"As long as I have the opportunity to examine what goes out and what comes in I see no reason to object to our arrangement."

James bowed again and without a backward glance excused himself.

"There is a guard at his door at all times," he reported back to Henry and Alison. "But we must think quickly for when I return our plans must be in place."

"How many servants would a man such as he have?" wondered Henry. "I would not guess at above two staying the night."

"The one who admitted me was elderly and feeble, to say the least."

"Though feeble elderly men should not be underestimated," Henry murmured, with a mischievous glint in his eye. Alison smiled. She had been greatly impressed by the way her old flame was rising to this occasion. "And presumably there are kitchen staff," he went on. "Our task is by no means an easy one. Meanwhile we must set in place two passages across the Channel. There will only be one chance, Allomore's son, and there will be no room for error." He looked grimly across at Alison. "So let us set our minds to it with no delay."

* * *

As soon as Donald and Euan crossed into the Glen of the Black Cattle they sensed that all was not well. It was not that the outward signs were any different. The herd still wandered over the green fields and ripe corn waved golden in the soft breeze. But an eerie silence hung over the land, making both men hesitate as they approached the overgrown gates of the house. Beyond the doorway the servants stood aside, not in respect, but with solemn, almost hostile, stares. Donald and Euan stood on the threshold but neither presumed to take a step inside.

"Is your master at home?" asked Donald.

He sensed a movement behind them, and then his ears caught an erratic scraping, a scuffling and a rasping breath. Someone was making his way slowly from the shadows, someone leaning on a crutch, someone in pain. The cripple stopped some feet inside the doorway and with a sinking heart Donald recognised Malcolm, Helen's elder brother, a man he had last seen at Falkirk in a British soldier's uniform.

"I am master here for the present," he snarled.

"Your father...?" Donald began.

"Is with your wife."

Euan felt his heart grow cold. He took a step closer to Donald's side and flexed his fingers. Malcolm's expressionless eyes stared back at them.

"Where..?" breathed Donald. But other footsteps were hurrying down the staircase. Malcolm hopped aside to let the woman push past. For a moment she could only stare at the two men in the doorway, as she might have stared at ghosts, but at last sobs began to tear from deep inside her. Donald reached out his arms and drew her into them.

"Eilidh!" he soothed. "Eilidh!"

Euan gazed on helplessly, not daring to imagine what terrible grief lay behind her sobbing.

"You could say, MacSomhairle," Malcolm said softly, "that here in Cairnill we have lost more than our lives. We have lost our hearts and our faith, perhaps even our souls. We have become a place of the living dead."

Donald let his cheek rest against Eilidh's tangled hair. He closed his eyes as this new wave of misery sweep over him. When he opened them his father in law was standing before him, a man stranded in the same empty world.

"Helen ..?" Donald breathed.

"Is here, but not here," the old man said. Although Euan could not define the expression on his face a chill ran through him. "Come inside, MacSomhairle," Cairnill went on in the same smooth and level tone. "You must see for yourself."

Euan waited as Donald gently unravelled himself from Eilidh's arms. He watched him follow the old man across the hall and up the staircase, then slipped quietly behind them. Malcolm grabbed his arm.

"They should be alone."

But Euan shook him off. There was a presence of evil in this house, a creeping sickness that threatened them all. Euan had no intention of letting Donald out of his sight.

Eilidh was again at his elbow. "It is bad, Eochain," she whispered. "It is very bad." They stood together in the doorway of Helen's room, where she had once played out her childhood and dreamed her dreams of Glenshellich, where she now gazed from the open window across the untouched policies of Cairnill. Secure as it might have been from the soldiers' raids the Glen of the Black Cattle was surely reaping its most bitter harvest.

"She was its heart," breathed Euan, and Eilidh nodded sadly.

"Not the father nor the brothers," she agreed, looking on sadly as Donald crossed the room to stand at Helen's shoulder. "And she will not know the husband," she added, as they watched him ease her around to face him. There was no recognition on her face. The hope she had clung to in Glenshellich through the long months of his absence was now fulfilled, but it brought her no comfort. The memory of it all had gone. She had become a ghost of the child she once was, treasured and safe in the artificial world her father had created. Eilidh had begun to fear that nothing might ever be real to her mistress again.

"The child?" Euan whispered.

"A baby girl. In Glenshellich with your mother."

Euan felt tears of relief spring to his eyes. "Safe?"

"They were safe when we left. But the clachan and the house are burned to the ground."

"And Christie?"

"Safe too and with them."

"Who else?"

Eilidh whispered the names as she and Euan kept their eyes on their chieftain, standing at the window, his hands on his wife's shoulders, searching her vacant eyes for some sign of recognition. Her father watched too, with a kind of bitter satisfaction. Euan had no doubt that Cairnill was not finished with them, that he needed them to share his torment, perhaps even to execute his vengeance. At last Eilidh crossed to her chieftain's side.

"She is safe with me," she whispered. "One day I will bring her back to you."

Donald turned away. His frantic eyes sought his foster brother. Euan's gaze was steady, but Cairnill's voice intruded again, softly persuasive. "Are you ready to hear the story, MacSomhairle?" Euan shuddered at the prospect. "Come," Cairnill went on. "Let us take some refreshment, and I will tell you all you need to know."

Still in his trance Donald followed the old chieftain back down the staircase and into the study. His son was ready to close the door behind him, but Euan was already inside. Both men raised their eyebrows.

"I go nowhere without Euan," Donald told them.

The room stank of whisky. It seemed to Euan that its fumes had licked the brocaded walls clean of all comfort and all hope. He could feel no hint of compassion in the House of Cairnill, no warmth and no forgiveness, only bitterness and the thirst for revenge. Euan was afraid of the old man's madness, the son's unhealed wounds, the daughter's empty stare, but he was more afraid still of their effect on his chieftain. He moved to stand beside Donald's chair.

"He is among friends here," Cairnill assured him, but Euan remained where he was. Cairnill shrugged. "What matter?" he muttered. "What matter any of it?"

He fixed Donald with his dangerous stare and swallowed a large mouthful of whisky. "You are much changed yourself, MacSomhairle." But he was unable to keep the passion from his voice as he added. "I gave her to you to protect: to protect and to place above all else. You failed in that duty."

"I placed her above my life," Donald told him. "As I do still."

"Yet we have both lost what gave meaning to our lives." He reached out to refill Donald's glass. "I sought to play a wise hand, but I have two sons dead and another in exile. I have a daughter who has lost her mind –" He nodded towards the chair where Malcolm sat. "And him."

"I am sorry for your injuries," Donald said softly, but Malcolm's only response was to drain his glass.

Euan looked from one to the other and knew they must escape from this place. Cairnill poured more whisky and his next words were slurred with its effect.

"There is just one thing left for us, MacSomhairle. I am to old for it and he is too weak, but you still have the power. Let hatred sharpen the sword of the son of Samuel."

Donald stared back at him. What did he see? thought Euan. A broken warrior? His father's oldest friend? He prayed it was an enemy more dangerous than any redcoat.

"It is too late to talk of revenge," Donald said at last.

"So what will you do?" Cairnill hissed. "Flee to France to lick your wounds and die a sad old fool like Allomore?" His bloodshot eyes were full of scorn. "Is that what your father would expect?" Again Donald turned away and Euan's hand stroked the handle of his dirk. "Then let me ask you one last thing," Cairnill went on. "Do you know who it was that burned your glen? Do you know who it was left my daughter to die in the burning shell of your home?"

"One fugitive cannot fight an army," Donald said sadly.

"He can fight another man." Cairnill's eyes were narrow with hatred. "Do you not know who led those soldiers, MacSomhairle? Who as we speak scours Appin for every last rebel, and for one rebel in particular? He does not seek you for the price that rests on your head." In a few seconds the atmosphere of the room had altered. Cairnill leaned back in his chair and almost smiled. "It was George Campbell of Kilclath," he said softly. "The man who cut short your father's life has brought about the ruin of your glen. He has forced your wife to the brink of madness. So tell me again, MacSomhairle, that it is too late for revenge."

Euan bent low and whispered in Donald's ear. "MacAlister has lost his own mind."

Donald studied the old man as he gazed into his glass. "Maybe," he whispered back. "But perhaps he is showing me the only way to keep mine."

* * *

Slightly before dusk descended over the city of London, a young man made his casual way through the Southwark streets. The first rusty leaves were beginning to drop from the trees and he paused for a while to watch them. Those rubbing shoulders with him would have seen a figure in no particular hurry, with nothing of great urgency on his mind. They would not have guessed how rapidly he heart was pounding as he paused on a street corner and slowly drew out his pocket watch. A lamplighter setting out on his regular round of duty bade him good evening and he glanced up for a moment at the grim walls of the New Gaol, stark and quiet in the changing light. But James Hamilton did not wait for long to consider the plight of its inmates, close to his heart as their sorrow might have been. He continued his leisurely stroll and as he rounded the corner into Brook Street he barely glanced in the direction of Messenger Howard's residence. A carriage trundled past him, the black-coated coachman staring fixedly ahead and the elderly gentleman inside doing the same. James watched as the carriage pulled to a halt under a tiny attic window that opened to the early moon. Aided by the coachman the elderly gentleman squeezed himself through the door and onto the street. He took some deep breaths and looked about him before making for the front door. Once facing it he raised his stick and gave three loud raps. The door opened and quickly closed behind him. James wandered over to the coach and stood behind it, well out of sight of any of the windows of the house.

"Mr Matheson," cried the messenger, looking up from the desk where he had been attending to accounts. "This is an unexpected pleasure."

"I hope I do not disturb you, Mr Howard," Henry announced as he hobbled across the room. He positioned himself in front of the grate where an apology for a fire spluttered. "I was passing this way and decided to call to enquire if you have received any word of Mr Stewart's trial. I am damned if I can get a decision out of any of my associates."

Messenger Howard was flattered to be so consulted. "I did hear a suggestion that a date was being considered for the week after next," he answered, "which may be the reason for Mr Stewart's spirits not being of the highest today." He paused, remembering his manners. "I must thank you, sir, for the gift of the claret, a remarkably fine vintage."

Henry brushed any thanks aside, but cocked his head expectantly. Messenger Howard took the hint.

"Barrow," he called to his servant. "Bring us some brandy."

Henry settled himself on the chair beside the fireplace and drew out his snuffbox. Barrow returned with the brandy and the two gentlemen raised their glasses in a silent toast.

Henry was on his second mouthful when it caught in his throat. He began to splutter and rose to his feet, his face purple and his eyes bulging.

"Water!" he gasped, clutching at his collar.

Messenger Howard rose in alarm. "I will fetch some immediately," he declared. "One moment."

One moment was all that Henry required. With remarkable alacrity he pulled a package from his waistcoat pocket and emptied its contents into the messenger's glass. He watched the powder sink and dissolve, and then sniffed it. The brandy was strong enough to disguise any foreign scent. Satisfied, Henry resumed his fit of coughing just as Messenger Howard reappeared with a large jug of water. Henry clutched at it with gratitude.

"Perhaps snuff is not advisable for a man prone to breathlessness," suggested the messenger.

Henry turned his streaming eyes his way. "You are right, Mr Howard," he gasped, as the water took effect. "You are most certainly right." His splutters subsided. "But an old man cannot lightly relinquish a lifetime's pleasure." He drew some more deep breaths. "There. You see how a little water restores me."

Henry sat back in his chair, watching approvingly as the messenger drank deeply from his own glass. "It is certainly unfortunate that Mr Stewart has had so long a captivity for dismal an outcome."

"I confess I will be sorry to see him go."

You will certainly be the poorer for it, thought Henry, as he watched the messenger take another deep mouthful.

"My ..." the messenger gasped. "The brandy seems exceeding strong..." and before he could finish his sentence he slumped forward and slid elegantly to the floor.

"Mr Howard! Mr Howard!" cried Henry in alarm, chuckling to himself as he moved to the door. "Barrow!" he called, and returned to make sure he was bending over the messenger when the servant appeared. "He passed out before my very eyes," he exclaimed. "The Lord only knows what can have taken him. My carriage is at the door. If you give my coachman instructions he will take you to fetch a doctor."

The servant did as he was bidden and soon the coach was lurching into the night. Henry waited at the door as James slipped inside and up the stairway, before taking himself to the kitchen quarters to ensure that particular coast was clear. By the time he found it empty James had climbed the main staircase. Above him were the narrow steps to the attic and a thin ugly face peering down from the top of it. Even as James drew his sword, he sensed he would be no match for this ruffian. The guard clattered to within sword arms length and James found himself lunging and stabbing furiously. It was with relief that he heard heavy feet on the steps below. Apparently rushing to the guard's aid, Henry dealt an expert blow to the back of his head and his extra weight helped to secure his wrists and ankles. James bound his mouth and eyes, then grabbed his key and turned it in the lock.

Andrew was sitting at the desk, a small candle burning before him and several neatly written pages beside it. He looked up in surprise.

"There is no time to lose, Andrew," James urged, and pulled him to his feet. They pushed past the unconscious guard and clattered down the stairs. Outside the drawing room door Henry grasped the hand of each young man before offering his own to be bound. "Freedom for some," he grinned, "and captivity for others!"

Seconds later James had pushed the freed prisoner out into the night to crouch in the shadows waiting for the return of Henry's coach. As soon as Barrow and the physician were safely inside they jumped aboard and the coachman cracked his whip.

James drew the blinds over the windows.

"Here," he said, thrusting pieces of cold fowl into Andrew's hand. "Eat what you can now and then you must change into these clothes. Our ship is docked in Greenwich and only waits for us to board. God willing by this time tomorrow we will be in France."

Still stunned Andrew gazed through the carriage window.

"For the voyage," James went on, "you are Mr Robert White, and I am Frederick O'Connor, both dealers in wine on a business venture to the Loire. That is as much as the captain of our ship has been told, though I am assured if he comes to suspect otherwise he will accept this purse to keep silent – it is more than the government would give him for our capture."

Andrew munched on the cold fowl and took a draught from James' brandy flask before studying the fine brocade suit. "We are wealthy merchants, I see," he smiled as he began to unbuttton his ragged prison clothes. "So what news from Glenshellich?"

James' face told Andrew this was a question he had dreaded.

"It is bad then," breathed Andrew. "And nothing to be done to change it. Then best let it wait until we are stowed aboard."

* * *

The House of the Eagle showed no sign of its recent occupation. The servant greeted Mhairi with little enthusiasm and the information that The Master had left hours before, galloping westward into the evening mist with Hughie at his side. Jean was weary with travelling and weary with Mhairi's fretful company. She declined the offer of supper and took herself upstairs to the Master's room.

As soon as she crept inside she knew that all was not well. She stood at the side of the four-poster bed and took deep breaths to steady herself, then lay down and stretched herself across it. She closed her eyes, and tried to summon his image, but somehow she felt further from him than ever before.

She could know nothing of the hours the Master had tossed on the counterpane, the nights he had paced the floor, tormented and dis-traught. She could know nothing of the years he had buried his pain as he searched every face on every street in every city for the one face that haunted his dreams. Neither could she know how he had longed to have her there beside him, the only one left in his life with the power to lead him back to the light.

Jean lay down on the cover and closed her eyes. The Valley of the Stones was empty and silent, its house cheerless and cold. She ran her hand across the swelling mound of her belly.

"Whatever happens," she whispered, "I will save you from this place."

* * *

The wine dealers uncorked two bottles and raised them to their lips. Andrew gazed through the porthole of their cabin into the darkness of the water and heard the ship draw anchor. Soon he recognised the familiar motion of waves and reached out and grasped James's hand.

"I owe you my life, Allomore's son."

James leaned back against the creaking cabin wall. For once he knew he had no reason to feel ashamed.

"So tell me everything," Andrew said softly.

As the boats bobbed alongside them in the calm water of the dark Thames James began his story, knowing how deeply each word of it struck at Andrew's heart. At last a silence a fell. They were rocking with the light wind that told them the vessel had entered the Channel.

"So we sail to an unknown future, you and I," whispered Andrew. "As our fathers did before us"

"We leave sicker country behind us."

"Perhaps we have finally seen the worst of it."

"Perhaps. But I fear we have not." The words escaped fiercely from James's lips. "I have vowed to seek a place where men can be free. And when I find it I will defend that freedom with surer weapons than guns and swords!"

As Andrew gazed at him he felt the trace of a smile touch his face. "Then I would defend it beside you, MacIain Mhor." At last he could fell the stirring of new lifeblood in his veins. His old dreams and his old obsessions were slipping past him quicker than the water beneath the boat's hull. The future was singing a new and beguiling tune. The waves slapped against the porthole and he heard the wind whip the sails. He raised the bottle to his lips and drank deep. "I toast friend-ship." His voice was strong like his spirit.

"And freedom," joined James.

"Friendship and freedom," Andrew echoed.

* * *

Two men scrambled from the tiny rowing boat: two men who had become outcasts in the their own land, one with a price on his head and a deadly score to settle. By day they slept on the hillsides and by night they edged closer to the lands that lay in the shadows of the Mountains of the Eagles: ragged, desperate men scavenging across a land of bare rocks and rough moor, a land where dangerous strangers had marched and destroyed.

But Euan MacMichael did not let bitterness cloud his purpose. He had his own dream now, and though he grieved for his country he would not abandon his hope. Donald's figure lurched ahead of him as each dusk fell, and staggered behind him into every dawn. They spoke barely a word, but Euan prayed constantly for Cairnill's vengeful image to be erased from his chieftain's heart. At last they entered the shadows of Kilclath through its narrow southern passes. From the foothills of Beinn Iolair they could see the sandstone walls of the House of the Eagle, the grazing herds, the trails of smoke from cottage roofs. If only this could be the end of it, Euan thought, if only they could learn from this moment to live in peace. But peace was impossible. Their lives were not made for peace. They settled to rest themselves for another night on another cold hillside against another hard rock.

* * *

From his hiding place on the mountainside Hughie McIvor watched them and his lips stretched into a grin. It was all turning out as the Master had predicted. MacSomhairle had indeed returned and soon would fall neatly into their trap. All it needed now was for the trap to be baited and the hunter would become the hunted, crossing the Bloody Burn, leading MacSomhairle into the very heart of his own glen, past the ruin that his own deeds had wrought. Hughie had no taste for wars like the one that had just been fought. His instincts cried out for the old ways, the hunt through the rocks, the quick thrust in the darkness, the silent death of an unsuspecting enemy.

When the next dusk fell they left their temporary shelter and steered their horses out of the Valley of Stones. The mist climbed upwards and drifted in the hollows as the Master and his servant rode on in silence. They were the lure, the bait, and time was on their side, a friend to them though an enemy to men exhausted with walking, thin with hunger, desolate with defeat. And Kilclath had another advantage: thirty years of heartache while MacSomhairle had lived with it for a few short weeks.

On the other side of the Bloody Burn they found a sheltered hollow and wrapped themselves in their plaids. The land was empty, leaderless and lost. They could afford to wait for another morning.

* * *

"It is a madness," breathed Euan. "A madness and an evil."

"He is trying to drive me mad," Donald replied. "But there is something he cannot know. Dead men can feel no madness."

Euan felt the cold fear rise inside him as he looked at his chieftain. He had seen him like this before, the black shadow of despair cloaking his heart, so that no anger, no bitterness, no grief could touch it. He could not believe that this would be the end of it all. MacSomhairle had not been brought back to life only to endure a worse anguish.

"Christie is in the glen." It was the first time in months that Euan had dared to mention her name.

"Christie is a dream," Donald whispered.

"She is a woman, MacSomhairle," Euan insisted and added softly, "She is your woman."

As the shadows of the evening stretched and merged around them Donald's eyes suddenly blazed into life. "Why do you speak of her now, at this of all times? Would you, too, drive me mad?"

Euan felt his body relax as the fear faded. The moment was over. "Dead men can feel no madness, MacSomhairle," he whispered. "No madness and no pain." Their faces were close. His eyes drilled into Donald's. "Dead men can feel no love."

Donald fell back into the heather and tears started from his eyes. "Then easier by far to be a dead man," he whispered.

"But not when your life is only half lived." Euan looked up. He could not see it but he knew the dark shadow of the cave's mouth beckoned. "So come, Domhnull MacSomhairle. We must look to Feodag to protect us tonight."

* * *

The boy was sharpening the skean dhu aimlessly on the rock at the cave's entrance. The day had been bright but dusk was falling fast. He would be lucky to reach the shielings before darkness. In only a few weeks he had grown the inch or two that gave him access to the quickest route down the mountain. He smiled to himself to think how relieved his great grandfather and the women would be to know he need never again face the perils of An Ciobar's Ridge.

He looked down on the scene below him: the glen, his glen, stretching into the distant northern hills and the wide ocean beyond, the grey water he sometimes felt drawing him. That evening he heard the beginnings of a new tune in his head, a slow, twisting melody that rose and fell like a heartbeat. He listened to it, letting his mind close around it and make it a memory, a memory he could bring later to his father's pipes. While he concentrated he did not notice the other sounds: the slither of small stones below him, the laboured breaths, but soon it was impossible not to be aware that someone, perhaps more than one person, was climbing closer.

"Someone is here, Euan."

415

Domhnull felt the blood surge through his veins. He scarcely dared to take a breath himself as he crouched behind the rock.

"How can that be?"

"I sense it. I know when Feodag speaks to me. Wait."

A hand clutched above the rock.

"You have not the strength. Wait and I will make a foothold."

Another tiny rock fall, then the hand found its grip. In a few seconds MacSomhairle lay just feet from him, sprawled on the ledge, heaving great gasps. Moments later Euan MacMichael was there too.

With eyes wide with wonder, Domhnull raised his head above the rock. Euan was the first to see him. For a long while he simply stared, then held out one arm and with the other roused his chieftain. Uncertainly, for this seemed too much like a dream come true, the boy crept closer. Euan clasped him to his chest, and then pushed him gently towards Donald.

"MacSomhairle!" the boy breathed.

For a long time Donald said nothing. The ache in his throat stopped any words leaving it, even if there had been words to describe what he felt. At last he tipped Domhnull's face so that their eyes could meet.

"I have come home," he whispered at last.

* * *

"What do you see in the embers, Catriona?" Christie asked softly.

Catriona raised eyes full of sorrow and looked at her across the spreading gloom. The shieling hut was bare and cheerless when the sun had slipped behind the mountain, the heather mattresses buzzing with insects and clouded by midge. There were no songs or stories this year to cheer their nights, no secret assignations on the path to the corrie, no children's laughter. Catriona shifted the baby in her arms and gazed down at her peaceful face. She, at least, was content, with her foster family and her devoted big brother. The shadows crept from the mountain across the huts and into the one that Christie, Catriona, Domhnull and the baby shared.

Catriona sighed. "I believe you know," she answered.

Christie moved to stand in the doorway, on the edge of the darkest shadow. Somewhere under the same sky James looked for Andrew. Perhaps by now he had found him. Somewhere Donald and Euan might be staring up at the same moon. Domhnull had still not returned and her anxious eyes scanned the steep shoulder of the ridge. He had taken to wandering further and further afield, and although she had no wish to confine him she constantly feared for his safety. The threat from Kilclath still hung over them. Both she and Catriona were certain that their business with the Master of the Stones was far from finished.

"Did he not know that in every smile, every tear, of Euan's and Donald's I thought of him?" Catriona whispered. "Not a day has passed since I left when he has not been there in my mind, in my heart."

Christie did not dare to tell her that from now on every day would be the same for her also. "You had no choice," she whispered.

A sob fell back in Catriona's throat. "I once thought so. But I have come to understand there must always be a choice. And I have come to realise how easy it can be to make the wrong one."

* * *

Domhnull made his way carefully down the mountainside. He was planning the feast he would carry to his chieftain and Euan in the morning: bannocks and milk, a rabbit fresh from the snare, shellfish from his great grandfather's nets. He knew where Fraser had hidden the bottles of wine he had rescued from the cellars. But he must be careful, they had told him, careful not to breathe a word of their coming, not to anyone, for the Campbell chieftain was prowling close and must be dealt with first. Domhnull's job was to bring them food and keep their secret.

The women were still awake when he crept inside the shieling hut.

"Where have you been, Domhnull?" Christie asked.

"Stalking a stag on the far side of the ridge," Domhnull lied. "His young one looked sickly so I will go back tomorrow and watch some more."

But when morning came Domhnull did not set out in the direction of the ridge. The sun was already bright when he woke and stretched himself in the clear air outside the hut. He looked back at the makeshift cradle where MacSomhairle's baby slept soundly and peacefully. MacSomhairle had been thrilled to hear how well she thrived and Domhnull had been thrilled to be the one to tell him. But MacSomhairle would see for himself soon. Domhnull set off towards the shore where he could already make out Iain and his grandfather preparing the boat. Perhaps he would sail out with them. It would be a good feeling to look up at the cave from the lochan and to know that his chieftain was inside it.

From the cave's entrance Donald could see him scampering along the shoreline. Inside Euan stirred but slept on, still exhausted, though Donald had climbed higher unaided than he had imagined possible. It was as if the air of home was renewing him with every breath. Below lay the blackened ruins of the clachan and the shell of his home, but distance disguised the reality and it seemed that his view from the cave was not much different than it had always been. The faint lowing of the cattle rose from the shielings and his heart warmed to think that Christie would be hearing that very same sound at the very same moment. Again he dared to let his thoughts stay with her, remembering the sensation of holding her close, of kissing her and feeling her body's response. And now he had a wife who had slipped from his reach, a glen he could no longer claim, an orphaned son he could never acknowledge and a baby daughter he might never see. He looked down at the calmness of Euan's sleeping face and thought of the only one who had been constant in both their lives, still here, cradling another child in her arms, waiting for her sons to return.

* * *

Hughie had been on the boy's trail from the early afternoon and quickly realised the purpose of his mission. He had left the Master concealed in a crevasse above the shielings, watching the women and thinking his thoughts, thoughts that were not for Hughie to concern himself with. He had his own thoughts, which mainly fixed on what he would do with the bitches from Allomore and the old fool from the city when the next chance arose. He had been thwarted once, but the Master would allow him a free rein now, he was certain. The Old Fox breathed into his son's ear through the lips of Hughie McIvor and at last there was none to stand in the way of his entreaties, no other voice to tempt him from his destiny. The curse had been laid on the House of the Eagle by Lachlan Mor MacCombie, seer to An Ciobar, on the very night the bodies of the Glenshellich's clansmen had damned the Bloody Burn and turned its waters crimson. *Redder by far will run this burn when the blood of Kilclath and Glenshellich is joined, and the son of the whore brings ruin to the House of the Eagle.* Hughie spat his contempt. The whore might have tricked the Old Fox, but sooner or later she too would be hunted down, just as the woman from Allomore had been. Soon they would all know what it was to feel the wrath of the House of Kilclath.

* * *

Evening burned in the cloudless sky and Domhnull MacCombie tried to set aside his impatience. The moon was full but its brightness could not compete with the orange sun, and the waters of the lochan, smooth as glass, reflected them both. Strangely Beinn Feodag cast no shadow, though a chill wind blew from its slopes. Above its whisper Domhnull sensed a breath that was not the mountain's. He shook it off and slipped past Angus' cottage, smelling the smoke that rose defiantly from the open rafters and hearing the thin rasp that told him his great grandfather was still awake. He risked running on, past the shoreline then upwards along the path to the shielings, the food wrapped tight in its bundle, the wine and the rabbit and the shellfish,

419

a feast for starving men. Domhnull felt almost happy. The world did not seem nearly so dark a place now that MacSomhairle was returned. He climbed through the twilight whispers, the fluttering of bats' wings, the distant hoot of an owl. The wind lifted his hair and for a moment he sensed the other breath again, but again he ignored it and scrambled on towards the steeper reaches where the clumps of heather gave way to bare rock. There the wind dropped slightly, but the other breath had grown stronger, warm and sour now at his back. His own breath came too late as a hand closed over his mouth and an arm tightened across his chest.

"Where might a boy be bound at so late an hour?" The voice that asked the question was rich and low. It was a voice that under different circumstances Domhnull might have wished to listen to longer. But not tonight: tonight was not the time to heed strange voices. The man stepped out from behind a boulder, a clansman, a chieftain by the look of his silk shirt and velvet doublet. Domhnull could not have answered his question, even if he had wanted to, for the rough hand, stinking of dirt and sweat, was still clamped across his mouth. He struggled and spat until the hand was removed with a curse, but he had no intention of uttering a word. The man repeated his question in Gaelic, and when Domhnull still did not reply he took some steps closer and squinted into his face. Even so, he was less threatening by far than the scowling clansman who maintained his painful grip on Domhnull's arm.

"Hughie." The chieftain nodded towards Domhnull's bundle. In a flash Hughie had snatched it and thrown it across to him. The chieftain made a thorough examination of the contents.

"So," he said at last, his eyes drilling deep into Domhnull's. "Now you will take us to MacSomhairle."

Archie Fraser made his way along the shoreline towards Angus' cottage. There was something uncanny in the moon's light, something he had never seen before. The water was unusually still and no sound came from it, no soft surge of waves, no gentle lapping onto the shore. The blackened walls of the crofts pointed accusing fingers, but not in his direction as he hobbled past. The smell of burning still hung in the air. He stopped, suddenly alert. He thought he heard a cry from inside the mountain, echoing through the gorge below the ridge. He listened again, but this time there was only silence.

Domhnull MacCombie remembered the story his mother had told him of the day MacSomhairle and Euan MacMichael had first crossed An Ciobar's Ridge. He knew the story well, but had always deliberately put it from his mind when he made the crossing. It was not sensible to think of falling when all your efforts must concentrate on clinging on. But often he had woken in the night and imagined how Euan must have dangled and kicked as he looked down the great drop from the ridge to the foot of the gorge. Perhaps he had seen a picture of himself plunging down to that dark, inaccessible hollow, never to be heard of again. Euan MacMichael would never reach Feodag's cave by that route a second time: no man would if they knew the other ways. But this chieftain and his man were not from Glenshellich. They could not know the safer paths. They must follow whichever way Domhnull MacCombie led them.

The moon was huge and gleaming in the midnight sky. Its beams turned the corries into unearthly craters, the scree into shifting mounds of silver. Soon they would approach the knife-edge, and the moon would illuminate a slice of the sheer descent, a thousand feet or more, to the boulder field below. What lay among those boulders no one knew, for no man could reach them, only the scuttling foxes and swooping birds of prey. They would have left the bones of their victims scattered among other bones: straying cattle, perhaps a headstrong dog or possibly even some unlucky boy of the clan. Domhnull stopped and listened. Behind him Hughie sniffed the air and Kilclath edged on all fours to the edge of the cliff.

"This is madness," he breathed.

Domhnull knelt down beside him.

"It is the only way to MacSomhairle," he whispered.

Domhnull would gladly have sacrificed his life for his chieftain, but tonight he was in no doubt that he would be of more use to him alive. There was no evidence that this enemy numbered more than two. Euan MacMichael had the strength of three men and Domhnull was certain that MacSomhairle could still put up a brave fight. Besides, he had quickly formed a plan of his own. It was a risky one, and would perhaps be impossible to execute, but he was anxious to give it a try.

He edged himself in front of the ragged clansman. Hughie was his name. The chieftain was MacIolair, son of the Eagle, and it seemed to Domhnull that he did indeed resemble that proud and ruthless bird.

"Who will lead the way?" he whispered.

Hughie scowled and looked uneasily at his chieftain. Domhnull waited, his head cocked to one side. He knew what the answer would be. A clansman would not let an enemy, even if that enemy were only a child, between him and chief. Slowly he crouched down on hands and knees and motioned his captors to do the same. The boulder field rose and beckoned in the silver light. Domhnull thought of Euan MacMichael hanging over it in the sunshine, gripping MacSomhairle's hand for his very life. He pushed the image from his mind and began to crawl inch by inch along the crumbling knife-edge. Behind him he heard the loose rocks tumble and the fear catch in the throats of his enemy.

"Slow down, brat!" Hughie spat.

Domhnull paid no attention. He crawled on, scrabbling, his agile limbs and experience finding a rhythm that theirs could not. He knew Hughie was still close on his heels, but he could sense MacIolair might be beginning to lag. Soon he would be far enough behind for Domhnull to set his plan in motion. His heart was pounding so loudly he was sure Hughie must hear it. He glanced down. Below them the treacherous bed of boulders lay like gleaming grains of sand. The breathing at his back grew faster, punctuated by curses. Domhnull increased his speed.

"Damn you!" cursed Hughie, "Slow down."

Domhnull did as he was told, conscious that Hughie was crawling too fast. There would be a moment, and it would come soon…

Domhnull stopped, dead in his tracks. He gripped the rock with his chafed fingers, hurled out his back leg and closed his eyes. He heard a scraping and a curse and a cry. Then he heard the desperate voice of MacIolair.

"Hughie! Hold tight. Hold tight and I will be there."

The moonlight showed Domhnull the fear in MacIolair's eyes. Now he must find the courage to complete his plan. He turned and the whole of Glenshellich spun below him. For a brief second he felt himself its master as he towered above the terror-stricken clansman who gripped and clutched with bleeding fingers. Hughie's legs kicked frantically for a hold as he screamed for his chieftain, and Domhnull stood, balanced precariously, waiting for the perfect moment. It could only come once. When he was steady he lifted his foot and stamped his tattered leather brogue down on the clutching fingers with all his force. Hughie's face twisted in agony, then his eyes filled with a desperate fury and disbelief. Domhnull stamped again, and again, until the crushed fingers lost their hold. He heard MacIolair's cry as Hughie tumbled like a rag doll, bumping then floating on a descent that seemed to last forever. Domhnull teetered on the knife-edge until Hughie was swallowed by the darkness. His plan had worked to perfection but it gave him no pleasure. It was not good to see a man die, especially in a death you had brought about yourself. He turned to look at the chieftain, spread-eagled ten yards behind him, his face pressed into the rock. He felt a strange surge of pity, but both he and the chieftain knew there was only one thing left to do. They continued to crawl along An Ciobar's Ridge towards the giant's cave.

* * *

Angus Ban heard the fading, falling cry, and hobbled to the door of his cottage. The mountain was bathed in moonlight and a single figure leaning on a stick was approaching along the shore. Angus waited and sent up a prayer of thanks that he had been spared to see this night.

The shingle slipped under Archie Fraser's feet. He too was gazing up at the mountain. A strange silence now hung over it.

"The silence of death," he breathed.

But Angus disagreed. "I do not think so," he said softly. "To my ears it sounds more like the silence of life."

* * *

In their shieling hut Christie laid the baby to sleep. It was not fair of Domhnull to stay out so late again. She crept to the door, afraid of wakening Catriona, but her eyes too were open.

"He has not come home," she whispered.

"I know," Catriona answered. "I have not been sleeping either. I feel as if my arm is being pierced by a hundred needles."

* * *

Euan MacMichael crept to the edge of the drop and his relief turned to alarm when he saw not one but two figures approaching. One was certainly Domhnull, but the other was a stranger, at once proud and downcast. Euan pressed himself against the rock. Donald was sleeping, and Euan wondered if this was business that could be settled without him. But when he next leaned his head forward again he saw the man violently grab Domhnull's wrist.

"MacIolair!" Domhnull screamed out.

Euan drew his dirk and stepped in front of them.

"No further."

The Master of the Stones held up his hand. "And you are?"

"I serve MacSomhairle."

"Euan MacMichael," breathed the Master, and kept his eyes fixed on Euan's face.

For a moment Euan drew back. Domhnull wriggled free of MacIolair's grip and ran to Euan's side where he looked desperately from one to the other.

"MacSomhairle is fortunate in his servants," the Master said softly. Euan's hand tightened on his dirk. The Master took a step towards him, still studying his face. "But I have come to claim him."

"Have you not claimed enough from Glenshellich?" Euan hissed.

The Master drew his sword. "Perhaps you should reverse that question," he murmured as Euan sprang to meet it. In the moonlight dirk and broadsword glinted silver and their clash echoed around the corrie. Domhnull watched, too afraid to draw breath, as they stumbled, crouched and parried on the ledge that broadened into the cave's mouth. Euan was the bravest fighter of all the clan. He had come through the battle without a single wound. But Domhnull knew in his heart that MacIolair was a different enemy and that this would be a fight to the death.

He crept behind them into the shadow of the cave mouth. Amazingly MacSomhairle still slept. Domhnull shook his shoulder, gently at first but with growing urgency, until at last his chieftain opened his eyes.

On the ledge outside Euan fought for his breath as his enemy's face bore down on him, black eyes drilling his. The Master of the Stones had pinned him between the corrie wall and the smooth rock floor. He had sheathed his broadsword and straddled Euan's chest, the point of his dirk sharp at his throat. Euan did not try to swallow the sob of despair that rose from his heart. He had battled so hard, learned and loved so much, and now it was to be snatched from him by this enemy whose strength must surely come from the devil himself. The piercing eyes seemed to search his very soul and Euan was powerless to look away as he waited for the final thrust. Their faces were so close that Euan could feel the sweet warmth of the Master's breath in his own nostrils. He closed his eyes, until he felt a different warmth, sticky and wet, spread across his throat where moments ago the dirk had trembled. He felt the weight of a head on his chest and when he looked up he saw that the eyes drilling his had turned to brown.

"Euan!" he heard Donald gasp, and saw the blade of the skean dhu, sharpened for its final purpose, glint in the moonlight. The weight of the Master of the Stones continued to press down on him as the warm blood from his gaping throat spread slowly across Euan's chest.

"Euan!" Donald's voice insisted, but Euan was still lost inside the Master's last breath, trapped by the extraordinary peace that came from the pressure of his body, so lost that when he felt Donald pull on the Master's shoulders his first instinct was to push him away.

* * *

It was left to Iain MacCombie's dog to alert the shieling. Its shrill barking shattered the first of the morning and the two women hurried to the door of their hut in time to see the sun creep around the shoulder of the ridge. For a moment its brightness blinded them, then out of the yellow glare a small figure came running and leaping around the last of Feodag's stones. Before they had time for relief they saw the figures that followed, at death's pace, the leader tall and muscular, the other bent and crooked. There could be no mistaking what they carried between them.

"MacSomhairle!" cried Domhnull as he reached them, pulling at their skirts with his excitement. "MacSomhairle and Euan!"

Catriona tried to take a step, but stumbled and clutched at the shieling wall. Then she reached out to Euan and held him close, tears streaming silently down her face while his body wrenched with sobs. Over his shoulder her eyes sought Donald, but he could not fathom the pain they held. When he dared at last look at Christie there was nothing in her expression either that he sought. Her stricken eyes were on the dark dead face of the Master of the Stones.

Then he felt a tug on his arm and turned to see Domhnull cradling the baby in his arms. Shyly the boy held her out to him. "She does not have a name until you give her one," he whispered.

Donald reached out and took his daughter into his arms. His finger teased back the blanket and he stared down into the tiny, perfect face. At last he laid his arm across Domhnull's shoulder. "Come, Domhnull," he said softly. "The three of us will go together to the clachan." As he limped away he turned for a brief backward look at the heads of

Catriona and Christie bowed low over the body of his enemy, and the grave figure of Euan beside them.

The moon still hung pale and ghostly beside the early sun as they threaded a path through the grazing beasts towards the roofless walls, the silent pens, the charred stones that stretched before them. Ahead loomed the black outline of his home. He closed his eyes and remembered what he once would have found there: the firelight flickering on panels of oak, the songs from the stables, his brother's laughter, Helen's shining eyes. He shifted the baby in his arms and gazed for a long time into her sleeping face. He could not bring himself to imagine how the House of Glenshellich had burned, or Beathag's crazed lament as she laid her last curse. He pushed at the splintered remains of the front door. It groaned ajar and a smell of stale burning slipped through.

"I remember all the things," Domhnull whispered, desperate to find some words of consolation. "My mother and father and the pipes in the morning; the horses and the hens, the voices, the songs."

Donald remembered them too and bitter tears streamed down his cheeks. He sank to his knees and sobbed against Domhnull's shoulder. For a moment the boy recoiled with disappointment, but only for the moment it took to understand that there could be no shame in tears such as these.

* * *

As daylight crept through the shieling hut Catriona MacMichael wiped the last trace of blood from the marble features of the Master of the Stones. Then she bent low and breathed her soft and private words into his ear.

Euan waited at a distance. The story his mother had told him was still very hard to believe. At last Christie appeared from the hut to join him. "*Wherever our life leads us, whoever we may pledge ourselves to....*" She thought of the sureness of the Master's seduction and her inescapable response. Never again, she promised herself, would she allow another person to have such power over her.

But Euan knew he should delay no longer. The sky blazed blue above the lochan and glinted in the ripples around Angus' boat. Iain MacCombie had discovered the horses from Kilclath grazing behind the ridge just after dawn. Euan glanced across to where they were tethered before he stepped inside.

"It is time," he whispered.

Catriona stood back to let him lift his brother into his arms. She followed him outside and watched him fasten the Master's body across the saddle. Then she kissed the cold forehead and brushed the dark hair from his face as Euan mounted and turned the horses' heads eastwards.

No wind breathed through the heather or sighed their passage through the silent land. They crossed the Bloody Burn unnoticed and held to the shade of the mountain until the field of stones stretched white before them. There Euan stopped and slid the Master's body from his horse. He leaned him against the rock that cast the longest shadow, turning his face to where the eagles soared with their glinting wings above the twin peaks.

"The herdsmen will find you before sunset," he whispered, "And take you the rest of your way. They will make the songs and stories of you now." He knelt closer, still reluctant to let the moment go, but at last he drew a final breath. "And there will be a song of you in Glenshellich, for my children and their children will tell of the night of no shadows when you spared my life. They will be of your blood. Perhaps one day they will help our lands find peace."

But first Euan knew he must make a different peace. He could not guess what longer journeys lay ahead or what further dangers they might hold. Yet, however long and however dangerous, his future could have but one destination. He swung into the saddle and pulled on the reins for Glenshellich.

About the Author

Born in Dorset, now settled in Moray, Liz has always had ambitions to be a writer. After her degree in English and History from Edinburgh University she taught English and now works part-time as a support for learning teacher. This is her first and only historical novel. It has been nearly thirty years in the making and through almost as many drafts!

Liz has had short stories produced on radio and is currently writing TV scripts and crime novels. Now that her family are grown up she is able to devote more time and energy to her projects. In her rare spare time she enjoys reading, walking her dogs and relaxing in the garden with a glass of wine.

Printed in the United Kingdom
by Lightning Source UK Ltd.
124216UK00002B/37-219/A